CLAUDIAN'S *IN EUTROPIUM*

JACQUELINE LONG

Claudian's *In Eutropium*

Or, How, When, and Why

to Slander a Eunuch

✦

THE UNIVERSITY OF NORTH CAROLINA PRESS

CHAPEL HILL AND LONDON

Library of Congress Cataloging-in-Publication Data
Long, Jacqueline. Claudian's In Eutropium : Or, how, when, and
why to slander a eunuch / by Jacqueline Long.
p.   cm.   Includes bibliographical references (p.   ) and index.
ISBN 0-8078-2263-9 (cloth : alk. paper)
1. Claudianus, Claudius. In Eutropium. 2. Rome—History—
Honorius, 395–423—Historiography. 3. Eunuchs—Rome.
4. Invective. I. Title.
PA6372.I7L66   1996   95-23507
873'.01—dc20   CIP

Jacqueline Long is assistant professor of classics at the
University of Texas at Austin.

00   99   98   97   96   5   4   3   2   1

For Bruce
(no resemblance)

CONTENTS

Contents

THIS BOOK HAD its first beginnings in spring of 1987, when Alan Cameron suggested Claudian's *In Eutropium* to me as a worthwhile topic for my doctoral dissertation. Some of his arguments in *Claudian: Politics and Propaganda at the Court of Honorius* (1970) had occasioned further debate, and the problems and antecedents of political literature had always intrigued me. I could not but leap at the chance to dissect the poem he had once called "the cruellest (and most entertaining) invective that has come down to us from the ancient world" (Cameron 1974, 144). A dissertation can be a daunting project, especially in the eyes of a graduate student just embarking on one; I reassured myself that whatever frustration I might ever feel, Claudian's ebullient nastiness would revive my spirits.

In I plunged. I began organizing my background research in the next year, while teaching Literature Humanities for Columbia College's core curriculum and collaborating with Alan on *Barbarians and Politics at the Court of Arcadius*. My application for a Junior Fellowship in Byzantine Studies at Dumbarton Oaks for 1988–89 happily found favor with the committee of Senior Fellows. It is a pleasure to thank them, the Trustees of Harvard University, and the then Director of Dumbarton Oaks, Robert Thomson, for the idyllic year of work I enjoyed there. Irene Vaslef and her staff in the Byzantine Library, particularly Mark Zapatka, kept a rich supply of texts and secondary studies at my fingertips. I cannot thank them enough. While in Washington I also enjoyed frequently the hospitality of Harvard's Center for Hellenic Studies, then under the direction of Zeph Stewart; to the Stewarts and to the Hellenic Center's library staff I am most deeply grateful. Colleagues at Dumbarton Oaks and the Hellenic Center enriched my life with their friendship and my work with good advice. Alessandra Ricci, Tom Dale, Berenice Cavarra, Robert Browning, Ioli Kalavrezou, Alexander Kazhdan, George Majeska, Michael McCormick, Lucas Siorvanes, Henry Mendell, and Hermann Schibli are only a few names out of many.

Meanwhile, Alan Cameron, Roger Bagnall, and Jim Zetzel heroically advised the dissertation by mail and telephone. They rescued me from many errors and infelicities. Peter Knox and Joan Ferrante joined them on the dissertation's examination committee and added valuable suggestions, which have helped to turn the dissertation into the draft of a book. I deeply appreciate their guidance.

Revisions have been a long project, carried out amid other research and teaching duties at the University of Texas at Austin. I should thank all my colleagues and students here for making it such a stimulating and friendly environment. The list would be unending; I will single out the successive chairmen of the Classics Department, Karl Galinsky, Michael Gagarin, and Tom Palaima, for holding it all together, and David Armstrong, Lesley Dean-Jones, Peter Green, Gwyn Morgan, Bill Nethercut, Doug Parker, and Paula Perlman, for thoughts that have helped to shape the final manuscript. Bonny Keyes of the Classics Library and Goldia Hester, the Classics bibliographer, have continually provided invaluable assistance. Alan Cameron and Roger Bagnall have also continued to offer kind and wise advice.

In 1990 I held a Summer Research Award from the University Research Institute of the University of Texas at Austin, and in 1992 a Summer Fellowship in Byzantine Studies at Dumbarton Oaks, both of which supported phases of revision. More thanks are due to all the library staffs involved, and to Dumbarton Oaks' current Director, Angeliki Laiou, and Director of Byzantine Studies, Henry Maguire, as well as to Eunice Dauterman Maguire, Alexandra Chekalova, Helene Saradi, and Elena Stepanova.

Lewis Bateman solicited the manuscript from me for the University of North Carolina Press. Through all my dealings with the Press, I owe him a great debt of gratitude for his interest and patience. The readers to whom the Press sent the manuscript for review, Barbara Saylor Rodgers and another who has remained anonymous, made many helpful and generous suggestions that informed the final revisions. I thank them most warmly. Ron Maner and Brian MacDonald have also helped tremendously.

Much of the final revising was done at the American School for Classical Studies in Athens, where I happily owe another huge round of thanks for all the help I received: to the Director, William Coulson, to the Secretary, Bob Bridges, to the Mellon Professor, John Camp, to Nancy Winter, the Librarian, and her staff, and to everyone else there.

Throughout the whole course of these labors friends and my family have unfailingly supplied me with humor and strength. From an immense list I recount to myself silently, I must mention Jean-Jacques Aubert, Jeri Fogel, Donna Hurley, John Lenz, Jon Roth, Lee Sherry, Glen Thompson, and Alex Tulin from our shared graduate school days, and Beverly Bardsley, Tim Barnes, Ted Champlin, Jim Coulter, Kevin Daly, David Dean-Jones, Rachel Friedman, Carin Green, Nicolle Hirschfeld, Richard Janko, Jack Kroll, Ralph Mathisen, Bill Metcalf, Joan and Gareth Morgan, David Olster, Carolyn Palaima, Miriam Pelikan, Matthew Santirocco, Hagith Sivan, Connie and Ron Stroud, and Leonardo Tarán from numerous places along the way. Above all, I thank my best friend, Jenni Sheridan, and my husband, Bruce LaForse, who have let me share myself (and Claudian) with them through thick and thin.

SHORTLY AFTER I sent the manuscript of this book to press, I received a query from Gary Brower, a doctoral student who had read my dissertation and wondered still what I thought were Claudian's real reasons for hating Eutropius. I would like to close this preface by quoting from my answer:

"My chief reason for neglecting the question you pose is that we know Claudian virtually solely from his poems. They are public statements about the expressly public topics of imperial politics. I'm not confident we have the evidence to identify a personal sensibility behind the public voice. If I were to speculate, I would work from the principle that people tend to hate most things they perceive as threatening them. A mere prejudice against eunuchs, even as degrading the symbolic post of consul, seems rather abstract in this connection, an argument Claudian could deploy rather than a motivating force. Eutropius's power over Eastern policy, particularly as it might touch the West and Stilicho, whose interests Claudian consistently promotes (not necessarily insincerely), seems to me to offer a likelier basis for real feeling, if one can be sketched.

"My second reason is sketchy and perhaps fanciful. Claudian so completely took possession of the figure of Eutropius, that I imagine it would have been difficult for him afterwards to distinguish fully the real eunuch from his artistic image. He represents the real eunuch damningly by an exuberant literary caricature. Where such creativity has been lavished, a pleasure results. I cannot but love the literary creation, having studied him; I suspect that Claudian felt the same."

I hope the reader will find some interest in my studies, if not perhaps the same curious pleasure. I do retain my claim to all errors and infelicities that remain.

The titles and numeration of Claudian's poems follow the edition of Hall 1985.

1. *Ol. Prob.*	*Panegyricus dictus Olybrio et Probino consulibus*
2. *Ruf.* 1pr.	*In Rufinum praefatio prior*
3. *Ruf.* 1	*In Rufinum liber prior*
4. *Ruf.* 2pr.	*In Rufinum praefatio altera*
5. *Ruf.* 2	*In Rufinum liber alter*
6. *3 Cons.* pr.	*Panegyrici dicti Honorio Augusto tertium consuli praefatio*
7. *3 Cons.*	*Panegyricus dictus Honorio Augusto tertium consuli*
8. *4 Cons.*	*Panegyricus dictus Honorio Augusto quartum consuli*
9. *Epith.* pr.	*Epithalamii dicti Honorio Augusto et Mariae praefatio*
10. *Epith.*	*Epithalamium dictum Honorio Augusto et Mariae*
11. *Fesc.* 1	*Fescenninum dictum Honorio Augusto et Mariae prius*
12. *Fesc.* 2	*Fescenninum dictum Honorio Augusto et Mariae alterum*
13. *Fesc.* 3	*Fescenninum dictum Honorio Augusto et Mariae tertium*
14. *Fesc.* 4	*Fescenninum dictum Honorio Augusto et Mariae quartum*
15. *Gild.*	*In Gildonem*
16. *M. Theod.* pr.	*Panegyrici dicti Mallio Theodoro consuli praefatio*
17. *M. Theod.*	*Panegyricus dictus Mallio Theodoro consuli*
18. *Eutr.* 1	*In Eutropium liber prior*
19. *Eutr.* 2pr.	*In Eutropium libri alterius praefatio*
20. *Eutr.* 2	*In Eutropium liber alter*
21. *Stil.* 1	*De Consulatu Stilichonis liber primus*
22. *Stil.* 2	*De Consulatu Stilichonis liber secundus*
23. *Stil.* 3pr.	*De Consulatu Stilichonis libri tertii praefatio*
24. *Stil.* 3	*De Consulatu Stilichonis liber tertius*
25. *Get.* pr.	*Belli Getici praefatio*
26. *Get.*	*Bellum Geticum*
27. *6 Cons.* pr.	*Panegyrici dicti Honorio Augusto sextum consuli praefatio*
28. *6 Cons.*	*Panegyricus dictus Honorio Augusto sextum consuli*
Rapt. 1pr.	*De Raptu Proserpinae libri primi praefatio*
Rapt. 1	*De Raptu Proserpinae liber primus*
Rapt. 2pr.	*De Raptu Proserpinae libri secundi praefatio*
Rapt. 2	*De Raptu Proserpinae liber secundus*
Rapt. 3	*De Raptu Proserpinae liber tertius*
CM 1–53	*Carmina Minora* 1–53
Carm. Spur.	
Susp. 1–24	*Carminum vel Spuriorum vel Suspectorum Appendix* 1–24

Secondary works are cited in the notes by the author's surname and year of the work, followed by page numbers; for full documentation, see Bibliography. Standard abbreviations are used to cite journals and works of reference. Exceptionally:

CLRE	Roger S. Bagnall, Alan Cameron, Seth R. Schwartz, and Klaas A. Worp, *Consuls of the Later Roman Empire* (Atlanta, Ga.: Scholars Press, 1987)
Ep. Imp. Pont. Al.	*Epistulae Imperatorum Pontificum Aliorum*, vol. 1, ed. Otto Guenther, Corpus scriptorum ecclesiasticorum Latinorum 35 (Vindobona: F. Tempsky, 1895)
Fargues, *Invectives*	Pierre Fargues, ed., *Claudien, Invectives contre Eutrope* (Paris: Librairie Hachette, 1933)
Fargues, *Claudien*	Pierre Fargues, *Claudien: Études sur sa poésie et son temps* (Paris: Librairie Hachette, 1933)
LSJ	*A Greek-English Lexicon*, ed. Henry George Liddell, Robert Scott, and Henry Stuart Jones (9th ed., Oxford: Clarendon Press, 1940; Supplement, 1968)
Lewis and Short	*A Latin Dictionary*, ed. Charleton T. Lewis and Charles Short (Oxford: Clarendon Press, 1879)
OLD	*Oxford Latin Dictionary*, ed. P. G. W. Glare (Oxford: Clarendon Press, 1982)
PIR	*Prosopographia Imperii Romani Saec. I, II, III*, ed. E. Klebs, H. Dessau, and P. de Rohden, 3 vols. (Berlin: Reimer, 1897–98); 2nd ed., ed. E. Groag, A. Stein, et al., issued in parts (Berlin: DeGruyter, 1933–)
PLRE	*Prosopography of the Later Roman Empire*, ed. A. H. M. Jones, J. R. Martindale, and J. Morris, 3 vols. in 4 pts. (Cambridge: Cambridge University Press, 1971–92)
TLL	*Thesaurus Linguae Latinae*, ed. International Committee of the Thesaurus Linguae Latinae, issued in parts (Leipzig: B. G. Teubner, 1900–)

CLAUDIAN'S *IN EUTROPIUM*

The Eunuch Consul and
the Court Poet

✦

THE YEAR A.D. 399 was unique in Roman history. As the sixth-century chronicler Marcellinus records,[1]

> XII. Theodori et Eutropii eunuchi.
> Hic Eutropius omnium spadonum primus adque ultimus consul fuit: de quo Claudianus poeta ait:
> > omnia cesserunt eunucho consule monstra.

> 12th [indiction, the consulate] of Theodorus and Eutropius the eunuch. This Eutropius of all eunuchs was the first and last consul. Concerning him the poet Claudian says:
> > All prodigies have given way, when a eunuch is consul.

At this time the Roman Empire was ruled jointly by Theodosius the Great's two sons.[2] The younger, Honorius, reigned in the West, with his court based at Milan; the elder, Arcadius, reigned from his court in Constantinople over the eastern half of the empire. Eutropius was Arcadius's grand chamberlain, or

---

1. *Chron. Min.* 2.66, quoting here Claud. *Eutr.* 1.8. On Marcellinus see Brian Croke, "A.D. 476: The Manufacture of a Turning Point," *Chiron* 13 (1983): 81–119, rpt. in *Christian Chronicles and Byzantine History, 5th–6th Centuries*, chap. 5 (Aldershot, Hamps.: Variorum, 1992), 87–90; *PLRE* 2.710–11, Marcellinus 9. See further Brian Croke, trans. and comm., *The Chronicle of Marcellinus*, Byzantina Australiensia 7 (Sydney, 1995), and R. A. Markus, "Politics and Historiography in Ostrogothic Italy: The Chronicle of Marcellinus and Its Continuation in the Light of Recent Work," in *ANRW* 3 (forthcoming). All translations in this book are my own except as otherwise noted.

2. The major histories of the period are Seeck 1913, esp. chap. 7; Bury 1923, vol. 1, chap. 5; Mazzarino 1942 = 1990; Stein and Palanque 1949–59, vol. 1, esp. chap. 6; Demougeot 1951; see also Alan Cameron 1970; Matthews 1975, chaps. 9–10; Liebeschuetz 1990, chaps. 7–9.

praepositus sacri cubiculi.[3] The post was often held by a eunuch, simply because
eunuchs made up much of the emperor's private domestic staff, just as they did
in the households of private citizens. Eutropius had served in the palace since
the time of Theodosius, and won his particular trust (Soz. *HE* 7.22.7–8). He
was able to capitalize still more on Arcadius's regard for him, and extended his
influence beyond the palace into imperial government. He completely ex-
ceeded the usual role of a civilian when in 398 he led a military campaign that
successfully repelled invading Huns from Armenia.[4] The victory won him the
consulate.

Before 399 was out, internal political relations of the Eastern empire forced
Arcadius to remove Eutropius from his office as chamberlain, revoke his honors, including the title of patrician, and eject him from the consulate. The law
deposing him describes his tenure with acrid censure: "His magnificence has
been stripped off and the consulate vindicated from the foul muck and from
the commemoration of his name and its filthy stains so that . . . all times may
grow silent and the degradation of our age may not be apparent by his being
listed" (*CTh* 9.40.17, quoted in full in Chapter 8.II).

The consuls of each year, although they had long ceased to hold any power
in the Roman state by virtue of the distinction, still gave their names to their
year. The great compilation of testimonia to the *Consuls of the Later Roman
Empire* documents how Eutropius's name disappeared when he was deposed.
Chroniclers like Marcellinus generally followed consular lists from which Eutropius had duly been deleted. Faced with only the Western consul, Mallius
Theodorus, some split off his first name and listed it as a separate person.[5] The
extant witnesses that were recorded permanently while Eutropius was still
recognized list him first, as the appointee of the senior emperor. From the fact
that Marcellinus lists Eutropius second, the editors inferred that his primary
source also omitted Eutropius, but Claudian's verse prompted him to reinsert
the Roman Empire's only eunuch consul in his entry. The Eastern law erasing
Eutropius's consulate was for Marcellinus annulled, ironically, by a Western
poem arguing that the consulate should never be recognized in the first place.

Modern historians who want to know the Roman Empire of A.D. 399 are

---

3. *PLRE* 2.440–44. On the office of *praepositus sacri cubiculi*, see Guyot 1980, 130–57;
A. H. M. Jones 1964, 566–70; DeGaiffier 1957; Dunlap 1924; on "The Political Power of
Eunuchs," see Hopkins 1978, 172–96.

4. See Albert 1979, particularly 626–31. Liebeschuetz 1990, 93–100, emphasized Eutropius's interest in keeping power out of the hands of regular generals.

5. *CLRE* 332–33 s.a., cf. 56–57. *PLRE* 1.900–2, Flavius Mallius Theodorus 27. On the
protocols of consular listings, see *CLRE* 22. Marcellinus's designation "the eunuch," of
course, would not have been part of Eutropius's formal titulature (cf. Dunlap 1924, 313–
14; Guyot 1980, 138–39), although it appears to have been used commonly, e.g., Eunap.
frr. 66, 72, 74 M = 65.1, 65.8, 66.2 Blockley.

subject to the same irony. The consulate of Eutropius, in and of itself, is memorable largely because Claudian the poet wrote two dazzlingly nasty books about it and about Eutropius's administration. The constitutional affront has dimmed, but the vituperation remains. It affords closely contemporary if wildly biased information. For many aspects of Eutropius's career it is our only source.

CLAUDIUS CLAUDIANUS's own biography consists of a stellar but very limited celebrity suddenly flashing forth from almost total obscurity. His own poetry provides the basis for inference.[6] Claudian's verse "Epistle to Gennadius" refers to "our Nile," suggesting he came from Egypt (*CM* 19.3).[7] His "Apology" to the Egyptian Hadrian narrows down his nativity to Alexandria, for he calls Alexander the Great "founder of my fatherland" (*CM* 22.20).[8] Claudian's date of birth may tentatively be put in the last third or quarter of the fourth century since he excuses himself to Hadrian on the grounds of "slippery youth" (*lubrica aetas, CM* 22.6), when Hadrian's career seems best to date the poem to 397.[9]

This origin and Claudian's appearance in history suggest that he set out to pursue a career relatively well attested among fifth-century poets, often, as it happens, native to Egypt: professional freelancers who traveled about seeking commissions for encomiastic verse to adorn ceremonial occasions.[10] Atypically, however, Claudian specialized in Latin, and took his career west. He received a spectacular commission at the Roman court in the New Year of 395: he presented a panegyric for the two young nobles Olybrius and Probinus, whom Theodosius had named consuls.[11]

Claudian later told Probinus (*CM* 41.13–16),

6. Relevant passages and the few testimonia are collected at *PLRE* 2.299–300.

7. Gennadius Torquatus, *PLRE* 2.1124. Sidonius Apollinaris refers to Claudian as "sprung of Pelusiac Canopus" and singing *De Raptu Proserpinae* (Sidon. *Carm.* 9.274–76). All my quotations of Claudian follow the text of Hall 1985; I note as they arise in my discussion controversies and reevaluations that other textual research makes appropriate, particularly the stemmatic research of Schmidt 1989.

8. *PLRE* 1.406, Hadrianus 2; Claud. *CM* 21 calls him simply *Pharius*, referring to the island and lighthouse defining Alexandria's harbor. *CM* 22.56–57, also refers to "the soil we share" and claims that the mouths of the Nile will groan over Claudian's death if Hadrian continues to persecute him. Suda, K 1707 also identifies Claudian as Alexandrian but other notices differ, erroneously; cf. Alan Cameron 1970, 2–7; 1965a.

9. On the date see Alan Cameron 1970, 397–401.

10. Alan Cameron 1965a assembled evidence and analyzed the careers of these "Wandering Poets" in an important article.

11. Anicius Hermogenianus Olybrius 2, *PLRE* 1.639–40; Anicius Probinus 1, *PLRE* 1.734–35.

Romanos bibimus primum te consule fontes
    et Latiae cessit Graia Thalia togae,
incipiensque tuis a fascibus omina cepi
    fataque debebo posteriora tibi.

I drank first from Roman founts when you were consul,
    and my Greek Muse yielded to the Latin civic robe;
beginning from your rods I took my omens
    and my later fortunes I shall owe to you.

It has been much debated whether Claudian means that he began to write in the Latin language as opposed to Greek, either at all or in major works for public recital, or that he began to treat Roman political as opposed to Greek mythological themes.[12] Only ventriloquism by the Muse would explain the elegance of Claudian's Latin in the panegyric and the complex density of his allusions to classical Latin poetry, if it were truly his first experiment with Latin at all.[13] A simple change of themes seems precluded by the appearance of Claudian's only major nonpolitical poem in Latin, *De Raptu Proserpinae*, to have been composed after his political invective *In Rufinum*.[14] The reference in the "Letter to Probinus" to Claudian's own fortunes is better understood to identify *Panegyricus dictus Olybrio et Probino* as having launched him professionally, in a career supported by the patronage of Latinate officials.

Specifically, Claudian passed into the ambit of Honorius's court in Milan. His next public work was an inaugural panegyric for Honorius's third consulate, in 396. For the next eight years he continued to produce major poems on Western political themes, as well as more private epigrams and the mythological *De Raptu Proserpinae*. Panegyrics by Claudian hailed consulates of Honorius in 396, 398, and 404, the consulate of Mallius Theodorus in 399, and the first consulate of Honorius's *magister militum* Stilicho in 400.[15] In 398 Claudian's Fescennine verses and epithalamium celebrated Honorius's marriage to Stilicho's daughter Maria.[16] His epics commemorate Western victories that

12. Birt 1892, viii–x; J. P. Postgate, "Editions of Claudian by Birt and Koch," *Classical Review* 9 (1895): 163–64; Glover [1901] 1968, 218; Platnauer 1922, 1.xiii; Fargues, *Claudien* 12; Romano 1958, 6–8, 20–21 n. 39; Alfonsi 1960, 131–32; Hall 1969, 101–2; Alan Cameron 1970, 457–59.

13. Birt 1892 collected *loci similes* in earlier and later Latin literature throughout Claudian's corpus. Gualandri 1969 explored "aspects of compositional technique in Claudian," especially allusion, concentrating on his public and private marriage-poems but also touching on his other works.

14. Alan Cameron 1970, 459–66. Both Hall 1969, 95–103, and Alan Cameron 1970, 453–57, convincingly refuted political readings that have been proposed for *Rapt.*

15. Stilicho, *PLRE* 1.855–58.

16. *PLRE* 2.720, Maria 1.

extinguished Gildo's revolt in Africa in 398 and that repelled the Gothic invasion of Italy under Alaric in 402.[17] Amid this laudatory output, Claudian also produced two sets of books attacking chief ministers of Arcadius, Rufinus[18] and later Eutropius. The panegyric for Honorius's sixth consulate, in 404, is Claudian's last datable work; presumably he died shortly after presenting it.[19]

Claudian's separate poems were collected after his death and began to circulate in groups. Theodor Birt in his monumental edition of Claudian's works, published in 1892, theorized that all Claudian's political poems except the panegyric for Olybrius and Probinus formed a single collection, the *carmina maiora*; it, the panegyric for Olybrius and Probinus, the three books of *De Raptu Proserpinae*, and the *carmina minora*, a collection of Claudian's shorter poems and fragments, each circulated separately (lxxvi–lxxviii). Birt's view reigned long, down to the most recent comprehensive edition of Claudian's poems, J. B. Hall's Teubner text of 1985.[20] Hall assembled the evidence of the more than 300 extant manuscripts that preserve Claudian's work, and concluded that several competing collections of various groups of poems descended independently from antiquity into the Middle Ages.[21] Without a single archetype behind the texts that thereafter lent readings to one another as they proliferated, further contaminating the tradition, Hall judged that stemmatic criticism was irredeemably frustrated. He took as his own editorial principles, "The truth is that only untrammelled eclecticism founded on a recognition of the inapplicability of stemmatics will permit full exploitation of the wealth of the tradition."[22] Peter L. Schmidt in 1989 challenged both these judgments.[23] Working from and acknowledging Hall's careful, thorough assembly of manuscript evidence (414), Schmidt showed that the several contaminations of the tradition most probably began in the twelfth century, when Claudian's works surged in popularity and began to be copied everywhere. The medieval transmission descended from a single collection in four separate codices: the *carmina minora*, the *De Raptu Proserpinae*, the panegyric for Olybrius and Probinus together with the panegyrics for Honorius, Theodorus, and Stilicho, and the invectives against Rufinus and Eutropius together with the contemporary epics *In Gildonem* and *Bellum Geticum*. A new reevaluation of the text of Claudian's works in the light of Schmidt's conclusions, unfortu-

17. Gildo, *PLRE* 1.395–96; Alaric, *PLRE* 2.43–48.

18. *PLRE* 1.778–80, Flavius Rufinus 18.

19. Alan Cameron 1970, 405–18; Merone 1954; Demougeot 1951, 288–94.

20. The very slender preface of Hall 1985 is supplemented by Hall 1986; Hall 1983 summarized his verdicts briefly.

21. Hall 1986, 67–68.

22. Hall 1983, 144.

23. "Die Überlieferungsgeschichte von Claudians Carmina maiora," *Illinois Classical Studies* 14 (1989): 391–415.

nately, still awaits. I shall discuss individual points as they relate to my own arguments in the chapters that follow.

Claudian won lasting renown, both at Honorius's court and before posterity. He received the senatorial rank of *tribunus et notarius*.[24] In 402 he could boast, in the preface to his epic about Alaric's defeat at Pollentia, that the Senate had awarded him a bronze statue (*Get.* pr.7–14). The still-preserved dedicatory inscription confirms that the emperors commanded the statue to be erected "at the Senate's petition."[25] These temporal honors might not have been motivated solely by considerations of art, but both abundant echoes in later literature and Claudian's lively manuscript tradition prove that his poems won and retained immense popularity in their own, literary right.[26] Claudian's innovations gave rise to the fifth-century genre of encomiastic epic, which persisted into the medieval period.[27] Late antique poetry's fascination with rhetorical magniloquence and brilliant visual imagery Claudian both typified and helped to fuel.[28]

THEODOSIUS HAD MARCHED from the East to take up the campaign against the usurper Eugenius in the summer of 394.[29] With him came the Eastern army and Stilicho, then Theodosius's *magister militum* and also the husband of Theodosius's niece and adopted daughter Serena.[30] They defeated Eugenius's supporters decisively at the battle of the river Frigidus on 6 September 394. Claudian sets at this scene Theodosius's decision to name Olybrius and Probinus consuls for the following year. The divine personification of the city of Rome, Roma, asks Theodosius to nominate them as he relaxes on the battlefield, garlanded and radiantly serene but still sweaty, hot, and breathing hard from the exertion of his victory (*Ol. Prob.* 113–23). On the one hand, Claudian's connection of the victory and the nomination may only mark a

24. On the office, see A. H. M. Jones 1964, 573–74.

25. The inscription is in Naples (Giovanni Garuti, ed., *Claudiani de Bello Gothico*, vol. 1, Edizioni e saggi universitari di filologia classica 23 [Bologna: Pàtron, 1979], 95 n. 8): *CIL* 6.1710 = Dessau, *ILS* 2949 = Moretti, *IGUR* 1.62, pp. 56–57.

26. On Claudian's Nachleben, see Manitius 1890 (cf. Max Manitius, *Geschichte der lateinischen Literatur des Mittelalters*, 3 vols. [Munich: Beck, 1911–31]); Birt 1892, lxxvi–cciv; Alan Cameron 1970, 419–51; Clarke and Levy 1976; Babcock 1986.

27. See Hofmann 1988.

28. See the important general study of Roberts 1989, *The Jeweled Style: Poetry and Poetics in Late Antiquity*.

29. He is last attested in the East on 20 June by *CTh* 16.5.23 at Hadrianopolis, then not in Italy (or anywhere else) until the battle of the Frigidus: Seeck 1919, 284. Fl. Eugenius 6, *PLRE* 1.293; cf. Matthews 1975, 238–46.

30. Serena, *PLRE* 1.824.

chronological fact: if the nomination was announced not long after Theodosius reestablished control over Italy, Claudian could reflect glory on his honorands by claiming that the decision was made at the very moment he won. But the connection also suggests a consideration that could have moved Theodosius to honor so tremendously two young men who had not previously held any public office. Their father, Petronius Probus, had been a prominent senator of Rome and had discharged numerous imperial posts; by bowing to his memory Theodosius could also signal to his whole social class that he would not hold their former support of Eugenius as a cause for estrangement.[31] Nonetheless, Theodosius otherwise functions in the poem only to voice admiration for Probus. All attention, human and divine, is fixed on Olybrius and Probinus, their noble parentage, the ceremony surrounding their inauguration, and the magnificent omens of their year. No other member of the imperial entourage figures at all, not even Theodosius's sons and fellow Augusti Arcadius and Honorius.

Not long after Claudian "drank first of Roman founts" with this panegyric, Theodosius died in January 395. Arcadius in the East was eighteen years old, Honorius in the West only ten. Neither brother ever dominated even his own court. As A. H. M. Jones observed, they performed an important function just by being alive.[32] The fact that they were Theodosius's sons and had already been Augusti with him made them his natural successors: they closed one avenue to usurpers. Dynastic loyalties helped to secure the empire. But the weakness of Arcadius and Honorius meant that true control would always be exerted by their ministers. Since their offices did not confer a basis of power permanently, rivalries were inevitable.

Naturally the greatest part of contention was contained within each court. But some of the most spectacular contests involved ministers of the two emperors. When Theodosius left the East in 394 to take the field against Eugenius's army, Zosimus records, "taking care for [Arcadius's] judgment in the future, because of his youth, [Theodosius] left Rufinus behind on the spot. He

31. So Alan Cameron 1970, 30–35; cf. Matthews 1975, 247; Matthews 1974, 84–85. Sextus Claudius Petronius Probus 5, *PLRE* 1.736–40, cf. Matthews 1975, 195–97. Compare too Matthews 1975, 224–32, on how Theodosius conciliated Westerners after suppressing the usurper Maximus in 388 (*PLRE* 1.588, Magnus Maximus 39).

32. A. H. M. Jones 1964, 173. He echoed and developed the thought of Stein and Palanque 1949–59, 1.225: "Both [Arcadius and Honorius] are representatives of a new imperial model, being the first Roman emperors of whom one could say, as of a sovereign of modern constitutional theory, 'The king reigns and does not govern.'" Oros. *Hist.* 7.36.3 says that Arcadius and Honorius survived to maturity only because "the guardianship of Christ brought them forward, on account of their father's and their own outstanding faith."

held at the same time both the praetorian prefecture and discretionary authority for every other matter of any kind, and managed as many things as the
power of authority gives an emperor."[33] After the victory over Eugenius, Zosimus reports that Theodosius made Stilicho "general of the ranks there [in the
West] and left him behind as guardian to his son [Honorius]." Theodosius
apparently had intended to return to the East, and so he prepared his way by
leaving behind one son and fellow emperor to forestall another usurpation; to
make up for his inexperience he put Stilicho at his side, just as he had done
with Arcadius and Rufinus when he left the East.[34]

Theodosius died in Milan in January 395, however, before further plans
could be realized.[35] Forty days later (Ambros. *Ob. Theod.* 3), the bishop Ambrose delivered a funeral oration which says that Theodosius "did not make a
will according to the common law, for concerning his sons, to whom he had
given the entirety, he had nothing new to establish, except that he commended
them to the parent who was still there" (*non communi iure testatus sit; de filiis
enim nihil habebat novum, quod conderet, quibus totum dederat, nisi ut eos
praesenti commendaret parenti*, Ambros. *Ob. Theod.* 5). "He had given the
entirety" clearly refers to the fact that Theodosius joined Arcadius and Honorius with himself as Augusti, well before he died. The "parent who was still
there" is evidently Stilicho; but it is unclear, and controversial, how much
Ambrose's verb "commend" truly means.

Claudian's inaugural panegyric for Honorius's third consulate in 396 suggests how Stilicho chose to understand Theodosius's legacy of a relationship
with his sons. The poem declares that Theodosius's last act on earth was,
having dismissed all other company, to entrust to Stilicho alone care of both
Honorius and Arcadius (*3 Cons.* 142–43, 152–53):

> ut ventum ad sedes, cunctos discedere tectis
> dux iubet et generum conpellat talibus ultro . . .

---

33. τὸ λεῖπον εἰς φρόνησιν αὐτῷ διὰ τὴν νεότητα θεραπεύων ἀπέλιπεν αὐτόθι
Ῥουφῖνον, ἅμα τε τῆς αὐλῆς ὕπαρχον ὄντα καὶ ἐς πᾶν ὁτιοῦν ἕτερον τῆς ἑαυτοῦ
κυριεύοντα γνώμης, πράττοντά τε ὅσα βασιλεῖ δίδωσιν ἡ τῆς ὑπεροχῆς ἐξουσία,
Zos. 4.57.4; cf. Eunap. frr. 62, 63 Müller = 62.1, 62.2 Blockley; Joh. Ant. frr. 188, 190 init.;
Philost. *HE* 11.3 (134.9–14 Bidez and Winkelmann); Oros. 7.37.1.

34. Στελίχωνα στρατηγόν τε ἀποφήνας ἅμα τῶν αὐτόθι ταγμάτων καὶ ἐπίτροπον
καταλιπὼν τῷ παιδί, Zos. 4.59.1; cf. Zos. 4.59.4; Philost. 11.2 (133.22–24 Bidez and
Winkelmann). The value of Zosimus's report about Stilicho has been contested, but see
Alan Cameron 1968b. Presumably Theodosius intended Stilicho to remain in charge
only of the troops normally stationed in the West, and the Eastern army to return with
himself.

35. *Chron. Min.* 1.245; Socr. *HE* 5.26; Zos. 4.59.4. Thus the Eastern army remained
under Stilicho's control.

tu curis succede meis, tu pignora solus
nostra fove: geminos dextra tu protege fratres.

On arrival at the palace, the general bids them all
depart from the building and of his own will he addresses his son-in-law
   with words like these . . .
You, succeed to my cares; you alone, foster
my children: you, protect the twinned brothers with your right hand.

The privacy of the scene, the adverb "of his own accord," the emphasis on family relations,[36] and phrases like "succeed to my cares" and "foster my children" all fit together into a picture of affectionate intimacy; but if the dispensation was to have practical effect over the empire, the absence of witnesses is suspicious and the adjective "alone" becomes aggressive.[37] Added to the powers with which Theodosius publicly invested Stilicho, to advise and supervise Honorius, appears a similar involvement with Arcadius in the East, setting aside or subordinating Rufinus. Zosimus says bluntly that Stilicho resented Rufinus's having power corresponding to his, wanted to exert his own control over Arcadius, and claimed that Theodosius had given him authority to do so (Zos. 5.4.3). Claudian's version of events supports these ambitions.

Stilicho's rivalry with Rufinus was cut short in November 395 when the Eastern troops that he returned to Eastern control assassinated Rufinus on their arrival in Constantinople.[38] Claudian commemorated the event with a poem that portrays Rufinus as a monster of evil sent by Hell to destroy the unity of the empire, who invited barbarians to invade and ravage it, and whom Stilicho opposed (*Ruf.* 1). In this book Claudian merely foreshadowed Rufinus's death; later, in a second, he claimed that Rufinus treacherously demanded the return of troops just when Stilicho was on the verge of crushing

36. "Son-in-law," "children," "brothers" just in these lines; the parts of the speech that I skip over invoke Stilicho's and Theodosius's shared campaigns and Stilicho's marriage to Serena.

37. See particularly Alan Cameron 1970, 37–45, and 1968b. Gnilka 1977, 29–30, associated *3 Cons.* 142–62 with 162–88 in which the star that Theodosius becomes shines over both brothers, and 189–211 in which Claudian prays the "brothers who share one soul" to rule in victorious prosperity over the world. In Gnilka's view, "all three main pieces of the final part accommodate themselves to a single idea . . . the idea of the unity of the Empire." Imperial unity is certainly an element of Theodosius's injunction, but entrusting the care for it to a single subject goes far beyond the pious hope that the empire may not be divided. Better the emphasis of Paschoud 1967, 134–35: "The core of the Stilichonian propaganda which expresses itself in the verses of Claudian is the theme of imperial unity under a Western precedence."

38. Claud. *Ruf.* 2.336–439; Socr. *HE* 6.1.3–7; Soz. *HE* 8.1.2–3; Philost. *HE* 11.3 (134.17–23 Bidez and Winkelmann); Zos. 5.7.5–6; Joh. Ant. fr. 190 *init.*

the rebellious Goth Alaric in Thessaly and that they murdered him in righteous revenge.[39]

Rufinus was succeeded in influence over Arcadius, however, not by Stilicho but by an imperial chamberlain, the eunuch Eutropius. Eutropius had belonged to Theodosius's household, and Sozomen reports that Theodosius entrusted a special mission to him in preparation for the campaign against Eugenius.[40] He remained at Constantinople thereafter. Zosimus reports an entertaining story of his intrigues against Rufinus (Zos. 5.3). Rufinus wished to marry Arcadius to his daughter, but Eutropius privately wooed Arcadius with praise of Eudoxia, the daughter of Theodosius's general Bauto; she was then living at the house of a son of another of Theodosius's generals, Promotus.[41] Eutropius persuaded Arcadius to marry her instead. He prepared the festivities. Rufinus knew nothing of Arcadius's changed designs until the wedding procession stopped at Promotus's son's house instead of his own. The tale doubtless has received some editorial shaping to bring out the drama, but it well illustrates the resources of the chamberlain's intimate relationship with the emperor.

Eutropius at first was less openly antagonistic toward Stilicho than Rufinus; they may even have coordinated to some extent the defense of Illyricum against Alaric.[42] On the other hand, Eutropius did not accommodate Stilicho's interests in Arcadius. In *In Eutropium* Claudian makes his personification of the Eastern empire tell Stilicho that at Rufinus's death "a brief and false freedom shone forth then; I hoped that I could again be governed by the reins of Stilicho" (*Eutr.* 2.543–45). Whatever its reality, the hope was not realized. About two years passed, however, before overt hostility is witnessed. In 397 Stilicho campaigned again against Alaric in Eastern territory, now in the Peloponnese. This invasion of authority doubtless roused suspicions of Stilicho's ambitions in the East, perhaps even more so since he withdrew without definitely defeating Alaric. Eutropius finally managed to halt the Goths' predations by naming Alaric *magister militum per Illyricum.*[43] This promotion of the erstwhile enemy roused converse resentment in the West, as Claudian illustrates (*Eutr.* 2.214–20).

---

39. The dates and functions of the two books of *Ruf.* are treated more fully in Chap. 5. On Stilicho's campaigns against Alaric in 395 and 397, see Heather 1991, 199–206; Alan Cameron 1970, 156–80, 474–77.

40. Soz. *HE* 7.22.7–8, quoted in Chap. 6.

41. Aelia Eudoxia 1, *PLRE* 2.410; Bauto, *PLRE* 1.159–60; Promotus (who quarreled violently with Rufinus in 391, earning a transfer to Thrace where he was ambushed by barbarians later that year), *PLRE* 1.750–51.

42. Heather 1991, 202.

43. See Demandt 1970, 730.

Meanwhile during 397 Gildo, a native Moor holding the Roman office of *magister utriusque militum per Africam*, began to reduce the normal grain shipments to Rome.[44] In the autumn he declared that he owed allegiance to Arcadius in Constantinople rather than to Honorius, and cut the West off entirely. The Roman Senate, at Stilicho's behest, declared Gildo a "public enemy," *hostis publicus*. Gildo's own brother Mascezel,[45] with whom he was already involved in a homicidal feud, was dispatched in winter 397–98 at the head of an expedition against him. Meanwhile Eutropius had the Constantino-politan Senate decree Stilicho *hostis publicus*. Whether Gildo or Stilicho was outlawed first is debated. The archaic form of censure better fits the Roman Senate's traditionalism and the strength of the senators' concern for the city of Rome, which Gildo threatened pressingly; it seems more likely that the East would have responded in kind than originated the move.[46] Regardless of the decrees' sequence, however, their effect on both sides was to entrench relations between the two courts officially at nadir.

Mascezel quickly defeated Gildo and the Western government took posses-sion of Gildo's estates (*CTh* 7.8.7, 7.8.9, 9.42.19), so that the immediate crisis was resolved; but overall relations did not improve. Later in 398 Eutropius led his campaign against Hunnic invaders in Armenia. The West refused to recog-nize the consulate with which his victory was rewarded, in 399. This strong form of diplomatic rebuke was customarily reserved for times when the em-peror who named the consul was himself denied legitimacy. The last time a consul had been rejected by emperors who recognized one another was over fifty years before, amid the increasingly fratricidal rivalries of the sons of Constantine.[47] Claudian responded with *In Eutropium* 1.

Later in 399 a Roman general of Gothic origins, Tribigild, led a revolt of Gruthungian Goths who had been settled in Phrygia as *laeti*, aliens settled in Roman territory on condition that they provide men for the Roman army.[48]

44. On Gildo's revolt, see Alan Cameron 1970, 93–123; 1974, 139–46; Demougeot 1951, 173–88; Stein and Palanque 1949–59, 1.231–33; Mazzarino 1942, 264–68 = 1990, 191–94; Seeck 1913, 282–91; and further discussion in Chap. 8.I.

45. *PLRE* 1.566.

46. So Seeck 1913, 285–86; Paschoud 1971–89, 3¹.113–15. Symm. *Ep.* 4.5 reporting the Senate's vote to Stilicho emphasizes the order's concerns for "ancestral custom" and for the grain supply to Rome; cf. Arnaldo Marcone, ed., *Commento storico al Libro IV dell'epistolario di Q. Aurelio Simmaco*, Biblioteca di Studi Antichi 55 (Pisa: Giardini Editori e Stampatori, 1987), 42–44. On senatorial conservatism more generally, espe-cially as reflected in Symmachus's letters, Matthews 1974, 68–80, 86–88; McGeachy 1942, 30–41; on senatorial concern for Rome, Matthews 1975, 12–31.

47. See *CLRE* 24–26 and s.a. 346; cf. s.aa. 307–13, 399, 400, 404, 405, 424, 451–53, 456, 458–59, 461.

48. Tribigild, *PLRE* 2.1125–26; cf. Alan Cameron and Long 1993, 112–16; Heather 1991,

Eutropius dispatched two forces under the generals Leo and Gaïnas, another Goth.[49] Tribigild defeated Leo's troops easily, killing Leo.[50] Gaïnas soon reported to Arcadius that Tribigild could not be defeated and must be appeased. The terms settled on were that Eutropius should be deposed and exiled to Cyprus, despite Arcadius's affection for him (cf. Joh. Chrys. *Hom. Eutr.* 4 = *PG* 52.395). The law officially deposing him and confiscating his property, 9.40.17 of the Theodosian Code, is transmitted as having been issued on 17 January 399, but since Claudian makes plain that Tribigild did not revolt until that spring (*Eutr.* 2.95–96), Otto Seeck emended the date to 17 August.[51]

The news of Eutropius's deposition Claudian greeted with *In Eutropium* 2, actually begun before the revolt was thus resolved but finished after the exile (see Chapter 5). Claudian shows no awareness of any subsequent events: Gaïnas demanded that Eutropius be executed, later demanded that the prefect whom he had used to secure this execution be exiled, and in summer 400 rose in open rebellion himself.[52] He was defeated and driven beyond the borders by yet another Gothic general in Roman service, Fravitta,[53] and finally killed by Huns. They signaled their wish to cooperate with the Roman Empire by sending Gaïnas's head back to Constantinople. It arrived and was paraded in the city no earlier than 3 January 401.[54]

Stilicho's status as *hostis publicus* presumably lapsed along with Eutropius's other policies annulled on his deposition in 399 (*CTh* 9.40.17); Eastern documents recognize the consulate Stilicho took in 400.[55] Yet contemporary West-

---

74, 207 (brief notice of the revolt, as a relatively insignificant affair in Gothic history); Liebeschuetz 1990, 100–103. Claudian calls Tribigild Tarbigilus, but I use the form now conventional (M. Schönfeld, *Wörterbuch der altgermanischen Personen- und Völkernamen* [Heidelberg: Carl Winter, 1911], 220–21, was inclined to prefer Tarbigildus over Tribigildus, but consensus is hard to win from the sources). On *laeti*, see A. H. M. Jones 1964, 620, 1256–57 n. 26: the term is attested in Gaul and Italy, not in the East, but since the arrangements seem to be the same, I shall adopt it as a convenient shorthand. Liebeschuetz (12–13) tentatively proposed that the Phrygian Gruthungi might have been federate troops, but the evidence he discussed (101) implies that federate status would have improved the Gruthungi's position, had they accepted it to settle their revolt.

49. Leo, *PLRE* 2.661–62; Gaïnas, *PLRE* 1.379–80.

50. Claudian claims, while Leo fled from battle (*Eutr.* 2.440–55), but perhaps really in combat.

51. Seeck 1895, 1146–47.

52. Gaïnas's coup and related Eastern internal and barbarian affairs are explored by Alan Cameron and Long 1993.

53. *PLRE* 1.372–73.

54. This date is given by *Chron. Marc.* s.a. 401 (*Chron. Min.* 2.66.21–30), and is followed by Seeck 1913, 325, 570. Different reconstructions of events would have to date the arrival later: cf. Zos. 5.22; Philost. 11.8; Maenchen-Helfen 1973, 59.

55. *CLRE* s.a. 400.

ern inscriptions all omit Stilicho's Eastern colleague Aurelian. Claudian's second consular panegyric for Stilicho refers darkly to "an unmoving and undutiful throng . . . using the royal name as a screen for its own madness" at Arcadius's court (*Stil.* 2.79–80); Claudian insists that Stilicho's loyalty to Arcadius is unshaken, but it did not extend to recognizing his consul that year. In 401 mutual recognition of consuls resumed. The rifts stemming from Eutropius's predominance were at last repaired.[56]

IN THE CORPUS OF Claudian's political poems as a group, after his panegyric for Olybrius and Probinus, Stilicho remains the uncontestably central figure. He always receives praise. That Claudian did not merely admire Stilicho and his achievements, and approve of his plans, but set out systematically to promote them as "Stilicho's official propagandist" is the fundamental thesis of Alan Cameron's important study published in 1970, *Claudian: Poetry and Propaganda at the Court of Honorius.* Claudian expressly addresses political topics throughout a large body of his works, so that their political function demands investigation. Cameron definitively set the terms for this discussion, whether or not later investigators have agreed with his conclusions. In the main, they have, although Siegmar Döpp, whose *Zeitgeschichte in Dichtungen Claudians* (1980) compares with Cameron's book in scope, and Christian Gnilka have criticized Cameron's approach in their reviews.[57] Gnilka in his 1976 article, "Dichtung und Geschichte im Werk Claudians," particularly rejected the applicability of Cameron's model of "propaganda" to *In Eutropium.*[58] I shall address aspects of this debate further in the chapters that follow. The traditions of political invective in which *In Eutropium* is rooted, the events and information to which its parts respond, its possible audiences and the ways in which it engages their literary and political sensibilities, all relate to the invective's operation in the public sphere.

The political implications of *In Eutropium* in no way preclude, and must not obscure, its literary, artistic quintessence. Rather, the invective works through

---

56. The victorious Fravitta and Fl. Vincentius (*PLRE* 2.1169; perhaps still *PPO Galliarum* to receive the high honor of the consulate; his successor does not appear till 25 June 401, *PLRE* 1.63–64, Andromachus 3) were recognized jointly throughout the empire in 401, Arcadius and Honorius, each for the fifth time, in 402, and the baby Theodosius II with the otherwise retired general Rumoridus in 403 (*PLRE* 1.786 inferred from the honor that he took part in defending Italy against Alaric in 402). Honorius did not recognize the Eastern colleague of his sixth consulate in 404, Aristaenetus (*PLRE* 1.104–5), but that is a separate story; Claudian does not seem to allude to the nonrecognition in *6 Cons.* Cf. *CLRE* s.aa.

57. Döpp 1975; Gnilka 1977.

58. Gnilka 1976.

its artistry. Claudian incorporates complex literary allusions in an epical and rhetorical matrix to create brilliant images of degradation, corruption, and incompetence; he binds them unforgettably about his invective victim.[59]

59. The literary operation of *Eutr.* has never before been the object of extensive study in its own right. Gnilka 1976 came closest, but his reading was subsumed by his thesis that *Eutr.* presents a program of "anti-Byzantinism" (119); see discussion, Chap. 8. Andrews 1931 focused on the text, chiefly in criticism of Platnauer 1922. Fargues's 1933 *Invectives* as a specific commentary complemented his general study of Claudian's life and works, *Claudien.* Schweckendiek 1992 has now produced a valuable commentary incorporating perspectives gained through more recent research. He and I each undertook our dissertations, from which his and this present work derive, independently at about the same time; we learned of one another and exchanged manuscripts only after these preliminary works were completed.

PART ONE

The Literary World
of *In Eutropium*

✦

CHAPTER ONE

Structure and Genre

✦

A FIRST STEP TOWARD understanding how *In Eutropium* struck its initial audiences, and what it reveals about Claudian's circumstances and aims, is to analyze its literary form. Both the tasks of identifying elements within a work and of recognizing their configuration as a whole presuppose a system of conventions that define elements and overall forms. These conventions are conveniently summarized by the labels of genre.[1] There is nothing about generic categories that is absolute, for they are determined organically by evolving literary traditions. A given work shifts the nucleus of the genre even as it participates in it. Moreover, formalized generic criteria merely pick out salient components from a more shadowy but significant aggregate: they alone do not tell the whole story. Nor does a work's conformity with any particular generic tradition mean that it may not also share in others. Genre is useful as it classifies clusters of features that coalesce distinctively at certain points in the continuum of literary history. Current combinations may guide the author in realizing his original conception; they do not prevent him from varying conventional patterns or introducing new elements. Generic affinities, as they emerge within a new work, prompt the audience to recall impressions left by other works of similar form. They do not block perception of the author's innovations; they rather supply a provisional model in terms of which the new composition can be apprehended. As it unfolds it progressively redirects its audience's expectations.[2] The model finally arrived at also broadens the basis on which to understand how elements function within the whole.

1. See generally Fowler 1982, who underlined the points that follow.
2. Thus I treat genre as producing associations that inform the process of reading, not as excluding possibilities; generic criticism does not have to fall into the restrictive traps Duncan F. Kennedy criticized in " 'Augustan' and 'Anti-Augustan': Reflections on Terms of Reference" in Powell 1992, 46–47. I shall return to the question of how *Eutr.* was received in Part III.

PROSE ORATORY conventionally treated the same types of political subject as Claudian's poems. Occasions for it proliferated with late antique court ceremonial. Rhetorical treatises such as the second ascribed to Menander detail ways to organize formal speeches for numerous public and private occasions.[3] The format prescribed for the *basilikos logos*, or imperial speech, could be used to praise the emperor on virtually any occasion; many preserved speeches follow its main lines closely. The same scheme also was adapted for praising lesser officials in the "address," or *prosphonetikos logos*, and for funeral eulogies, *epitaphioi logoi*.[4] This basic format was a flexible and powerful literary model.

But although Claudian delivered his political works at the court of Honorius, at consular inaugurations, victory celebrations, and other occasions that ceremonial orations commonly adorned, one difference would immediately have struck his hearers: these pieces were not prose but poetry. Claudian composed in dactylic hexameters of great purity.[5] They necessarily resonate with long traditions of epic: members of his audience who had enjoyed a literary education could instantly appreciate the noble antiquity of Claudian's metrical form. Many specific allusions within his poems sharpen these associations.[6]

Latin satire shared the hexameter line, although its versification was less regularized than Vergilian or Ovidian epic. Peculiarities such as an occasional accented monosyllable placed last in the line or spondaic fifth foot validate Horace's claim to write "pure conversational speech" (*sermo merus, Serm.* 1.4.48).[7] They may also be considered to evoke the more archaic verse of the first satirists, Ennius and Lucilius. Claudian does not follow this metrical

3. Russell and Wilson in their edition and commentary dated both Menandrian treatises to the reign of Diocletian (1981, xxxiv–xl). On the proliferation of rhetorical forms, see Kennedy 1983, 68–70.

4. *Basilikos logos*, Men. Rh. 368.1–377.30; *prosphonetikos*, 414.31–415.5; *epitaphios*, 419.1–15; cf. Theon, Spengel 2.109.20–24.

5. Also the lyric Fescennines and elegiac prefaces to some hexameter pieces; they share the same purity. See further Birt 1892, ccxi–ccxix; Duckworth 1967, 117–26; Alan Cameron 1970, 287–92.

6. On the content, currency, and effects of literary education in late antiquity, see Kaster 1988, esp. chaps. 1 and 2. I discuss allusions within *Eutr.* in later sections.

7. See George E. Duckworth, "Horace's Hexameters and the Date of the *Ars Poetica*," *TAPA* 96 (1965): 73–95, and "Five Centuries of Latin Hexameter Poetry: Silver Age and Late Empire," *TAPA* 98 (1967): 109–17, comparing "Variety and Repetition in Vergil's Hexameters," *TAPA* 95 (1964): 9–65; Adolf Kiessling, ed., *Q. Horatius Flaccus: Oden und Epoden*, 11th ed., revised by Richard Heinze, supplemented by Erich Burck (Zurich: Weidmann, 1964), xxvii–xlv; G. Eskuche in Ludwig Friedlaender, *D. Junii Juvenalis Saturarum Libri*, 2 vols. (Leipzig: S. Hirzel, 1895), 57–80.

byway; his hexameter has a purely epic cadence.[8] But the subject of *In Eu-tropium* did inspire satirical handling in other ways. Eutropius was a eunuch. He had risen in the domestic service of the palace to its top, as *praepositus sacri cubiculi.*[9] He had developed great influence over Arcadius, extending well beyond the domestic concerns of the palace. He won the consulate for 399 by actions even less expected of a eunuch chamberlain: he took command of the Eastern army and drove back from Armenia a band of invading Huns.[10] In attacking Eutropius, Claudian exercises a sharp sense of paradox and bitter wit to accentuate the incongruity of his person and political position. Juxtaposi-tions and expostulations often recalling Juvenalian satire make Eutropius ap-pear reprehensibly ludicrous.

Theodor Birt raised the question of whether *In Eutropium* is satire, in *Zwei politische Satiren des alten Rom* (1888). The first problem he faced was defining the genre of satire.[11] He found too many exceptions to the distinctions drawn in the scholarly literature of his time. Juvenal's famous tag *facit indignatio versum* (*Sat.* 1.79) compellingly supplies one view of satire, but Birt noted that Horace and Lucilius are not always indignant.[12] Horace's Canidia and many of Lucilius's victims belie the notion that satire attacks generalities rather than individuals. Birt found more fully characteristic the idea that satire combines a serious purpose with a jesting or mocking technique. In keeping with this idea, he singled out Claudian's declaration, "examples are born to outdo the jokes of comedy and the woes of tragedy" (1.298–99), as the motto of *In Eutropium* and pronounced it a satire; a century later, Severin Koster still applauded Birt for the motto.[13] Koster nonetheless discussed *In Eutropium* as invective.

Whereas the definitions Birt rejected exclude some pieces generally regarded as satires, Birt found his "seriocomic" combination in works belonging to virtually every ancient genre as defined by other criteria.[14] Although *In Eu-*

---

8. Exceptionally, *Eutr.* 1.229, *iamque oblita sui nec sobria divitiis mens* ("his mind forgetful of itself and drunk on riches"), where the lurching line apes Eutropius's instability.

9. On the office, see Guyot 1980, 130–57; A. H. M. Jones 1964, 566–70; DeGaiffier 1957; Dunlap 1924; on "The Political Power of Eunuchs," see Hopkins 1978, 172–96.

10. Albert 1979; Liebeschuetz 1990, 96–100. On the historical dimensions of *Eutr.*, see Parts II and III.

11. Birt 1888, 6–35.

12. Even Juvenal relaxed his indignation in his later books: see, e.g., W. S. Anderson 1982, 277–92 = "The Programs of Juvenal's Later Books," *Classical Philology* 57 (1962): 145–60, and 293–361 = "Anger in Juvenal and Seneca," *California Publications in Classi-cal Philology* 19 (1964): 127–96; Braund 1988.

13. Birt 1888, 40; Koster 1980, 323.

14. Compare the survey of Lawrence Giangrande, *The Use of Spoudaiogeloion in Greek and Roman Literature* (The Hague: Mouton, 1972).

tropium qualifies handily, the standard too easily embraces too many things to define a class bound by significant affinities. Mockery in *In Eutropium* appears readily, but Birt identified no standard for seriousness of purpose. His discussion shows that he was willing to recognize it on almost any grounds. He delineated a theme or style, which can operate within many genres. He did not establish a defining criterion of satire alone.

Ulrich von Wilamowitz-Moellendorff notoriously declared that there is no genre of satire, but only Lucilius, Horace, Persius, and Juvenal.[15] Wilamowitz himself did not rest great weight on this observation. It supports merely an incidental contrast of archaic and classical Greek with Roman authors, in whom he perceived more individuality; but he adduced satire first, as his strongest case. Nonetheless, these writers themselves and ancient as well as modern readers have sensed the connections of a tradition between them. It arises from the confluence of several factors.

Satura became a Roman literary term when Ennius applied it to his books of miscellaneous informal poems.[16] Ancient grammarians derived it variously:[17] they connected it either with satyrs, for their ridiculous and shameful activities; with *lanx satura*, a platter offering to the gods a diverse abundance of first fruits; with *satura* as the name for a stuffing composed of numerous foods; or with omnibus legislation known as *lex satura*. Modern scholars generally consider the association with satyrs secondary. The other three etymologies all limn a form that brings multitudinous disparate elements into a new unity. The primary cohesive force in ancient satire, from Ennius onward, was the strongly personal vision the authors projected.[18] Horace calls attention to how intimately and completely his chief model, Lucilius, reveals himself in his books. He and Persius and Juvenal similarly present their satires as personal responses.[19] Thus, ancient views of satire embraced both variousness and just the vivid individuality of the poet's persona that moved Wilamowitz to declare genre inapplicable to satire.

15. Ulrich von Wilamowitz-Moellendorff, *Griechische Verskunst* (Berlin: Weidmann, 1921; rpt. Darmstadt: Wissenschaftliche Buchgesellschaft, 1958), 42 n. 1.

16. B. L. Ullman, "*Satura* and Satire," *Classical Philology* 8 (1913): 172–94; more cautiously, Waszink 1972, 101–5.

17. Diom. 3.485.30–486.16 Keil I. See discussion by Van Rooy 1965, 1–29; cf. 124–43. C. J. Classen, "Satire—the Elusive Genre," *Symbolae Osloenses* 63 (1988): 95–121, took issue with Van Rooy on the etymological vicissitudes of *satura* and *satiricus*, but upheld "the heterogeneity of its elements" (104) as satire's essential characteristic.

18. Waszink 1972, 112–19, on Ennius and Lucilius; Van Rooy 1965, 30–89.

19. Horace on Lucilius, *Serm.* 2.1.30–34; he claims that his own satires record good and bad examples of conduct for himself (*Serm.* 1.4.103–40), or gratify a compulsion to versify (*Serm.* 2.1.24–34). Persius introduces his satires as a secret kept from all the world (*Sat.* 1.114–34), Juvenal his as his revenge on contemporary literary taste (*Sat.* 1.1–21).

Lucilius added a distinctive current of personal attack.[20] Horace and later satirists, however, although they explicitly referred to Lucilius's aggressiveness when characterizing their own satires, transmuted it to general moral or philosophical admonition. In particular, they moved away from Lucilius's contemporary political criticism. One factor was the changed political environment of the Roman Empire as opposed to the Roman Republic. Tacitus, looking back on more than a century of imperial government, remarks that eloquence has transferred its attentions from politics to the courts, because the emperors have stilled political contention.[21] Quintilian similarly notes that forensic speeches more seldom need rhetorical figures to mask criticism of the powerful than do speeches criticizing a tyrant (*Inst. Or.* 9.2.67–68); he is discussing school exercises, but the exercises trained students for practical situations.[22] His choice of a model for political discourse reflects both the artificial tradition of the schools and present risks in the face of absolute power. Satire in the imperial period veiled its political component and diffused it over broader ethical issues.

Horace in the programmatic *Sermo* 4 of his first book gives the change a pedigree, or at least an analogue, from Attic comedy. He cites Eupolis, Cratinus, and Aristophanes as models for Lucilius, but declares that his own satires follow the pattern of his father's moral instruction: as Eleanor Winsor Leach has shown, Horace casts as his father a persona shaped by Terence and Attic New Comedy.[23] Old Comedy assailed individuals, especially politicians, openly, by name, with fantastic vehemence; New Comedy focused on more realistic domestic plots enacted by characters who represent types.[24] Horace implies that his satire too will avoid polemic and address social interactions generally. I. M. LeM. DuQuesnay has argued that book 1 of Horace's *Sermones* does bear a political message, which advocates acquiescence to Octavian's new regime;[25] but such a quietistic exhortation strengthens itself by promoting alternative concerns. When Horace imitates Lucilius's great journey-satire (book 3) in his "Journey to Brundisium" (*Sermo* 1.5), which was occasioned by

20. Waszink 1972, 112; Van Rooy 1965, 51–55; Knoche 1975, 32–33; cf. Hor. *Serm.* 1.10.3–4; Pers. 1.114–15; Juv. 1.165–67.

21. Tac. *Dial.* 36–41, esp. 38.2; cf. Ronald Syme, *Tacitus*, 2 vols. (Oxford: Clarendon Press, 1958), 100–111. I am grateful to Barbara Saylor Rodgers for emphasizing this point. Townend 1973, 150–52, argued that Juv. 7 refers to *Dial.*

22. On ancient rhetorical training, see further in Chap. 3.II. Ahl 1984 acutely elucidated Greco-Roman doctrines of figured speech.

23. Eleanor Winsor Leach, "Horace's *pater optimus* and Terence's Demea: Autobiographical Fiction and Comedy in *Sermo* I,4," *American Journal of Philology* 92 (1971): 616–32.

24. F. H. Sandbach, *The Comic Theatre of Greece and Rome* (London: Chatto and Windus, 1977), 41–54 and 55–75, nicely summarized qualities of Old and New Comedy.

25. DuQuesnay 1984.

Maecenas's embassy to Antony in 37 B.C. on behalf of Octavian, the urgent mission is adumbrated only obliquely. Horace unleashes no political vituperation. Instead he depicts the travelers' friendly enjoyment of one another's company, resuming the thematic focus of *Sermo* 1.3. At the same time, the various stages of travel link up a virtuoso display of satiric episodes. Horace's technique implicitly corrects Lucilius's, in fulfillment of his literary critique in *Sermo* 1.4.[26]

The ancient *Life* of Persius and scholia to his *Satire* 1 identify Nero as the author of verses Persius decries.[27] He fully equates stylistic with moral criticism; morality potentially comprehends capacity to rule, which forms the point of departure for *Satire* 4. But the Stoic paradigm of the Wise Man who alone is truly King pertains to anyone governing his own life.[28] Persius consistently resolves issues at the universally applicable level of the individual soul. When he touches on an imperial event expressly, it is incidental (*Sat.* 6.43–52). A victory occasions festivity. *Satire* 6 considers neither the emperor nor the victory nor even the festivity itself, but the propriety of spending from one's estate on any occasion rather than hoarding it all for a future heir. Persius nowhere satirizes political practice.

Juvenal attacks Domitian in *Satire* 4, but comments on his death at its close (*Sat.* 4.150–54): he explicitly ranks Domitian with the inoffensively remote ostensible targets he promises in *Satire* 1 to select from among the dead (*Sat.* 1.162–71). Even though Juvenal depicts Domitian and his courtiers very specifi-

---

26. On the multiple objectives of Hor. *Serm.* 1.5, see Sallmann 1974; cf. C. J. Classen, "Die Kritik des Horaz an Lucilius in den Satiren I 4 und I 5," *Hermes* 109 (1981): 339–60.

27. *V. Pers.* 54–59 Clausen; Σ ad *Sat.* 1.93, 99 Jahn; cf. Σ ad *Sat.* 1.121 Jahn. Sullivan 1985, 74–114, drew the strongest case for political implications: they remain very general. Vasily Rudich, *Political Dissidence under Nero: The Price of Dissimulation* (London: Routledge, 1993), 60–62, argued that, although the *Satires* hold aloof from politics (cf., however, forthcoming work promised in his note, 278–79), Persius's lost juvenilia were pointedly Republican. Emily Gowers, "Persius and the Decoction of Nero," in *Reflections of Nero: Culture, History and Representation*, ed. Jás Elsner and Jamie Masters (London: Duckworth, 1994), 131–50, impressionistically related some of Persius's images to other views of the Neronian age.

28. Ludwig Edelstein, *The Meaning of Stoicism*, Martin Classical Lectures 21 (Cambridge, Mass.: Harvard University Press for Oberlin College, 1966; rpt. 1968), 1–18, conveniently outlined the ideology of the Stoic sage; Miriam Griffin, "Philosophy, Politics, and Politicians at Rome," and Elizabeth Rawson, "Roman Rulers and the Philosophic Adviser," both in *Philosophia Togata: Essays on Philosophy and Roman Society*, ed. Miriam Griffin and Jonathan Barnes (Oxford: Clarendon Press, 1989), 1–37 and 233–57, assessed the complex and limited relevance of philosophy in late Republican and early imperial politics. On Persius's stoicism, see generally Dessen 1968; Ramage, "Persius, the Philosopher-Satirist," in *Roman Satirists and Their Satire: The Fine Art of Criticism in Ancient Rome*, by Edwin S. Ramage, David L. Sigsbee, and Sigmund G. Fredericks (Park Ridge, N.J.: Noyes Press, 1974), 114–35.

cally, they fit the program of his first book of satires by embodying a type of situation rather than their individual historical selves. On the one hand, his pose of fearing execution if he named living sinners (*Sat.* 1.150–57) prompts readers to consider contemporary specifics; on the other, his representation of one set of evils by another refracts his criticism over more than one object. The first place given in *Satire* 4 to Crispinus's lust and extravagance also pulls its focus back from Domitian's court alone.[29]

Although a satire immediately directs its criticism outward upon an other, the audience becomes implicated in its process of reflection. The act of reading casts the reader in the role of "you" whom satirists confront. Sometimes they demand agreement, as when Persius praises an addressee who does not share the vice he is reprobating (e.g., *Sat.* 2.3–4), or when Juvenal puts his addressee in a situation that merits satirical resentment (e.g., *Sat.* 1.37–39). Adversarial at other times, they charge "you" with varied misconceptions. Horace claims in *Sermo* 1.1 that his narratives match the behavior of his audience, if identities were changed (*mutato nomine de te fabula narratur, Serm.* 1.1.69–70). Self-reflective reading also enables satires to provide instructional models, just as Horace says his father pointed out to him good and bad models of conduct (*Serm.* 1.4.103–26; cf. 78–103, 126–43).[30] The way he represents himself writing satires exemplifies a way for the reader to take and apply them. Persius too, most clearly in the dialogue of *Satire* 5 between himself and his teacher Cornutus, offers an image of himself posing paradigmatically before a reader whom his satires may instruct. Even a satirist like Juvenal, whose extreme stance repels a reader from identifying with him, can indirectly prompt moral contemplation. William Anderson in several papers has profitably applied to Roman satire Alvin Kernan's model of how the satiric authorial persona operates.[31]

Kernan identified "the Satirist" as a dramatic character created within individual satires. He showed that it remains highly consistent in works from classical antiquity to the English Renaissance, and argued that it cannot corre-

29. On Crispinus in Juv. 4, see esp. Townend 1973, 155–57. F. M. A. Jones 1990 recently provided a valuable discussion of the whole satire with full references to earlier studies. Edwin S. Ramage, "Juvenal and the Establishment. Denigration of Predecessor in the 'Satires,'" *ANRW* 2.33.1 (1989): 640–707, read Juvenal's references to former emperors as disparagement indirectly praising the current regime.

30. Birt 1888 ignored both implicit and explicit instructional stances taken by Horace but credited Persius and Juvenal with instructing.

31. Conveniently assembled in W. S. Anderson 1982, particularly 3–10 = "Roman Satirists and Literary Criticism," *Bucknell Review* 12, 3 (1964): 106–13; 169–93 = "Persius and the Rejection of Society," *Wissenschaftliche Zeitschr. W. Pieck-Universität Rostock, Gesell. u. Sprachwiss. Reihe* 15 (1966): 409–16; 293–361 = "Anger in Juvenal and Seneca," *California Publications in Classical Philology* 19 (1964): 127–96. Kernan [1959] 1971; on the Satirist, 1971, 252, 258–69. The quotations that follow come from 264.

spond precisely to the true character of so many authors. It assumes a pose of righteousness and denounces vice. Yet behind this avowed "public personality" of the Satirist, Kernan noted, there stands "a darker side to his nature, a private personality which the author may or may not allow his Satirist to discuss openly, and this personality is, like the public personality, consequent upon the Satirist's function in satire." For example, the Satirist claims that other forms of literature are all lies and that he himself alone tells the truth, and yet he gives only a one-sided and distorted picture of a reality in which vice is threateningly ubiquitous. He claims to speak plainly, but is a master of rhetorical persuasion. He reviles vice, yet glories in recounting its lurid horrors. He abhors the intemperance and unreasonableness of his targets, but he himself exhibits much worse as he intemperately decries them. Given these inconsistencies, a morally suspect Satirist may well undercut his own raillery at the vice of the world. But even when he does, doubts about the character's sincerity and self-knowledge broach ethical questions. The expressed moral purpose supplies a moral frame for any response. Arguably, the author provokes more profound examination of the Satirist than of his ostensible targets. John G. W. Henderson has even proposed that satire can function as a "paradigm of '*bad*' criticism . . . it could well be a standard feature of 'Satire' that you be expected to ask yourself continuously whether you agree, are supposed to agree, keep catching yourself agreeing, and so on (or whether you *dis*-agree, etc.)."[32] Satire in which the Satirist expressly targets himself, like Horace, even more plainly submits his character for analysis.[33]

Epic travesty, which appears intermittently in Persius and Juvenal and more extensively in Horace's *Sermones* 1.7 and 2.5, can satirize a literary target. Kernan tied mockery of high style to the Satirist's effort to present himself as a plain speaker (260). Persius and Juvenal, professing to disdain the heroic topics and inflated language of epic and tragedy, competitively insist that their more mundane genre is superior because it considers issues of more real importance.[34] High epic style and the lofty associations of epic characters and situations can also accentuate the baseness of topics they frame, as when Teresias teaches Ulixes how to hunt for legacies in Horace's *Sermo* 2.5.[35]

The Roman satirists, as Birt observed, variously exploit humor as they animadvert on their topics. Leon Guilhamet, who focused on English satire but furthered Kernan's work across the whole satiric tradition, observed that

32. John G. W. Henderson, "Not 'Women in Roman Satire' but 'When Satire Writes "Woman,"'" in *Satire and Society in Ancient Rome*, ed. Susan H. Braund, Exeter Studies in History 23 (Exeter: University Publications, 1989), 90.

33. E.g., Hor. *Serm.* 1.3.19–28; cf. Kernan [1959] 1971, 268–69.

34. E.g., Pers. 5.1–4; Juv. 1.1–14, 51–54. Cf. Winkler 1989; Bramble 1974, 12–13, 164–73.

35. Sallmann 1970, 181, 184, noted that Hor. *Serm.* 2.5 is not directed primarily against epic as a genre.

the combination of reproach with humor distinguishes satiric from comic perspective.[36] Simple reproach is invective, but invective too sometimes exploits forms of humor in stirring animosity against its targets. Conversely, satire sometimes calls for harsh condemnation along with reflection. Amy Richlin has emphasized the antagonism with which Roman satirists call their audience to laugh with them at some denigrated absurdity.[37] By their laughter they affirm a shared superiority to the target. In order to differentiate invective and satire, Guilhamet adopted the argument of Barbara Herrnstein Smith's essay "Poetry as Fiction."[38] Smith defined "natural discourse" as any "verbal acts of real persons on particular occasions in response to particular sets of circumstances." "Fictive discourse," on the other hand, represents verbal acts artificially, and is recognized by its audience as an imitation of speech; if an audience fails to recognize the imitation, the fiction ceases to operate as such. Guilhamet (12–13) insisted that fictive discourse fundamentally circumscribes satire. If fictive techniques such as irony, combination of genres, or an authorial persona pervasively mark a whole work, it is framed off as a literary artifact. Instead of transparently stating its manifest content, it artistically represents such a statement. Then it can be satire, if it otherwise operates satirically. "If, however, the fictive devices remain subordinate to the purposes of natural discourse, there is no deformation and, consequently, no generic change from rhetoric to fiction" (13). A work may employ satiric modes of expression without so transforming itself.

Guilhamet's definition relies on a determination that in some works will be very subtle indeed. The rigorous questioning of assumptions demanded by modern critical theory makes it as hard to measure pervasive fictiveness as Birt's seriousness of purpose. But Claudian at the close of *In Eutropium* 1 includes a detail that definitely places his poem in relationship to historical reality.[39] He pictures Roma begging Honorius and Stilicho not to recognize the eunuch consul (*Eutr.* 1.431–99). In actuality, they did not.[40] Roma is an artistic personification, and Claudian seems to have published the poem with this

---

36. Guilhamet discussed basic generic criteria in his introductory chapter (1987, 1–17).

37. See particularly Richlin [1983] 1992, 59–63.

38. B. H. Smith, "Poetry as Fiction," *New Literary History* 2 (1971): 259–82; rpt. in *New Directions in Literary History*, ed. Ralph Cohen (Baltimore: Johns Hopkins University Press, 1974), and in B. H. Smith, *On the Margins of Discourse: The Relation of Literature to Language* (Chicago: University of Chicago Press, 1978), 14–40. I quote Smith's definition of natural discourse from 15 and paraphrase her definition of fictive discourse from 24–25, 28. I emphasize the reader's collaboration in the fiction a little more sharply than Smith; Guilhamet did not address the issue.

39. Koster 1980, 353, emphasized historical concreteness as the essence of invective.

40. Cf. *M. Theod.* 265–69; *Eutr.* 2.122–32; *Stil.* 2.291–311; *CLRE* s.a. 399.

request after it had been fulfilled,[41] but these types of fictitiousness do not obscure the essential practicality of the request itself. It prevents the recontextualization Guilhamet described as creating satire from rhetoric. The request also presupposes, within the structure of Claudian's poem, an immediate, unique target. It implicitly supplies the same target to his audience. It does not provoke contemplation of wider political problems. It directs hostility against Eutropius, and it suggests that this hostility is to be answered by specific political acts. Roma's second plea, that Stilicho move to depose Eutropius, was never realized, nor was the parallel request of Aurora in book 2; but they too manifestly contemplate real action.

The question of Claudian's historical purpose is more complex, and I shall return to it, but this blunt statement of the surface of the text does not misrepresent his fundamental concerns in a way that would affect the generic classification of *In Eutropium*. His text is directed not at literary abstraction, nor yet at political, ethical, or philosophical reflection, but at political action in the real world.

Arthur H. Weston, surveying modal satire in Latin literature after Juvenal, correctly placed in its context Claudian's remark about comedy and tragedy that Birt quoted as a motto.[42] It is evoked by another paradox immediately preceding it, which also concerns Eutropius's holding high offices: "anything that is an adornment of men, as a eunuch's is a crime" (1.297–98). In this connection, the idea that "examples are born to outdo the jokes of comedy and the woes of tragedy" does not evoke the seriocomic in the abstract, programmatically. It affirms that Eutropius, debased below the figures of comedy, commits wrongs more lamentable than those of tragedy. Claudian moves immediately to describe how ridiculously vile Eutropius looks in his glorious consular robes. This visual paradox is the goal at which the two verbal paradoxes aimed. It reiterates the same idea that Eutropius is unsuited to his position. Although Claudian uses satiric humor, he exploits his audience's ethical sensibilities and sense of the ridiculous only as these things serve his attack.

WHAT FORM DOES the attack take? Claudian begins with a catalog of portents, all of which pale in comparison with a eunuch consul. This is an even more eerie union of contraries than "half-beast births" and the rest (1.1). He considers what new disasters such a prodigy may signal and concludes that the omen must be averted by sacrificing the unnatural thing itself: "whatever the fates are preparing by this omen, may Eutropius expiate it with his neck" (1.22–

---

41. On the date of publication of *Eutr.*, see Chap. 5.
42. Weston 1915, 117.

23). This movement concisely introduces the subject of book 1, the catastrophe represented by Eutropius's consulate. It constitutes a proem (1.1–23). Eutropius is identified as eunuch, as consul (1.8), and finally by name (1.23). He is also a *monstrum* (1.8), a *prodigium*, and an *omen* (1.22), who threatens disaster for the state. He must be removed.

Claudian next explains in what senses Eutropius is a prodigy, focusing primarily on the social incongruities that he unites. A rebuke to Fortuna modulates the transition. In second-person address, she is more personified than the fates evoked in the proem, but reference to her as to them denies any human agency in Eutropius's rise. If she insists on making criminal slaves consul,[43] Claudian complains, she might at least restrict herself to those who have served only one master. Eutropius's were innumerable. Claudian next briefly summarizes Eutropius's slave career and increasing decrepitude: this synopsis constitutes a subsidiary proem introducing the section, of the type known as *theoria* (1.23–44).[44] The section as a whole recounts the experiences that shaped Eutropius's character (1.23–137). It advances him to the condition in which he entered the public life of the empire, in which he remains fixed from that point on, and which informs his malicious abuses.

Claudian begins with the shocking scene of Eutropius's castration. It marks his life indelibly. Virtually at birth, Claudian claims, "he was snatched for castration from the very breast; punishments took him up after his mother's guts" (1.44–45). His early career is launched: he serves first as a catamite. When his beauty fades, he becomes a pander. When he loses his effectiveness in that capacity he is made into a lady's maid. Finally, when he can do nothing at all, his masters turn him loose as a castoff into the world. Claudian deftly sketches each position. Eutropius's sexual role fixes an image of debased morality, and a point from which Claudian clocks his increasing physical debility.

Another subsidiary proem divides off the next section (1.138–50, 1.138–284). "There is a point where disdain helps too much." After having been rejected by all his masters, Eutropius is received into the palace. Claudian again ascribes the reversal to superhuman caprice, now Olympian. No process of events is shown to explain this mad favor. It occurs; and Eutropius appears suddenly at the height of his power and ferocity. The picture is timeless. Chronologically fixed incidents in the remainder of the section illustrate it with specific detail but do not fully activate it as true narrative.

The main body of the section falls into two parts. In the first Claudian terms Eutropius *iudex* (1.208, cf. 286; 1.151–228). It was a standard term for an impe-

---

43. Insofar as it defiles the civil honor of the consulate, slavery itself is a "servile crime" (*servile crimen, Eutr.* 1.26–27; cf. *Stil.* 2.324–25); Claudian takes the thought yet farther by imagining chain-gang and workhouse slaves (*compede*, 1.27; *ergastula*, 1.28).

44. Viljamaa 1968, 71–72, discussed the types of preface in early Byzantine encomia.

rial official whose competency included administration of the laws, so that it subsumes both strictly judicial and broader magisterial functions.[45] Abundantius's fall and the confiscation of his property typify how Eutropius abuses the former.[46] He had been Eutropius's patron (1.151–70); Eutropius's ingratitude heightens the injury. Throughout the subsection cruelty and avarice intertwine. Eutropius rages on more widely, filling prisons with nobles and distant lands with exiles. Claudian asserts that his having been a slave himself intensifies his savagery. Worse yet is his greed. Castrated, he lusts only for gold. His avarice itself is cruel, specifically, "bloody" (cruentam, 1.192). It thus recalls the "bloody tortures" to which "his earliest cradle-days were owed" (cunabula prima cruentis / debita suppliciis, 1.44–45) in Claudian's earlier account of his castration. Such echoes evaluate the influence on Eutropius's official career of the character formed by his career as a slave.

Besides abusing his capacity as judge, Eutropius as a magistrate also feeds his covetousness by prostituting the provinces. Claudian first depicts Eutropius's sales office and catalogs the dominated lands fallen to Eutropius's service. Finally he evokes the exotic luxuries in which Eutropius horridly wallows (1.190–228).

In the second part of the section, Claudian shifts to Eutropius's misdeeds in war (1.229–84). His eunuchry unfits him for martial deeds too. "He is a prodigy, whatever he does."[47] Having defiled civil office,[48] he now "prepares to violate arms as well, and heaps omens on portents" (1.236–37). Sweeping images of military disaster introduce the scene of Eutropius's return from war against the Huns, a travesty of a triumphal procession. Further expostulation at the close of the section urges Eutropius to resign from war for a more appropriate career: he should serve Minerva domestically, or direct violence at himself as one of Cybele's castrate priests, or at least, having been a pander,

45. TLL s.v. iudex, IBγ. On the appropriateness of this term for Eutropius's office, see Chap. 4.III.

46. Abundantius, PLRE 1.4–5. David Jordan has consulted Alan Cameron about an unpublished curse tablet from Tyre against Abundantius's son Uranius. The tablet identifies Abundantius as a στρατηλάτης, and names his wife Ava.

47. prodigium, quodcumque gerit, Eutr. 1.232. Platnauer 1922, 1.157, Andrews 1931, 51, and Koster 1980, 241, took prodigium as accusative, but in a context that discusses Eutropius's roles (iudicat eunuchus; quid iam de consule miror?, 1.231), it is parallel, as well as more forceful and concordant with the proem, to identify Eutropius himself as the prodigium (cf. 1.23).

48. The nonrhetorical analysis of Albert 1979, 624, identified Eutr. 1.229–34 as a separate section. But its reference to Eutropius's judicial role merely summarizes the previous section, and in the same breath Claudian looks ahead to Eutropius's culminating role as consul: these transitional lines slot Eutropius's military acts between his civil abuses and Claudian's next major topic.

bring Arcadius and Honorius together rather than splitting their fraternal harmony.

Crowning his other enormities comes Eutropius's demand for the consulate. Claudian formulates this transition much as he did the transition into deeds in war, alleging that Eutropius specifically purposed to pollute every possible sphere of activity (1.284–86). This idea forms a subsidiary proem to the next section (1.284–370). "He demands the year in reward for such achievements" as his campaign, so that the honor culminates his political career. The prospect of him as consul epitomizes all the monstrous incongruities his person and his public honors have represented hitherto. It brings together all the associations accumulated by Claudian's pictures of his rise. The comment it elicits thus refers summarily back to the whole portrait of Eutropius's career and forms the climax of Claudian's book.

The comprehensive evaluation is carried out through comparisons. Claudian exclaims how much worse this prodigy is than the archetypal sins of myth (1.287–99). Next he imagines the inauguration. He compares Eutropius in his consular robes to an ape a boy has dressed up in silk while leaving his back and buttocks bare, in order to amuse dinner guests (1.300–316). Claudian further decries the bad omens of the year in his own voice. He compares the prospect of this year to one hypothetically taken by a woman: it is worse, for there are women queens and goddesses and priestesses, whereas eunuchs are unfit for all these roles (1.317–45).[49] Finally, he turns to envisage reactions to the news (1.346–70). Implicitly, the first speaker compares the eunuch consul to traditional adynata. The second, with a series of lewd puns, compares Eutropius's honors to his supposed sexual proclivities. They too weigh Eutropius's consulate against broadly established norms of Roman social behavior and history, and find it impossibly debased.

The final section of book 1 turns from contemplating the unedifying spectacle of Eutropius to propose a practical reaction to his consulate (1.371–513). The personified goddess of Roman tradition, Roma herself, demands of Honorius and Stilicho that the abomination of the eunuch consul not be recognized in the West. Her scene climaxes the immediately preceding pair of human reactions as a third and higher response. She also recapitulates ideas raised earlier, explicitly opposing Eutropius to the achievements of Roman history and espe-

---

49. Schmidt 1976, 61, identified the omens as a first category of response, nature's, before the human reactions and Roma's that follow. But the omens occupy only three lines, in the final two of which they are subordinated to Roman divinity: "Cries of birds clamored, the year stood aghast / at the name. From his twin mouth Janus proclaims / it insane, and forbids a eunuch to be added to the fasti," *Eutr.* 1.317–20. These natural or supernatural and Roman responses introduce the competing possibility of a woman consul, on which the passage as a whole focuses.

cially of Honorius's own reign. At the same time, she impels a new movement in the book. Hers is the first named voice to speak in opposition to Eutropius: she therefore possesses a new dramatic concreteness, for all that she personifies an abstract concept. She acts as a character, more truly than even Eutropius, who rather is displayed through a series of tableaux. Moreover, her call to respond to Eutropius's consulate involves her audience within the poem, Stilicho and Honorius, in its concerns as the recital of complaints up to that point had not. By the sympathetic magic of dramatic representation, the emotions of the audience hearing the poem are also engaged the more. Roma gives a direction to the emotions roused by the whole book.

In a subsidiary proem, Roma exclaims in outrage to herself, flies to Honorius's court and admires the young and warlike prince (1.371–91). She begins to speak in good rhetorical form, with a *prolalia* that both introduces her main topic and seeks her addressee's goodwill:[50] she praises the good state to which he has brought the West (1.391–411). Yet now, she complains, Eutropius's prominence affronts her majesty and all the patriots of the ancient republic. Let him have the East if need be, but the dishonor must not cross the Alps (1.432–33; cf. 319, 436). She elaborates the plea in peroration to Honorius (1.488–99). Her request had a practical correlate. The West did not recognize Eutropius as consul, although Claudian later credits the refusal to Stilicho rather than Honorius.[51] Finally Roma asks Stilicho to depose the slave and take over the East: the crack of a whip will suffice to cow opposition (1.500–513). This request went unfulfilled. Claudian places a similar one in Aurora's mouth at the conclusion of book 2. The relationship of the requests and actions, and Claudian's purpose in voicing the requests, are questions to which I shall return. For structural purposes, it is enough to observe that Roma's two requests direct toward practical ends the indignation Claudian arouses throughout the book.

Subsidiary proems articulate the movement of *In Eutropium* 1 into discrete steps. They each introduce a new topic for discussion; each section as a whole then dilates upon that topic. Claudian marks this essentially demonstrative impulse most clearly in the first instance, where the action covered by the section is briefly previewed (*Eutr.* 1.23–44). Once this principle of movement is established, he can introduce subsequent sections a little more loosely. Yet albeit less pointedly, a subsidiary proem delimits each section to come. Roma's concluding scene adapts this principle to its fundamentally different character. Its subsidiary proem introduces her speech through narrative. It does not literally forecast the action to follow, but by a corresponding function it foretokens the last section's change in movement and its opening out of the poem.

50. On rhetorical *prolalia*, see Viljamaa 1968, 71–72; G. Anderson 1993, 53–55.
51. *Eutr.* 2.123–32; *Stil.* 2.291–311; cf. *M. Theod.* 265–69; *CLRE* s.a. 399.

With this one, partial exception, the subsidiary proems endow *In Eutropium* 1 with a movement of statement and demonstration. The sections themselves remain essentially static. This dynamic corresponds well to that of the epideictic speeches whose place in imperial ceremonies Claudian's poems so often filled. They too are designed essentially to demonstrate a series of assertions about the official whose character and achievements they treat. Indeed, Menander Rhetor specifically recommends subsidiary proems within a speech of praise for an emperor's accomplishments: "You must learn and observe the precept that, when you are about to pass from topic to topic, it is necessary to make a preface about what you are going to take up, so that you make the hearer attentive and do not let the investigation of your topics go unnoticed or get hidden away" (δεῖ προοιμιάζεσθαι περὶ οὗ μέλλεις ἐγχειρεῖν, Men. Rh. 372.14–18). Does the content of the specific sections also correspond?

The fundamental modern study of ancient epideictic literature was carried out in 1902 by T. C. Burgess. Burgess surveyed its development from Gorgias to Christian homiletic, in both prescriptive theoretical works and actual epideictic texts. He found the tradition remarkably consistent. Throughout antiquity, epideictic literature remained broadly but primarily concerned with moral character, and it continued to use very much the same structures to accommodate praise and blame. Basic formulas corresponding well to the patterns of epideictic works are abstracted by, for example, Anaximenes, Dionysius of Halicarnassus, Theon, Menander Rhetor, Aphthonius, and Nicolaus of Myra. They vary only slightly in detail. All instruct the speaker to accommodate the basic scheme to the qualities of his subject and the circumstances under which he presents his speech: certain topics should receive more or less emphasis, or at times need to be omitted entirely. Even when presenting their model prescriptively, rhetors emphasized its adaptability. Speakers did not all slavishly follow arbitrary instructions, nor did rhetors deliberately reproduce one another's work. Rather, consistent impulses shaped a strong but flexible generic model.

From the ancient prescriptive and practical texts Burgess synthesized his own outline of the primary headings for an epideictic work.[52] The proem may involve whatever the subject suggests, but protestations of inadequacy before so grand a subject are customary. *Genos* covers the subject's immediate and remote ancestry, including his city, country, or nation. Any or all may be treated. *Genesis* concerns his birth, particularly any omens or dreams that accompanied or preceded it. *Anatrophe* relates the circumstances of his youth, paying attention to early indications of his character such as love of learning, natural ability, or special aptitudes. His *epitedeumata* are actions considered as they relate to personal choice. Different authors either connect this topic with

52. Burgess 1902, 122–26.

the subject's choice of profession, or use it to discuss generally how his deeds reveal his character; such a treatment of *epitedeumata* may be included in discussion of the subject's major achievements, his *praxeis*. They are the chief topic. They are most often divided into deeds in war and deeds in peace. The deeds are not meant to be treated fully or chronologically, but selected to illustrate the Socratic virtues of courage, justice, temperance, and wisdom; philanthropy is "often added as a second or more comprehensive virtue." The discussion always looks to character, even when it concerns external or physical qualities. *Synkrisis*, comparison, is an important but discretionary element of encomium. It may be used incidentally, of a single item or quality, when it is really a technique for amplifying another topic rather than a topic itself. It also may be used comprehensively, near the conclusion: this *teleiotate synkrisis* compares the whole of the subject's achievement with something else of the same order.[53] Finally, the epilogue like the proem will depend on what is being treated. A common pattern is to summarize the subject's life and urge the audience to imitate his virtues. It was generally thought most appropriate to end on a prayer.

In 1919 Lester B. Struthers enshrined a topic by using Burgess's synthesis as a standard to analyze Claudian's panegyrics, including the unfinished encomium of Stilicho's wife Serena and the encomium of Hercules doubtfully assigned to Claudian.[54] In all of them he found sections according with most of the major topics, in the standard order. When Claudian omitted a topic, Struthers found a reason to invoke the rhetors' exception. He concluded, "while it would be impossible to maintain that the poet had always set out with the well defined intention of writing this or that poem according to a body of fixed rules, the study of his panegyrics does show that Claudian has been continually guided in his workmanship by the precepts of the *rhetores*" (87). Struthers's procedure and conclusions were echoed by Pierre Fargues in his comprehensive study of Claudian.[55]

Naturally in an invective the standard topics organize revilement rather than praise.[56] But *In Eutropium* for a while defied formal study. While investigating how well Claudian's other invective, *In Rufinum*, fits the rhetorical pattern, Harry L. Levy declared flatly, "A study of the *In Eutropium*, however,

53. Cf. Men. Rh. 376.31–377.9.

54. Serena, *CM* 30; Hercules, *Carm. Spur. Susp.* 2 (as Alan Cameron 1970, 203, observed, its metrical irregularities make it most unlikely to be Claudian's). Struthers did not discuss *Stil.*, but claimed that it conforms fully to the pattern of the others (Struthers 1919, 53 n. 3).

55. Fargues, *Claudien* 191–218.

56. Cf. Theon, Spengel 2.112.17–18; Hermog. *Prog.* 7.36 (15.9–11 Rabe); Alex., Spengel 3.3.20–29; Aristid., Spengel 2.502.3; Aphthon. *Prog.* 8, 9 (21–31 Rabe); Nic. Soph., Spengel 3.482.11–14.

discloses no indication that its composition was influenced by the ψόγος pattern."[57] Distinguishing the two books allowed more positive conclusions. Alan Cameron recognized book 2 as a parody of epic, which apes its structure while debasing its themes. Book 1, on the other hand, he judged "scarcely qualified, by either subject-matter or treatment, as an epic, but basically a narrative all the same."[58] Within its chronological progress he did not perceive the topical arrangement of rhetorical invective.

Both Levy and Cameron differentiated topical and chronological arrangements as criteria for categorizing *In Rufinum* and *In Eutropium* as rhetorical invective or as epic. But chronological organization does not in itself invalidate rhetorical structure. Quintilian prescribes chronological and topical arrangements for encomium as alternatives (*Inst.* 3.7.15). Libanius's *Epitaphios* in praise of Julian (*Or.* 18) steps by the standard encomiastic progression in stages from family to upbringing to education, and then to Julian's deeds as emperor. This arrangement conforms to the precepts ascribed to Menander for a funeral speech (Men. Rh. 418.5–422.4). Libanius follows Julian's imperial career chronologically too, thus concentrating on his military deeds as Caesar with brief notices of civil and personal activities interlarded,[59] then on the peaceful activities with which he began his sole rule as Augustus, and finally on his great campaign against Persia. Julian's death concludes the narrative. Libanius laments; he closes with consolation. At every turn he evokes Julian's martial and social virtues, as rhetorical precepts require, but he does not organize his presentation by the virtues. Instead he continues throughout the speech the biographical narrative inaugurated by the formal scheme's progression from ancestry to birth to childhood development of innate character. Similarly Libanius's autobiographical *Oration* 1 "on his own Fortune" in its original form proceeded on the encomiastic model from praise of his birthplace Antioch to his family to his education to his mature achievements, and arranged them too in chronological order; he summed up with a triple *synkrisis* of Fortune in relationship to his private affairs, teaching, and performances, and finally ended on a prayer.[60] The compendious student of ancient rhetoric, George Kennedy, identified its technique simply as "that of an ordinary encomium which follows chronologically through the life of the subject."[61]

---

57. Levy 1946, 65 n. 31.

58. Alan Cameron 1970, 257.

59. Lib. *Or.* 18.52, 74, 82–87 (Julian's grain dispositions reported in 18.82–83 follow on a victory, and after he restores Heraclea in 18.87 he returns to campaigning); 18.90–110, the section beginning with the jealous intrigues against Julian that led his soldiers to proclaim him Augustus and advancing to the point of his departure on campaign against Constantius, is more civil than military but cannot be classified strictly.

60. The *synkrisis* spans Lib. *Or.* 1.145–55; cf. Norman 1965, xii–xvii and 191–94.

61. Kennedy 1983, 153.

Strictly topical arrangement may suffice to preclude epic, but it is the literary or argumentative end served by incidents arranged chronologically that determines whether they constitute an epic or rhetorical narrative.

Peter L. Schmidt recognized basic epideictic patterning in *In Eutropium* 1, first after Levy and Cameron denied it.[62] He allowed that it is "freely adapted" but not compromised by the biographical arrangement of material. In fact, if the book is analyzed according to the divisions marked by its subsidiary proems, it proves to conform even more closely and more completely than Schmidt discerned.

Claudian's proem to the whole of *In Eutropium* 1 does not protest his own inadequacy before a great subject, as encomiastic proems commonly do. But it clearly suits the subject he takes for invective. The motif of omens introduced in the proem recurs when the year reacts to Eutropius's polluting it as its consul (1.1–23, 317–19). Omens embody in the natural world a supernatural reaction to human events. They mark the interconnection of nature, humanity, and the gods. Roma picks up the theme as she concludes her argument to Honorius, when she demands sarcastically what wars can be waged and what fertility expected from marriages or the earth, under a eunuch's auspices (1.493–96). Divine interest in Eutropius's rise is ascribed to the fates in the proem, to Fortuna in the subsidiary proem immediately following, and to an Olympian god in the next subsidiary proem (1.22, 24, 140); divine interest in his fall is manifested extensively by Roma in the concluding section of the book. The proem thus undergirds the whole.

The first subsidiary proem encapsulates the endless cycle of Eutropius's masters, which is detailed more fully in the ensuing scenes of his slave career (1.23–44). He is seen first when his prospect of mature fertility is cut off by the castrator's blade (1.49–51). Repeated sales are briefly evoked. In the next series of vignettes Eutropius's effeminate beauty, his powers as a pander, and finally his ability to perform even mechanical tasks all fail. The end of the line is reached when he has deteriorated to "bare bones" (1.121–22), and is turned loose into the world like a dog who can do nothing but die. This progression encompasses the only changes Eutropius undergoes in book 1. It shapes both his physique and his character into a fixed form, in which he takes up the public activities depicted in the remainder of the poem. In just the same way education and physical training in youth, the normal topics of encomiastic *anatrophe*, mold their subject into the beauty, strength, wisdom, and virtue that inform his mature deeds. The section embraced by this subsidiary proem relates an *anatrophe* for Eutropius's professional career.

Schmidt (61) obscured the structural distinctions by attaching the subsidiary proem of the *anatrophe* to the proem of the whole, bringing it down to

---

62. Schmidt 1976, 61.

line 44. But the section's recapitulation of the ideas evoked in the subsidiary proem makes the two a unit. Another subsidiary proem and section intervene before the book advances to Eutropius's monstrous consulate. Schmidt also cut off the *anatrophe* with Eutropius's last slave job at line 109, excluding his physical description and final expulsion (1.110–37); but the summary encompasses them too (1.38–41). Having pushed the description outside of the rhetorical scheme, Schmidt was forced to apologize for it as "a biographical *topos*." In a formal biography it is, to be sure, but such *topoi* belong to encomiastic and invective schemes also. The rhetorical exercises ascribed to Hermogenes, for example, direct the student to discuss the subject's *physis*, both spiritual and bodily, between his *anatrophe* and *epitedeumata* (Hermog. *Prog.* 7.37.1–38.8 Rabe). Aphthonius recommends discussing *praxeis* as they relate to the soul, to the body, and to the fortune of the subject, and specifically includes physical appearance among the bodily topics (Aphthon. 22.5–9, 27.17–28.2 Rabe). Claudian instead subsumes this topic within the *anatrophe*.

Claudian's *anatrophe* of Eutropius also encompasses a scene that corresponds functionally to the typical encomiastic *genesis*: Eutropius's castration (1.44–52). The normal topic of this section, divine signs accompanying a birth, clearly identifies the encomiastic subject as more than human; it may also align him gloriously with a historical or legendary hero (cf. Men. Rh. 371.4–10). Eutropius's castration analogously makes him less than human (cf. 1.51, 56). Phrases in the first lines of this passage, "his first cradle-days," "from the very breast," "after his mother's guts," attach it closely to the moment of Eutropius's birth (1.44–46). What *In Eutropium* 1 lacks is any section that corresponds to *genos*. Technically a slave was not a person under Roman law, so that his personal origins might be dispensed with if an author did not choose to make any additional slanders of them; artistically, by beginning directly with Eutropius's castration, Claudian avoids buffering its harsh impact.[63]

The section embraced by the next subsidiary proem discusses in turn Eutropius's misconduct as *iudex*, in both strictly judicial and broader magisterial functions, and his misconduct of war as a military leader. These subsections clearly correspond to the conventional subdivisions of *praxeis* in the rhetorical scheme, between deeds in peace and deeds in war. Schmidt (61) blurred the transition from *anatrophe* to *praxeis* by grouping Eutropius's emancipation together with his entry into imperial service and first crime against Abundantius in a separate, transitional section. I have already argued that the disdainful dismissal of Eutropius from servitude he can no longer perform rather concludes his professional *anatrophe*, because the subsidiary proem introducing

---

63. I would modify the claim of Schmidt 1976, 61, that the descriptions of Eutropius's castration, slavery, and pandering "represent . . . the usual parts on origin, birth and upbringing."

the section extends so far. Eutropius's entry into imperial service, ascribed to a vicious joke of Fortune, furnishes the transition (1.138–50). It constitutes a subsidiary proem embracing the section to follow, because it elevates Eutropius to the position in which he perpetrates these misdeeds. The next division comes when he claims the consulate. Koster correctly identified the ruin of Abundantius as Eutropius's first misdeed in peace;[64] it is indeed the one concrete instance of misconduct that Claudian lists. His other abuses of judicial power are alleged vaguely. The idea that he sold governorships is suggested memorably but imaginatively by the vision of his sales office, not through specific facts.

Between the two sets of charges against Eutropius's civil administration Claudian attributes his ferocity to his past slavery and his castration (1.181–90). Similarly the next lines derive his greed from his castration, bridging the transition into the charge of sale of offices (1.190–93). Showing how the training of *anatrophe* has formed the subject's character and produced the choices revealed in his mature deeds is the function of *epitedeumata*. These observations work fully within the rhetorical scheme.

Finally Schmidt grouped together the remainder of the book under the rubric "The Scandal of the Eunuch-Consulate." I dispute his division, because it overlooks how Roma's intervention changes the dynamic mode and rhetorical direction of the book. The differentiation affects both the book's argumentative structure and its artistic texture. That the consulate crowns the book, however, Schmidt is entirely right to underline.

Claudian's subsidiary proems delimit this group of comparative statements as the penultimate section of book 1, the usual position of *teleiotate synkrisis* in the standard rhetorical scheme. The comparisons evaluate what Eutropius's consulate represents, thus also performing the function of *teleiotate synkrisis*. Rhetors emphasize the power of comparisons to magnify or diminish a subject by measuring it against a separate standard (e.g., Men. Rh. 376.31–377.2, Aphthon. 22.9–10 Rabe). Such measurements in themselves help to define the subject. Moreover, while they support a simple verdict of greater or less, they also furnish images that fill in the picture of the subject in more complex ways. Julian's second oration in praise of Constantius, for example, does not only assert that Constantius is more kingly than Agamemnon, more successful in victory than Achilles, braver than Ajax, Hector, or Sarpedon, wiser than Nestor, and more eloquent than Odysseus. It also implicitly enrolls Constantius among the Homeric heroes. Julian's comparisons reflect onto Constantius the luster of centuries-long cultural tradition. Its associations themselves glorify him. They also give his victories and government in peace new meaning, as renewing and improving on the heroic age.

64. Koster 1980, 320.

So too Claudian's comparisons both debase and illustrate Eutropius against various cultural standards. The incestuous marriages of Oedipus and Thyestes, the catastrophic history of legendary Thebes, the destruction of Troy, and the transformations of Tereus, Cadmus, Scylla, and others, are appalling or impossible things that tradition records have happened; yet never has a eunuch been a consul or a magistrate or a general (1.287–97). The simple comparison asserts that Eutropius's achievement is more impossible than all these traditional monstrosities. The comparison also endows Eutropius with some of their monstrousness, even though the abominations listed do not share very much else in common with him. Claudian does not stop with the profoundly upsetting horrors of literature and myth, however, so that they do not complete his associative portrait of Eutropius. He is also measured, in his consular robes, against an ape dressed up to parody humanity, against the lesser affront of a woman consul, against conventional natural impossibilities, and against the promiscuous sexual complaisance earlier ascribed to him as a slave. The comparisons render Eutropius appalling, subhuman and ludicrous, effeminate, inconceivable, and sexually debased. Ideas of him already presented in different scenes are recreated and projected through a new kaleidoscope of likenesses. They assess him comprehensively.

The final section of *In Eutropium* 1 recapitulates themes of the whole book, with a new emphasis. It plays especially upon emotions attached to Roman traditions so as to develop yet another argument against Eutropius. It is a substantial and complex unit. Conversely, the term epilogue may seem to designate an afterthought.[65] In rhetors' sample exercises and in actual speeches, epilogues are not always closely integrated to the whole.[66] Yet even the most perfunctory message that the speech has drawn to a close performs an important function. The listener has been exposed to a continuous structure of words. The words create their own world or illusion of reality. At the end of the speech the structure ends; the listener is returned to the world outside the words. The epilogue by announcing the change more or less explicitly locates the speech within that exterior context. Closings frequently recommended by rhetors seek to integrate the two worlds yet more extensively. Prayers for the continued life, strength, and good fortune of the subject enact involvement. They co-opt the community attending the speech into their wishes. Exhortations to imitate the subject's virtues call on listeners to pattern their realities upon the world of the speech. Roma's request here implicitly solicits the audience, along with Honorius and Stilicho, to reject Eutropius. Her scene moves the book into a more epic mode, suggesting a change from exposition to action. Her speech incorpo-

---

65. Thus Schweckendiek 1992, 19–20 n. 15, against my analysis of Roma's scene in my dissertation.

66. Aphthonius's *progymnasmata* afford some of the clumsiest examples. Compare his sample invective of Philip, discussed below in Chap. 3.II.

rates the internal structure of deliberative oratory. This form, as Aristotle says, calls upon the auditor to make a decision about the future (Arist. *Rhet.* 1358b). Roma's additions to the book's generic mixture help to turn it outward so that its argument faces its auditors. In this way as well as by her recapitulation, her scene fulfills the fundamental task of an epideictic epilogue.

In Eutropium 1 conforms fully to the rhetorical formula for an invective speech. Subsidiary proems articulate it into sections. Each item of the indictment is distinguished and stated briefly before being demonstrated with specific details. This progression of statements and proofs gives the book a quintessentially epideictic movement. Its dynamic, in this sense, is even more basic to the epideictic nature of book 1 than the topics of the particular sections; yet they too follow a standard rhetorical scheme for formal invective. The proem lays a foundation for the whole book. There is no section on *genos*; but the rhetors never required any section that did not suit an author's purposes. A section on *anatrophe* includes a modification of *genesis* within it. The formative experiences discussed in these sections ground Eutropius's mature *praxeis*. They are presented in two subsections, deeds in peace and deeds in war; some remarks on Eutropius's *epitedeumata* are subsumed into the former. Eutropius's *praxeis* won him the supreme honor of the consulate. The subsidiary proem that introduces this fact thus in one sense concludes the account of his achievements, but in crowning them it also establishes how the imagery of Eutropius as consul sums up the whole of his career. The comparisons that it introduces comprehend the entire book. They effect a many-faceted *teleiotate synkrisis*. Finally, by both summarizing the book and opening it out to the audience, Roma's concluding scene functions as an epilogue. Claudian elaborates individual sections beyond the rhetors' minimum requirements, but he maintains the logic of their structure.

THE PREFACE TO *In Eutropium* 2 announces and exults at Eutropius's fall from power. Koster divided it into three parts as he thought they focus on Eutropius's past (2pr.1–32), present (2pr.33–54), and future situations (2pr.55–76).[67] This division would make the preface correspond, albeit in third- and second-person speech, to the rhetorical exercise of first-person *ethopoeia* defined by Aphthonius (35.13–14 Rabe), but Claudian does not so distinguish the last two sections Koster claimed. *Erit* (2pr.54) is no less future than *terrebis* (2pr.55) and *agitabis* (2pr.56). *Caruit* (2pr.57) asserts that the Byzantine Senate already has been missing Eutropius.

It is better to divide the preface into two parts. The first celebrates the turn of fortune that has brought Eutropius back down again (2pr.1–32). The em-

---

67. Koster 1980, 345–50.

blems of his consulate change relation to demean him; the prodigy has turned on itself. The effeminate has been driven from his bedchamber citadel. All repudiate him. His former masters want to buy him in order to punish him. This part recapitulates the motifs of book 1. A division is marked when Claudian turns to address Eutropius in second person. The idea of repudiation bridges the transition. The rest of the preface gloats over Eutropius's exile, now his only refuge (2pr.33–76). Not the East, not Eutropius's former access to prophecy, not his sister, not his crimes, not his sham paternity to Arcadius[68] will help him now. Claudian bids Eutropius say farewell to arms and to the Byzantine Senate. Cyprus and the service of Venus wait to welcome him back (2pr.55–62); this jibe too recalls rebukes in book 1 (1.271–84). But perhaps the Tritons will detain him to teach them how to seduce the Nereids, or the winds wreck Eutropius as they did Gildo. No dolphin will save him. And so may all eunuchs be warned. The mention of Gildo recalls his revolt two years earlier, when he cut off the grain supply of Rome and transferred the allegiance of Africa to Constantinople. In *In Eutropium* 1 Claudian had accused Eutropius of supporting Gildo; the recollection sharpens the present allusion.[69] The preface's informal arrangement corresponds to the rhetors' discursive *lalia* (cf. Men. Rh. 391.19–28). Claudian's prefaces for *In Rufinum* 1, *Panegyricus dictus Honorio Augusto tertium consuli*, *De Consulatu Stilichonis* 3 and *Bellum Geticum* also fall into parts. None observes the more orderly and complex schemes in which Claudian molds his major works.

CLAUDIAN'S SUBSIDIARY proems within *In Eutropium* 1 clearly divide it into sections. Apart from omitting *genos*, they follow formal invective's regular sequence of topics. The proems also create a distinctively epideictic momentum: Claudian urges each point briefly, then illustrates it at greater length before passing to the next. Each discrete section demonstrates its own thesis. Collectively, they remain static. *In Eutropium* 2, in contrast, moves smoothly from one section to the next. Though much derisive material is included, it does not divide into the headings of the formal scheme. Rather it flows along with the course of events, and their sequence dictates the dynamic structure of the poem. Defamatory effects no more nullify the dynamic structure of epic than the biographical detail of book 1 keeps it from being fundamentally expository. Moreover, Claudian targets some of Eutropius's subordinates as well as himself.

68. So Claudian interprets Eutropius's title *patricius* (cf. *Eutr.* 2.561), which was specifically revoked by *CTh* 9.40.17.
69. *Eutr.* 1.399–411; cf. *Stil.* 1.7–8, 275–81; Zos. 5.11.2. Claudian does not make the accusation in *Gild.* (see Alan Cameron 1970, 110–11, and my discussion in Chap. 8.I). In *Eutr.* 1 he cites Gildo's retribution at Tabraca, which is also recalled in the preface to book 2, 2pr.71.

Their bad qualities reflect on him, of course, but they also broaden Claudian's canvas to a more epic scope. And his subject is the epic one of war. This war too, the revolt of the Gothic general Tribigild and the Gruthungian Gothic *laeti* he commanded in Phrygia, in cause and conduct has many aspects that damn Eutropius; but despite this controlling purpose, it generates its own momentum in the narrative. Book 2 shows itself to be a true epic, with satirically handled invective implications.

Its proem reviews the disastrous portents of the year in which a eunuch was consul (2.1–94). They have been realized. The epimethean regret of the East will not avert them; more drastic measures than the exile of Eutropius are called for (2.1–23). Dire omens greeted his inauguration and yet folly prevailed (2.24–58). Not only did Eutropius become consul, he was received adoringly. Claudian expatiates indignantly over Eutropius's fawning callers, titles and statues, his dissoluteness, the accolades of his sister, and his incestuous relationship with her (2.58–94). As both sister and wife of a eunuch she is prodigious (2.88), a quality that aligns her too with the proem's focal motif.

This developing portrait of luxury and obscene honors establishes the moral basis for divine reaction in a more pervasively epic style than personified Roma's formal protest. Momentum shifts from the proem's montage of images to an episode developing action (2.95–173). Mars takes offense at the sight of the Eastern court preparing its annual vacation to Ancyra, another of Eutropius's diversions. He exclaims to Bellona at the softness of the East. It refuses to learn the lessons of war. Worse yet, it has even promoted a eunuch consul; at least Stilicho has preserved Rome itself from the insult to tradition. The East, however, deserves what it has chosen. Mars begs Romulus and Brutus to forgive him for being so slow to avenge the fasces, then commands Bellona to stir up rebellion among the Ostrogoths and Gruthungi settled in Phrygia: "Let barbarian arms relieve the Roman shame" (2.159). He seals the injunction by thundering his shield and casting his spear into the fields of Phrygia.

In the next dramatic scene (2.174–237), Bellona obeys. She comes to Tribigild disguised as his wife, greeting him when he returns empty-handed from negotiations with Eutropius. She kisses him and asks what gifts he brings. When she hears his tale of failure, she reviles his weakness. Other barbarian husbands adorn their wives with spoils. He should use the arms he bears. The cities are unguarded. The example of Alaric shows that raids can even win Roman honors.[70] "War will render allies" to bolster his forces (2.222). Most advantageous of all, the Roman defense has been entrusted to eunuchs. With a last rallying cry, she turns into a horrid bird. Once Tribigild recovers from the shock, he reports his vision and rouses the barbarians.

---

70. Claudian specifies Alaric's devastation of "Achaea and recently Epirus" in 396–97, *Eutr.* 2.214–15.

The next scene completes the divine preparation for war (2.238–303). Claudian gracefully draws the mythical antiquity and pastoral beauty of Phrygia, then shatters it with the barbarian attack. In parallel, Cybele's turreted crown falls from her head while she is watching her Curetes dance. She recognizes the omen that presages Phrygia's destruction. She mourns and bids the land a final farewell.

Now the action moves to the human plane. Eutropius first tries ostrichlike to ignore the crisis, then tries to woo Tribigild with belated gifts. But the barbarian has recalled his old lust for plunder and considers honor from a eunuch consul to be an insult (2.304–22). This exchange introduces Eutropius's council meeting, but unlike the subsidiary proems of book 1, it does not anticipate anything that transpires there. Claudian first describes the assembly (2.322–53). The courtiers are all gluttons for exotica. They are interested only in their toilette, the theater, their houses, dancing, and chariot racing. Some are plebeians, some former slaves still scarred with fetters or brands. Eutropius holds first place; his second is Hosius,[71] an estate-born slave and former cook. This expertise still marks his administration. The councillors instantly forget about Phrygia and start arguing about the theater. Eutropius calls them to order and reminds them that affairs are in crisis, but begs off serving himself (2.354–75).

Now Leo, the corpulent former weaver, springs up and urges boldness (2.376–401).[72] His speech is pivotal: it both concludes the meeting and introduces his lamentable campaign (2.402–61). The councillors applaud, and Leo marches off to dismal omens. His army is equally bad. Ill led and indisciplined, it wanders about lost. Tribigild attacks while the troops are all sluggish from banqueting. Leo flees, but sinks in a swamp because of his bulk. Claudian gleefully compares him to a pig Hosius might prepare to butcher. A breeze stirs the foliage behind him; thinking it is a weapon, Leo dies of fright.

As the Easterners react to the peril into which Eutropius has thrust them, they propel the final grand movement of book 2. First, rumors of Tribigild's advance stir terror (2.462–73). Then another rumor claims that Persia is planning to attack (2.474–84). The people are demoralized. Like Epimetheus they recognize their error after its consequences have struck them. They call for Stilicho, like children when their father has gone from home. Eutropius's lictors shudder, the fasces are thrown away, and the axes drop of their own accord. The citizens are like Maenads when the Bacchic frenzy leaves them stained with Pentheus's blood. The string of comparisons (2.485–526) gives images to the major thesis of the book, penultimately to Aurora's concluding

71. The Eastern *magister officiorum, PLRE* 1.445. Claudian's claim that Hosius was an estate-born slave of Spanish *penates* suggests that he had belonged to Theodosius's household; so Strohecker 1963, 116.
72. *PLRE* 2.661–62.

summation; thus in technique and function it corresponds to the *teleiotate synkrisis* of rhetorical invective. But in notable distinction from invective, the invective victim is not the subject of comparison, and the comparisons substantially motivate action, which follows.

Now Aurora gives voice to the general desires (2.526–602). She flies to Italy and addresses Stilicho. She has missed him since the defeat of Eugenius.[73] First Rufinus and then Eutropius have prevented Arcadius from joining Honorius in fraternal harmony under him. This flattery is the *prolalia* of her address (2.534–52). Then she tells how Eutropius rose to dominate the East, first getting rid of good men while lurking inside the imperial bedchamber, then bursting into public view with Hosius and Leo in his train. He defiles the offices he sells; those he holds himself he defiles even worse. Under his auspices, the instruments of war have grown soft. The East falls an easy victim even to barbarians it had once defeated. The court cares for nothing so long as its pleasures are not curtailed; Eutropius has divided the remaining provinces to preserve his profits. Finally, Aurora tells Stilicho that hope rests in him alone. Her need must apologize for the slights he has suffered. She does not seek to draw him from Italy, but begs him to defend both halves of the empire together (2.553–602).

The epic *In Eutropium* 2 moves straight from one end to the other. Each scene directly motivates the action of the next, far more fluidly than in the chronological progression of topics in book 1. The one anomaly is that the conclusion of book 2 does not advance the action as far as Eutropius's exile, which is envisaged in the book's proem. This point raises questions that figure in dating the books, which I shall address in Chapter 5. For now the structure and distinctions of the two books have been sufficiently sketched. It remains only to summarize the outline:

In Eutropium 1
    1–23 Proem: Eutropius as *monstrum*
    23–137 *Anatrophe*: Eutropius as slave
        23–44 Subsidiary proem: Fortuna in Eutropius's rise, synopsis of slave career
        44–57 Pro-*genesis*: castration
        58–77: castoff catamite
        77–97: pander
        98–109: lady's maid
        110–37: final rejection in ultimate decrepitude
    138–284 *Praxeis*: Eutropius in imperial service
        138–50 Subsidiary proem: paradoxical elevation from being despised
        151–228 Misdeeds in Peace

73. Against whom (*PLRE* 1.293) Stilicho marched west in 394 under Theodosius, whom Aurora omits mentioning.

151–70: Abundantius
170–80: generalized ferocity
181–90 *Epitedeumata*: ferocity results from having been a slave and being a eunuch
190–228: sale of offices
229–84 Misdeeds in War
  229–51: absurdity of eunuch trying to act in war; enemy success
  252–71: travesty triumph
  271–84: expostulation by poet: more appropriate roles than warrior
284–370 *Teleiotate synkrisis*: Eutropius as consul
  284–86 Subsidiary proem: consulate as reward for generalship, culminates pollution of civil and military offices
  287–99: mythical comparisons
  300–316: scene of inauguration; comparison to bare-assed monkey
  317–45: poet's assessment of omens of year: comparison to prospective consulate of a woman
  346–70: human assessment in West (implicit comparisons): inconceivability; sexual puns
371–513 Epilogue: the reaction of Roma
  371–91 Subsidiary proem: reacts privately to the consulate, flies to court, admires Honorius
  391–513: speech
    391–411 *Prolalia*: good state of West after Gildo
    412–99: begs Honorius not to recognize Eutropius as consul
    500–513: begs Stilicho to crush the upstart

Preface to *In Eutropium* 2
  1–32: rereversal of fortune, reprise of motifs from book 1 (third-person)
  33–76: second-person address: exile to Cyprus
    33–54: repudiation; Cyprus is only refuge
    55–66: return from inappropriate roles of Constantinople to appropriate roles at Cyprus
    67–76: possible shipwreck en route to Cyprus

In Eutropium 2
  1–94 Proem: omens of year with a eunuch as consul
    1–23: exile insufficient expiation
    24–58: omens did not forestall inauguration
    58–94: obscene success of Eutropius
  95–303: epic divine machinery of war
    95–173: Mars declares war, rouses Bellona

174–237: Bellona inspires Tribigild
238–303: rape of Phrygia and Cybele's prophecy
304–461: Eutropius's reaction
304–22: preliminary to meeting, ostrich act and failed conciliation
322–53: assembly of base, frivolous courtiers
354–75: several incapacity of courtiers and of Eutropius
376–401: speech of Leo[74]
402–31: bad omens, errant army
432–61: Tribigild attacks; death of Leo
462–602: Eastern reaction
462–526: demoralization at rumored threats returns populace to its senses: the people long for Stilicho
526–602: Aurora: conclusion
526–33 Subsidiary proem: she flies to Italy, addresses Stilicho
534–52 *Prolalia*: her longing for Stilicho, oppression by Rufinus and Eutropius, and resulting friction with West
533–83: Eutropius's rise to power and her victimization
591–602: plea for help and forgiveness of unwilling slights: protect both halves of empire

CLAUDIAN FUSED epic and rhetorical invective more fully in his earlier *In Rufinum*. Although he despaired of *In Eutropium*, Levy was able to analyze *In Rufinum* largely in terms of the rhetorical form.[75] Claudian's reflections on divine providence clearly identify the proem (*Ruf.* 1.1–24). Most of the Furies' council (1.25–175) seemed to Levy to fall outside the rhetorical sections, but Megaera does explain how she fostered Rufinus, providing an *anatrophe* (1.92–115).

Levy explained Claudian's omission of a *genos* by the rhetors' exemption for tact: "ethnically, Rufinus was a Gaul, and Claudian was bound to treat the Gauls with respect as constituting an important element in Stilicho's army, as well as the court of Honorius."[76] His point is valid, but does not address all the possibilities. Claudian could have omitted Rufinus's remoter connections, for example, and invented a scandalous family history. Since his testimony is the most detailed information preserved about Rufinus's origins,[77] no obstacle to

74. Leo's speech both concludes the meeting and introduces the campaign, which otherwise form separate subsidiary units.
75. Levy 1946.
76. Levy 1946, 60; he was followed by Alan Cameron 1970, 83.
77. Megaera comes to him in Elusa, which thus appears to be his native town, *Ruf.* 1.137 (see Levy 1971, 39–40); Zos. 4.51.1 merely reports that he was a Gaul. *PLRE* 1.778–81.

his invention appears; he felt free to fill in the obscurities of Eutropius's past with febrile creativity. Conversely, if Rufinus's background had been known and unassailable, Claudian could have reproached him by the contrast. The *Rhetorica ad Herrenium* recommends precisely this tactic (3.13), for example, and Cicero exemplifies it to devastating effect when he evokes Appius Claudius against Clodia in his *Pro Caelio* (34). Rather, Claudian chose to let no human details muddy his portrait of Rufinus as the product and agent of Hell. The theme of divine justice in Claudian's proem foretokens his focus on the idea that Rufinus was supernaturally evil: his crimes stir the remote gods to retribution (cf. *Ruf.* 1.354–87). Megaera claimed him for herself at his birth (1.92–93). She nursed him. Her snakes shaped his limbs. The Hell Council agrees to launch him as its instrument against the good harmony of the world. He rises magically, because demons have sent him. No rational explanation is needed.[78] Similarly, at the end of the second book, after his death he is condemned beyond the farthest reaches of the underworld. Even the archetypal sinners of myth are less bad. Any ordinary *genos*, however scabrous Claudian made it, would have detracted from the superhuman magnificence of Rufinus's evil stature. As in *In Eutropium*, artistic considerations that have their own rhetorical effects govern how Claudian manipulates rhetorical formulas.

Claudian also omits *epitedeumata* of Rufinus, from the same desire for concentration. He does not blunt the impact of his mature deeds by any practicing before the moment Megaera activates the rapacity she bred into him (1.123–75). The boasts Levy cited within Megaera's speech involve only hypothetical feats of avarice and discord, not favorite "pursuits" ever really practiced (1.101–11). They properly belong to the potentiality that *anatrophe* matures.

At this point Levy's rhetorical analysis breaks down. Fusing both books together, he identified a section on Rufinus's misdeeds in peace (1.176–258) and a long section on his misdeeds relating to military activity, arising from and interspersed with comparisons with Stilicho (1.259–2.383). Yet this contrast extends the discussion of deeds rather than summarizing it, as the comprehensive rhetorical comparison should.[79] More important, the directions and emphases of these comparisons radically differ from the invective model. Lines

---

78. Barr 1979, 187, complained that a "full-scale invective" of Rufinus ought not to have neglected "the evil arts by which he secured office" or the embarrassing story of how Eutropius preempted his marriage plans for Arcadius (Zos. 5.3). But although such topics could serve an invective, they need not if the author chooses otherwise. Compare Men. Rh. 405.15–412.2 on the *kateunastikos logos*, where he lists many topics as potentially appropriate, but emphasizes repeatedly that the speaker must limit himself to treating only a few of them.

79. Barr 1979, 186, objected that a general comparison comes after deeds in the rhetorical scheme, not in the middle.

1.251–56 contain genuine *synkrisis* of Rufinus with archetypal tyrants. Stilicho is introduced in lines 1.259–300, which Levy identified as *synkrisis* with Rufinus. Yet Stilicho is not compared with Rufinus here, but with the people he terrorizes (1.256–60). Unlike them Stilicho is not cowed. Where Rufinus threatens, he defends (1.260–67). This thought contrasts Stilicho and Rufinus in a sense; but then the passage breaks to describe Rufinus's reaction to Stilicho's onset (1.267–72), turns again to praise Stilicho directly, and finally turns the contrast with Rufinus to Stilicho's praise (1.273–300). Levy's structural chart (65), revealingly, continues to trace the action back and forth between Rufinus's *praeis kata polemon* and *laus Stilichonis* down to line 383 of book 2.[80] This alternation, as Levy said, "encompass[es] the entire theme of the work" (64), but it extends far beyond the illustrative function of a rhetorical *synkrisis* focused on the invective subject. The intercutting of scenes dynamically builds expectations for an epic clash of hero and archenemy.

Levy recognized that sections of *In Rufinum* exceed the functions that the rhetorical scheme would assign them. The Hell Council frames Megaera's report on Rufinus's nurture, but it also propels his actions and endows them with cosmic significance. Megaera involves herself intimately in the action of the poem in just the ways that gods and demons do in epic, as William Barr rightly urged. She exerts dynamic force for epic action. Even her relatively static confrontation with Iustitia at the end of book 1 recalls Tisiphone's confrontation with Pietas before Eteocles and Polynices finally fight hand to hand at the climax of Statius's *Thebaid* (11.457–96). Levy could regard Rufinus's induction into Hell as epilogue, but felt that "the famous account of Rufinus's murder and dismemberment (2.384–453) . . . [the poem's] emotional climax . . . could not be classified under any of the six τόποι without doing wholly unwarranted violence to their interpretation" (59). In fact, however, rhetors did include the subject's death as a topic, when it had occurred. Theon numbers a good death among the encomiastic subject's external advantages, for example. Hermogenes makes it a denouement between *praxeis* and *teleiotate synkrisis*. Libanius includes it in many sample encomia and invectives. Menander places grieving over the death at the emotional climax of a funeral speech, for which he prescribes the standard encomiastic arrangement interspersed with lamentation.[81]

But although Rufinus's gruesome death could be accommodated within the

---

80. Schmidt 1976, 59, identified a "constant oscillation back and forth between polemic and panegyric" of Rufinus and Stilicho in Claud. *Ruf.* 1.259–2.256, overlapping with the narrative of events from 392 to 395 in *Ruf.* 1.201–2.439.

81. Theon, Spengel 2.110.2–6; Hermog. *Prog.* 7.38.18–40.1 Rabe; Lib. *Prog.* 8.2.25, 8.3.22, 8.5.17, 9.2.17, 9.3.14, 9.4.12; cf. Aphthon. *Prog.* 9 (30.15–20 Rabe). Men. Rh. 419.11–16, 421.10–14.

invective scheme, the way Claudian's narrative advances to that climax more fundamentally determines *In Rufinum*'s generic identity. From Megaera's report of *anatrophe* to Rufinus's death and condemnation beyond Hell, the action drives itself. While it advances more or less through the same stages as the rhetorical model, the narrative is not called forth in short bursts, as in panegyric or invective, to illustrate formulaic topics. The rhetors deploy narrative for this greater end, not as the primary mode of exposition dominating the whole speech. Even in the informal *lalia*, where Menander recommends inserting narratives to add charm, he speaks of them only as illustrative examples (389.9–390.4).

Heinz-Günther Nesselrath has now analyzed *In Rufinum* and its dynamic progression of events, more successfully, as epic.[82] Book 1 develops in two complementary movements. The first part installs Rufinus in imperial government as the agent of Hell; the second galvanizes the heroic Stilicho against him. Notably, the parts do not merely contrast statically: the action of the second springs from the first. The end strains forward further, looking for Iustitia's prophecy to be fulfilled at Rufinus's death, as the proem anticipates (1.1–24). Within this framework, Nesselrath traced the action from a superhuman level to human and back again. The Hell Council (1.25–122) precipitates Megaera's incitement of Rufinus (1.123–75), where supernatural power acts in the human world. Rufinus in turn commences a reign of terror within the terrestrial empire (1.176–256). Stilicho takes arms as the populace's savior (1.256–322), then fights against Rufinus's barbarians with the support of his own supernatural familiar, Mars (1.323–53); finally, at the divine level again, Megaera taunts Iustitia only to be answered by her triumphant prophecy (1.354–87). In book 2 the action proceeds linearly. In the human plane, Rufinus intrigues with barbarians (2.7–99), Stilicho again campaigns to save Greece (2.100–129), Rufinus forces Arcadius to demand Stilicho's troops from him (2.130–70), Stilicho loyally remits them, although they protest (2.171–276), and they return and execute Rufinus at the moment he has been planning to usurp a share of the imperial throne (2.277–453). Finally Rhadamanthys exiles Rufinus beyond Hell (2.454–527).

Nesselrath rightly underscored the differences between the symmetrical development of *In Rufinum* 1 and *In Rufinum* 2's linear trajectory, but throughout both books each event propels the next. This dynamic movement fundamentally characterizes epic. Books 1 and 2 cohere not only because book 2 details the murder predicted by the proem of book 1 and Iustitia at its close, or because Claudian sets in parallel courses the campaigns of Stilicho he describes in each book, that of 392 against the Bastarnae and that of 395 against the

82. Nesselrath 1991.

Goths.[83] Epic momentum also helps to bridge the chronological gap. *In Eutropium* 2 also displays epic dynamism. It contrasts markedly with the stepwise epideictic movement of *In Eutropium* 1. The disparate artistic texture of *In Eutropium* 1 and 2 marks a change in Claudian's artistic purposes between the two books; its implications extend beyond purely literary considerations, however, so I postpone further discussion to Part III.

IN BOTH *In Rufinum* and *In Eutropium*, the function of narration is the most decisive generic criterion. In panegyric or invective it illustrates a point, whereas in epic it carries the tale. Cameron rightly drew this distinction, but he like Levy trusted too rigidly in a chronological disposition of material to determine that a tale was being narrated for its own sake.[84] Nothing in the topicality of the rhetorical scheme demands that the topics be treated in an arrangement that violates the order of time. Indeed the regular progression of rhetorical topics from ancestry to birth to upbringing to mature achievements encourages a biographical scheme. What classifies the genre is rather how narrative as such relates to the quality of movement with which a poem is endowed.

Schmidt underlined the biographical aspect of *In Eutropium* 1 correctly, though he was wrong to distinguish it from the rhetorical elements in his structural analysis. In fact the chronologically determinable incidents of Eutropius's career, as reported by Claudian in book 1, progress in order as they and other unfixed details illustrate the standard rhetorical topics. Eutropius is traced from bad to worse in the stages of his slave career. Then, suddenly translated to imperial office, he does wrong in civil and military capacities. Claudian less narrates Eutropius's official career than evokes its qualities, as the rhetorical emphases demand. Cruelty and avarice unite in civil administration, vainglory and incompetence in generalship. It happens that Claudian chose Abundantius, whom he calls Eutropius's first victim (*Eutr.* 1.155), to stand for his whole judicial administration. Even that *primum* may only have been emphatic: Zosimus recounts the ruin of Timasius first (Zos. 5.8–9).[85] The fact that Abundantius had been Eutropius's patron won him Claudian's attention. Eutropius campaigned in Armenia at a later date, but it was because this campaign won him the consulate, his crowning enormity, that Claudian treats it later in his poem, when he reaches his climax. Abundantius and Armenia are the only datable *praxeis* that Claudian uses. They give an impression of chron-

---

83. On how Claudian represents the campaigns, see Alan Cameron 1970, 71–75; Levy 1971, 87–89.

84. Alan Cameron 1970, 84; Levy 1946, 59.

85. See Paschoud 1971–89, 3¹.105–6, 112–13. Timasius, *PLRE* 1.914–15.

ological ordering, but only superficially. Chronology is incidental to the emphases of Claudian's argument.

Argumentation essentially defines the movement of epideixis. Specific points are cited and then demonstrated. They cumulate toward an overall verdict. The specific topics identified by ancient rhetoricians were developed and followed by living oratory throughout classical and later antiquity; but even long-standing convention does not determine the essential impulse. The impulse propels the conventional scheme. *In Eutropium* 1, with its divisions and subsidiary proems, follows both.

I do not mean to suggest that the rhetorical model of formal invective exerted an abstract force to dictate Claudian's form. Nor did he copy it simply and reflexively. As Jasper Griffin has remarked, "rhetorical set pieces . . . are at most only one in [the poets'] armory of devices."[86] But the device is available. It lies close to poetic ones. D. A. Russell and N. G. Wilson in their commentary on the treatises ascribed to Menander Rhetor emphasized that poets and speakers independently developed conventions for treating certain types of event.[87] Some similarities were dictated by the common occasions. These resemblances made it possible for poets sometimes to adopt rhetorical usages: Russell and Wilson cited Theocritus's *Idyll* 18 as an early example of a "rhetoricized wedding-poem" (xxxiv). Teachers of rhetoric in their turn cited poets as authorities for conventions of the oratorical tradition (e.g., Men. Rh. 405.19–24). The two traditions kept themselves mutually available, even though it would overstate the case to claim that either depended on the other. Literary schooling, with its extensive grammatical and rhetorical exposition of epic, may well have encouraged hearers to perceive rhetorical elements in literature generally.[88] Long experience of rhetorical conventions in late antique panegyric inevitably familiarized court audiences like Claudian's with the form that *In Eutropium* 1 inverts. Rhetoric provided an especially useful device to this poem: dispraise of a consul stands out the more strikingly against a format normally used for praise. Claudian took advantage of rhetorical conventions to fortify his poetic purposes.

86. Griffin 1981, 48.
87. Russell and Wilson 1981, xxxi–xxxiv. Cf. Cairns 1972.
88. See D. A. Russell, "Rhetoric and Criticism," *Greece and Rome* n.s. 14 (1967): 130–44, on the development of rhetorical theory, its teaching and its influence on literature and criticism. On the educational method, Stanley F. Bonner, *Education in Ancient Rome* (Berkeley: University of California Press, 1977), 227–49. Curtius 1953, 443–44, remarked on Macrobius's rhetorical reading of Vergil. Frederick Ahl, "Homer, Vergil, and Complex Narrative Structures in Latin Epic: An Essay," *Illinois Classical Studies* 14 (1989): 1–31, like Russell, recommended a rhetorical perspective to modern criticism of ancient poetry, on the grounds that it most closely approximates the approach of ancient audiences.

In Eutropium 2, on the other hand, gains its impact from its dynamic action. Its preface establishes a temporal context that controls the interpretation of the book. Schmidt noted correctly that the main narrative illustrates Eutropius's incapacity,[89] but its incidents develop from one another organically, without the summary statements and transitional steps of *In Eutropium* 1. Mars sees Eutropius wallowing in the luxury of office depicted by the proem, and tells Bellona to act. She inflames Tribigild. He attacks. There is an interlude as the beauty of Phrygia is evoked. But the pause does not halt the narrative to introduce an allegation to be illustrated: it releases tension in order to emphasize the shock and brutality with which the war begins. Cybele's lament reiterates the rape of Phrygia, but it also moves beyond to confirm with divine authority how serious the disaster is. The narrative does not leap magically ahead to Leo's campaign, or even to Eutropius's meeting, as it did between *anatrophe* and *praxeis* in book 1. First Eutropius attempts and fails to cope by other means. Mars, Bellona, and Cybele have already taken epic roles as gods motivating and reacting to human events, and in Tribigild a human martial antagonist has been introduced; now Claudian spreads his narrative wider to include subordinates on Eutropius's side. The contrast to *In Eutropium* 1 is striking. There, up until Roma's appeal, Eutropius was really the sole character, and even Honorius and Stilicho merely receive Roma's words. Now Hosius steps to Eutropius's side as a shabby second, and Leo blusters forth a travesty of epic heroism. Typically of this book, his speech cannot decisively be classed as part of the Council scene or as the introduction to his campaign: it pivots between the two. The narrative progresses smoothly. The East as a whole reacts to Tribigild's advance after defeating Leo. Aurora then entreats Stilicho on behalf of the whole East to save them. Her speech gathers up the developing strand of the narrative hitherto; yet she too looks forward to a new stage beyond the frame of the poem. It moves forward continually. Both books are metrically *epos*, that is dactylic hexameter. But only book 2 lives up to epic standards in scope and treatment.

89. Schmidt 1976, 61–62.

CHAPTER TWO

Traditions of Roman Satire

✦

In Eutropium 1 and 2 generate different momentums, which control the audience's reception of the poems. The generic labels I have attached to them mark that difference. Yet the two books are not entirely disparate. Both the stepwise demonstration of book 1 and the driving movement of book 2 convey outraged mockery of Eutropius. The mode of attack recalls satire generally; Claudian reinforces the resemblance with various specific allusions. His contemporary audience was doubtless well equipped to appreciate echoes of satire. At least Ammianus Marcellinus, sourly assessing why serious history was neglected by Roman aristocrats at the close of the fourth century, asserts that they read nothing but Juvenal and the racy biographer Marius Maximus.[1] Whether it was satire or scandal that drew readers, *In Eutropium* offers much to appeal.

Birt chose a specific precedent for *In Eutropium* as a political satire.[2] He supposed that Claudian based *In Eutropium* particularly on a satire about the Numantine War that he thought he detected in the fragments of Lucilius's twenty-sixth book. Naturally his argument rests on his reconstruction of this putative satire, and all arguments concerning the arrangement of Lucilian fragments are hotly disputed; to detail them would extend far beyond the scope of this chapter.[3] Suffice it to say that Birt's proposals have won little

1. Amm. 28.4.14; on Marius Maximus, see Barbieri 1954.
2. Cf. Chap. 1.
3. On the problems, see Christes 1971, 18–23; Charpin 1978–91, 1.41–64; Charpin, "Nonius Marcellus et le classement des fragments de Lucilius," *RPh* 52 (1978): 284–307 (also, alas, e.g., H. D. Jocelyn, *CR* n.s. 30 [1980]: 16–18, on Charpin 1978–91; F. R. D. Goodyear, *CR* n.s. 25 [1975]: 206–9, and D. C. White, *CP* 68 [1973]: 36–44, on Krenkel 1970; C. J. Fordyce, *CR* 53 [1939]: 187–88, on Warmington 1938). Garbugino 1990, 129–31, relied on the principles of W. M. Lindsay, *Nonius Marcellus' Dictionary of Republican Latin* (Oxford, 1901; rpt. Hildesheim: Olms, 1965), as formulated by Francesco Della

acceptance.[4] It may be doubted whether a text of Lucilius survived intact to the later fourth century: Emil Luebeck demonstrated even before Birt's study that all Jerome's references to Lucilius derive from Cicero or Horace.[5] Reconstructors of book 26 since Birt have not found a satire on the Numantine War.[6] Nonetheless, Birt's arguments provide a convenient point of departure for illustrating some of the affinities *In Eutropium* bears with satire, and also with other currents of humor in political abuse. After introducing both these topics here, I will develop them further in Chapters 3 and 4.

Birt began by trying to establish that Claudian knew Lucilius. He adduced first a fragment from book 1, in which Lucilius puns on *ius* to the disadvantage of his butt Cornelius Lentulus Lupus. Ostensibly, the line refers to various kinds of fish and so to "broth": it would suit a satire on gluttony, and Marx understood it thus.[7] But Servius's description of the satire (*ap. Aen.* 10.104) suggests that it was political, so that "lawsuits" or "rights" of the "small fry" Lupus oppressed also applies:[8]

occidunt, Lupe, saperdae te et iura siluri.

The juices-rights of sardines and catfish are killing you, Lupus.

As Birt pointed out, Claudian makes the same pun about Eutropius's second, Hosius (*Eutr.* 2.347–49):

dulcior hic sane cunctis prudensque movendi
iuris et admoto qui temperet omnia fumo,
fervidus, accensam sed qui bene decoquat iram.

He is sweeter than all of them, for sure, and expert at stirring up
law-broth, one to mellow everything by putting it on the smoker,
a hot one, but good at rendering down wrath flambé.

Corte, "La lex Lindsay e i frammenti di Varrone," in *Varrone: Il terzo gran lume romano* (Genova: Istituto Universitario di Magisterio, 1954), 321–77.

4. Even in Birt's own time: e.g., E. Zarncke, *Litterar. Centralblatt* 1888, 35, 1195–97; F. Marx, *Deutsche Litztg.* 1888, 18: 662–63; J. Stowasser, *Zeitschr. öst. Gymn.* 39 (1889): 984–85; J. Proschberger, *Blätter bayr. Gymn.* 25 (1889): 334–38; cf. Romano 1958, 97. L. Jeep (*Berl. Phil. Wochenshcr.* 10 [1890]: 664–65) found Birt's arguments "likely" if not demonstrable, but gave no reasons.

5. Emil Luebeck, *Hieronymus quos noverit scriptores et ex quibus hauserit* (Leipzig: B. G. Teubner, 1872), 116. Marx 1904–5, 1.lx–lxi, and Knoche 1975, 39, suggested that extracts of Lucilius were preserved in a moralistic florilegium; cf. Wiesen 1964, 3–6, on the satirists' survival into the fourth century.

6. For discussion, see Cichorius 1908, 101–42; Christes 1971; Garbugino 1990.

7. Marx 1904–5, 2.27–28; Lucil. fr. 54 Marx = 46 Warmington = 55 Krenkel = 1.33 Charpin. Lupus is "Cornelius 224," *RE* 4 (1901): 1386–87.

8. Cichorius 1908, 231–32, explicated the associated puns on "Lupus" (both "wolf" and a type of fish ["bass," *OLD* s.v. 3]).

Hosius had been a cook before he and Eutropius began to "rule the laws" (*iura regunt*, 2.344); Claudian asserts that he reapplies his old skills to his second career. Without the context surrounding Lucilius's line it is impossible to know how he developed his punning image, but even within the context of the line itself he appears to have applied it differently from Claudian. Hosius is master of the law-broth, whereas it threatens Lupus. And the pun itself has little force as a specific link, for it is used not only by Varro, whom Birt cited (*Rust.* 3.17.4), but also by Plautus, Cicero, Martial, Vespa, and Donatus.[9]

Cicero uses the pun most similarly to Claudian when he reports the Sicilians' bitter joke, "no wonder *ius verrinum* ['Verres' justice' and 'pork broth'] is so bad." In both cases the pun refers to the invective victim's abuse of office. Cicero's further jest that Sacerdos, Verres' predecessor, was cursed for leaving behind "such a worthless Verres-pig," *verrem tam nequam*, could have helped inspire Claudian's fantasy of Hosius preparing to butcher a hog like which Leo squeals (2.445–55):[10] Cicero's gibe is phrased so as to convey the complaint that Sacerdos ought to have lived up to his name, "Priest," and sacrificed the "Pig." Claudian develops the idea utilizing the different proficiency of another figure from his context. The Sicilians, if Cicero credits his pun to them accurately, also demonstrate how common it was. Such language belongs to any genre in which wit may serve attack, not only satire and rhetorical invective but also popular lampoon.[11]

In the twenty-sixth book of Lucilius, Birt laid great weight on a fragment in which Lucilius declares "part is blown away by the wind, part stiffens over with cold" (*pars difflatur vento, pars autem obrigescit frigore*).[12] As Birt pointed out, Plautus's Miles Gloriosus is flattered that he can "disperse [*difflavisti*] legions with a breath, like wind on leaves" (Plaut. *Mil. Glor.* 17). Birt claimed that *obrigescit frigore* "only fits people." Then, since *difflare* can be used of troops, he insisted that it must be understood in that sense here, so that the line describes the defeat of an army under one of the generals who failed to take Numantia in the campaign seasons before Lucilius's patron Scipio besieged it successfully. Birt then related the line to Claudian's claim that "a light breeze struck the leaves behind Leo's back" (*Eutr.* 2.452), so that he died of fright. The connection is ingenious but hardly compelling, since it is with Plautus not Lucilius that

9. TLL s.v. *ius*² 3 (vol. 7, 2 col. 705.67–706.4): Plaut. *Cist.* 473, *Epid.* 523, *Poen.* 586, *Pseud.* 197; Cic. *Verr.* 2.1.121, *Ep. Fam.* 9.18.3; Mart. 7.51.5; Vespa 29; Claud. Don. ad *Aen.* 8.180 p.142.13. On other puns in Claudian's passage, see Chap. 4.III.

10. It is always possible that that Claudian took the idea not directly from Cicero but from a compilation of rhetorical jokes such as Macrobius's (*Sat.* 2) or Cicero's own in *De Oratore* (2.220–30, 240–88); or, of course, that he reinvented it independently.

11. See in general Richlin [1983] 1992, 86–96 and 279–82.

12. Lucil. fr. 666 Marx = 654 Warmington = 646 Krenkel = 26.37 Charpin = 36 Garbugino; Birt 1888, 99, 113.

Claudian shares the conjunction of wind and leaves. Even that conjunction is trivial. Claudian does not use the same verb: his wind strikes (*concutit*), not blows away. Moreover, Leo's army is no longer there to be dispersed when the wind destroys him. Cold is nowhere apparent. Birt's interpretation of the fragment in Lucilius's context too may be doubted: Friedrich Marx and E. H. Warmington referred it simply to Lucilius's estate, Conrad Cichorius, Johannes Christes, and Giovanni Garbugino deemed it the complaint of a publican about harvests generally, Werner Krenkel thought it described the emotional devastation wrought by Lucilius's sarcastic satires, and François Charpin declared it impossible to tell whether the complaint was literal or metaphorical.[13]

Claudian's scenario shows closer similarity to Plutarch's story that Demosthenes, fleeing from Chaeronea, felt a bush catch his cloak behind him and cried out, "Take me alive!" (Plut. *Mor.* 845F). Both Demosthenes and Leo deepen the disgrace of running away from the field of battle by panicking at insignificant, natural actions of shrubbery. Yet shared cultural attitudes derisory of cowardice sufficiently explain the partial correspondence; Claudian need not have borrowed from Plutarch either.

That Lucilius gave space in the twenty-sixth book to some thought of composing a poem about the Numantine War seems certain from the fragment "Noise about Popilius's battle, sing the deeds of Cornelius" (*percrepa pugnam Popili, facta Corneli cane*).[14] M. Popilius Laenas was defeated by the Numantines in 138 B.C., and Cornelius Scipio Aemilianus capped the series of generals the Romans sent unsuccessfully by taking Numantia in 134.[15]

But the fragment gives no indication of who uttered its imperatives, or of what response they met. Birt argued that Horace could represent Trebatius as bidding him to "dare to tell the achievements [*res*] of unconquered Caesar" (*Serm.* 2.1.10–11) only if Lucilius had already established such a topic in satire.[16] Lucilius is indeed mentioned in the context of this advice, as Birt observed. But Lucilius is mentioned after Horace declares that he lacks the strength for battle scenes: Horace makes his refusal, and Trebatius replies, "Yet you could write of a man both just and brave, as wise Lucilius did of Scipio" (*Serm.* 2.1.16–17). *Res* in Trebatius's first suggestion is neutral; Horace willfully applies it to military action. But now the emphasis shifts explicitly to moral qualities, and it is at this point that Lucilius is invoked.[17] Only with this shift does Horace consider

13. Marx 1905, 2.243; Cichorius 1908, 103; Warmington 1938, 209; Krenkel 1970, 1.84; Christes 1971, 29; Charpin 1978–91, 2.283, Garbugino 1990, 171–72.

14. Lucil. fr. 621 Marx = 714 Warmington = 689 Krenkel = 26.26 Charpin = 2 Garbugino.

15. Liv. *Per.* 55 (67.2–4 Rossbach); see A. Schulten, "Numantia," *RE* 17 (1937): 1254–70.

16. Birt 1888, 89–90 n. 1; Charpin 1978–91, 2.278 ad 26.26, took essentially the same view.

17. As noted by Porphyrion ad loc.; quoted by Charpin 1978–91, 2.278.

satire as such; he refuses to write not martial satire but epic. Numerous later parallel refusals are made from within genres metrically distinct from epic, by the elegists and by Horace himself in the lyric *Odes*. Persius and Juvenal both mock the epic poetry of their days in programmatic satires.[18] Marx argued that Lucilius rejects epic in the same way as Horace, choosing to write satire instead when someone bids him, "Noise about Popilius's battle, sing the deeds of Cornelius"; most scholars since him have concurred.[19]

Cichorius set the command in still a third relationship, neither as a recommendation Lucilius proceeds to fulfill nor as a course he rejects, but as a project he enjoins on someone else.[20] Cichorius grouped it with a series of fragments as addressing a young historian friend of Lucilius; the key to the reconstruction is Lucilius's remark, "Led on by zeal you write ancient history addressed to your own darlings."[21] The injunction to "sing" the martial deeds of Popilius and Scipio in this connection would propose an even nobler literary alternative, celebrating contemporary Roman history in epic instead of recording remoter deeds in prose. Cichorius emphasized the close link of this recommendation with the subjunctive "may you [or perhaps, if you would] take up this labor, which would bring you praise and advantage."[22] Christes has more recently underscored the fact that among the Romans history typically was written by experienced statesmen, so that Cichorius's interpretation defies Roman literary convention as well as erotic probability; Cichorius showed that the Romans could sometimes use erotic language of chaster regard, but his fundamental assumption is anomalous.[23] Christes judged *veterem historiam* here to mean narrative of traditional mythology, a more romantically promising subject. Removing the occasion for Lucilius to recommend that someone else treat the Numantine War in poetry weakens the case for Cichorius's scenario. Marx shepherded Lucilius's satire into closer parallelism with Horace's under the best guidance of literary tradition. Nonetheless, nothing in the fragment itself invalidates any of these interpretations. Birt is not to be faulted excessively for testing a hypothesis that ultimately fails.

Birt did emphasize rightly that *In Eutropium* displays close affinities with the sort of military satire he postulated. Leo's inept campaign, the rout of his army and his humiliating death sardonically mimic heroic themes. More kindly than

18. Pers. 1.50, 92–106; Juv. 1.7–11, 162–64. Cf. Bramble 1974, 126–31; Winkler 1989.

19. Marx 1904–5, 2.230 ad frr. 621, 622; e.g., Knoche 1975, 41; Christes 1971, 72–76; Garbugino 1990, 138–39.

20. Cichorius 1908, 109–27.

21. *Veterem historiam, inductus studio, scribis ad amores tuos*, Lucil. fr. 612 Marx = 700 Warmington = 672 Krenkel = 26.23 Charpin = 6 Garbugino. This association is followed by Warmington 1938, 220–21, and Krenkel 1970, 1.86.

22. *Hunc laborem sumas, laudem qui tibi ac fructum ferat*, Lucil. fr. 620 Marx = 713 Warmington = 690 Krenkel = 26.30 Charpin = 1 Garbugino.

23. Christes 1971, 26–27; Cichorius 1908, 110.

Claudian, Horace exemplifies epic travesty as a variety of satire in the "Rex" joke of *Sermo* 1.7 and the briefer battle of wits on the journey to Brundisium (*Serm.* 1.5.50–69).[24] In these poems petty combats humorously contrast with the epic language in which they are described.[25]

In Eutropium 2 shares the same type of dissonance. Its scenes progress with the fundamental dynamism of epic, as I have shown (Chapter 1). Gods take epical parts in inciting war, by the same means they employ in epics. The sight of Eutropius journeying to Ancyra stings Mars to take action against him, just as for example Juno inspires the first storm of the *Aeneid* in protest at Aeneas's safe voyage from Sicily (*Aen.* 1.34–75). Bellona approaches Tribigild in disguise, just as Allecto disguises herself as the priestess Calybe to inspire the fury of war in Turnus (*Aen.* 7.323–474). Phrygia is pastorally described before the gods lay it open to "Gothic devastations" (*Eutr.* 2.274);[26] to similar effect Vergil describes a pet stag and then has Allecto cause Ascanius to shoot it, so that he sets off the first combat of Trojans and Italians.[27] Cybele's prophecy recalls epic recognitions of omens (e.g., *Aen.* 7.112–34) and divine prophecies of future events (e.g., *Aen.* 1.257–94). Scenes of war of course are quintessentially epic; although Claudian renders Leo's campaign a ludicrously feeble travesty, Tribigild's first strike echoes Vergil and Lucan.[28] The epic conventions surrounding Tribigild ring true.

On the other hand Eutropius's response is farcical. First he tries to disregard the crisis, like an ostrich burying its head in the sand (*Eutr.* 2.310–16). Cameron pointed out that Claudian is the first and perhaps the only ancient author to exploit this image;[29] its novelty for Claudian's audience would have redoubled the incongruity of the picture itself, a giant bird idiotically ignoring its pursuers, with the grave martial prospect it answers. Claudian shares with satiric technique both disconcerting abasement of epic tone and unheroic animal comparisons.[30] He operates in the same way when he compares Leo's army to a whale without its pilot fish (2.425–30).

When Tribigild's revolt proves impossible to ignore entirely, Eutropius calls a meeting of imperial councillors (2.322–401). Birt observed that this scene is

---

24. See Schröter 1967; Sallmann 1974; cf. Bramble 1974, 29–34.

25. Horace also uses epic devices for satiric dissonance with a noncombative subject when Teresias instructs Ulixes in hunting legacies, *Serm.* 2.5; see Sallmann 1970.

26. *Populatus* is a nonclassical word borrowed from Luc. 2.534; also at *Eutr.* 1.244.

27. Verg. *Aen.* 7.477–539; the metamorphosis of rustic to military tools is remarkable.

28. *Eutr.* 2.276, *spes nulla salutis, nulla fugae:* Verg. *Aen.* 9.131, 10.121; Luc. 10.538 (Birt 1892, 106 ad loc.; Fargues, *Invectives*, and Andrews 1931 followed).

29. Alan Cameron 1970, 300.

30. Horace's town and country mice supply a famous extended example, *Serm.* 2.6.77–117 (on its delightful complexities, David West, "Of Mice and Men: Horace, *Satires* 2.6.77–117," in *Quality and Pleasure in Latin Poetry*, ed. Tony Woodman and David West (Cambridge: Cambridge University Press, 1974), 67–80.

modeled on the council of Domitian in Juvenal's fourth satire.[31] This part of that satire too parodies epic, specifically, Statius's lost *De Bello Germanico*.[32] Juvenal calls upon Calliope to tell the tale, but instantly deflates his invocation by saying that she may tell it sitting down, and by bidding the Muses to appreciate his compliment in calling them "maidens" (Juv. 4.34–36). High-sounding periphrasis and hypallage[33] describe the catching of an immense turbot. The fisherman journeys through an ornately wintry and noble land-scape to present his catch to the emperor. No dish is large enough for it, and so the council is summoned to debate the problem. The councillors assemble; each is described separately. One praises the fish especially fulsomely, even though being blind he turns in the wrong direction to look at it. Another flatters Domitian more directly by declaring the fish an omen of victory. Another displays his culinary expertise, a common satirical target, by analyz-ing the fish's native country and age.[34] Finally Domitian calls for a decision. Montanus, the greatest gourmand, proposes that a larger dish be made. The councillors are released from where they had been summoned in fear and haste, "as if he were going to say something about the Chatti or the grim Sygambri, as if from distant parts of the earth an anxious letter had come on rushing wing" (2.147–49). Thus Juvenal's council travesties an epic council of war by the triviality of the crisis it addresses; Claudian's faces a war, but the councillors themselves are frivolous and ineffectual. In both, the solemn framework of the setting heightens the debasement of the characters and their actions.

Lucilius supplies a precedent for satirical displacement of councils from epic, in his divine council over Lupus (book 1); his use of the council is paralleled more closely by Seneca's *Apocolocyntosis* and Claudian's judgment of Rhadamanthys over Rufinus than by Juvenal or *In Eutropium*. Conversely, their modally satirical subversion of the council itself may have been influ-enced by an arguably subversive epic, Ovid's *Metamorphoses*, in its initial council of the gods over Lycaon.[35] I will discuss further Claudian's echoes and inversions in Chapter 4.

31. Birt 1888, 56. On Juv. 4 see now F. M. A. Jones 1990.

32. See F. Buechler, "Coniectanea," *RhM* 39 (1884): 274–92, 283–85; Griffith 1969; Townend 1973, 153–58; Courtney 1980, 195–96.

33. Cf. Serv. ad *Aen.* 3.61.

34. Juv. 2.129; cf. 139–43, Hor. *Serm.* 2.4, 2.8. Such connoisseurship varies the broader theme of gluttony, as does the extravagance Juvenal attacks in Crispinus in the first part of the satire; for further citations, including satirical prose authors, notably Ammianus and Jerome, see Wiesen 1964, 24–25 (further on Jerome alone, Wiesen 27, 43–44, 51–53, 77–79, 134–35, 139–40). Jerome passes from satire to invective when he charges heretics and personal enemies with gluttony (see Wiesen 182–83, 192, 211–12).

35. On Ovid's council, see William S. Anderson, "Lycaon: Ovid's Deceptive Paradigm in *Metamorphoses* I," *ICS* 14 (1989): 91–101.

More often than satire travesties epic, it seeks to excite an audience's attention against a social or ethical problem. Satire and *In Eutropium* use similar
mechanisms. Amy Richlin has affirmed that Sigmund Freud's theory of jokes
fits well much Roman satire, relatively restrained Horatian mockery as well as
Juvenalian violent denunciation.[36] This analytical model explains humor as an
economical expression of aggression, which does no material harm but claims
superiority competitively. The joker enlists the audience with him against an
other about whom the joke is made. They enjoy together the joke's confirma-
tion of their common values, as it defines them at the other's expense. The
other is excluded. *In Eutropium* too is fundamentally exclusionary. Claudian
chiefly contends that Eutropius offends Roman traditions and decent sensibilities by being what he is and holding the power that he does, so that he
must be removed. As a subsidiary argument, Claudian also remarks several
times that Eutropius's castration makes him neither a man nor a woman. He
demonstrates Eutropius's disqualification through several scenes (see further
Chapter 4).

Alvin Kernan instructively characterized the confrontational mood of satire.[37] "The scene of satire is always disorderly and crowded." Examples of vice,
folly, and their appurtenances swarm malignly; often the contrasting ideal is
evoked, but if so it is always severely threatened or already destroyed. Satire is
sometimes superficially realistic and sometimes openly symbolic, but in all
cases it distorts the world by its single-minded concentration on vice. The
Satirist, an imaginary entity through whose sensibilities the satiric view is
presented, claims to be a simple, honest individual who would prefer to live in
quiet moderation minding his own business, but whom the ills of the world
drive irresistibly to protest. So extreme are they, however, that he does not
really expect to win out against them; rather, he will, still protesting bitterly,
ultimately be crushed. The violence with which he has to meet the world
makes him no less extreme than it. The plot of satire consequently becomes "a
stasis in which the two opposing forces, the Satirist on one hand and the fools
on the other, are locked in their respective attitudes without any possibility of
either dialectical movement or the simple triumph of good over evil. Whatever
movement there is, is not plot in the true sense of change but mere intensifica-
tion of the unpleasant situation with which satire opens."

Claudian revels in detail as concrete illustrations underline his points again
and again, so that in this respect *In Eutropium* closely resembles satire; but it

36. Richlin [1983] 1992, 59–63. She emphasized the aggressive element, which Freud
[1905, rev. 1912] 1960, 236, stated (in his conclusion) more circumspectly; but cf. Freud
96–102 and 102–15, 117–19, 132–38, 150–56. Important observations in Freud 198, 200,
distinguish "the comic" per se from the aggressive impulse that may be involved in the
decision to make another person comic.

37. The quotations that follow come from Kernan [1959] 1971, 253, 270–71.

also resembles any other genre where rhetorical exuberance can play. Ovid, for example, is no less abundant in epic or in erotic elegy. Claudian argues for a normative position too, from which Eutropius is excluded. He has no expectation of changing Eutropius by this attack. But neither does he face the same futility as the Satirist, for he does not aim to persuade Eutropius himself. He seeks to have him eliminated by outside means. The goddesses' requests at the ends of the two books apparently expect fulfillment; Roma's first request, not to recognize Eutropius as consul, had been met by the time Claudian performed. Although in book 2 he inveighs harshly against Eastern vice, by the end of the book he asserts that the will of the people has reformed (see Chapter 8.II).

As Horace's famous warning implies, the moral discourse of satire has the potential of applying to the audience the Satirist addresses: "What are you laughing at? Change the name, and the story is told about you" (*Serm.* 1.1.69–70). Claudian speaks in the second person not in order to engage his audience but to isolate his target: the apostrophe adds forcefulness to his derision. Of the twenty-three times Claudian uses the pronoun "you" in his own voice in *In Eutropium*, seventeen instances address Eutropius with some rebuke.[38] Two times he uses the pronoun in telling the East that it is not sufficiently cleansed by Eutropius's exile (2.20, 22). He also addresses the lamentable Leo twice (2.456, 461). He addresses one rebuke to Fortuna for raising Eutropius (1.26), and once speaks more neutrally to Roma in the course of a historical exemplum (1.215). He makes the term of address strongly confrontational.

Specific premises on which Claudian confronts Eutropius also operate in ethical satire. Juvenal's second satire, for example, not only influenced Claudian in many phrases and juxtapositions of ideas, but also in its attack on hypocritical inconsistency.[39] Juvenal begins with a general denunciation of

38. Christiansen 1988, 398 s.v. *tu: Eutr.* 1.224, 225, 226, 271, 273, 274, 275, 283; 2pr.35, 39, 41, 44, 52, 53, 62, 67, 69; 2.151 (at 1.271 he calls him "most foul," *turpissime*, at 1.283 "mad," *demens*, etc.). Other instances of "you" make reported speech more vivid: 1.391, 435, 485, 487, Roma to Honorius; 1.453, Roma to Serranus among Republican heroes (the audience may somewhat identify with these addressees, all complimented and distinguished from Eutropius); 2.221, 222, 226, 227, Bellona to Tribigild; 2.534, 537, 538, 591, 592, 599, Aurora to Stilicho.

39. Birt 1888, 52–63, assembled Juvenalian echoes in Claudian. On Juvenal see Courtney 1980; Mayor 1901 (who omitted *Sat.* 2, 6, 9); cf. John Ferguson, ed., *Juvenal: The Satires* (New York: St. Martin's Press, 1979); W. S. Anderson 1982, 197–254 = "Studies in Book I of Juvenal," *YCS* 15 (1957): 33–90 (*Sat.* 1–5); Gilbert Highet, *Juvenal the Satirist* (Oxford 1954; rpt. New York: Oxford University Press, 1961). Ferguson followed Highet 59 in considering Juv. 2 to be directed simply against homosexuality, but this view cannot account for all the poem's targets (cf. Ferguson 133 ad 2.143–48; Highet 63–64 approached a broader political emphasis). More precisely, Juvenal attacks falseness to one's own position: the moralists deserve censure more than the others they attack, so that their attack constitutes an imposture; men betray their masculinity by effeteness,

those who "look like Curii and live like Bacchanals" (2.3). They are uneducated, but they collect statues of sages. Pathic homosexuality belies the severity they cultivate. Several hypothetical inversions are topped by the incestuous Domitian's revival of Augustus's legislation on adultery. The former all relate to political crises,[40] but now the scale narrows to personal sexuality.

Juvenal reports the adulteress Laronia's rejoinder to accusation: men practice homosexuality but women do not.[41] Women do not argue law and few women are athletes, but men spin as finely as their slave-mistresses.[42] Again, men keep male lovers and wives profit from not complaining.

Juvenal resumes the attack in his own voice, now turning on one Creticus. He inveighs against adulteresses, and yet wears transparent robes. He will

---

transvestitism, and homosexuality, or their class by their sport; and both the false moralists and the open immoralists betray the austere martial traditions of Rome (which is what the moralists pretend to uphold: e.g., 2.37 lamenting the Julian law; brought out though with different emphasis by W. S. Anderson 1982, 209–19 = 1957, 45–55).

40. In the inversions, the Gracchi denounce sedition, Verres thieves, Milo murderers, Clodius adulterers, Catiline his fellow conspirator Cethegus, and the second triumvirate (identified as "Sulla's three pupils") proscription. Juv. 2.83–90 points to Clodius's famous transvestite infiltration of the rites of Bona Dea celebrated in Julius Caesar's house, allegedly to seduce Caesar's wife: thus his supposed denunciation (2.27) comprehends national religion and Caesarian politics as well as private morality. Cf. Juv. 6.335–41.

41. Cf. Judith P. Hallett, "Female Homoeroticism and the Denial of Roman Reality in Latin Literature," *YJC* 3 (1989–90): 209–27 = Dynes and Donaldson 1992, 179–97.

42. Apparently the sense of Juv. 2.57, the *paelex* being specified to rebuke male infidelity; but the text is not entirely satisfying (see Courtney 1980, 131 ad 57). Exemplifying derogatory charges of male spinning, Courtney ad 54 cited Ar. *Nub.* 831 (of Cleisthenes); Ctesias, *Frag. Gr. Hist.* IIIC, 1.688 (444; of Sardanapallus, an archetypal figure originally of wealth [Hdt. 2.150] but later of luxury [e.g., Ar. *Av.* 1021]; see further Weißbach, "Sardanapal," *RE* ser. 2, 1A [1920]: 2436–75); Cleomedes *De Motu Circulari* 2.1 (166.25 Ziegler; of Sardanapallus); Plut. *De Alex. Fort.* 1.2.326–27 (of Sardanapallus); Clearchus (ap. Athen. 12.516b, fr. 43a Wehrli, *Schule des Aristoteles* 3, of Midas); and Hercules when subject to Omphale (the insult is Roman too, e.g., Cic. *De Orat.* 2.277; Claudian makes it an adynaton, *Eutr.* 1.497–99). Courtney concluded, "Probably Laronia is thinking of these rather than any actual cases at Rome." Certainly Juvenal exploits the negative connotation, but a stronger correlation with fact would strengthen Laronia's point. She contrasts male spinners with women who pursue masculine public and private activities (law and wrestling), and it is a fact that traditionally woolworking was a domestic occupation of women; but it also became a common business for men (for evidence on classical Athens and Pompeii, see Wesley Thompson, "Weaving: A Man's Work," *CW* 75 [1981–82]: 217–22; for later antiquity, A. H. M. Jones, "The Cloth Industry under the Roman Empire," *Econ. Hist. Rev.* 2nd ser. 13 [1960]: 183–92). Juvenal could be twisting a relatively ordinary circumstance to fit the inversions of gender and social roles throughout *Sat.* 2. The "slender thread" Laronia says that men spin also foretokens the "sheer garments" of Creticus in the next section of the satire (Juv. 2.66).

progress from this garb to even worse scandal, Juvenal avers, full transvestitism and worship of the Bona Dea. Amplifying the spread of this disease, Juvenal ironically pretends that now genuine women are barred from the rites.[43] His catalog of the effects of the celebrants descends to "a mirror, the vademecum of pathic Otho" (2.99) and Otho's defeat of Galba in civil war: male effeminacy, especially sexual, is associatively bound with political sedition. Juvenal concludes by describing the feast of Bona Dea (2.111–16):

> Here are Cybele's vile men, and license of speech with broken
> voice, and an aged devotee with white hair,
> the high priest of the rites, a rare and memorable example
> of great voraciousness, who ought to be hired as a teacher.
> Yet what are they waiting for, when long since it was time that, in
>   Phrygian fashion,
> they cut off their excess flesh with knives?

From this unedifying spectacle Juvenal turns to describe another atrocity that he asserts is now being practiced secretly but will soon become common and public: marriage between two men. A male bride is not just a moral scandal calling for the censor, he protests, but a prodigy for the haruspex. "Hah! Would you be horrified and think it a greater monstrosity [*monstra*], if a woman gave birth to a calf, or a cow to a lamb?" (2.122–23). Yet worse, the bride Gracchus is a Salian priest of Mars; Juvenal rails at Mars for failing to protest this dishonor. On the other hand, he is pleased that Nature denies male brides all hope of offspring. Gracchus makes himself an even greater *monstrum* when despite his noble birth he enters gladiatorial competition as a *retiarius* (2.143–48).

Finally Juvenal returns to the political aspect of his complaints. He holds up against the present moral degeneration the spirits of republican heroes and present military success. Ironically, Rome now overcomes subject peoples morally, by effeminizing and seducing its hostages, so that they may return home with "their morals dressed like Roman boys" (*praetextatos mores*, Juv. 2.170).[44] At the surface of the text, Juvenal has been distracted from hypocrisy

---

43. I judge the Bona Dea passage (Juv. 2.82–90) to expand on Juvenal's assertion in 2.78–81 that Creticus's fashion for transparency has spread by contagion like a plague or blight: not only will Creticus advance deeper into effeminacy and scandal until he joins the celebrants, but they already represent the infected. Courtney 1980, 135, presumed that "Juvenal actually did know of some secret society which carried out such a parody of the rites of the Bona Dea," analogously to the Eleusinian parody alleged against Alcibiades.

44. See Courtney 1980, 149–50, on the overtones of *praetextatos* and the grammatical interpretation of *Artaxata* (in any case, a traditional patriotic cliché is tellingly reversed, when Rome now corrupts Eastern barbarians.)

onto sexual scandal, but the last string of comparisons confronts sexual scandal with traditional Roman military and imperial ideals. Implicitly Juvenal asserts that the greatest hypocrisy is for Romans who tolerate such scandal to think that they are any better than anyone else. The rebuke demands that reform correct this state of shame.

A great deal more than hypocrisy or inconsistency is criticized in the satire, and Claudian models many points of his invective after it. I shall analyze specifics in Chapter 4. It is worth noting now that together with the broader common features of indignation, sexual themes tied with gender and class prejudices, and reproach cast against a background of religious violation, Claudian also adopts the satiric device of making a rebuke from the opponent's own person. Whereas Juvenal blasts various individual targets so as to delimit his topic from different angles, Claudian assails manifold iniquity in Eutropius.

A narrower example of reproach from the self[45] appears when Claudian accuses Eutropius of sowing discord between Arcadius and Honorius and bids him consider his own past career as a pander: it would be more appropriate for Eutropius to bring them together (1.281–84). Nothing in the passage presses the potential sexual overtones of this "joining" of the brother emperors. Claudian otherwise rejoices in their fraternal unity, and blames Eutropius for breaking it (e.g., 2.543–52); here he sharpens the same rebuke for violating the imperial ideal by claiming that Eutropius violates his own nature too.[46] Secondarily, the charge recalls the fact that Eutropius more closely acted the pander to Arcadius in persuading him to marry Eudoxia.[47] So too in his epithalamium for Honorius and Stilicho's daughter Maria, Claudian makes Honorius boast that he did not chose his bride from a picture (*Epith.* 25–27), clearly glancing at Arcadius's choice and its sponsor.[48]

Claudian concentrates his satirical denigration strongly on Eutropius. He alone figures in book 1; in book 2 his cronies reproduce the status and predilections already established for him cardinally. Contrary to the technique of *In Rufinum*, no positive hero takes action against Eutropius. Stilicho foils him implicitly but distantly, when Roma and Aurora at the close of the two books wish him to rescue the East. Just as Roma begs Honorius not to let Eutropius pollute the consulate in the West (e.g., 1.429–31) and Mars rejoices that Stilicho has protected the Western fasti (2.123–32), Claudian abases Eutropius too far to sully Stilicho by any direct engagement. Roma assures Stilicho that he need only crack a whip to prostrate Eutropius (1.505–13). The essential frivolity of

45. Hor. *Serm.* 2.3.307–11 is comparable in scope. Juvenal applies the adage "know thyself" (γνῶθι σεαυτόν) differently at *Sat.* 11.27–45.

46. Cf. *Eutr.* 1.77–97 and Chap. 4.III.

47. Zos. 5.3.2–3; Aelia Eudoxia 1, *PLRE* 2.410.

48. Alan Cameron 1970, 53–54.

this remedy satirically rejects rather than solves the problem; Horace, Persius, and Juvenal in programmatic satires similarly answer literary challenges with dismissive jokes.[49] Aurora, on the other hand, by leaving her plea to Stilicho completely open urges an intervention that is more conceivable in practical terms. The final note of book 2 thus advances beyond book 1 in treating Eutropius as a genuine political enemy.

49. Kenney 1962. Lucilius seems to have confronted literary adversaries more belligerently; John G. Griffith, "The Ending of Juvenal's First Satire and Lucilius, Book XXX," *Hermes* 98 (1970): 56–72.

CHAPTER THREE

Literary Traditions of
Political Invective

✦

CLASSICAL GREEK and Roman politics generated many bitter conflicts, which in turn inspired much eloquent vituperation. Claudian still exploits the topics and techniques of ancient authors, although he does not often allude particularly to individual political works. The first interest of this chapter will be to sketch what kinds of attacks became established, and what relevance they bore for political issues.

The milieux and forms of political criticism changed from classical to late antiquity. Macedonian dominance first and later Roman suzerainty quieted the political ferment of democratic Athens; emperors stilled the political contention of republican Rome. In the Roman imperial period throughout the Mediterranean region, deliberative oratory lost its currency. Judicial oratory too ceased to serve as a vehicle for essentially political attacks. Epideictic oratory alone retained its public platform. It increasingly occupied the focus of rhetorical treatises and practical training, and it too influenced Claudian. I have already shown that a standard rhetorical formula applicable to either encomium or invective underlies the structure of *In Eutropium* 1. The second part of the present chapter reviews late antique training in the use of this form and how orators applied it to practical situations.

Other late antique works use similar techniques outside of strictly rhetorical genres. In the third part of the chapter I explore this material, so that the chapter as a whole may indicate the range of traditions of political abuse on which Claudian draws in *In Eutropium*.

1. Political Contumely in Athens and Rome

Political detraction was vociferated from many platforms in classical Greece and Rome. Political and courtroom speeches attacked adversaries directly. In fifth-century Athens, Old Comedy did too. At Rome, contemporary references both hostile and favorable were read into the lines of plays; audiences cheered and booed politicians in the audience just as they did the shows and performers.[1] Political heckling by individuals and crowds employed simple name-calling and more elaborate wit, literary allusions and original verses.[2] In all these forms of abuse, over disparate political issues, from widely different places and times, similar behaviors and propensities consistently bear the brunt of attacks.

These phenomena have been studied before, from various perspectives over different fields of inquiry. In 1910 Wilhelm Süß investigated Greek traditions of rhetorical characterization, including invective. Severin Koster in 1980 studied invective in both oratory and poetry, from archaic works to Claudian. Koster still deemed fundamental Süß's ten categories of derogatory imputations employed by Greek orators:[3] (1) service as a slave or slave parentage;[4] (2) barbarian origin;[5] (3) banausic occupation; (4) criminality; (5) reprehensible sexual practices; (6) hostility toward kin, friends, or city; (7) ill temper; (8) peculiarities of appearance, dress, or behavior; (9) military desertion;[6] and (10) bankruptcy. R. G. M. Nisbet appended to his edition of Cicero's *In Pisonem* a handy survey of conventional topics of abuse: it highlights lowly origins, physical appearance, dissipation, avarice and pretentiousness, and key words associating the victim with animals, dirt, malign omens, tyranny, violence, and madness.[7] Ilona Opelt has surveyed Latin vituperative terminology.[8] Her categories of reproach against the public activity of politicians include criminality, corruption, autocratic tendencies, treachery, hostility or dangerousness to the state, and likeness to historic enemies of Rome. She reviewed accusations against politicians' private lives under the headings origin, occupation and rank, financial dealings, age and appearance, crimes, sexual dissipation, glut-

1. Some examples are surveyed by Alan Cameron, *Circus Factions: Blues and Greens at Rome and Byzantium* (Oxford: Clarendon Press, 1976), 158–61, 170–71; *HA Marc.* 29, *HA Commod.* 3.3, *HA Maxim. Duo* 9.3–5 record similar later incidents. See further Bollinger 1969; Edwards 1993, 98–136; W. J. Slater, *Class. Ant.* 13 = *Cal. Stud. Class. Ant.* 25 (1994): 120–44, on the "Pantomime Riots" under Tiberius, sparked in part by young knights.

2. Richlin [1983] 1992, 83–104 and 278–84, surveyed Roman examples. Gleason 1986 discussed Antiochene political lampoons. Cf. *HA Pert.* 9.5–6; *HA Opell. Macr.* 12.9, 14.2; *HA Gord. Tres* 19.4.

3. Koster 1980, 2; Süß 1910, 247–54.

4. On the social background of this attitude in classical Athens, cf. Dover 1974, 39–40, 283–84.

5. Cf. Dover 1974, 83–87.

6. Evading military service legally disenfranchised an Athenian in the classical period: MacDowell 1978, 160.

7. Nisbet 1961, 192–97.

8. As used in political contexts, Opelt 1965, 125–89.

tony and high living, and evil associates. For monarchs she added tastes un-suited to the dignity of their office. Other important studies relevant to politi-cal invective include Katherine A. Geffcken's of the comic techniques exploited by Cicero against Clodia in his defense of Caelius and her appendix on Cicero's apparently similar attack *In Clodium et Curionem*,[9] Amy Richlin's investiga-tions into sexual themes in Roman humor, including invective wit,[10] and Catharine Edwards's survey of *The Politics of Immorality in Ancient Rome* from the mid-first century B.C. to the early second century A.D.[11]

IT IS WORTH briefly reviewing some examples of political criticism from classical Athens and Rome, to give a sense of the tradition. Political malfea-sance naturally constitutes a most important target. Andocides in his defense *On the Mysteries*, for example, discredits his prosecutors by listing their crimes against democratic Athens.[12] Cephisius defaulted on public rents he had farmed, keeping huge profits for himself (Andoc. *Myst.* 92–93). Meletus ar-rested Leon, whom the oligarchical Thirty Tyrants executed without a trial (*Myst.* 94). Epichares actually held political office under the Thirty (*Myst.* 95).

Lysias prosecutes Eratosthenes for having been one of the Thirty (Lys. *Or.* 12). The first part of his speech describes simply but powerfully how Lysias himself was arrested by Peison, another of the Thirty, and managed to escape, while his brother Polemarchus was arrested by Eratosthenes, killed without

9. Katherine A. Geffcken, *Comedy in the Pro Caelio*, Mnemosyne Suppl. 30 (Leiden: E. J. Brill, 1973), 2–8, discussed social and psychological attitudes to comedy, 66–70, to invective.

10. Richlin [1983] 1992, esp. 96–104 and 282–84, on sexual slanders in rhetorical invective, particularly in the late republic.

11. Edwards 1993; in particular, her chapter on "*Mollitia*: Reading the Body," 63–97, lucidly integrates the perspectives on sexuality of Michel Foucault and others into her study of "Roman discourses about sexual behaviour and how those discourses were deployed in the pursuit of non-sexual (as well as sexual) ends" (67). I focus here on hostile political deployments. Interesting narrower studies include Marilyn B. Skinner, "Parasites and Strange Bedfellows: A Study in Catullus' Political Imagery," *Ramus* 8 (1979): 137–52, on metaphorical sexual slanders; Ronald Syme, *The Roman Revolution* (Oxford: Clarendon Press, 1939), 149–61, on late republican themes of abuse, singling out "disgusting immorality, degrading pursuits and ignoble origin," and an introduc-tion to positively valued political catchwords; and on charges and countercharges between Antony and Octavian, Kenneth Scott, "The Political Propaganda of 44–30 B.C.," *MAAR* 11 (1933): 7–49, M. P. Charlesworth, "Some Fragments of the Propaganda of Mark Antony," *Classical Quarterly* 27 (1933): 172–77, and cf. Zanker 1988, 33–77, "Rival Images: Octavian, Antony, and the Struggle of Sole Power," and Maria Wyke, "Augustan Cleopatras: Female Power and Poetic Authority," in Powell 1992, 98–140.

12. See Douglas MacDowell, ed., *Andokides: On the Mysteries* (Oxford: Clarendon Press, 1962).

trial, and denied decent burial by his family. Lysias highlights the implacable greed with which the oligarchs and their agents seized all the money and valuables they could, even taking the earrings out of Polemarchus's wife's ears. This narrative not only establishes a personal grievance against Eratosthenes, but also characterizes the regime of Thirty for the whole speech. The remainder details how Eratosthenes from first to last helped to establish, promote, and preserve the oligarchy. Lysias argues that Eratosthenes supported one faction competing for power within the group, but never opposed any of its corporate oppressions. He repeatedly evokes the jury's resentment at the ravages of the Thirty: homes invaded (*Or.* 12.30), property confiscated (12.83), relations killed without trial and their funeral rites blocked (12.36, 39, 52, 82, 83, 87–88, 96, 99–100), defenses dismantled and armies betrayed (12.36, 39, 40, 63, 68, 70, 99), citizens exiled (12.33, 57, 58, 95–98), and democracy overthrown (12.43–48, 65–67, 71–78).

Demosthenes' speech for Diodorus against Androtion primarily castigates his proposal to honor the outgoing Boule although it had failed to build triremes. Thus condoning omission of this duty will encourage future councillors to leave Athens defenseless, he argues (Dem. *Or.* 22.19). Furthermore, allowing Androtion's decree to stand will release councillors from a due audit of their acts in office (22.38–39). Demosthenes further charges Androtion with unnecessary abusiveness in collecting back taxes, so as to forestall Androtion's chance of claiming that condemning him now will encourage defaulters; rather, in insulting and imprisoning citizens and resident aliens Androtion surpassed the tyranny of the Thirty (22.42–64). Writing for Euthycles against Aristocrates' proposal that the person of the mercenary leader Charidemus be decreed sacrosanct, Demosthenes argues that the decree contravenes existing laws, works generally to Athens' detriment, and protects someone who has long injured Athens (23.18). The speech as a whole focuses on dangers posed by Charidemus, but Demosthenes also blames corrupt Athenian politicians for cheapening the city's honors by peddling them for personal gain, and complaisant citizens for acquiescing to their disadvantage (23.196–214). Aeschines he continually accuses of selling his voice in Athenian politics to the interests of Philip of Macedon (18.133, 136, 139–59; 19.8, 16, 27, 28, 47, 77, 88, 90, 96, 100, etc.). Eventually the speakers who convicted Demosthenes of taking a bribe from the fugitive Macedonian treasurer Harpalus alleged that Demosthenes too betrayed Athenian interests for Philip's gifts.[13]

Similar charges of cruelty and corruption in political office were also exploited at Rome. Cicero charges that in his judicial capacity the former gover-

13. Hyp. *Dem.* cols. 14.9–25.28; Din. *Or.* 1.28–29; see Ian Worthington, *A Historical Commentary on Dinarchus: Rhetoric and Conspiracy in Later Fourth-Century Athens* (Ann Arbor: University of Michigan Press, 1992).

nor of Sicily Verres executed the innocent, tortured and crucified citizens, and, accepting bribes, released guilty pirates (Cic. *Verr.* 2.1.9). Torture and crucifixion violated the victims' rights as citizens as well as demonstrated Verres' savagery.[14] Cicero also accuses Verres, in his administrative capacity, of embezzlement and extortion (*Verr.* 1.11–14, 2.1.11, etc.). He claims that when Verres' own affairs were at stake he did what he could to pack the court with biddable partisans (*Verr.* 2.1.18), and further bribed electors and judges (e.g., *Verr.* 2.1.19, 20). Cicero poises the whole first speech against Verres' reliance on bribery to buy himself safety from prosecution, either directly in the court or through the prestige of political office secured by bribing voters (*Verr.* 1.1–10, 15–32, 36, 38–42, 47).

Cicero as consul began his counterattack on the revolution of Catiline by denouncing him in the full Senate. He charges that Catiline planned to assassinate the chief men of the state (*Cat.* 1.7, 9, 11, etc.). This accusation expands into claims that Catiline intended then to "attack openly the entire republic, the temples of the immortal gods, the buildings of the city, the life of all the citizens, calling all Italy to destruction and devastation" (*Cat.* 1.12). Cicero later claimed that subtler threats to the state were posed by his political enemy Marc Antony: he charges that Antony intimidated the Senate, abused his augurate, and forged decrees as memoranda of Julius Caesar so that they might take force as his *acta* (e.g., *Phil.* 1.16, 2.81). The political accusations range from relatively demonstrable facts to emotive fantasies of unrealized intentions, but all concern specific acts in public affairs producing identifiable consequences.

A BROADER FORM of political slander is represented by Aristophanes' complaints against Cleon in *Knights*.[15] They constitute the central topic of the play, so that it demonstrates especially clearly political vituperation operating within Old Comedy. Cleon and other Athenian politicians are represented as slaves of the anthropomorphized Demos. Cleon is alleged to beguile Demos's worst instincts, manipulating him with bribes and oracles. He lusts after glory and power. He steals the credit for more honorable leaders' achievements and has them persecuted (e.g., Ar. *Eq.* 46–70). Personal profits he skims off from state revenues (e.g., *Eq.* 716–17, 1218–23). Furthermore he prolongs the war (*Eq.* 1388–95), implicitly for the sake of these profits; but throughout the play Aristophanes concentrates as much on the process of corruption as on its ends. Consequential charges are relatively vague. Paphlagon, the character repre-

14. They were routinely used on slaves in both investigation and punishment; Cic. *Verr.* 2.1.9 concerns a penal use, cf. *Verr.* 2.1.13–14. Cf. P. Brunt, "Evidence Given under Torture in the Principate," *ZSS* 97 (1980): 256–65.

15. Lowell Edmunds, *Cleon, Knights and Aristophanes' Politics* (Lanham, Md.: University Press of America, 1987), discussed Aristophanes' political message in *Knights*.

senting Cleon, competes against a new rival, the Sausage-Seller, in flattering
Demos with oracular delusions of grandeur and in catering opulently to his
gluttony. The last part of the duel ends on yet another allusion to Cleon's
filching the achievement of Demosthenes at Pylos, a past scandal whose practical results had already been realized. Pylos is an issue only as it contributes to
Cleon's prestige.

In more practical political confrontation, prestige is similarly at stake and
similarly embraces the contested issue without directly touching on it, when
Demosthenes complains that Aeschines deprived him of credit for ransoming
prisoners from Philip (Dem. *Or.* 18.39–40). For a Roman example, Cicero
disputes prestige when he huffs that he will not treat Antony as a consul since
he has not treated him as a former consul. He adds that Antony's way of life,
conduct of office and manner of election deny him qualification as a consul
"whereas I without any question am of consular rank" (Cic. *Phil.* 2.10). Both
Cicero and Demosthenes deride their adversaries' abilities as public speakers.
Demosthenes often refers to Aeschines' career as an actor in ways that impugn
his oratory now: he bellows pointless, grandiose exclamations "as if in a tragedy" (Dem. *Or.* 19.127) and he quotes poetry but avoids lines too apt to himself
(18.243–50). He relies on his good voice to carry his argument, but even as an
actor he was hissed offstage (18.337). Cicero mocks logical incoherence in
Antony's counterinvective (Cic. *Phil.* 2.28–32).

ANOTHER TACTIC of political slander much used in Athens and Rome, com-
prehending still more of the victim's character, assails personal details arguably
irrelevant to public concerns. Aeschines' speech against Timarchus technically
does not exemplify this procedure because its personal charges are the crux of
Aeschines' case, but it both affords an explanation for the prevalence of such
charges and vividly exemplifies them.[16] A substantial section of the speech
relates an elaborate tale of lust and degradation (Aeschin. *Or.* 1.39–70). Here as
in Lysias's speech against Eratosthenes, vivid narration fixes the allegations in
memory. Aeschines claims that when Timarchus emerged from boyhood he
became a prostitute. At first he served a wide clientele from a doctor's house in
Piraeus, but later he successively attracted the citizens Misgolas and then Anti-
cles, next the public slave Pittalacus, and finally Hegesandrus, a citizen who
had in his day been whore to Leodamas, to maintain him in their houses in
return for his services. But although Timarchus took their money for his
gambling and female prostitutes, he still encouraged other men's attentions to

16. K. J. Dover, *Greek Homosexuality* (London: Duckworth, 1978), 19–109, discussed
issues relevant to "The Prosecution of Timarkhos" at length. MacDowell 1978, 174,
outlined the legal basis; Meulder 1989 discussed Aeschines' rhetoric; see too Halperin
1990, 88–112, on "Prostitution and Citizenship in Classical Athens."

himself and provoked scandalous brawls. He also wasted his father's estate (1.94–105). He bought public posts illegally and abused them, molesting the women of allied cities, extorting money from allies and embezzling from Athens (1.106–15). In connection with these abuses Aeschines argues that "a man who commits outrage, not only against others but even against his own body, at Athens," in the face of the laws and his fellow citizens, can only be expected to behave worse when he has the power and immunity of a public office (1.108). Moral and political misdeeds are two sides of the same coin.

The circumstances of Aeschines' suit correspond. He arraigned Timarchus for a political purpose, in order to impede Timarchus's and Demosthenes' suit against him for treason; he brought the case under laws that disqualified profligates from participating in the public life of Athens (1.19–21, 28–32). These laws reveal how intimately the Athenians connected personal and public activity. They licensed sexual accusations in all sorts of legal action and in any context of political defamation.[17]

Speakers did not always bring formal charges as Aeschines did, but they might hope at least to arouse prejudice against their opponents. Andocides claims that Epichares has prostituted himself cheaply to all comers, for example, and that he should therefore have been barred from serving as an informer under the Thirty (Andoc. *Myst.* 95–101). The allegations both of prostitution and of sycophancy and allegiance with the Thirty seek to bias jurors against Epichares' present prosecution of Andocides. Demosthenes' speech against Androtion refers to charges against him under "the law of prostitution" (Dem. *Or.* 22.21). Aeschines accuses Demosthenes of effeminacy (Aeschin. *Or.* 1.131, 2.99, 2.179).[18]

Aristophanes' humorously inverted claim that pathic sexuality qualifies a citizen for political life (e.g., Ar. *Nub.* 1089–90, 1093–94; *Eccl.* 112–14) implies that accusations were made ubiquitously; exaggeration is part of the joke, but the accusations must have been fairly common to inspire it. Aristophanes implicitly applies the charge himself when the Sausage-Seller in *Knights* boasts among his qualifications to replace Cleon the fact that he has been pathic as an adult (*Eq.* 1242).[19]

---

17. David Cohen, *Law, Sexuality, and Society: The Enforcement of Morals in Classical Athens* (Cambridge: Cambridge University Press, 1991), discussed extensively the complicated relationship between Athenian laws and social attitudes connecting sexuality and public life; chap. 7 is especially relevant to Timarchus. Cf. "*Mollitia*: Reading the Body," in Edwards 1993, 63–97, on classical Roman attitudes.

18. See Dover, *Greek Homosexuality*, 75–76.

19. Possibly in this context "sausage-selling," the other half of the Sausage-Seller's boast, takes on sexual overtones; the sausage is introduced to the play as a symbol with emphasis on the fact that it is long and full of blood (207–8; but this reading need not apply to every passage where it is mentioned).

OTHER SEXUAL, moral, and class slanders abound. In the second parabasis of
Knights Ariphrades, evidently a constant speaker in the Ecclesia (cf. *Eccl.* 129),
is reviled as a cunnilinctor (*Eq.* 1281–89).[20] Cleonymus takes a brief hit for
gluttony (*Eq.* 1290–99). When it is proposed that Hyperbolus command the
fleet, the very ships protest in disgust: one of them suggests that he set sail on
the trays from which he used to sell lanterns (*Eq.* 1300–1315). Personal habits
and lowly former careers in trade, not substantive argument, bear the burden
of the attack.

Aristophanes derides Cleon for his father's business, as a "leather-seller"
(Ar. *Eq.* 136; cf. 449, 740, 868, 892); his Paphlagon threatens the Sausage-Seller
in terms that pun on leather tanning (*Eq.* 369–73). The name (*Eq.* 2, 6, 44, 54,
etc.) stigmatizes Cleon's noisy style of speaking, for it is coined on παφλάζειν,
to boil or splutter.[21] More extended comments recur: he is compared to a noisy
river or a storm;[22] he and the Sausage-Seller try to outshout one another (*Eq.*
274–77, 285–87); epithets and descriptions accuse him directly (*Eq.* 303, 830).
In an extreme instance of gratuitous degradation it is imagined that he may
have anal polyps, a disease of swine.[23]

Aristophanes' comedy might seem a fantastic genre, granting greater license
in attack than more straightforward political invective, and correspondingly
less apt to be taken seriously: Ariphrades evidently survived long despite
Aristophanes' repeated attacks, as did major targets like Cleon. But political
oratory in antiquity was no less superfluously scandalous.[24] Andocides defends
himself against a new charge of offending the Eleusinian mysteries by a narrative showing that Callias had contrived the charge and was not even qualified
to interpret the religious law. This reasonable argument is reinforced by the
assertion that Callias made his wife's mother his mistress and maintained them
both in his house at once, and later sought to marry the grandmother. Andocides gleefully details the ensuing complications (Andoc. *Myst.* 124–29).

Demosthenes emphasizes the lowly professions of Aeschines' parents. His
mother was priestess of an orgiastic cult (Dem. *Or.* 18.259–60; 19.199, 249, 281),
whom in *De Corona* Demosthenes describes as a whore as well (18.129–30).
Aeschines' father taught grammar, and is said in *De Corona* to have been a slave
(18.129; 19.249, 281). Demosthenes relates how Aeschines assisted in the school,

20. Cf. Ar. *Vesp.* 1280–84, *Pax* 883–85; O. Crusius, "Ariphrades," *RE* 2 (1896): 845. It is
unclear whether the things that he does with his mouth in brothels are to be taken
literally or as a metaphor for his public speaking, but in either case the abuse relies on
transference of associations from sexual to political spheres.

21. Cf. Ar. *Eq.* 919–20. The epithet passed into common speech, and was eventually
applied to Claudian himself by John the Lydian: Birt 1892, iv–v; Alan Cameron 1970, 3.

22. Ar. *Eq.* 137 (cf. *Ach.* 381 and schol.); 429–41.

23. Ar. *Eq.* 375–81; cf. Arist. *HA* 603b21.

24. Cf. Dover 1974, 30–33.

"holding the position of a household slave, not a free child" (οἰκέτου τάξιν, οὐκ ἐλευθέρου παιδὸς ἔχων, 18.258).

Cicero accuses Verres of sexual crimes against other men's wives and children (*stuprum*, Cic. *Verr.* 1.14). He declares artfully that in the interests of time he will omit much that he could adduce (*Verr.* 2.1.32–33):

> He will hear nothing from me about the sins of his childhood, nothing out of his well-known impure youth. . . . Let there be silence about his nocturnal orgies and stakeouts; let no mention be made of the pimps, the dice players, the seducers; the damages and disgraces borne by his father's property and his own youth, let them be passed over; he may have for free the traces of his old dishonor: the rest of his life permits me to jettison this great a part of the charges.

However terrible any of these activities might be, none of them bears directly on Verres' extortion in Sicily. The most Cicero might do by substantiating them would be to stain Verres' character in a general way by their associations; by preterition he achieves the same effect through bare enumeration, without getting bogged down.[25]

On Catiline Cicero pours a similar stream of accusations, again focusing on moral charges beside the political crisis actually at hand (*Cat.* 1.13–14). He makes one positive claim, that except for Catiline's fellow conspirators, a crew of derelicts (*perditorum hominum*), everyone in Rome hates and fears him. The reproach extends to no more than an attitude that Cicero alleges. Rhetorical question and preterition raising other issues avoid substance even as they accentuate Cicero's indignation. "What mark of private degradation is not branded on your life?" The vocabulary and images are strong enough to conceal their lack of content. "What lust [*libido*] has ever been absent from your eyes, what crime [*facinus*] from your hands, what sin [*flagitium*] from your entire body?" Catiline is permeated by moral and social wickedness. Its classification is less important than its extent.

The series of questions parallels Cicero's technique overall. He asserts the corruption of a few notable parts of the body, and extrapolates from there the corruption of the whole. The broader conclusion is no better proven, but colors the judgment of any other part. Similarly, the strictly irrelevant but spectacular vices that Cicero mentions suggest by induction that Catiline is totally evil. The totality carries an unreasonable conviction onto more relevant but less emotive charges.

25. Aeschines, prosecuting Timarchus on the grounds of his sexual history, lets go "all the sins that [Timarchus] committed against his own body when he was a boy" without hinting at them further; preterition shows its barbs more when he says that he omits listing the clients of Timarchus's prostitution in youth in order to avoid appearing "excessively precise" (*Or.* 1.39–40).

Cicero goes on to suggest that Catiline has seduced youths into wanton violence or sexuality, and that he murdered his wife in order to free himself to take a new one. "This I let go and easily allow to pass in silence, so that the enormity of so great a crime may not seem either to have existed or to have gone unpunished. I omit the ruination of your fortunes which you feel threatening you, completely, on the next Ides." Violence and corruption of others compound sexual and financial dissoluteness. From these topics Cicero returns to his account of Catiline's conspiracy.

Toward the end of the second Catilinarian oration Cicero catalogs Catiline's partisans (*Cat.* 2.17–25). The first four classes he discerns consist of assorted debtors: still ostensibly respectable ones, who hope to escape dishonor and yet retain their property by a cancellation of debts; others who crave power but see no way to win it except through revolution; Sullan veterans who failed as colonists, having begun with excessive luxury and ambition; and desperate wastrels already beset by judgments against them. The partisanship of all these men blackens Catiline, for implicitly only their desperation and antisocial instincts incline them to his side. Their inability to manage their own affairs honestly reveals their worthlessness. Catiline shares it. The final class comprises Catiline's closest friends (*de eius dilectu, immo vero de complexu eius ac sinu*). Naturally such affection betokens great affinity of character. They number "parricides, assassins, and, in short, all the criminally minded" (*Cat.* 2.22). In describing them Cicero found a new way of reiterating moral and criminal accusations against Catiline. Suggestively, the moral accusations predominate (*Cat.* 2.22–23):

> You see them with their hair well groomed, the slicks, either beardless or bushy-bearded, with long-sleeved ankle-length tunics, clad in sails, not togas. All their life's enterprise and wakeful effort is brought to bear on predawn banquets. In these gangs all the dice players, all the adulterers, all the impure and unchaste spend their time. These boys, so charming and delicate, have learned not only to love and to be loved, nor to dance and sing, but also to shoot daggers and sprinkle poisons. Unless they leave, unless they die, even if Catiline dies, know that there will be this seedbed of Catilines in the state. But still, what do these wretched fellows want? Surely they aren't about to take their little girlfriends into camp with them? Yet how will they be able to be without them, especially now during these nights? Yet how will they endure the Apennines and that frost and snow? Unless perhaps they think they will bear winter more easily, because they have learned to dance naked at banquets!

Grooming, frivolity, and debauchery make up a much larger part of the indictment than actual criminality. And even the claim that these pretty boys are also fledgling assassins is framed in such a way as to emphasize less the unsubstantiated fact than the casualness with which they are supposed to murder, just as they perform their other activities. It is their general wantonness, more than specific acts, that Cicero expects to stir his audience.

Against Antony Cicero proceeds along the same lines, with yet more lurid detail. His allegations, both sexual and financial, loosely parallel Aeschines' against Timarchus. Cicero begins with the fact that Antony went bankrupt before he came of age. Although the fact itself might be cast back upon his father, only Antony's own insolence led him to defy the social laws to which bankruptcy subjected him. As soon as he assumed the *toga virilis*, he made it *muliebris*, that is to say, he took on the role of a whore.[26] This observation demonstrates the pungency of word play. "But soon along came Curio and took you out of the whore's business, and, as if he'd given you a matron's robe, settled you down in stable, secure marriage" (*Phil.* 2.44). Curio's father disapproved and repeatedly threw Antony out of the house, but lust and profit kept him coming back. Cicero vividly sketches Antony being let down through the roof, the elder Curio taking to his bed and the younger Curio wildly begging Cicero to defend his lover against his father (*Phil.* 2.45).[27] Cicero parades Antony's mime mistress Cytheris throughout the second *Philippic* for the sake of the scandal created by their relationship (*Phil.* 2.20, 58, 61–62, 69, 77). He also recurs to an incident when Antony vomited in public, Cicero claims from drunkenness (*Phil.* 2.63, 84).[28] He sinned against the memory of greatness in daring to buy up at auction the property of Pompey; then he gambled and drank it all away until he needed to try to sell off the few bedraggled remnants (*Phil.* 2.64–69, 73). Further effrontery was displayed when he sought or rather requested the consulate clad in Gallic slippers and a cloak instead of Roman shoes and toga (*Phil.* 2.76). When Antony urged Caesar to accept the title of king, as a Lupercal of course he was naked, and Cicero rebukes him for that sartorial failure as well (*Phil.* 2.111).

MUCH OTHER vituperative material plays within the broad tradition of politically motivated abuse in classical Greece and Rome. This quick profile of a few major works illustrates the wide range of considerations accepted as appropriate. Besides matter directly relating to the political issue under contest, Verres'

---

26. *OLD* s.v. *toga* 2.c.

27. On Cicero's relations with the Curiones, see William C. McDermott, "Curio *Pater* and Cicero," *AJP* 93 (1972): 381–411 (on Cic. *Phil.* 2.44–46, 401–2).

28. Cf. *crapulam . . . exhala*, Cic. *Phil.* 30; *vini exhalandi*, 42; *explere* ⟨*haurire quod statim effundas*, 50; *convomeres*, 75 (not immediately referring to the incident, but potentially recalling it to the minds of an audience which knew of it). Cf. Kenneth Scott, "Octavian's Propaganda and Antony's *De Suo Ebrietate*," *CP* 24 (1929): 133–41, on the later life of this slander.

extortion in Sicily, for example, or Catiline's revolutionary conspiracy, more profound questions of political character also come into play. The cruelty and rapacity a governor might evince generally suggest his capacity to abuse his office in the present case (e.g., *Verr.* 2.1.9). One unconstitutional act of a magistrate reveals his willingness to bend the law to his own ends (e.g., *Phil.* 2.84). Prestige, won for whatever reasons, influences the audience's estimations; therefore it must be claimed for one's own side and denied to the other.[29] But perhaps at the very criterion of prestige, the invective argument steps beyond the immediate political concerns into a morass of personal scandals. Lowly origins, misspent youths, gambling, debts, gluttony, drunkenness, shamelessness, dancing, effeminacy, adulteries, pederasty, catamitism, casual murders, and revolutionary ambitions are alleged with great representational vividness and sometimes very little rational support. Nor need they reflect fact. Cicero in his dialogue *De Oratore* explicitly recommends inventing material, if necessary, to make a characterization sufficiently lively (*De Or.* 2.240–41). As Nisbet remarked, even highly circumstantial descriptions might be "largely or completely fictitious . . . inventions were meant to cause pain or hilarity, not to be believed."[30] The speaker sought to make an unforgettable impression, not to win full acceptance for every charge; or so one must infer from the fact that speaker after speaker supported his essential theses with such overwrought images.

The theory describing how the images operated has been elucidated by students of political propaganda, and I shall discuss these matters in greater detail. To summarize briefly by a classical analogy, like Platonic myth the invective portrait concretizes something the speaker wants to propose as a spiritual reality. It fixes a certain estimation of his opponent's character. This general estimation, rather than specific credence for the details by which it is produced, was the speaker's true goal. As Richlin commented about accusations of naked dancing, "The idea was that a man who would do such things was a bad man and would have stooped to whatever the case was about—and vice versa: whole cases depended on such arguments (e.g., *Rosc. Am.* 38–39, *Mur.* 11)."[31] The present charges might concern specific acts, but the whole

29. Cf. Süß 1910, 243–45. Cic. *Phil.* 2.10 (cited previously) explicitly contrasts titles and rights; more subtly, Cicero's many boasts of the effects of his influence (e.g., *Phil.* 2.46), self-reported sagacity (e.g., *Phil.* 2.24), and claims to be endorsed by other prestigious persons (e.g., *Phil.* 2.11, 12) also affirm his superior worth. Ar. *Eq.* 1192–1205 enacts the conceit satirically. Here prestige comes on the grounds of having served Demos better; Demos's cynical conclusion, "the credit doesn't belong to the server," οὐ γὰρ ἀλλὰ τοῦ παραθέντος ἡ χάρις, aptly characterizes any such contest for prestige.

30. Nisbet 1961, 196–97.

31. Richlin [1983] 1992, 101; cf. 284. Edwards 1993, 9–12, similarly observed that the rhetorical moralizing of Roman authors was often factually false, but on the other hand took as "a central premise . . . that accusations and descriptions of immorality

man acted. His character in total was relevant to any case, and so therefore were the most wide-ranging slanders.

The Greek and Roman orators and Aristophanes, who represents Attic Old Comedy in extant literature, employ remarkably similar techniques of political attack. Direct influence need not be supposed, since the authors shared kindred cultural structures and social attitudes. It is natural that their methods echo and complement one another. Claudian is fully in step with the classical traditions of political revilement when he emphasizes Eutropius's base origins, sexual ambivalence, avarice, cruelty, luxury, effrontery, and incompetence.

But the orators, comic poets, and Claudian also are separated by significant differences of form and purpose. The classical orators were politicians. They dueled for advantage in their speeches, whether the speeches actually were delivered before a political assembly or in the courts, or were published as pamphlets imitating the form of a speech. What wit or other devices an orator used—for example, Cicero's sarcastic joke, previously quoted, about naked dancers' training for the hardships of a winter camp (Cic. *Cat.* 2.23)—subserved practical purposes external to the literary entity of his attack. Aristophanes and other comic poets who used political themes composed their attacks for performance as comedy. Comic choruses often voice explicitly the wish to win the playwrights' competition that framed their performance.[32] Plays had to succeed as plays, whatever other effects they might essay; their raillery at some level must subserve wit.

Claudian too frames the matter of political invective in a poetic form with recognized artistic ramifications of its own. The practical goal enunciated within the text of *In Eutropium* is political. Its themes and handling also recall satire. The structure and essential mode of discourse in book 1 conform to rhetorical handbooks' model of epideictic invective, not the more fluid structure of the classical political and judicial speeches. The material so organized is expressed in the dactylic hexameters of epic. The more comprehensive vituperation of book 2 develops within epic narrative. The static, expository book and the more dynamic, epical book both echo the sound of their metrical heritage. This sound influences the ways the books can be perceived: in that regard even *In Eutropium* 1 operates differently than might a prose invective.

The distinction of political and aesthetic goals does not mean that authors did not pursue both. The classical examples demonstrate that function is not limited to a single form. To appreciate fully the artistry or the political relevance of any work, one must understand how they both interact within it.

---

were implicated in defining what it meant to be a member of the Roman elite, in excluding outsiders from this powerful and privileged group and in controlling insiders" (12).

32. E.g., Ar. *Eq.* 546–50; *Pax* 765–74; *Nub.* 520; *Eccl.* 1154–62; cf. *Vesp.* 1051–59.

11. Rhetorical Invective: The Formal Model

The epideictic model which *In Eutropium* 1 follows structurally was actualized mostly in encomium. Rhetors taught invective as an inverted form: it should be organized in the same way, but with the topics turned to vituperation instead of praise. They trained their students in it as in other forms of rhetorical composition by means of exercises called *progymnasmata*.[33]

Aphthonius, who taught rhetoric in Antioch in the later fourth century, both provides instructions for his *progymnasmata* and embodies them in sample exercises. Interestingly, his sample invective on Philip of Macedon follows a typical pattern but not exactly the one Aphthonius describes in his instructions.[34] This inconsistency confirms that the rhetorical forms were flexible, even within a single rhetor's schoolroom. Aphthonius's proem primly announces that it is right to censure the wicked, and Philip outdoes all other bad men. Aphthonius methodically if baldly asserts in turn that Philip's nation, city, ancestors, and father are each more demeaned than the last. These statements match the headings into which Aphthonius subdivides *genos*. Philip's *anatrophe*, next according to plan, was experienced as a hostage in Thebes; he still practiced barbarity in his *epitedeumata*. Instead of subdividing *praxeis*, deeds, by his own scheme according to the spirit, to the body, and to fortune, each with further subdivisions of its own, Aphthonius simply disparages Philip's *praxeis* in war, through a list of the places he evilly subjugated. He next avers that Philip died shamefully, not in war but amid pleasures that bear witness to his dissipation. Aphthonius appears to stray into an alternative arrangement despite his own instructions, which do not mention the subject's death among the topics for discussion; but other rhetors do.[35] Then Aphthonius shortly compares Philip to Echetos, who lost merely his fingertips, whereas Philip crippled his whole body. The epilogue abruptly announces that Philip never knew when to stop, but the speech must. The sample invective gives the student little more guidance than the instructions, since it so perfunctorily

33. On *progymnasmata*, see generally S. F. Bonner, *Education in Ancient Rome from the Elder Cato to the Younger Pliny* (London: Methuen, 1977), 250–76 (on the application of such lessons to life, 288–327); Kennedy 1983, 54–73. The rhetors' precepts for invective were cited in Chap. 1: Theon, Spengel 2.112.17–18; Hermog. *Prog.* 7.36 (15.9–11 Rabe); Alex., Spengel 3.3.20–29; Aristid., Spengel 2.502.3; Aphthon. *Prog.* 8, 9 (21–31 Rabe); Nic. Soph., Spengel 3.482.11–14.

34. Aphthon. *Prog.* 9 (28–31 Rabe), cf. *Prog.* 8, 22.1–11 Rabe. On Aphthonius, Kennedy 1983, 59–66.

35. It is barely possible that *praxeis* in peace occupied a lacuna: Spengel suggested that Phocis fell out of the text after the cities of Thessaly (Spengel 2.iv ad 2.42.3 = 30.11 Rabe). Death in a rhetorical plan, e.g., Hermog. *Prog.* 7.38–40 (16.18–17.1 Rabe; cf. Chap. 1); Aphthonius describes Philip's so loosely as to distort it.

relies on plain assertion rather than demonstrating its points. It outlines a standard design at work.

Aphthonius's teacher Libanius demolishes Philip more fully and colorfully (Liban. *Prog.* 9.3). Most of the ideas associated with such a well-known historical subject were widely current; still, the personal connection between Libanius and Aphthonius and the many parallels between their sample exercises together suggest that Aphthonius condensed Libanius's, and partially assimilated it to his own structural plan. Libanius's structural preferences too obey the common impulse and underlying logic of other rhetorical plans. Physical descriptions appear in several different places within different models; Libanius appends one to his account of Philip's *praxeis*, which he divides between war and peace.[36] In all his invective *progymnasmata* Libanius summarizes the career of his subject with one especially significant act rather than with a *synkrisis*. He also likes to report his subject's death, which provides him with a natural context for a final verdict.

Libanius's proem declares that it is just and praiseworthy to revile evil men, that tyrants are the worst of bad men, and that Philip was the worst of tyrants. There is nothing good to be said about him. His country was barbarian. His city was wretched Pella. His ancestors seemed to rule but in reality were slaves who received their assignments from Persia and paid tribute to Athens. His father Amyntas was, being a barbarian, crude, drunken, gluttonous, and given over to pleasures, with not a qualm at the most shameful. Philip learned all these habits in his own *anatrophe*, and served as a hostage in Thebes because of his father's weakness and his own ill fortune. He learned nothing from his exposure to superior culture. Pammenes used him as a catamite. Philip's *praxeis* in war display ingratitude, deceit, treachery, imposition of tyranny, outrage of the gods, and disregard of treaties. Personal debauchery and shamelessness mark his *praxeis* in peace. Libanius summarizes the *praxeis* with moral analysis: Philip sought peace at times for war, and made warlike acts at times for peace, thus demonstrating his weakness and wickedness (ὧν τὸ μὲν ἀσθενείας, τὸ δὲ πονηρίας δεῖγμα, *Prog.* 9.3.11). His body is deformed by a limp, an eye knocked out, and numerous serious wounds in his limbs. His victory at Chaeronea is admired by some as his greatest achievement, but truly typifies his conduct: he failed twice before succeeding through treachery. At last the gods avenged the Hellenes by having Pausanias, whom too he had outraged, kill him.[37]

Students of rhetoric practiced many such exercises. The *progymnasmata* as

36. Cf. Chap. 1.
37. The sordid story is given most fully by Diod. Sic. 16.93.3–94.4 (cf. Just. 9.6.4–8). Ov. *Ibis* 295–96 indicates a simpler variant, in which Philip raped Pausanias; this version might be reflected by Libanius's emphasis in saying that Pausanias "shamed his own youth" (ἑαυτῆς, Lib. *Prog.* 9.3.14). Either way, more accurate than Aphthonius.

well as the classical literature they read with their teachers and sought to imitate trained them in numerous techniques of disparagement. Using the same derogatory themes as classical speeches within the biographical and moral divisions of the rhetorical scheme, Libanius's invective against Philip successively despises barbarian origins in and of themselves, mocks dependency, rebukes failure to learn cultural values, snidely notes catamitism, drowns practical achievements in the immorality alleged to have won them, and further damns character with accounts of unproductive vice, detests physical deformity, and enrolls the gods against the victim. Such masterful displays forcefully imprinted on students' minds both the types of attack and the basic structure of the invective formula.

But once they graduated, the students' opportunity to apply these lessons directly and fully was limited by the circumstances of life that called real speeches forth. As Libanius remarks about Caesarius, in a grateful panegyric for his handling of the Riot of the Statues in Antioch in 387 (*Or.* 21.4),[38]

> If one wanted to recall all the things that he has done in his whole life, his self-control as a child, when he emerged from childhood his courage in the circumstances that needed it, his judgment, his general affability, how he could make others fear but was not seized by any fear himself, and how he served now one emperor and now the next with the same praise, each ruler valuing the abilities of Caesarius—if we touch on all these points now, we will seem to disparage the present issues as not sufficient for our speech [κατεγνωκέναι τῶν παρόντων δόξομεν ὡς οὐκ ἀποχρώντων εἰς λόγον]; but if on this, by not introducing anything extra [τῷ μηδὲν ἐπεισάγειν] we will seem to honor his help.

The passage amounts to *recusatio* of the full formal encomium, with complimentary preterition to make up the default. When the orator faced such a ceremonial occasion as a consular inauguration, on which pure display was appropriate, he could develop a character in full according to the rhetorical scheme. But when he addressed a particular issue, it was better to stick to the point.[39] And although there were occasions consecrated to decorative praise, blame is less easy to ritualize. It generally has an end in view.

One might, for example, as Libanius does in *Oration 37*, have occasion to

---

38. On the Riot of the Statues, see Glanville Downey, *A History of Antioch in Syria from Seleucus to the Arab Conquest* (Princeton, N.J.: Princeton University Press, 1961), 426–33; Petit 1955, 238–44; Browning 1952; on Caesarius, *PLRE* 1.171 (he is to be identified as Typhos in Synesius's *De Providentia*, however: see now Alan Cameron and Long 1993, 149–97).

39. Cf. Men. Rh. 414.32–415.5 on the address to an official (*prosphonetikos logos*); Libanius focuses yet more tightly than Menander's scheme suggests.

renounce a personal friendship. Polycles[40] had repeated accusations against Julian which Libanius refused to countenance, namely that he made excessive gifts to eunuchs and that he gave away jewelry of his mother's to a doctor in return for poisoning his wife. Narration of this quarrel and refutation of Polycles' side fills the first half of the speech (Liban. *Or.* 37.2–11). In the second half Libanius takes up the offensive against Polycles. By supporting Helpidius[41] in these false accusations of Julian, he is seconding a catamite against a chaste man (ἀνθρώπῳ κιναίδῳ κατὰ ἀνδρὸς σώφρονος, *Or.* 37.12). He displays ingratitude for Julian's appointing him to govern Phoenice, the first appointment of Julian's sole reign; Julian had been misled in making it (*Or.* 37.12). Libanius does not regret losing Polycles' friendship, for he used to disrupt Libanius's school (*Or.* 37.17). He also has wooed other friends at Libanius's expense, hoping to profit from their evil machinations (*Or.* 37.18–20). Libanius recounts discreditable behavior, but at no point does the speech blossom into a full invective. It is rather structured according to points of conflict in his and Polycles' conduct toward one another.

Libanius's *Oration* 38 against Silvanus similarly deploys adverse comments as they relate to personal grievances.[42] Silvanus's son had studied with Libanius. Silvanus later transferred him to a Latin teacher, but when the young man was disgracefully beaten by the relations of a youth whom he had assaulted, Silvanus tried to blame his son's bad behavior on Libanius's influence. The narratives of Silvanus's son's activity as "both whore and pander" (*Or.* 38.8) and disgraceful beating (*Or.* 38.11) defame the son just as Aeschines' similar tales defame Timarchus; most important, they support Libanius's argument that Silvanus is at fault. He excites additional prejudice against Silvanus by recalling that he was a slow and difficult student himself (*Or.* 38.2), and that he mistreated his father (*Or.* 38.1, 14). Libanius says that he has suffered at Silvanus's hands virtually as from a parricide, evoking for his own quarrel the extremely strong emotions attached to familial violence (ἔστι γὰρ ἡμῖν ὁ γενναῖος Σιλβανὸς πατραλοίας, ὡς μέν φασί τινες, *Or.* 38.13). Sexual dissolution and hostile behavior to kin are classic invective themes. Alleged ineducability exactly reverses encomium's praise of childhood application in *anatrophe*; both Libanius and Aphthonius exploit it in their sample speeches against Philip.[43] But Libanius makes these charges serve his immediate argument rather than developing a freestanding invective portrait.

Libanius's *Orations* 37 and 38 concern essentially private disputes, although

---

40. *PLRE* 1.712.

41. *PLRE* 1.414, Helpidius 4.

42. *PLRE* 1.841, Silvanus 3.

43. Synesius similarly develops an invective *anatrophe* for Typhos in his allegorical tale *De Providentia* (90C–91C); see further Chap. 2.III.

he concludes the latter with the recommendation that Silvanus be made to perform curial liturgies. The emperor Julian's *Misopogon* occupies a more public sphere. It is addressed from the emperor to the citizens of Antioch, and it was posted publicly in a square of the city. Herbert Hunger tentatively classified it as invective.[44] Certainly it uses typical themes, and sections within it can be abstracted, combined, and paraphrased to make invective statements. Albeit interruptedly and with different argumentative ends served by the passages in their immediate contexts, Julian does include sections that trace his own progress from uncouth origins through a roughening education to mature feats of wrongheadedness and failure. His ancestors were "the Mysians on the very banks of the Danube . . . a totally uncouth race, austere, gauche, graceless, and sticking immovably to its judgments, all of which are indications of terrible uncouthness" (Jul. *Misop.* 348D). His tutor Mardonius, a barbarian and moreover, despicably, a eunuch, hardened these native qualities into even more rigid inelegance (351A–353A). Julian's attempts to revive the pagan worship of Antioch and to regulate the city's public life met with resistance and failure (361B–364B, 366B–371B). Julian also incorporates physical description and moral characterization suitable for invective. The "lice who run about [my beard] like wild animals in a thicket" leave a disgustingly indelible image (338C). He repeatedly castigates his awkward, scowling nature (e.g., 342D, 359B). But these themes do not structure the whole of *Misopogon*.

Arnaldo Marcone has shown that several sections of *Misopogon* correspond negatively to topics prescribed by rhetors for formal praise of a city.[45] Such an "inverted panegyric" would constitute an urban invective. Where an encomium would glorify the city's founders, Julian relates an unfavorable story about the eponymous Antiochus (*Misop.* 347A–348A; cf. Men. Rh. 353.19–30): he was consumed by an incestuous passion for his stepmother and sought to indulge it soon after his father died. Julian also ironically praises the Antiochene system of education, another standard topic (e.g., Men. Rh. 361.4–10, 363.28–364.9, 385.22–28; *Misop.* 356B–D). With first their women and then their children liberated from all social controls, the citizens have learned to reject every form of slavery (δουλείαν): to the gods, to the laws, and to the emperor as the guardian of the laws. But *Misopogon* is far from addressing all the topics that rhetors prescribe to give a full picture of the city. Julian says nothing about Antioch's location, for example, or any aspects of its foundation (cf. Men. Rh. 346.27–351.19, 353.5–359.15). Its internal government, natural resources, and piety are treated only obliquely, as they relate to Julian's difficulties with the city; he focuses particularly on its grain shortages and his

---

44. Hunger 1978, 121. Gleason 1986 set *Misopogon* in its social context; cf. Amm. 22.14.2; Socr. *HE* 3.17. On its literary operation, see Marcone 1984 and Long 1993.
45. Marcone 1984, 233–38.

religious revival (cf. Men. Rh. 359.18–367.8). These omissions are too extensive to ascribe merely to rhetors' exceptions for unsuitable topics. *Misopogon* cannot be described adequately as an invective of Antioch.

Moreover, *Misopogon* does not display Julian and Antioch statically in the demonstrative epideictic mode but opposes them dynamically. The text develops almost through dialogue. Julian not only joins the Antiochenes in inveighing against his own austerity, but even borrows an Antiochene voice for one long passage (*Misop.* 342D–344B). References to the Antiochenes' lampoons against him punctuate the whole (e.g., 338D, 357A). Invective sections are scattered throughout the loose, digressive structure of Cynic diatribe. As Julian relates, his official acts had failed to rouse the Antiochenes even to cooperate very much with his policies; he attempts fresh exhortation under a form that evokes a different social context.

Once Julian died, Gregory Nazianzen had an opportunity for comprehensive formal invective of the sort that Libanius's and Aphthonius's *progymnasmata* exemplify. But as noted the recent editor of his two orations against Julian, Jean Bernardi, Gregory does not choose to follow the rhetorical form.[46] His introduction and conclusion to the second describe them as two posts like the Pillars of Hercules, the one blazoning Julian's acts of impiety and the second the retribution they received (*Or.* 5.1, 42). Bernardi remarked how Gregory repeats his image of stelae pillorying Julian's apostasy. The speeches proclaim a posthumous Christian indictment, vindicating Julian's death and the failure of his government as God's sentence of execution (39). Gregory reviews Julian's character and deeds entirely in the light of his religious dereliction.

Within this ideological territory, Gregory deploys the resources of secular oratory. Biographical incidents illustrate spiritual wrong.[47] Gregory identifies as Julian's cardinal sin (ἐν μὲν καὶ πρῶτον, *Or.* 4.21) his failure to return gratitude to God or to Constantius for preserving him along with his half brother Gallus when, after Constantine died, his soldiers massacred their other relatives.[48] The one he answered with apostasy, the other with rebellion. Greg-

---

46. Bernardi 1983, 15 n. 8. Kennedy 1983, 221–22, noted "various compositional segments having their origins in progymnasmatic forms." In the orations Gregory assails among other things Julian's attempt to exclude Christians from traditional, pagan rhetorical education: on this legislation, see recently Banchich 1993 (including full bibliography) with Walter E. Kaegi, "An Investigation of the Emperor Julian: Retrospective and Prospective Remarks," *AncW* 24 (1993): 45–46; Bernardi 1983, 51–57; cf. Yves Courtonne, *Saint Basile et l'Hellenisme* (Paris: Firmin-Didot, 1934).

47. Cf. Bernardi 1983, 38–50, on the value of Gregory's evidence about Julian.

48. A. Olivetti, "Sulli stragi di Costantinopoli succedute alla morte di Costantino il Grande," *Riv. di fil.* 43 (1915): 67–79, assembled evidence on the massacre of 337 and reviewed previous scholarship; J. W. Leedom, "Constantius II: Three Revisions," *Byzantion* 48 (1978): 132–45, attempted to distance Constantius from responsibility.

ory projects through the crisis of Julian's early life a vision of its perverse culmination in illegitimate seizure of empire and the blasphemous attempt to resuscitate paganism on the strength of his power. So too, throughout Gregory's account of Julian's career, each moment reverberates his ultimate verdict.

Gregory raises hypothetical questions of assigning responsibility for Julian's actions elsewhere, in order to return it more forcefully to Julian himself. A long section weighs whether to inculpate Constantius for elevating first the savage Gallus and then Julian to the rank of Caesar (4.33–45). Gregory resumes thoughts of Julian's rescue from the massacre after vividly describing how during Julian's reign a pagan mob brutally lynched Mark of Arethusa, the bishop who had hidden Julian from the soldiers (4.88–91). The one misdeed Mark committed that could possibly justify the murder was to have saved someone who would cause so much harm to the world, he opines; but then he represents Julian's praetorian prefect Salutius, a pagan but otherwise a good man,[49] as rebuking Julian for condoning the mob's cruelty. Julian stands condemned from his own side.

Gregory also uses formal invective's technique of characterizing his subject morally through emotionally affective physical description. He shows Julian in their student days in Athens unable to regulate his body or speech (5.23–24). He twitches spasmodically. His remarks tumble over one another nonsensically. This frenzy reflects the frenzy of his soul, for his secret purpose in coming to Athens was to consult "sacrificers and deceivers" about his fate, "since sacrilege did not yet have freedom of speech" (οὔπω παρρησίαν ἐχούσης τῆς ἀσεβείας). From this sight Gregory claims that even then he could foretell what an evil Julian would be to the Roman state. Recreating the image verbally enforces his vision on his audience. His speeches follow a looser structure than formal invective, borrowing homiletic reflection on particulars as they arise, but in mode Gregory effectively creates a new genre of Christian invective to vaunt over the dead Apostate.

Circumstances closer to those of *In Eutropium* arose when an orator spoke against a live minister, for instance a local governor, in order to have him restrained or deposed. The appropriate form then was an address to the emperor, which bolstered a specific request with general admiration for imperial

49. Gregory's surprisingly favorable comment here may only heighten contrast with Julian, but on the other hand Ammianus reports that Salutius was offered the succession after Julian died, as a candidate acceptable both to Julian's Gallic soldiers and to courtiers once attached to Constantius (he refused: Amm. 25.5.3; on the doublet of this incident when Jovian died, Zos. 3.36.1–2 and Zonar. 13.14 [3.218A–B Dind.], see Paschoud 1971–89, 2¹.238–39). Salutius continued to serve as praetorian prefect of the East under Jovian and again under Valentinian and Valens to 367, thus in the period to which Bernardi (1983, 11–37) dated Gregory's orations against Julian. Cf. *PLRE* 1.814–17, Saturninius Secundus Salutius 3.

benevolence. Menander recommends dividing the "ambassador's speech," *presbeutikos logos*, between praise of the emperor, especially his philanthropy, and the miseries of one's city (Men. Rh. 423.6–424.1). As for the offending official, it normally sufficed to detail his misdeeds in office. The damning possibility that he had been badly brought up in a barbaric milieu by craven and licentious parents might stir hostile emotions, but had little meaning within the confines of the late Roman administrative bureaucracy. The comprehensive picture of full invective would diffuse the practical focus.

Emphasis on the administrative sins of an official did not wholly preclude invective's generalizing tactics. Despite their structures, Hunger classified as Libanius's invectives *Oration 46* to Theodosius against Florentius and the similar petition-speech *Oration 56* against Lucianus, as well as *Oration 37* against Polycles (discussed earlier).[50] Among Libanius's many complaints against Florentius figures one that he had had court policemen beat to death certain tradesmen while imposing the full penalty of fifteen lashes (Liban. *Or.* 46.7–9). Libanius takes care not to cloud his pathos by suggesting any reason why the tradesmen might have incurred this penalty: they are simply "wretched men [ἀθλίους] . . . rounded up by the policemen." He observes sarcastically that Florentius "supposed, like his father, that beaten men have backs of iron." Of course Florentius's father has nothing to do with the present case; he serves to entrench the impression of Florentius's brutality. Tatianus and Proculus are dragged into the speech to evoke evil memories of their cruelty.[51] Libanius claims he had hoped Florentius would not follow their example or "be a beast rather than a man," a simple incidental *synkrisis* elegantly expressed through the negative (μηδ' ἀντ' ἀνθρώπου θηρίον ἔσεσθαι). Florentius, however, seems to think that brutality is a necessary part of his post, and that it is shameful to be or be called benevolent. Libanius adds, "together with you" (μετὰ σοῦ), not merely flattering Theodosius in the recommended fashion, but also carefully dissociating him from his subordinate. For pathos again highlighting Florentius's callousness, Libanius pictures the victims' horrible welts: they scare off doctors, who can do nothing to help them. Florentius rejoices to hear it. Finally, Libanius demands if Florentius thinks himself innocent of murder, just because he did not use a sword. No, he is doubly a murderer, for killing the men and, moreover, for doing it painfully. The Romans are superior to the Persians for many reasons, but particularly for employing a quick method of execution. Florentius's local cruelty, in effect, betrays his nation.[52]

50. Hunger 1978, 120. On the historical context of Lib. *Or.* 56, see Seeck 1920–24. *PLRE* 1.364–65, Florentius 9; 516–17, Lucianus 6.

51. *PLRE* 1.746–47, Proculus 6; 876–78, Tatianus 5.

52. Lactantius applies to Galerius the same conceit of "Persian" cruelty, *Mort. Pers.* 21.2–4.

Florentius justifies himself by the fact that the barkeepers had been defrauding customers with short measures, so Libanius moves on to counter him by describing luridly how soldiers and their hangers-on abuse them (*Or.* 46.10–16); but the passage just paraphrased sufficiently indicates how the lessons of invective *progymnasmata* were put into practice. Libanius divides his attention between the harsh penalty itself and Florentius's attitude. The first is established through graphic images, the second through nasty supposition, association with others including a suggestion of paternal influence, comparison to animals, and a charge of barbarism that comes close to insinuating treason. But though the moral indictment steps onto paths leading away from the immediate issue, Libanius never strays far. He is embellishing and pointing his thesis that Florentius abuses his office and oppresses the city, not launching into the systematic character assassination of full formal invective.

Paul Petit argued that Libanius wrote *Oration* 46 in 393 at the request of Rufinus, then praetorian prefect, for him to show in justification of executing Florentius; he explained *Oration* 56 similarly as having been written in 388 for Tatianus against Lucianus.[53] That speech too is structured to present a clear argument. Libanius introduces it by saying that he is but one of many complainants (*Or.* 56.1). The main body of the speech details how Lucianus misuses his power (*Or.* 56.2–14). He has restricted the curia's access to himself. He piles up cushions to prop himself higher than his fellows on the judicial bench: this gesture symbolizes arrogance realized in judicial brutality. He is supported only by the theater partisans, whose insolence ought to damn him with them (*Or.* 56.15–20). Finally, Libanius turns to praise Tatianus for the relief he has afforded and to seek that it be reinforced by more permanent measures against Lucianus (*Or.* 56.21–32).

Only two of Libanius's antagonistic speeches closely follow the rhetorical invective form, and both of them appear to have been written under unusual circumstances. *Oration* 33, against Tisamenus, is one of a pair with *Oration* 45 addressed to Theodosius about illegal imprisonments of citizens accused of crimes.[54] *Oration* 45 asserts boldly that "the governors sent out to the provinces are murderers" (φονέας, *Or.* 45.3), but Libanius never names the murderous governors. He depicts his own frustrations in trying to get them to hear a plea for redress (*Or.* 45.16–26): they waste time on lesser matters, both petty claims and recreation. One unnamed governor deferred a murder case for seven months, and when finally it was to be heard, fled the courtroom at the advent of a group of monks singing hymns. Libanius also laments the misplaced clemency that encourages officials to prefer unreasonable incarceration to

53. Petit 1956, 499–502 = 1983, 114–19.
54. Tisamenus, *PLRE* 1.916–17. On *Orr.* 33, 45, see Pack 1935, 70–120; Petit 1956, 504–5 = 1983, 122; Norman 1969–77, 2.155–58.

proper judicial examination or execution of the guilty, even though "streams of blood flow in the courtrooms" from their judicial floggings and men they have had imprisoned are driven to suicide (*Or.* 45.27–29). Yet although he represents some incidents with particular detail, the anonymity of the narrative generalizes them. Petit argued that this is the one of the pair that was sent to court through ordinary channels, and that its doublet, *Oration* 33, was circulated as a pamphlet to a very restricted number of sympathizers.

Oration 33 is far more specific and forceful than *Oration* 45. Tisamenus is named in the first sentence as a governor who has forced Libanius to speak out, although he would rather praise Theodosius's governors. With this proem (*Or.* 33.1–2), Libanius begins the structure of formal invective. Tisamenus's grandfather participated in many learned discourses (*Or.* 33.3); this statement nods briefly at Tisamenus's *genos*. Tisamenus himself pursued rhetorical training to a rudimentary level, just as far as he was forced, but soon resorted to dancers instead. He composed songs for them and depended on them to have his songs performed. Suddenly he became governor of a province; his term was undistinguished. A few years later he became assessor to a military governor. He had no experience in law, but he helped out with his chief's dissipation and drinking. This section seems to constitute an *anatrophe*, although it extends beyond education itself to career offices, because the offices occasion little comment and in the next section Libanius cites them as the basis for Tisamenus's promotion as *consularis* of Syria; in that office he begins his true *praxeis* (*Or.* 33.3–4, 5).

Tisamenus evidently boasted of having served well under hard conditions, overseeing purchase of grain in Euphratensis. Libanius belittles the duty, since, after all, slaves and donkey-drivers attached to Tisamenus's staff endured the same hardships, less mitigated (*Or.* 33.6–7). Tisamenus ignored his judicial duties there and on returning to Antioch continues to ignore them, either avoiding the courts or wasting time on irrelevancies. He pays far too much attention to games, the theater, and acclamations. He might claim to acquit himself well as a governor in his relations with the local decurions, but in fact he persecutes and demeans them: he has them publicly flogged, and when he could not coerce any of them to hold the Syriarchate, he gave the liturgy to a Beroean.

To this point in the speech Libanius can be seen to follow standard invective structure; particularly strikingly does it organize the first sections of the speech, whose information does not relate closely to his complaints against Tisamenus as governor. But now Libanius interrupts his litany of Tisamenus's official misdeeds to address Theodosius directly, praise him and demand that Tisamenus be deposed (*Or.* 33.24–25). His speech takes on dicanic tones when he anticipates Tisamenus's objection that he had been insulted by a decurion who failed to invite him to games he was giving (*Or.* 33.26–27). Then he returns to how Tisamenus abused his duties as judge. He deferred court busi-

88   THE LITERARY WORLD

ness in favor of his daughters' weddings and, again, subjected decurions to imprisonment and floggings. Libanius then breaks off to request that Tisamenus be deposed and to refute claims Tisamenus might make of having bene-fited Antioch. He admits that Tisamenus does not take bribes himself, but asserts that he has abused his office to the point where people seeking relief offer bribes, which other members of Tisamenus's household do take; justice is corrupted all the same (*Or.* 33.38–40). Libanius pictures again the suffering of defendants Tisamenus has imprisoned and refuses to release, since he will not determine their cases. He closes requesting a new governor of completely different character (*Or.* 33.43). From Libanius's first interruption the initially epideictic structure of his speech devolves into the argument of a petition. Even though, circulated privately, *Oration* 33 pursued its practical goal by a less direct route than *Oration* 45 genuinely addressing the emperor, it too relied on a more stirring mode than static epideixis to deliver its final exhortation. The sections corresponding to formal invective merely help to lay a broad founda-tion for the ultimate request.

Only in *Oration* 4, "On Not Prating,"[55] or, Against Eutropius,"[56] does Li-banius incorporate the complete form of rhetorical invective in an argument related to real events, as opposed to a *progymnasma*. Eutropius had refused to hear his pleas that he issue an overdue judgment, and called him a bore (*Or.* 4.40); Libanius in turn denounces him systematically. He starts by claiming that Eutropius has often rejected his arguments with this insult (*Or.* 4.1). He debates whether old men really prate or may be blamed if they do. He observes that Eutropius is the only one who has accused him. He demonstrates the soundness of his wits by proclaiming his knowledge of Antioch, imperial administration, and his own students. But why waste time on these matters, he asks; he can best prove himself by showing how well he knows Eutropius (*Or.* 4.14). Thus Libanius turns a response to the issue at hand into the proem of an invective.

Libanius first attacks Eutropius's father, inaugurating the invective proper at *genos*. He was born in a village, but fled from his obligations as a farmer into the service of a homosexual magistrate; Libanius packs with innuendo the idea that he made himself invaluable. When he fathered Eutropius he again defrauded the land of services owed by enrolling his son with literary teachers; by refusing to pay their fees, he defrauded the Muses as well as Demeter. Thus *genos* smoothly introduces *anatrophe*. Eutropius was too blockish to profit from the pains he caused his instructors. He turned to the dullards' study, law, but could

55. The key terms in the oration are "talk nonsense," φλυαρεῖν, in the insult to which Libanius responds with his speech (πάλιν οὗτος ἥκει κόψων ἡμᾶς οἷς φλυαρήσει, *Or.* 4.40) and "prate/r," ληρεῖν/λῆρος, everywhere else.
56. Not the eunuch: see *PLRE* 1.318; Martin 1988, 105–8.

never persuade a prospective client that he would be worth employing. Libanius boasts that Eutropius cannot accuse him of prating inaccurately now (*Or.* 4.19). He next assaults Eutropius's *praxeis* as a magistrate. Cynegius enrolled him in the curia but by unjust assistance he escaped these duties. Instead he appeared as the governor. He bought his office, borrowing so heavily that he became a slave to his creditors. He repays them by administering the law unjustly. He also collects taxes rapaciously: he brutalizes those who cannot pay and profiteers from those who can. He has escaped official investigation for malfeasance by bribing the investigator with part of his profits. When he cannot abuse the curia he settles for flogging artisans. He fixes prices so as to encourage merchants to bribe him. Libanius concludes that Eutropius's every word, act, or thought is set on money. He marks the end of a section by referring again to his supposed "prating." In one last *praxis* thus marked off, Eutropius intimidates bakers who had complained to Libanius when Eutropius wanted them to pay an excessive fee for mill-water. The next section performs the function of *synkrisis*: it justifies Libanius's calling Eutropius Scylla on the grounds that, although he alone holds office, all the members of his family, even the women, share his abuses of power (*Or.* 4.30–31).

Libanius imagines that these people encourage Eutropius to slight him. This idea returns him to his personal grievances against Eutropius. His protests against injustices, among which he now highlights judicial floggings, have gone unheeded. At most they have provoked the insult on which the whole oration turns, which he recounts at the oration's conclusion. In terms of formal structure, this passage serves as an epilogue. It and the proem contain the substantive, specific charges of the speech. The central invective they frame amplifies their implications. It also pads them out to the dimensions of a full speech. It subserves Libanius's real complaints with its completeness as a rhetorical form, lending the dignity of a broader perspective to an otherwise private attack.

In contrast to *Oration* 33, *Oration* 4 while relating general complaints against Eutropius seems to seek no more than personal vindication. Libanius never even calls for Eutropius to be deposed, although he gloatingly anticipates his retirement outside of Syria in self-imposed exile (*Or.* 4.39). This limitation has suggested to the most recent editor of *Oration* 4, Jean Martin, that Libanius delivered it to only a few close friends.[57] He compared *Orations* 54 and 57, which Petit argued are too wildly prejudiced to have served Libanius's stated ends by public performance.[58] Friends who sympathized over Eutropius's insult to Libanius could rejoice to hear it answered with a rhetorically comprehensive counterinsult.

57. Martin 1988, 109; 118 n. 1.
58. Petit 1956, 503–4 = 1983, 120–21.

The circumstances Libanius faced in *Oration* 4 offer the closest parallel to those of Claudian's *In Eutropium*. There is no reason to suppose that Claudian did not deliver it before a Western court audience, as he did the other Stilichonian poems with which it shares its hexameter form and manuscript transmission.[59] Especially in book 1, he principally addresses Western concerns. But this audience like Claudian himself had no direct practical connection with Eutropius. He served a separate administration. His outlawing Stilicho had already set the governments of East and West as deeply in official enmity as was possible short of actual war. Claudian had for years closely identified himself with Stilicho's policies. He had nothing left to lose in the East. At the same time, although both Roma in book 1 and Aurora in book 2 call for Eutropius to be deposed, Claudian could not expect to achieve this end by means of his poem alone. Thus separated from his subject and from his ultimate objective, Claudian faced a perfect occasion for epideixis. Eutropius's crucial offense was to hold the consulate. Since it conveyed the highest honor possible, by associating the consul with republican traditions still felt as ideals and by immortalizing him through the eponymy of the year,[60] Claudian could treat it as the culmination of Eutropius's career. As such, it bears a relationship with every aspect of his person and his past; and Claudian declares that every aspect so contrasts with the honor as to forbid the consulate. A full systematic portrait supports this argument. Claudian had the opportunity, so commonplace for panegyric but nearly unexampled in living invective, to realize and elaborate the scheme prescribed by his rhetorical education.

III. Diverse Contexts of Late Antique Invective

The techniques which school practice in invective fostered did not atrophy outside fundamentally hostile speeches, whether formally constructed or more pragmatically focused on a particular set of misdeeds. Even laudatory speeches could find advantage to saying bad things: as Aphthonius points out, *synkrisis* of good with bad twins encomium with invective, heightening the effect of both (Aphthon. 2.42.22–28 Spengel). Invective techniques continued to develop as they subserved other ends.

The late antique Gallic panegyrics often magnify their subjects by portraying their adversaries as criminal, monstrous, brutal, or insane.[61] In his pan-

59. On Claudian's audience, see further Chap. 7.I.

60. Cf. *CLRE* 1–12.

61. *HA Quadr. Tyr.* 2.2 comments that "great princes always call [usurpers] brigands" (*latrones*); Ramsay MacMullen, "The Roman Concept Robber-Pretender," *Rev. intl. de l'antiquité* 3rd ser. 10 (1963): 221–25, demonstrated the fact; cf. Robin Seager, *Ammianus Marcellinus: Seven Studies in His Language and Thought* (Columbia: University of Missouri Press, 1986), 120, 127–29, on "tyrant" and its cognates. On the form and

egyric of 289, Mamertinus compares Maximian's success in suppressing ma-
rauding peasant rebels to Hercules' victory over the Giants, "monsters of
double shape" (*monstrorum biformium, Pan. Lat.* 10[2].4.3; cf. 11[3].3.4).[62]
Scarcely had their "madness" (*furor,* 10[2].5.1) been quelled, when barbarian
invaders threatened to destroy the Gallic provinces. Maximian saved them
virtually single-handed, fighting everywhere in the line at once, so promptly
that his own soldiers could hardly follow him with their eyes. Now he faces
Carausius, "that pirate," and Mamertinus anticipates swift success against him
too (10[2].12.1; cf. 13.5). Maximian's Herculian heroism is intensified by the
contrast with his opponents. So too in his panegyric of 291, Mamertinus passes
with compact preterition over how "by your valor the republic was liberated
from the most bloodthirsty domination" (*virtute vestra rempublicam dominatu
saevissimo liberatam,* 11[3].5.3), that is, how Diocletian, with whom Mamertinus's addressee Maximian is now joined, displaced the reigning emperor
Carinus. Virtuous valor is defined by opposition to cruel tyranny. Mamertinus's epithets establish basic judgments of value.

The Gallic orators routinely label the western barbarian tribes, who regularly threatened their region, as treacherous and feral. Their attitudes remained applicable to barbarians generally, for Claudian and his audiences.
Mamertinus in 289 applauded Maximian for punishing as they deserved "that
slippery and deceitful race of barbarians" in a bloody seaside battle.[63] In 291 he
found proof of Maximian's and Diocletian's *felicitas,* good fortune confirming
divine favor of their reign, in the fact that barbarian nations were now slaugh-
tering one another: "now spontaneously they requite the punishment of their
stubborn savagery" (*obstinataeque feritatis,* 11[3].16.5). The panegyrist of Constantius in 297 credits him with having once captured "a king of the most
ferocious nation, in the midst of the very ambush he was devising" (8[4].2.1).
Eumenius rejoices in freedom from the "savagery of the Franks" (9[5].18.3, of
298).[64] Constantine's panegyrist in 310 commends Constantius's settling
Franks on Roman territory, "so that they were forced to put down not only
their arms but also their savagery" (6[7].5.3). Constantine began his career of

---

nature of the *XII Pan. Lat.,* see Pichon 1906; MacCormack 1976; Nixon 1983; Nixon and
Rodgers 1994. Lassandro 1981 surveyed the panegyrists' denigrating tactics; Seager 1983
the ideals upheld by the panegyrists and how they inform particular political aims of
individual speeches. Barbara Saylor Rodgers has graciously advised me on this section.

62. On the rebellion of the Bagaudae, see William Seston, *Dioclétien et la Tétrarchie*
(Paris: Boccard, 1946), 67–69.

63. This phrase, *lubrica illa fallaxque gens barbarorum* (*Pan. Lat.* 10[2].11.4), reverberates fourteen years later with reference to a different incursion, *ruperat fidem gens levis
et lubrica barbarorum* (12[9].22.3).

64. At *Pan. Lat.* 9[5].4.1 Mynors preferred Lipsius's emendation assigning "brigandage" to the "Bagaudan rebellion," but Galletier 1949–55, 1.124 n. 1, gave reason for
preferring the transmitted reading and barbarian rebels, *latrocinio Batavicae rebellionis.*

defending the Roman state when "on some low barbarian band, which tested the auspices of your rise by sudden attack and unforeseen brigandage, you visited the penalty of their temerity" (6[7].10.1). Constantine's execution of the two Frankish kings Ascaric and Merogaisus "punished their past crimes and bound with fear the slippery loyalty of the whole race" (7[6].4.2, of 307; cf. 6[7].10–11, of 310). Nazarius compares Constantine to the infant Hercules: "Thus did you, Emperor, in the very cradle-days of your reign, as it were slaughter twin snakes, sporting by notorious punishment of most bloodthirsty kings" (4[10].16.6, of 321).

Maxentius, who was proclaimed emperor in Rome but who died in battle against Constantine in 312, is painted as a usurping tyrant. The panegyrist of 313 refers to him variously as a "monster," a "prodigy," and a "native-born slave, empurpled" (*monstrum, prodigio, vernula purpuratus*, 12[9].3.5, 7.1, 16.3). He contrasts him with Constantine, Constantius's true son, as supposititious to Maximian (12[9].4.3).[65] His supposed father himself tried to wrest the purple from him but was forced to recognize that his line had passed to that "disgrace" (*dedecus*, 12[9].3.4). The panegyrist reinforces these slanders on Maxentius's paternity, status, and humanity by physical description (12[9].4.3): "he is of very despicable littleness, his limbs twisted and disjointed, his very name mutilated by an abusive pronunciation." Not only do the deformities alleged make him contemptible. His own defective speech annuls his name's dynastic echo of Maximian's. This symbolic disparagement underscores more substantive charges. In itemized contrast to Constantine, Maxentius is undutiful to his supposed father, cruel, debauched, and influenced by "superstitious maleficence"; moreover, he bears responsibility for temples being despoiled, the Senate butchered, and the Roman plebs slain by famine (12[9].4.4). Nazarius evokes similar charges in his panegyric of 321 (4[10].8.3).[66]

The panegyrist of 313 envisions Roma personified finally stretching out her hands entreatingly to Constantine (12[9].14.2). Nazarius, also using images that tend to personify Roma, hails Constantine's desire to avenge her, who is "gashed by so many wounds" (4[10].13.2). Base pusillanimity keeps Maxentius within the city walls, where he boasts emptily to his soldiers (12[9].14.6) and suppresses reports of his defeats (12[9].15.1).[67] He amasses provisions from Africa, Sicily, and Sardinia for an infinite siege, ruinously (12[9].16.1). When at

65. As Galletier 1949–55, 2.126 n. 1, noted ad loc., Aurel. Vict. *Epit.* 40.13 and Anon. Val. *Exc.* 4.12 also report Maxentius supposititious, whereas Mamertinus at *Pan. Lat.* 10[2].14.1–2 of 289 confidently anticipates Maximian's "son . . . divine and immortal offspring," triumphantly fulfilling his birth and nurture.

66. Nor are these accusations confined to the panegyrical tradition: e.g., Vict. *Caes.* 40.19–24.

67. Cf. Moreau 1954, 2.428.

last he must meet Constantine in battle, he draws up his line so that his army is hemmed in by the Tiber; the panegyrist speculates that he wants to destroy as many as possible along with himself, the last revenge of the doomed tyrant,[68] "so that all might be companions of his death who had stood out as partici-pants of his crimes" (12[9].16.4). And so Tiber swallows down Maxentius's "impious" troops (12[9].17.2; cf. 7.1) along with the "false Romulus and par-ricide of the city" himself (12[9].18.1). The people of Rome joyfully mutilate and befoul Maxentius's corpse (12[9].18.3; cf. 4[10].31.4–5).[69]

The younger Mamertinus, in his *gratiarum actio* to Julian for the consulate of 362, perpetuates traditional slanders against barbarians (3[11].4.1) and usurpers (3[11].13), but he also extends the charge of brigandage from these malefactors to provincial governors appointed by Constantius II (3[11].4.2).[70] He avoids criticizing Constantius directly, as did Julian himself after he had succeeded him, but he blames subordinates for poisoning Constantius's ears to Julian while he was his Caesar (3[11].4.4–5.2; cf. Jul. *Misop.* 357B). In more general terms Mamertinus extols Julian for abolishing imperial courtiers' old business of peddling their ability to influence high official appointments and honors (3[11].19–21).

> [Political aspirants] used to lobby, not even men but little females; and not only women, but eunuchs too, whom either nature's origination or a catastrophe of the body has cut off from the community of human kind, as exiles from either sex. Even the outstanding bearers of well-established names used to fawn on the most squalid and most disreputable members of the imperial retinue. And when these men had been sent into the provinces, they would ravish off both sacred things and profane, con-structing themselves a road to the consulate with money. (*Pan. Lat.* 3[11].19.4–5)

Conventional disparagement of effeminacy grows even sharper when men literally effeminized acquire a role in traditionally male political transactions;

---

68. So too, e.g., Claud. *Ruf.* 2.17–21; cf. Levy 1971, 123–24 ad loc. and *TGF* Adesp. F513; Cic. *Fin.* 3.19; Sen. *Clem.* 2.2.2; Luc. *BC* 7.654–55; Suet. *Ner.* 38.1; Dio 58.23; Synes. *Prov.* 122B.

69. Abusing corpses was not only a heroic *topos* (e.g., *Il.* 22.395–404, Hector), but also, sporadically, Roman historical reality, e.g., Juv. 10.85–86, Dio 58.11.5 (Sejanus); Tac. *Hist.* 1.49 (Galba); *HA Heliog.* 17.1–3 (Elagabalus); for the spirit, cf. *HA Commod.* 19, purported acclamations of the Senate calling for Commodus's corpse to be mangled (quoted from Marius Maximus). Claudian takes full advantage of the abuse practiced on Rufinus's corpse, *Ruf.* 2.427–39: cf. Jer. *Ep.* 60.16.1; Philostorg. 11.3; Zos. 5.7.6; *Chron. Marc.* s. ann. 395.5 (*MGHAA* 11.64).

70. On Mamertinus, *Pan. Lat.* 3[11], see Blockley 1972; Lieu 1989, 3–38 (with transla-tion by Marna M. Morgan).

Mamertinus voices a common abhorrence that such people should be involved in public decisions.[71] The monetary corruption in which they trade spawns further abuses.

Pacatus, when he addressed Theodosius in summer 389 after the defeat of Maximus, faced the delicate task of absolving his fellow Gauls from having appeared to tolerate the usurper.[72] He blends with his praise of Theodosius's *praxeis* in war an account of how the Gauls suffered under his tyrannous opponent (esp. 2[12].23–31). He refers to Maximus as an "empurpled executioner" (2[12].24.1). Fear of persecutions stripped the towns of their citizens and filled the woods with nobles. Maximus confiscated their property and auctioned it off; he put a price on their heads. No one dared to grieve, lest he call attention to himself. Maximus's greed was insatiable. "He used to stand, purple-clad, by the scales: the movements of the weights and the noddings of the pans he would examine, pale and gaping. . . . Here was weighed gold pulled from the hands of matrons, over there amulets stolen from the necks of orphans, there silver dyed with the blood of its owners" (2[12].26.1–2). Of all his gains he never yielded up anything, not even to buy allies; he disdained performing even the most shallowly specious acts, lest he give any slight appearance of virtue. He had generals assassinated in fear of their loyalty to Gratian, and he cruelly executed even women. He encouraged informers. He was the aggressor in 388 when he and Theodosius finally came to combat; Pacatus says so explicitly, as well as accusing Maximus of breaking his treaty and "violating fetial law" (2[12].30.1). Ferocity, greed, and impiety render him a new Phalaris (2[12].29.4). Claudian imputes the same vices to Eutropius and even exploits the same type of images. He too is both avaricious and cruel in administration. His greed too evokes debased mercantile figures. He too bears the blame for conflict and religious violation, which is cast in terms of ancient Roman traditions.

Having built Maximus up as a monster the Gauls could not withstand, Pacatus proceeds to abase him before Theodosius. Shame at all he had done should have conquered him instantly, if Theodosius came to the battle alone. Pacatus compares the revolt of Scythian slaves before the Persian Wars:[73]

> Once masters going to fight against their rebellious slaves brought whips
> onto the battle line. So great was the force of conscience that the armed
> were reversed by the unarmed, so that men who had offered their breasts

71. I shall discuss further how other authors portrayed the malign influence of eunuchs.

72. See the general introduction and notes of Nixon 1987, 6–11, 71–91.

73. Pacatus, *Pan. Lat.* 2[12].30.5. Cf. Hdt. 4.1–4; Justin 2.5.1–7. Ronald Syme, "The Date of Justin and the Discovery of Trogus," *Historia* 37 (1988): 358–71 = *Roman Papers*, edited by Anthony R. Birley (Oxford: Clarendon Press, 1991), 6.358–71, dated Justin's epitome ca. 390.

to death gave their backs to the lash. Should not you too have managed
the whole affair on being seen, leaving your legions at ease?

Claudian has Roma cite the same incident when she encourages Stilicho to
whip Eutropius from office (*Eutr.* 1.505–13).[74] He does not take the image
straight from Pacatus, however, but follows Herodotus in identifying the rebels
as "servile youth" (*servilis pubes*), that is, the children the Scythian women
bore to their slaves during their husbands' generation-long absence on campaign in Asia. Pacatus follows the Latin tradition preserved in Justin's epitome
of Trogus, which identifies the rebels as the slaves themselves. The generation
of the rebels is reconciled with the term of absence: Herodotus says the Scythians were away for twenty-six years, Justin and Trogus, eight.

In the final part of this section Pacatus outlines Maximus's character in
synkrisis with Theodosius. Maximus was once a slave. He could not name his
father. He has been a dependent of noble houses. He was "exiled from the
world and a fugitive from his homeland" when he rose in revolt (*Pan. Lat.*
2[12].31.1).[75] Neither the legions nor the provinces nor the gods consented to
his elevation. Contrasting with Theodosius quality by quality, he stands allied
to perfidy, sin, injury, impiety, lust, cruelty, and all the league of crimes and
vices. Again the topics and commonplaces of rhetorical encomium and invective rule Pacatus's conceptions. Again, many parallels reveal the same influences operating on Claudian.[76]

Claudian in *In Eutropium* shows closest affinities with the invective techniques of the anonymous panegyrist of 313, Mamertinus in 362, and Pacatus in
389. Whereas the older Mamertinus and other earlier panegyrists rely more on
epithets to attach opprobrious characteristics to their emperors' adversaries,
these authors often dramatize their kindred charges in emblematic scenes. The
sample provided by the Gallic collection is extremely selective, but if it represents contemporary epideixis fairly, it shows a taste for literary enactment
gaining ground toward the end of the fourth century. In any case, Claudian
capitalized on the possibility as he exploited a poetic form with its own strong
tradition of dramatic representation. He differs with such subtlety from even

74. The common reference was noted by Fargues, *Invectives* 84 n. 508; Galletier 1949–
55, 3.97 n. 2; Nixon 1987, 91 n. 103.

75. Homelessness is a rebuke because it attests weakness and ill fortune, or else such
worthlessness that one is rejected: cf. Libanius of Philip, *Prog.* 9.3.4; Synesius of the
Goths, *Reg.* 25C; Claudian for the same effect compares Eutropius to a mangy dog
turned loose to die, *Eutr.* 1.126–37.

76. Another similar set of disgraces is recorded by *HA Opell. Macr.* 4.3 against
Macrinus: he was "a freedman, a prostitute, busied in servile duties in the imperial
house, of salable loyalty, his life squalid under Commodus, by Severus removed from
his most miserable duties and relegated to Africa." See below on how invective motifs
are shared between oratory and other genres.

his closest parallel to the preserved panegyrics, Pacatus's exemplum of the Scythian slaves, that the variation cannot have conferred much advantage; general taste and confluent traditions of rhetorical exemplification may therefore be the surest links between them, rather than direct borrowing.

HOSTILE MEANS of presenting characters were not only perpetuated in school exercises and the panegyric speeches whose form Claudian inverted in *In Eutropium* 1. Other literary forms also had villains to portray. Working from common cultural grounds, they devised similar formats.[77] Rhetoric resonated in Greco-Roman literary culture more and more plangently with the Second Sophistic.[78] Schools' *progymnasmata* and declamation entrenched rhetorical patterns of thought in students' minds.[79] The exercises also, drawing on traditional myth and history for their subject matter, exploited material from other genres and tempered it to rhetorical ends. Sophistic performances brought these conventions before public audiences.[80] Orators did not alone transmit cultural standards, nor need they even have been regarded as especially authoritative sources, yet they gave currency to rhetoricized versions. Audiences absorbed patterns of thought and expression, and the need to accommodate their expectations reinforced rhetoric's reciprocity with other literary forms.

In later antiquity, taste for ceremony proliferated, and with ceremony

77. Cf. Russell and Wilson 1981, xxxi–xxxiv, on rhetoric and poetry.

78. See G. Anderson 1993 (survey of cultural influences, with an excellent bibliography of particular studies); Penella 1990 (sophistic of fourth century A.D.); Vito A. Sirago, "La seconda sofistica come espressione culturale della classe dirigente del II sec.," *ANRW* 2.33.1 (1989): 36–78 (review of major theories about the Second Sophistic, bibliography including late antique successors); B. P. Reardon, *Courants littéraires grecs des IIe et IIIe siècles après J.-C.* (Paris: Les Belles Lettres, 1971; cf. Ewen L. Bowie, "Greek Sophists and Greek Poetry in the Second Sophistic," *ANRW* 2.33.1 [1989]: 209–58; D. W. T. C. Vessey, "Challenge and Response," *Cambridge History of Classical Literature*, vol. 2, *Latin Literature*, ed. E. J. Kenney with W. V. Clausen [Cambridge: Cambridge University Press, 1985], 2.497–502; Eduard Norden, *Die antike Kunstprosa*, 5. Auflage, vol. 1 [Stuttgart: B. G. Teubner, 1958]); Bowersock 1969 (social and political significance of the sophists).

79. See G. Anderson 1993, 47–53 (*progymnasmata* and their influence); D. A. Russell, *Greek Declamation* (Cambridge: Cambridge University Press, 1983); Kennedy 1983, 52–103 (rhetorical theory), 133–79 (Greek schools in later antiquity); G. Kennedy, "The Sophists as Declaimers," in *Approaches to the Second Sophistic*, ed. G. W. Bowersock (University Park, Pa.: American Philological Association, 1974), 17–22; S. F. Bonner, *Roman Declamation in the Late Republic and Early Empire* (Berkeley: University of California Press, 1949), esp. "Some Indications of Declamatory Influence on the Literature of the Early Empire," 149–67.

80. See Graham Anderson, "The *Pepaideumenos* in Action: Sophists and Their Outlook in the Early Empire," *ANRW* 2.33.1 (1989): 79–208, esp. 89–104, on performance; Penella 1990, 79–117, on fourth-century sophists and their activities.

speeches proliferated too. The second treatise ascribed to Menander partially illustrates the range of occasions that might require an address of greater or lesser formality. The *basilikos logos* comprehensively praises the emperor. The *epibaterios logos* celebrates arrival at one's native city after travel, arrival at a city one is visiting, or the arrival of a governor at one's city. The informally structured *lalia* can be shaped to almost any theme; it corresponds to the display speeches of traveling sophists like Dio Chrysostom in the High Empire.[81] In particular, the *propemptike lalia* bids farewell to a traveler and varies according to the speaker's and the traveler's relative status. The *epithalamios* or *gamelios logos* for a wedding can be composed in both "strict" and "relaxed or prosy" styles. The *kateunastikos logos* dispatches the newlywed couple to the bedroom. The *genethliakos logos* celebrates a birthday. The *paramythetikos logos* mourns a death, again in strict or prosy style. The *prosphonetikos logos* praises a governor, but differs from full encomium by its greater focus on the actual deeds of the subject. The *epitaphios logos*, unlike the *paramythetikos*, applies the full encomiastic scheme to the deceased, of course incorporating lamentation. The *stephanotikos logos* presents *aurum coronarium* to the emperor.[82] The *presbeutikos logos* conveys one's city's plea for help from the emperor. The *kletikos logos* invites a governor to a festival. The *syntaktikos logos*, which may also be composed as a *lalia* or in prosy style, takes one's leave of a city. The *monodia* is a short private speech of mourning which, Menander directs, should always be composed in the relaxed style. The *sminthiakos logos* hymns Apollo. Private and public, religious and secular occasions each called for a peculiar type of speech. Rhetorical treatments burgeoned. As they did, they multiplied the interchange linking rhetoric with other genres.

All the types of attack already discussed, on professional conduct and personal character, were current in a wide range of genres. Yet another, found extending from oratory to history and fantasy, transfers the initiative for an evil action from the actor to his wife. It inverts encomium's praise for good wives who are helpmeets sometimes able to intercede for mercy beyond strict justice.[83] For example, Libanius uses it to vilify Theodosius's praetorian prefect

81. On whom see generally C. P. Jones 1978.

82. On *aurum coronarium*, a nominally voluntary gift from cities in celebration of special events, in later antiquity particularly accession and the quinquennial *vota*, see T. Klauser, "Aurum coronarium," *Röm. Mitt.* 59 (1944): 129–53 = *Gesammelte Arbeiten*, 292–309, Jahrbuch für Antike und Christentum Ergänzungsband 3 (1974); Millar 1977, 140–42; Barnes 1986, 105–6; Delmaire 1989, 387–400.

83. E.g., Jul. *Or.* 3, of Constantius's wife Eusebia; Them. *Or.* 19.231a, of Theodosius's wife Flacilla and young son Arcadius; cf. Men. Rh. 376.9–13 and Holum 1982, 21–44, on Gregory of Nyssa's funeral oration for Flacilla and how a philanthropic ideology was developed for women of Theodosius's family. Claudian claims Serena surpassed even Flacilla in soothing Theodosius when he was angry, *CM* 30.135–38; cf. Consolino 1986, 105 ad loc.

Cynegius in his oration *Pro Templis* (Lib. *Or.* 30.46).[84] He was the one, Libanius asserts, who misled Theodosius concerning the destruction of pagan temples. He is "vile, hateful to the gods, cowardly, avaricious, and most hostile to the earth that received him at his birth." Moreover, he is "a slave to his wife, obliging her in everything and thinking she is everything." "Vile," "hateful to the gods," "avaricious" and "most hostile" seem to assign him malign potency, but at the same time "cowardly" and his subjection to his wife belittle him. The two lines of attack logically contradict one another. Nevertheless, their effects cumulate together in Cynegius's discredit.

Historians sometimes subject figures of whom they disapprove to the same double attack. Ammianus Marcellinus blames the Caesar Gallus's wife for encouraging his native cruelty: she secures unjustified executions in return for bribes, and she joins Gallus in encouraging informers (Amm. 14.1.2–3, 7.4). She exacerbates his worst tendencies. Ammianus explicitly contrasts her with the good helpmeet of "truculent Maximin" (Amm. 14.1.8). Eunapius says Jovian's wife induced him to burn a temple of Hadrian to the deified Trajan, in which Julian had had a library established (Eunap. fr. 29.1.17–22 Blockley).[85] The domestic impulse stated forestalls any policy from appearing to motivate the burning, so that it appears only as sacrilege against imperial traditions. Procopius demeans Belisarius even more thumpingly. He alleges that Belisarius killed Constantinus at his wife Antonina's persuasion, thereby earning himself great opprobrium (Procop., *Anecd.* 1.28–30):[86] she hated Constantinus because he faulted her for her adultery with her and Belisarius's adopted son, which Belisarius himself was so besotted as to ignore when he caught them virtually in the act (*Anecd.* 1.18–20, 24). Antonina's adulteries continue to hamper Belisarius's actions and subject him to general ridicule (*Anecd.* 2.21, 5.27).

84. On Lib. *Or.* 30, cf. Petit 1951; *PLRE* 1.235–36, Cynegius 3.

85. αὐτῶν τῶν παλλακίδων ὑφαπτουσῶν μετὰ γέλωτος τὴν πυράν (Eunap. fr. 29.1.21–22 Blockley) appears to heighten female participation, but may contain some textual corruption. Blockley translated, "his concubines laughing and setting the fire"; yet the plural αὐτῶν must mean "their" or, better, emphasize "the concubines themselves." Either interpretation sits oddly with the context. If the text is sound, it may attest a weakened sense for παλλακίς, possibly "young girl," like its cognate παλλακή at Aelius Dionysius fr. 172 (LSJ s.v.); if so, to follow out this line of speculation as far as it can be pushed, Eunapius perhaps attests daughters for Jovian, in addition to his sons (for whom see *PLRE* 1.461, Fl. Iovianus 3).

86. Procopius cross-refers this incident to "the business surrounding Praesidius and the daggers," i.e., *Goth.* 2.8, where he reports that Constantinus wrongfully confiscated a pair of gold-trimmed daggers from Praesidius, a citizen, when he was escaping from the Goths, refused to surrender the daggers when Praesidius repeatedly appealed to Belisarius, and finally attempted to assassinate Belisarius; nonetheless, when two of Belisarius's attendants execute Constantinus, Procopius editorializes, "This was the one unholy act done by Belisarius, and in no way worthy of his character" (οὐχ ὅσιον ἔργον, *Goth.* 2.8.18).

Perhaps the most spectacularly deplored wife of late antique and early Byzantine historiography is Justinian's wife Theodora in Procopius's *Anecdota*.[87] He introduces her with the remark that she destroyed the Roman state "to the roots" (*Anecd.* 9.1). She pilots Justinian's legislation by appealing to his greed (13.19–20). She manufactures false charges against any who oppose her and manipulates the judges (15.20–23); Justinian professes ignorance, but scoops up the property of her victims (16.10, 17.4). Theodora controls official appointments, both raising the unworthy candidates she desires (17.27, 22.5, 22.22–23, 22.33) and ruining her personal enemies (17.38–45). Procopius claims she controls Justinian himself by witchcraft (22.28). She even receives proskynesis and welcomes foreign embassies with monetary gifts, scandalous innovations that Procopius couples with her and Justinian's insistence that they be addressed as "Master" and "Mistress," and magistrates be referred to as their "slaves" (δέσ-πότην, δέσποιναυ, δούλους, 30.24–26; cf. 15.13–18). Procopius depicts Theodora both as inciting and as embodying Justinian's despotism. *Anecdota* outdoes earlier histories in its concentration of invective motifs, but in so doing only the more abundantly exemplifies the same types of denigration. Messalina's vendettas show Claudius both hastily savage and oblivious, for example (Tac. *Ann.* 11.1–2), and when he marries Agrippina, she institutes "a sort of masculine thralldom" (*quasi virile servitium*, Tac. *Ann.* 12.7).[88]

In his hostile *De Mortibus Persecutorum*, Lactantius does not blame wives for his villains' actions, but he does claim that the harshest instigator of persecution, Maximian Galerius, was spurred by his mother Romula (*Mort. Pers.* 11.2). She used to entertain her neighbors at sacrificial feasts, Lactantius explains. Christians rejected her hospitality; "from this cause she conceived a hatred against them, and with womanish complaints stirred her no less superstitious son on toward destroying people." Galerius's susceptibility to feminine whining demeans him, adding emotional force to Lactantius's religious censure. The persecution appears the more wanton and outrageous. This degrading line of attack reinforces Lactantius's more direct assaults on Galerius's outstanding ferocity, which he also traces back to Romula's barbarian blood (*Mort. Pers.* 9.2).

The *Historia Augusta*, part biography, part fantasy, replicates these other forms' overdetermined narrative patterns, including a few slurring references

87. On *Anecdota*, see Averil Cameron 1985, 49–66; on how Procopius treats Theodora throughout his works, 67–83.

88. Claudius was long reviled for subservience to his wives and freedmen, e.g., Tac. *Ann.* 11.28; Suet. *Claud.* 29; Vict. *Caes.* 4.5, 12. On historical evidence for "Women's Power in the Principate" see MacMullen 1990, 169–76 (= *Klio* 68 [1986]: 434–43), esp. n. 1 for references on strong imperial women. Cf. Mary R. Lefkowitz, "Influential Women," in Averil Cameron and Kuhrt 1983, 49–64, on classical Greek and Roman attitudes that ordinarily constrained women's access to power.

to powerful women.[89] Although it generally portrays Marcus Aurelius favorably, it records that he was held at fault for promoting four lovers of his wife (*adulteros*), even one he had caught breakfasting with her (*HA Marc.* 29.1). This gross image of complaisant cuckoldry reinforces other censures of Marcus's indulgence toward his family (e.g., *HA Marc.* 15.3, 16.1–2).[90] A reiterated charge against Elagabalus is that he permitted his mother a role in public business, or indeed was wholly dominated by her (*HA Heliog.* 2.1–2, 4.1–4, 18.2–3). She even attended the Senate openly. The author emphasizes that Elagabalus was the only emperor to allow a woman to attend the Senate; for comparison, Agrippina outraged propriety by listening from behind a curtain when Nero met in the palace with senators (Tac. *Ann.* 13.5). The especially fabulous *Quadriga Tyrannorum* reports that the libidinous if brave usurper Proculus was driven to the "madness" of seizing imperial power by his wife Samso (*HA Quadr. Tyr.* 12.3).[91] The epithet *virago* assigns her further masculine potency. The fact that such structures inform invented narratives demonstrates that they were well-established patterns of thought.

Synesius of Cyrene composed his *De Providentia*, a political allegory based on the Egyptian myth of Typhos and Osiris, along the lines of a twinned encomium and invective of his Osiris and Typhos.[92] The fantastic milieu permitted him full liberty in exploiting rhetorical conceits, and he invented a superbly manipulative wife for his villain. Typhos is wicked, but forceless. He falls into despairing torpor when Osiris rather than he is elected king of Egypt (*Prov.* 104C–105A, 106D–107C). "But now his abominable wife . . . rescues herself and her husband, managing him with ease as always [ἀεί ποτε αὐτῷ ῥᾳδίῳ χρωμένη]" (107C). She devises elaborate orgies which restore his spirits, or at least distract him, preserving him for the next stage of action. Vile as her methods are, in marked contrast to him she is effectual. Still more when they plot against Osiris, all the initiative and planning are hers (108B–110B). Typhos makes a single suggestion only to have another conspirator nobly reject it (110C–D). And once their coup succeeds, Typhos remains "tame and

89. The literature on the *HA* and its author or authors is vast: see Merten 1985–87.

90. Cf. Vict. *Caes.* 16.2 and Dufraigne 1975, 112–13 ad loc. Indulgence is Marcus's one trait that Julian blames in his *Caesars* (312A–B).

91. Ronald Syme, *The Historia Augusta: A Call of Clarity*, Antiquitas Reihe 4, Beiträge zur Historia-Augusta-Forschung 8 (Bonn: Habelt, 1971), laid great emphasis on *Quadr. Tyr.* for his case that a single author, whom he identified as a "rogue scholar" (112), although reproducing good sources in some parts, in the whole perpetrates a massive hoax. Syme characterized *Quadr. Tyr.* as "continuous fiction: nothing except the names of the four usurpers deserves credence" (87; cf. Syme, *Emperors and Biography* [Oxford: Clarendon Press, 1971]; *Ammianus and the Historia Augusta* [Oxford: Clarendon Press, 1968]).

92. See Alan Cameron and Long 1993, 271–81, comparing the remainder of their chap. 7 for other generic affinities.

submissive [τιθασὸς ἦν καὶ χειροήθης] toward the women's quarters, especially since he was grateful for their having obtained his throne for him"
(112D). It is even possible to win his favor, through her, by cuckolding him.[93] At
every point Typhos is emasculated and demeaned. In the rhetorical fashion,
Synesius condemns him not so much by the facts he alleges against him, as by
the emotions that his allegations stir. On the one hand Typhos is blamed for
overthrowing Osiris's good government; yet he is also despised for being weak.

Claudian alludes to wifely instigation in retrospect in his epic about the
battle of Pollentia in 402 (*Get.* 623–34). He gloatingly pictures Alaric suffering
not only defeat but also the wails of his wife at having lost the "jeweled
necklaces of Ausonian matrons for her proud neck and Romans as her slave
girls" that she had demanded.[94] Claudian could not have considered that such
a base motive for Alaric's revolt in any way reduced either the horror of the
revolt or Stilicho's glory in victory; it merely blackens Alaric further. He committed his atrocities for the sake of ignoble vanity and greed, which he did not
even conceive himself. He merely yielded to his wife's nagging. Her insanity in
the aspiration (*demens*) underscores the senselessness of Alaric's motives.

Accordingly, the scene in which Bellona obeys Mars's instructions to rouse
the Gruthungi to revolt, so that they may avenge the shame of a eunuch's
consulate (*Eutr.* 2.141–43, 159), may be seen in the light of this invective device.
Taking on the guise of Tribigild's wife, Bellona rebukes him for having fallen
from the traditions of warlike barbarian manhood (*Eutr.* 2.194–229). Other
wives, she complains enviously, are decorated with the spoils of towns their
husbands have sacked and are served by captive Argive and Thessalian women.

Claudian's basic structure comes from epic: a god goes disguised to a mortal
in order to inspire a specific course of action. So for example Athene goes to
Telemachus disguised first as Mentes and then as Mentor (*Od.* 1.05, 2.268),
Aphrodite goes to Helen disguised as an old servant (*Il.* 3.386–89), and Hera
encourages Diomedes and his men disguised as Stentor (*Il.* 5.784–86). More
specifically, Bellona in her disguise inspires impious aggression that begins a
new movement of war, just as Athene in the guise of Laodocus inspires Pan-
darus to break the truce (*Il.* 4.86–87) and Allecto in the guise of Calybe inspires

---

93. Synesius says only "intercourse" (ὁ ταύτῃ διειλεγμένος), but the sexual nature of
her court establishes the double meaning (*Prov.* 112C–D; cf. Alan Cameron and Long
1993, 373–74 and notes).

94. In the "Argive, Corinthian and Spartan slave-girls" of whom Claudian sarcastically imagines Alaric's wife had grown tired (*Get.* 629–30), there may be a distant
echo of the "Spartan, Argive, Attic and Corinthian slave-women" Atossa urges Darius
to obtain for her in a related scene, Hdt. 3.134.5. Heleen Sancisi-Weerdenburg, "Exit
Atossa: Images of Women in Greek Historiography on Persia," in Averil Cameron and
Kuhrt 1983, 20–33, argued that Greek sources' scenes of Persian women exercising
pernicious influence are the product of Greek ideologies.

Turnus (Verg. *Aen.* 7.415–19).[95] Bellona also echoes Cupid disguised as Iulus to beguile Dido (Verg. *Aen.* 1.709–22; cf. 1.683–88), in instilling the destructive passion she conveys through a specious embrace (*Eutr.* 2.187–88).

It is the fact that Bellona disguises herself as a nagging wife, as in the derogatory cliché, that aligns her intervention with invective. As in *Bellum Geticum*, petty instigation does not soften the military force of the barbarian attack, as Claudian tells it, or the emotive force of his telling. Tribigild presses on inexorably from the first strike past Leo's defeat. The terror he inspires in the Easterners begins to turn them away from Eutropius and makes them prey to rumors about the Persians, so that at last "in Stilicho shines their only salvation" (2.501–2). At the end of *In Eutropium* 2 Tribigild remains a threat. Had events worked out differently, the story might have been continued in a third book of more straightforward epic, celebrating Stilicho's victory; in that case Tribigild would have been more extensively vituperated, as was Alaric a few years later in *Bellum Geticum*. As it is, Bellona's complaints play against the epic setting. She foreshadows the complete epic travesty achieved by the death of Leo. Furthermore, she nags in terms that recall Roman prejudices about the savagery native to barbarians (cf. 2.318–20), and she reawakens this savagery in Tribigild. She underlines the nature of the threat faced by the East.

Bellona first appears not in her disguise, but in her native state as an "implacable divinity," wearing blood-spattered clothing and combing out her hair of "snakes fattened on Illyrian slaughters" (2.109–11). When she has roused Tribigild, she turns herself into a "dreadful bird . . . with wings darker than infernal shadows" (2.230–31). These attributes emphasize her affinities with Allecto, whose activity instigating the Italian war of the *Aeneid* she broadly imitates (Verg. *Aen.* 7.323–29, 346, 408, 447–57). The idea of demonic influence also had applications to invective.[96]

From a very early time the Greeks shared a belief in spirits who could oversee human affairs.[97] Generations of philosophers refined their theories to

---

95. As Birt 1892 noted ad loc., *centumque vias meditata nocendi* ("having pondered a hundred ways of injuring," *Eutr.* 2.174) echoes *mille nocendi artes* ("a thousand arts of injuring," Verg. *Aen.* 7.338); so too Clemens Weidmann, in a review of Schweckendiek 1992, *Wiener Stud.* 106 (1993): 271–72.

96. Lassandro 1981, however, despite his title, discussed "demonization" of political enemies in *Pan. Lat.* only in the looser sense of tactics for blackening human opponents.

97. See "Geister (Dämonen)," *Reallexicon für Antike und Christentum* 9 (1976): 546–797, esp. "Hellenistische und kaiserzeitliche Philosophie" (640–68, C. Zintzen) and "Volksglaube" (761–97, C. D. G. Müller). A survey and selection of texts up to the period of Iamblichus are provided by Georg Luck, *Arcana Mundi* (Baltimore: Johns Hopkins University Press, 1985), 163–225. A survey of "Chaldaean Demonology," in fact covering much wider popular and philosophical ground, is provided by Hans Lewy, *Chaldaean Oracles and Theurgy: Mysticism, Magic and Platonism in the Late Roman*

define demons as a class of intermediate beings who link human and divine realms; they can help bring humanity into closer relationship with the divine, but by other views, they are related to the imperfect human world not through merely partial goodness but through actual evil. Meanwhile popular belief continued to emphasize the demons' caprice and malice. The late anonymous treatise *Peri Politikes Epistemes* uses demonic intervention to describe the apparently spontaneous origins of civil war (*Pol. Ep.* 5.104).

When attached to individuals, the supernatural evil of malevolent demons not only connotes tremendous power, but also repels any sense of human sympathy. Lactantius says Domitian was incited by demons to persecute Christians (*Mort. Pers.* 3.2).[98] Synesius as bishop calls his adversary Andronicus a locust, a scourge, a murderer, an agent of "the Tempter," and finally, repeatedly, a demon himself.[99] In Synesius's *De Providentia* evil demons oppose Osiris and the gods, and they fasten on the kindred spirits of Typhos and his wife in order to overthrow him (*Prov.* 107D–108B). Procopius demonizes both Justinian and Theodora, claiming in proof that only demons could have devastated mankind so greatly.[100]

Invective demonization is not limited to contexts with Christian overtones. Ammianus calls Gallus's wife a "mortal Megaera" (Amm. 14.1.2). Pacatus calls Maximus's brother Marcellinus, one of his generals, a "Megaera of civil war" (*Pan. Lat.* 2[12].35.1). Guy Sabbah linked Ammianus with Pacatus, claiming that both echo an "epic cliché"; he cited tentatively Vergil's *Tartaream . . . Megaeram* (Verg. *Aen.* 12.846).[101] But this passage merely names Megaera herself, sister of the Dirae. It is in applying the name to someone else that it takes on invective force. Invective implications give to Megaera her relevance for both Pacatus and Ammianus, as to more vaguely evoked masses of demons for other authors. Such epithets reveal how essentially rhetorical these attacks are, even when they appear in other genres of writing. They make no argument but quickly affix emotive labels.

Empire (Cairo, 1956; rpt. with addenda and indices, ed. Michel Tardieu, Paris: Études augustiniennes, 1978), 259–309. I am grateful to Lucas Siorvanes for advice about the philosophical background.

98. Creed 1984, 83–84 n. 2, assembled evidence and further references on whether Domitian did persecute.

99. Synes. *Ep.* 57 = 41 Garzya: τὴν ἀκρίδα, 55.16; τῇ πληγῇ, 56.1; τὸν παλαμναῖον τῆς χώρας ᾽Ανδρόνικον, 56.9–10; διὰ τούτου μέτεισιν ὁ περάζων, 56.14; δαίμων, 59.16–18, 60.4–6, 61.1–2. Synesius's decree of excommunication against Andronicus also equates him with the Devil (*Ep.* 58 = 42 Garzya, 74.9–75.7). PLRE 2.89–90, Andronicus 1.

100. Procop. *Anecd.* 12.14–17; 12.32; 18.1; 18.36–37 (the disasters reported in the remainder of the book are adduced to support the contention); 22.28–32; 30.34 (τῶν δαιμόνων ἄρχων). See Averil Cameron 1985, 56–59.

101. Sabbah 1978, 325.

Claudian makes greatest use of demonization in his attack *In Rufinum*. Rufinus's whole career is launched when Allecto calls the denizens of Hell together to see how best they can wreck the new Golden Age inaugurated by Theodosius (*Ruf.* 1.51). They do not quite dare to overturn the world directly, as she suggests (*Ruf.* 1.62–65); Megaera recommends using Rufinus instead. She describes how she nursed him and how her snakes formed his limbs. Even physically he is her product. Her lessons in viciousness formed his character too. And now, she concludes, he has surpassed her: "he alone has every particular of sin that we all possess" (*Ruf.* 1.111). He is a superdemon. By this device, as Alan Cameron has observed, Claudian relieved himself of all need either to suggest motives for Rufinus's acts or to explain how he had won the favor of Theodosius: insatiable malevolence and demonic potency cover everything.[102] So too in *In Eutropium* demonic inspiration, very much in an epic model, adds its power to Tribigild's attack.

The invective motifs of wifely and demonic instigation, applied to the villain of the war of *In Eutropium* 2, harmonize its epic form with its overall invective purpose. Eutropius continues to bear blame for the revolt, since his failure to conciliate Tribigild is its mundane inspiration (2.177–80, 191–92). The hostility Claudian excites at other butts rebounds on his central target as well.

Much the same prejudices that make a wife who impels her husband to commit evil into an effective invective device also operate against what was seen as the relentlessly malign backstairs influence of eunuchs.[103] Women might soften their husbands' severity, but they ought not to hold power personally; when they did, they seemed to emasculate their men and to deserve independent animosity. Procopius's Theodora of the *Anecdota* most fully exemplifies both tendencies. Even Zenobia of Palmyra, whom the *Historia Augusta* exceptionally admits transcended her sex's capabilities, ruled "longer than befitted a woman" (*HA Tyr. Trig.* 27.1).[104]

Eunuchs fall still further beyond the pale. The passage of Mamertinus's panegyric of Julian quoted earlier (*Pan. Lat.* 3[11].19.4–5) reflects a common attitude that eunuchs' alien form takes them out of the "community of human kind," let alone out of the realm where political decisions should be made.

102. Alan Cameron 1970, 69–70.

103. Compare Bird 1984, 116–21, on Victor's strictures about "Women, Eunuchs and Sexual Morality."

104. Septimia Zenobia, *PLRE* 1.990–91. *HA Tyr. Trig.* 30 both praises and disparages her; cf. *HA Aurel.* 25–30. The *HA* directs the denigratory implications of Zenobia's power chiefly against Gallienus: even women surpass him (*HA Gall.* 13.2–3; *HA Tyr. Trig.* 30.23, 31.1, 31.7; *HA Claud.* 1.1–2). On traditional ideas behind these negative judgments, cf. Maria Wyke, "Augustan Cleopatras: Female Power and Poetic Authority," in Powell 1992, 98–140; William Blake Tyrrell, *Amazons: A Study in Athenian Mythmaking* (Baltimore: Johns Hopkins University Press, 1984).

Similarly, Severus Alexander is praised by the *Historia Augusta* for having removed almost all eunuchs from palace service, except a few slaves for his wife; "he used to say that eunuchs were a third type of humans, that must be neither seen nor held in use by men, but scarcely by women" (*HA Alex. Sev.* 23.7). The singular exception Ammianus finds to the general run of eunuchs, scarcely to be credited even if Numa Pompilius or Socrates vouched for him, is Julian's chamberlain Eutherius (Amm. 16.7.4–10).[105] Interestingly, Ammianus casts Eutherius in an admonitory role similar to that conventionally envisaged for good wives: "had the emperor Constans heard him in times past . . . recommending honorable and upright things, he would have been guilty of no sins, or at least only ones deserving pardon." Eutherius even used to correct Julian's occasional fits of Oriental lightness. Typically, however, eunuchs in imperial government were notorious for plotting, selling favors, and fortifying their position by closing off others' access to the emperor.[106] Some censure attaches to emperors who succumbed to eunuchs' machinations, as when Ammianus notes in summary of Constantius's life that he was "a great deal too much enslaved to his wives and the piping voices of his eunuchs" and the flattery of certain yes-men among his courtiers (*nimium quantum addictus*, Amm. 21.16.16), or when Synesius in his speech *De Regno* says that Arcadius, shut away from the real events of his realm by Eutropius, "lives the life of a jellyfish" (Synes. *Reg.* 14D).[107] But even more lively detestation is left over for the eunuchs themselves.

105. *PLRE* 1.314–15, Eutherius 1.

106. E.g., *HA Alex. Sev.* 23.4–8, 45.4–5, 66.3; *HA Gord. Tres* 24.2–4; *HA Aurel.* 43.4 (cf. 43.1); Jul. *Ath.* 272D, 274A–B; Liban. *Or.* 62.9–10; Amm. 14.11.3, 15.2.10, 18.4.3–4, 20.2.4, 21.16.16, 30.4.2, 22.3.12; Synes. *Reg.* 15B (cf. Barnes 1986, 107–8); Socr. *HE* 2.2, 3.1; *AOC* 1.4.224, 293 Schwartz; Prisc. fr. 3.1, 2 Blockley; cf. Lact. *Mort. Pers.* 14.2, a false rumor that readily found credence. See further Stroheker 1970; Hopkins 1978, 172–96; Guyot 1980, 160 and generally 157–76; Albert 1984, 53.

107. On Ammianus's judgment of Constantius, see Blockley 1975, 38–41; on Synesius's handling of Arcadius in *Reg.*, Alan Cameron and Long 1993, 130–32, 137–40.

How to Slander a Eunuch

✦

1. Graphic Images

Ancient invective, from the freewheeling attacks of democratic Athens and republican Rome to the formalized epideictic theory of late antiquity, always centered on the person of its victim. Authors presupposed that the character of an opponent determined all his acts. Not only his conduct in the practical issue at hand, but also his private life, childhood, and family origins entered the argument. Wild allegations mingled freely with verifiable facts. Authors sought to persuade by emotive portraits as much as by rational means.

For Claudian, the central fact of Eutropius's person was that he was a eunuch. Simple references to his lack of virility recur continually in both books of *In Eutropium*; I count 58 separate references.[1] Key terms include "castrate" (*castrare*, 4 times), which Claudian uses only in this poem, "eunuch" also here only (*eunuchus*, 28 times; *spado*, 4 times), "soft" or "effeminate" (*mollis/mollescere/mollire/mollitia/mollities*, 9 times), "woman" (*muliebris*, once), "old woman" (*anus/anilis*, 4 times), "half man" (*semivir*, 2 times), "man" and "manly" in hostile contrast (*vir/virilis* 9 times), and in various combinations "male" (*mas*, here only, 3 times).

But Claudian and his late antique audience associated eunuchism with much more than the clinical fact alone. Eunuch slaves were a long tradition. They had served in private households since at least the fourth century B.C. in Greece and the Augustan period in Rome.[2] They were still conspicuous luxury

---

1. *Eutr.* 1.8, 10, 29, 39, 45, 56, 99, 145, 152, 171, 190, 193, 214, 231, 234, 240, 252, 255, 296, 298, 315, 319, 324, 326, 337, 419, 425, 438, 461, 462, 467, 494, 497; 2pr.21, 26, 33, 43, 45–46, 51, 74, 75; 2.22, 55, 62, 74, 80, 90, 112, 122, 138, 157, 192, 223–24, 415, 550, 552, 555, 563. Cf. Guyot 1980, 37–42.

2. Guyot 1980, 52–57; cf. A. H. M. Jones 1964, 851–52 and notes. On eunuchs in the Byzantine period, see Judith Herrin, "In Search of Byzantine Women: Three Avenues of Approach," in Averil Cameron and Kuhrt 1983, 171.

items. Claudian's contemporary Ammianus vividly pictures the "armies" of servants aristocrats marshaled to escort them about the streets of Rome (Amm. 14.6.16–17). Bringing up the parade would be

> the throng of eunuchs, from the old men down to the boys, sallow and deformed by the misshapen fitting of their limbs. Wherever anyone goes and sees the lines of mutilated humans [*mutilorum hominorum*], he will abhor the memory of that ancient queen Semiramis: she was the first of all to castrate unhardened males [*teneros mares*], doing violence to Nature, as it were, and throwing her back from her established course— Nature, who among the very cradles of growth, through the primordial founts of seed, shows by some silent law the routes for propagating posterity.

As in satire or diatribe, Ammianus dwells on the ugliness, cruelty, and unnaturalness that belong to this display of wealth; these qualities rebuke the aristocratic masters. He uses emotive, graphic language for maximum impact. The details conveyed by his rhetorical bombast are precise and medically correct. Modern spectrophotometric studies of hypogonadal and castrated men confirm that their low androgen levels cause lower than normal circulation of blood to the skin, lower than normal levels of hemoglobin in the blood, lower than normal supply of melanin and higher than normal amounts of carotene in the skin, all of which would contribute to the "sallow" complexion that Ammianus notes.[3] Those who observe such men often remark on the softness, pallor, and pastiness of their skin, and the mesh of fine wrinkles that it develops even at early ages.[4] Prepuberal castration causes the long bones of the legs and arms to grow several inches longer than is normal, because androgens hasten the epiphyseal closure that puts an end to bone growth. Therefore eunuchs have abnormally long limbs and can fall victim to osteoporosis, curvature of the spine, and joint deformities in middle age.[5] Ammianus notes correctly "the misshapen fitting of their limbs." Although in humans castration does not necessarily result in caponism, both prepuberal and postpuberal castrates tend to distribute fat in a feminine pattern, depositing it especially on the hips, buttocks, breasts, and abdominal wall.[6] Much more than their genitals marked eunuchs as "mutilated men."

3. Dorfman and Shipley 1956, 208–9, 316; with references to clinical studies.
4. E.g., Bremer 1958, 82–83, 109, 111, 307; cf. Dorfman and Shipley 1956, 316.
5. Dorfman and Shipley 1956, 315. The same is also true of hypogonadal men, photographs of whom illustrate the chapter. Some individuals are strikingly malproportioned.
6. Dorfman and Shipley 1956, 210, 315–16; Bremer 1958, 82–83, 110–11, 307. Adrenal androgens normally suffice to cause an adult growth of axillary and pubic hair, but in postpuberal castrates as well as hypogonadal men and prepuberal castrates it grows in a

Members of a society that used such men in daily life at all commonly would have had ample opportunity to observe their deformities.[7] Ammianus's description gains effectiveness from being accurate. Eunuchs did look abnormal, and their strangeness could be perceived as unpleasant. Claudian takes full advantage of this perception; indeed he does everything that he can to emphasize Eutropius's condition and, through it, induce a visceral reaction against him.

He opens his invective with a catalog of traditional portents of disaster (1.1–7):

> Semiferos partus metuendaque pignora matri,
> moenibus et mediis auditum nocte luporum
> murmur et attonito pecudes pastore locutas
> et lapidum diras hiemes nimboque minacem
> sanguineo rubuisse Iovem puteosque cruore
> mutatos binasque polo concurrere lunas
> et geminos soles mirari desinat orbis.

> Half-beast births, and babes to frighten their mothers;
> in the midst of the city walls the murmur of wolves, heard
> in the night. Sheep that spoke to their astonished shepherd.
> Dire winter storms of stones. With bloody cloud,
> a threatening Jove grew red. Wells were transformed
> with gore. Double moons run about the pole,
> and twin suns—at these things the world ceases to wonder.

"Half-beast births" joins human and animal. Pliny uses the same phrase to describe the offspring of bestial unions among the Indians (Plin. *NH* 7.30). He also lists kinds of births that were considered portentous: births of more than three children at once, of hermaphrodites, and of animals or half animals to human parents (7.33–35). *Pignus*, originally a legal metaphor, ought to convey

---

feminine rather than masculine pattern, with the pubes a clearly defined triangle (Dorfman and Shipley 1956, 317; Bremer 1958, 82–83, 109–10, 307). Other readily apparent abnormalities of prepuberal castrates and hypogonadal men are immature genitalia, retained juvenile voice (although it was observed of the operatic castrati that "many castrati passed through a difficult period, vocally speaking, during the years in which their voices would have broken, had they not been what they were, and some of them were never able to sing again," Angus Heriot, *The Castrati in Opera* [London: Secker and Warburg, 1956; rpt. New York, 1975], 172), and a juvenile hairline ("an uninterrupted curve without the usual wedge-shaped indentations which are present over the sides of the forehead in the normal adult. Extensive simple baldness does not occur," Dorfman and Shipley 1956, 319).

7. For ancient observations, see Danilo Dalla, *L'incapacità sessuale in diritto romano*, Seminario giuridico della Università di Bologna 76 (Milan: Giuffrè, 1978), 29–67; Guyot 1980, 16–17, 37–42 and notes. Lucian, *Eunuch*, epitomizes ancient prejudices.

the sense that a child validates the bond between its parents,[8] but these *pignora* are so horrible that they repel their mother. Both the limits of natural fertility and the human bonds consequent on fertility are ruptured. With his first words Claudian introduces a theme that runs throughout his indictment.[9]

Claudian's catalog continues with other weird conjunctions: wolf howls being heard inside the city, sheep speaking to their shepherds, rains of stones, bloody clouds, wells turned into gore, doubled moons and suns. He is echoing, as Birt observed and Richard Bruère detailed, Lucan's catalog of portents when Caesar arms for civil war and Pompey flees from Rome.[10] Lucan begins with meteorological omens, unusual behavior of cult fires, floods, and weeping and sweating cult statues. The omens that interested Claudian come in the middle of Lucan's list: wild animals make their lairs inside Rome, sheep begin to speak, and deformed human babies terrify their mothers (Luc. 1.559–63):

> accipimus, silvisque feras sub nocte relictis
> audaces media posuisse cubilia Roma.
> tum pecudum faciles humana ad murmura linguae,
> monstrosique hominum partus numeroque modoque
> membrorum, matremque suus conterruit infans.

> We hear that bold wild beasts, deserting the woods
> at night, have put their dens in the middle of Rome.
> Then the tongues of sheep grow apt to human murmurs,
> and births of men are monstrous in both the number and the manner
> of their limbs, and her own child terrifies a mother.

Then dire Sibylline oracles are circulated, Bellona's and Cybele's self-mutilating priests sing of the gods and human disaster, and warlike ghosts begin to walk. Claudian evokes Lucan's horrific atmosphere, but eliminates the directly religious omens and the ones that transparently indicate civil war. Instead he gives pride of place to events that overturn laws of nature; the social disruptions they may imply, particularly in light of Claudian's allusion to Lucan, darken foreboding subliminally. The violations appall the senses directly. Children should belong to a single species, and should bond with their mothers. The wilderness should avoid civilization. Sheep should be silent while shepherds speak.[11] The elements should remain constant, not interchange with one

---

8. The *OLD* and Lewis and Short s.v. indicate that the meaning "child" is post-Augustan: first in elegy (Prop. 4.11.73; Ov. *Her.* 6.122, 12.192), though soon passing into prose. Cf. *3 Cons.* 152, *Eutr.* 1.74.

9. Claudian here improves on Africa's complaint that Gildo has married his black barbarians to "Sidonian matrons," "a discolored infant frightens his cradle" (*Gild.* 193).

10. Luc. 1.524–83; Birt 1892, 74 ad loc.; Bruère 1964, 239.

11. In neat verbal interlock, *attonito pastore* contrasts with *pecudes locutas, Eutr.* 1.3 (quoted previously).

another or with animal life. The heavens should remain single. A new and ghastlier abomination, plainly, awaits.

The world no longer marvels at the omens, Claudian continues (*Eutr.* 1.8.):

omnia cesserunt eunucho consule monstra.

All prodigies have given way, when a eunuch is consul.

"All" and "prodigies" frame the line. "Eunuch" is centered and set off by the caesura and diairesis; momentarily the line appears to make an even more grim statement, "all things have given way." A eunuch as consul is the ultimate incongruity. When these two things go together, only disaster can result. The highly charged portentous atmosphere sparks into Juvenalian hyperbole, dire but at the same time ambiguously undercut. Juvenal can discuss applying to Nero the horrible traditional Roman penalty for parricide, hold up the mythological example of Orestes for matricide and find Nero's motives more squalid, even before observing that he killed his sister and his wife as well, and finally cap these crimes with Nero's competing on the stage and composing an epic on Troy.[12] It is both an ironic deflation and a transition to a different level of consideration, where Nero's social and literary crimes imply even more awful lawlessness than do his murders.[13] A eunuch consul is both more horrible than the other monstrosities Claudian enumerates, and faintly silly in comparison. The imperceptibly self-conscious exaggeration here foreshadows the grandiose ridiculousness toward which Claudian develops his portrait.

Claudian turns now to the Sibylline Books, which Lucan makes contribute to the general panic as people relate oracles to one another.[14] Claudian calls for interpreters: pontiffs, augurs, and haruspices. Birt compared Juvenal's protests against Gracchus's taking a husband in *Satire* 2: he demands whether a censor or a haruspex should intervene, and whether births of one species to another would seem a worse portent.[15] In Claudian's combination, the sexual scandal of Juvenal informs the ominous structure of Lucan. As Isabella Gualandri has observed, Claudian frequently makes several different allusions at once. Not only has he assimilated a great breadth of literary tradition, but he joins disparate elements from the traditions to make new statements.[16] His catalog

12. Juv. 8.213–30; cf. Courtney 1980, 383–84; Mayor 1901, 2.48–53 (better than Courtney on Nero's murders). Aristophanes similarly leaps from sociopathy to artistic sin at *Ran.* 146–51.

13. Cultural terrorism is a crucial theme in Juvenal, which I hope to treat elsewhere; compare, e.g., Juv. 1.42–44 with the programmatic statements of that satire, esp. 1.1–21; Domitian's culinary council of Juv. 4; domestically, the literary critic of Juv. 6.434–56.

14. As Birt and Bruère noted, both use the periphrasis, "songs of the Cumaean priestess" (*Cumanae carmina vatis, Eutr.* 1.11; Luc. 1.564).

15. Birt 1888, 52–53; Juv. 2.117–23.

16. Gualandri 1969.

of portents is no less suggestively dire than Lucan's. But it also has distinct overtones of sexual violation, which point the book toward a theme it takes up in more detail later.

Claudian calls for the evil prodigy to be destroyed, in order to avert the omen it bears (*Eutr.* 1.19–23):

> quae tantas expiet iras
> victima? quo diras iugulo placabimus aras?
> consule lustrandi fasces ipsoque litandum
> prodigio; quodcumque parant hoc omine fata,
> Eutropius cervice luat.

> What victim will expiate such great
> angers? By what throat shall we placate the dire altars?
> With the consul must the rods of office be purified, and with the prodigy itself
> must the propitiating sacrifice be made; whatever the fates are preparing with this omen,
> let Eutropius make atonement with his neck.

The passage recalls Lucan's Arruns (Luc. 1.589–91):

> monstra iubet primum, quae nullo semine discors
> protulerat natura, rapi sterilique nefandos
> ex utero fetus infaustis urere flammis.

> First he bids the prodigies, which from no seed a jangling
> Nature had brought forth, to be snatched forth, and the unspeakable offspring
> from a sterile womb to burn with baleful flames.

This call for execution is the climax and immediate goal of Claudian's conceit that Eutropius is a prodigy. But the idea develops further. The thought of fate leads him to rebuke Fortuna, whose wanton whim has lifted Eutropius to culminating honor from the basest depths of slavery. Eutropius gets no credit for raising himself. His former position as slave at least matched his low nature, Claudian grants, but now "the crime of servility befouls the curule chairs" (*servili placuit* [sc. *Fortunae*] *foedare curules crimine*, 1.26–27). That is, socially too Eutropius is an incongruous prodigy. This quality is later recalled by the string of adynata to which the "more serious" Western mind compares the prospect of his consulate (1.350–57).[17]

Even as a slave, numerous resales attest that nobody wanted Eutropius or valued him. Claudian uses his whole account of Eutropius's slave career to

17. Cf. Birt 1890.

demonstrate this assertion. The obvious polemical end must cast doubt on the detail he alleges; he is our only source. To compare an example from a milieu where individual and family backgrounds must have been better known than the Easterner Eutropius's could have been in Milan, Cicero does not hesitate to call Piso "some unknown Syrian from the mob of new slaves" in the same speech that he mocks him for coming from Insubrian or even Transalpine Gallic stock.[18] The slanders are not consistent, let alone all true. Cicero adds that Piso has a "servile complexion" and lacks "any particle of the freeborn or free man" (Cic. *Pis.* 1; fr. viii). In the same speech he also dismisses scornfully "two tribunes bought off the stone," that is as slaves, who failed to support his return (*Pis.* 35).[19] Such people are worthless, the allegation implies; their opinions need not be taken seriously. Nor need individual slanders have been taken seriously either. They merely added to a cumulative, impressionistic sketch of character.

Claudian had more opportunity to press the charge of slavery literally, since eunuchs were normally slaves. He amplifies hyperbolically. Eutropius had as many masters as the sea has waves, or Libya grains of sand (1.32–33). Another favorite device is rhetorical exclamation: "How often was he stripped, while the buyer consulted the doctor, lest his loss lurk in a hidden fault!" (1.35–36).[20] The miniature scene sustains a momentary drama, in that respect alone enriching Claudian's work. Eutropius stands naked. The buyer doubts the value of his purchase, and fusses with the doctor. The aesthetic vividness of the scene makes concrete the fact that Eutropius has been a chattel, which is intrinsically demeaning; the same technique is applied to the same purpose when other writers claim that chalk still marks the feet of former slaves.[21] Moreover, the image enacts Claudian's other claims about Eutropius. While he is being exhibited as a chattel, within the scene and by it to Claudian's audience, he is degraded before them by the inspection.[22] The hesitation that prompts it adds an extra sting.

Other images function more viscerally. Eutropius could only be sold, of

18. Cic. *Pis.* 1 (cf. *Red.* 14); *Pis.* frr. ix, xi; 62. Cf. Koster 1980, 217–18, 226–27; Nisbet 1961, 194; Ronald Syme, "Who Was Decidius Saxa?," *JRS* 27 (1937): 130–33 (= *Roman Papers*, vol. 1, ed. Ernst Badian [Oxford: Clarendon Press, 1979], 33–38); on Gallic senators and Saxa as well as Piso; Süß 1910, 247.

19. Cf. Nisbet 1961, 97 ad loc.

20. Christiansen 1969 (see esp. 92–102) missed this image, and other such miniature scenes as well. The enumeration of Eutropius's masters, which he noted, uses concrete but very ordinary comparands and does not sustain the images.

21. See the references of Mayor 1901, 1.140 ad Juv. 1.111.

22. The remarks of Bella Zweig on the degradation of "The Mute Nude Female Characters in Aristophanes' Plays," in *Pornography and Representation in Greece and Rome*, ed. Amy Richlin (Oxford: Oxford University Press, 1992), 73–89, apply still more readily to Eutropius, in the unambiguously defamatory context of *Eutr.*

course, while he was still worth buying at all. But "afterward, he was left a misshapen cadaver [*deforme cadaver*], and all of him sagged down in anile wrinkles." His masters gave him away just to be rid of him (1.38–41). The image of them "contending [*certatim*] to drive him from the threshold," like the buyer's examination, illustrates a point that Claudian enunciates elsewhere. Epigrammatic paradox underlines the same point again at the close of the section, twice: Eutropius "never ceased, but nonetheless often began, a service ancient, but ever new" (1.42–44).

Eutropius himself is simply, directly repulsive. Any eunuch may be "misshapen," but deformity need not be unique to be horrid. The word *deformis* denotes an offense against the conventional ideals that identify beauty with worth:[23] Petronius's Encolpius marvels, for example, that Trimalchio's pet slave boy is "wizened, bleary-eyed, more misshapen than his master" (Petron. 28.4). Apuleius has Venus assign labors to Psyche on the grounds that being "so misshapen," she can hope to win lovers only by her service (Apul. *Met.* 6.10). The antierotic connotation often borne by *deformis* is not crucial in this passage of *In Eutropium*, but it is an element that figures elsewhere in the invective. I shall return to it. Eutropius, further, is a *cadaver.*[24] His life is already exhausted. Nothing more remains. "All of him" and "flows down" image extravagant collapse. "Anile wrinkles" suggests not merely old age but, by being female, also sexual repulsiveness: wrinkles feature prominently in antierotic poetry about old women.[25]

Yet more lurid is the scene of Eutropius's castration, which stands for *genesis* in Claudian's account of his *anatrophe* (1.44–57). The language is graphic and emotive. Castration is described as "bloody penalties," "bloody" being dramatically juxtaposed with "his earliest cradle." Assonance of *c* and *p* also bind the words together: *cunabula prima cruentis / debita suppliciis.* Or even before he reaches a cradle (1.45–51),

> rapitur castrandus ab ipso
> ubere; suscipiunt matris post viscera poenae.
> advolat Armenius certo mucrone recisos
> edoctus mollire mares damnoque nefandum
> aucturus pretium; fecundum corporis ignem

---

23. The adjective *deformis* is used by both Claudian and Ammianus in the passages already cited; cf. *TLL* s.v. II, for transferred, moral applications: it is used quite commonly of abstract qualities (5, 1, col. 368.79–329.39).

24. Cf. Cic. *Pis.* 19, *eiecto cadavere* of Piso, from whom no serious help could be expected, but who if propped up might at least sustain the name of consul.

25. E.g., Hor. *Epod.* 8.3 (description, discussed by Richlin [1983] 1992, 109–13); *Carm.* 4.13.11 (curse fulfilled); Prop. 3.25.12 (curse); Juv. 6.144 (anticipatory); transposed into prose with a gender variation, Petron. 23–24 (description of an aged and painted homosexual who rapes Encolpius).

sedibus exhaurit geminis unoque sub ictu
eripit officiumque patris nomenque mariti.

> He is snatched for castration even from
> the breast: punishments take him up after his mother's guts.
> An Armenian flies to him, who has well learned how to soften the males
> he trims with his sure blade, and who will by the injury increase
> the damnable price;[26] the body's fertile fire
> he drains from its twin seats and under one blow
> tears away both the office of a father and the name of a husband.[27]

Haste in "he is snatched" and "flies" heighten the brutality of the scene, and the disapprobation conveyed by "injury" and "damnable." *Damnoque nefandum / aucturus pretium* neatly juxtaposes the antithetical "loss" and "increase." Now the pace slows. "Uncertain of life he lay, and deeply into the top of his brain the severed sinews drew chills" (1.52–53). The newborn baby has been subjected to unspeakable violence by a greedy barbarian, and nearly dies in consequence. The scene should be pathetic. But with total unconcern Claudian asks, "Are we to praise the hand that took away strength from an enemy?" (1.54). No, finally: "he stands out the happier by his shame; he would be a slave still if he were stronger" (1.56–57). The smug rhetorical quibble abruptly defuses the pity aroused by the description.

Pity frustrated turns against Eutropius. He is an "enemy" who deserves "penalties" and "punishments." The only pity is that they did not incapacitate him further. The vividness of the scene fixes the castration in the audience's minds indelibly: from the beginning of his life Eutropius is damaged and effeminized. As in Ammianus's outburst against Semiramis, the initial injury was committed by an external force, but it becomes a fact of Eutropius's own flesh and mind. It changes him from the ordinary slave he otherwise would

---

26. In default of other information, *Eutr.* 1.47 and 58 are always cited as evidence that Eutropius came from Armenia or Syria (e.g., *PLRE* 2.440). Claudian may be right, but perhaps on no more basis than convention, since castration was illegal within the Roman Empire: in *CJ* 4.42.1 Constantine reiterated a ban originated by Domitian (see further Guyot 1980, 45–51).

27. Andrews 1931, 33, and Alan Cameron 1968a, 400, thought that the attributes of *Eutr.* 1.51 must be understood to be exchanged. But *patris* can be understood as predicative: by begetting children, a man performs the "office" that makes him a father, thus confirming that he has the relations with his wife that "the name of husband" recognizes merely verbally. *Nomenque mariti* recurs at *Stil.* 1.6 of Honorius, who never did father a child. (The occasional euphemism *officium* for sexual performance, e.g., Prop. 2.22.24, Ov. *Am.* 1.10.46, 3.7.24, cf. Sen. *Controv.* 4pr.10, lends an overtone of paradox that highlights the epigrammatic neatness of *Eutr.* 1.51.) Claudian follows ancient medical theory connecting production of semen with the brain (e.g., Hp. *Aër.* 22) in the fever that follows Eutropius's castration.

have remained into something ugly, contemptible, and more insidiously wicked. Claudian charges that he did not shame to profit by the injury too. *Suscipiunt* of the punishments taking up Eutropius "from his mother's guts" is a technical term that substitutes them for a father acknowledging paternity;[28] he is thus illegitimate too. And if the contested reading *debita* accepted by Hall is right,[29] the description is opened by the assertion that Eutropius's "bloody penalties" were deserved. In any case, it arouses a strong disgust that Claudian transfers to Eutropius.

Degradation and revulsion are fundamental aims of the images Claudian deploys against Eutropius. By the time his *anatrophe* concludes, he has been reduced to the lowly duties of a lady's maid (1.105–9). "The ruler of the East and future consul" impressively unrolls his future glory. It is the subject of a sentence that continues, "combs the hair of his mistress and often, when his fosterling is bathing, stands naked bearing pure liquid [*lympham*] for her in a silver dish." His future offices are undermined by his performance as a hair-dresser: even among servile duties, hairdressing seems to have been regarded as especially base.[30] The luxury of the silver dish contrasts starkly with Eutropius's exposure.[31] A similar ironic juxtaposition of future title and present duty, opulence and degradation, breaks about the caesura in the last line of the description, "the patrician fans with peacocks' rosy wings" (*patricius roseis pavonum ventilat alis*). "Patrician" is lofty. The rosy color bespeaks luxury. But the rest of the line corrects the perspective. All the luxury belongs to the pampered mistress. Eutropius is only an instrument who fans her in the heat.

Finally, Eutropius cannot perform even these tasks any longer. Claudian paints his decrepitude in great detail (1.110–14).[32]

28. *OLD* s.v. *suscipio* 4. Castration corrupting the whole person, e.g., Lucian, *Eun.* 8.

29. By Hall's report, at *Eutr.* 1.45 *debita* is given by four witnesses of the twelfth to thirteenth century (P_2, F_2, P after corr., F); Schweckendiek 1992, 69, preferred its vividness. Andrews 1931, 32 (approved by Alan Cameron 1968a, 400, though he found *debita* attractive), preferred *dedita* of six witnesses, one ca. 1050 and the others of the twelfth to thirteenth century (Γ, g, R *varia lect.*, W_1, J_3, n_1); Schmidt 1989, 407 located Γ closest to the archetype of his stemma. Birt 1892, followed by Platnauer 1922, read *debet* of three witnesses of the twelfth to thirteenth century (L in ras., P before corr., R).

30. Possibly because hairdressing was associated with adultery by the mistress: as an intimate servant, the hairdresser might act as a go-between (a commonplace of erotic elegy, e.g., Ov. *Am.* 1.11), and the mistress would want to be groomed especially well for a lover (e.g., Juv. 6.487–511). Julian *Caes.* 335B ranks hairdressing with pastry cooking, a Platonic image of base titillation, e.g., *Grg.* 464D–E, 521E–522A.

31. The combination of silver dish, eunuch, and bather parallels Trimalchio's entourage at the baths, Petron. 27 (cf. Mart. 3.87), but *lympham* sanitizes away the rich man's urine; Claudian emphasizes only the abasement of the slave.

32. As Birt 1892, 78, and Fargues, *Invectives* 48, observed on this passage, Juv. 10.191–209 describes similar ravages of old age: thickened skin, drooping cheeks (cf. *Eutr.*

iamque aevo laxata cutis, sulcisque genarum
corruerat passa facies rugosior uva:
flava minus presso finduntur vomere rura,
nec vento sic vela tremunt.

Now his skin is loosened with age. From the furrows of his cheeks,
his dried-out face had collapsed, more wrinkled than a raisin.
The golden country earth is less cloven by the plow pressed upon it,
and sails do not shake so in the wind.

Each image is fresh and different, so that its full impact is felt as it reiterates the same claims about its referents, the flapping wrinkles of Eutropius's drooping flesh. Peder G. Christiansen interpreted the images as wholly unfavorable: he asserted that "the helpless objects, disfigured by the plow and the wind, represent the mistreatment of Eutropius by his former masters."[33] But sails are not disfigured by the wind. They flap until they are drawn in and the ship takes off. The image is merely pictorial. The earth, in the georgic literature that *sulcis*, *flava rura*, and *vomere* suggest[34] and in the real life of an agricultural community, is not a passive, helpless object. It is plowed so that it may bring forth the crops on which life depends. *Flava*, as Andrews noted, is used of fields ready to be reaped.[35] Raisins were spread out to dry (*passa*) and become a sweet condiment. Thus Claudian's agricultural imagery suggests desirable fertility. It mocks Eutropius's sterility even as it describes his wasted face. The treatment he received as a slave does not enter into consideration.

Claudian goes on to claim that Eutropius's scalp has been chewed by grubs, so that there are gaps in his hair. Continuing his agricultural imagery, Claudian compares Eutropius's head to a cornfield stricken by drought (1.113–18).[36]

1.258–59, but also my note 41 on that passage), wrinkles, shaky voice and limbs, baldness, sniveling, toothlessness, impotence.

33. Christiansen 1969, 93.

34. In a general way; neither Birt, Fargues, Andrews, nor I have been able to detect strong specific echoes in the passage.

35. Andrews 1931, 39 ad loc., citing Verg. *Georg.* 1.316 and Gellius's definition, '*Flavus*' *contra videtur e viridi et rufo et albo concretus* ("compounded of verdant green, ruddy, and white," Gell. 2.26.12 [not 2.16.12]). Entries in *TLL* s.v. *flavus* show that when applied to soil the adjective was used of sand (*harena*), which would not have been plowed, so that Claudian's *flava rura* must anticipate the ripe grain, of which *flavus* was used commonly (*TLL* 6, 1 s.v. *flavus* II.A, 888.11–20; II.D, 889.34–40).

36. Andrews 1931, 39, said of *tineae*: "this word means 'worms,' and Harper's, Quicherat, and Platnauer are wrong in thinking that in this one place it has the meaning 'lice.' [Platnauer translated "grubs" here, "lousy" at 1.260.] Claudian's description shows that Eutropius was obviously a victim of partial alopecia, a disease which is commonly produced by a species of ringworm." Andrews is too precise: Claudian only

The wrinkles plowed in him cannot produce even a raisin. The simile's dried-out ears of grain mockingly imitate his own infertility. The imagery now accords with its object.

Claudian supplies another simile (1.117–18): "or as, with feather falling from frozen rimes, a swallow dies upon a winter tree's trunk" (*vel qualis gelidis pluma labente pruinis arboris inmoritur trunco brumalis hirundo*). A bird molting always looks unpleasant, as the Romans would know from their pets. It is another pungently graphic image. But Claudian pushes the image yet further, beyond ugliness and infertility finally to death.

Eutropius himself, when Claudian returns to him, has become a walking corpse or ghost.[37] "Pale image," "naked bones," "horror," and "bleached emaciation" (1.121–23) all suggest a specter. "A distressing corpse and shade baleful to its own family spirits" (1.130–31) makes it explicit. The imagery goes far beyond what Christiansen suggested, "a swallow is out of place in the cold frost of winter; Eutropius ought not to serve as consul" (93). Claudian indeed implies that Eutropius ought not to serve as consul, but not merely because he is out of place. He is virtually dead and unfit for anything. He is an evil omen for those he meets (1.125). He will bring destruction on the home (1.131).

This strong assertion legitimates the otherwise callous and cynical behavior of the shepherd in Claudian's next simile. He feeds his dog while he is fit to protect the flock, but "when the same dog, slower and dirty, lets droop ears now torn by mange, he undoes and keeps as profit the chains stripped from his neck"; thus is Eutropius set free (1.135–37). Claudian has just reiterated that Eutropius did not even guard when he was physically capable (1.128–30), so that as a slave he was less useful than the dog. Now when he can no longer perform even the most menial tasks, the kindest thing possible is to allow him

---

claims Eutropius's crop of hair looks infested. Related derogatory imagery, e.g., Jul. *Misop.* 338C (lice in the beard), Lact. *Mort. Pers.* 33 (worms in Galerius's rotting bowels, modeled esp. after 2Macc. 9: cf. Moreau 1954, 1.60–64, 2.383–87).

37. *Trunco* in the swallow simile alludes indirectly to Eutropius's castration and moribund state: cf. Verg. *Aen.* 2.557, 9.332 (death); Ov. *Am.* 3.7.15 (sexual impotence). Heinsius suggested it be applied to Eutropius directly at *Eutr.* 1.254, *truncum vexilla secuntur* for *tum cum* J_6 (before corr.; *tunc cum* g, P_2, R *var. lect.*, F; *tunc tum* σ); Hall accepted the emendation. R and other manuscripts Hall considered the best, including the stemmatically prior Γ (cf. Schmidt 1989, 407), read *peditum*, but as Schweckendiek 1992, 82–83, commented, that the units should consist of infantrymen adds little meaningful information. He preferred Koenig's *tumidum*, underscoring the farcical delusion of Eutropius's triumphing. Despite Schweckendiek's professed incredulity, I cannot see how "the standards follow a trunk" emasculates the army any more (or less) than Claudian's calling them "maniples of eunuchs" in the next line. Ovid's use of the image sets up a nice counterpoint for the hollow action of this "legion most worthy of Hellespontine emblems" (see subsequent discussion and in Chap. 8.I).

to skulk off and die by himself. His freedom in no way reflects anything good about him. Rather it passes a final verdict on his worthlessness.

Yet Eutropius does not skulk off and die. "There is a time when contempt helps too much," Claudian bitterly remarks (1.138). By some evil humor of the gods, from being rejected from slavery Eutropius is catapulted into power. He finds shelter in the palace like an "ancient vixen," an animal proverbial for cunning,[38] but he still is the same "venal cadaver" who has "crept into the sacred service," to the grief of all (*vetulam vulpem; inrepere sacris obsequiis . . . venale cadaver*, 1.145–47). *Sacris* at this point means no more than "imperial,"[39] but the sense of pollution is retained from the earlier comparison to a corpse.

Eutropius is not improved by success. When he returns from his Hunnic campaign, Claudian recalls his hair-grubs with him too (1.260),[40] as well as his drooping cheeks, sallow complexion, and high-pitched voice.[41] Such a hideous figure looks incongruous indeed at the focus of a public celebration. The evidence for late antique triumphal ceremonies, studied in detail by Michael McCormick, shows that the structure of Claudian's account fits the custom.[42] At least as Claudian portrays it, Eutropius reinforced his pretensions to victory by making his assertion in the public language of ceremony. Claudian belies the victory itself with his picture, immediately before the return, of barbarians with their ferocity unabated: they turn to slaughter merely because they are bored with plunder (1.250–51). Eutropius himself is appalling, but as "a slave and an effeminate" unashamed by anything (1.252). His army moves forward

38. E.g., Hor. *Serm.* 2.3.186; Pers. 5.117.

39. As early as the Augustan period (Ov. *Fast.* 6.810), and standard in later antiquity: *OLD* s.v. *sacer*.

40. Hall reported a marginal note in the *Isingriniana* of *tunicas* for *tineas*; but though the corruption would not be difficult paleographically, "his maggots sprinkled with dust" has the more force from its incongruousness, whereas "tunics sprinkled with dust" is pedestrian.

41. "He labored to puff out his flabby cheeks" (*Eutr.* 1.258–59) betrays not simply old age (despite 1.110, "skin gone slack with age"), but also Eutropius's eunuchism, as do his "words broken beyond depravity" (1.260–62): modern studies have found that the skin of eunuchs shows "increased distensibility as determined by quantitative procedures" (Dorfman and Shipley 1956, 316), and observers remark on the "poor turgor and freshness" of the facial skin of castrates (Bremer 1958, 109). Werner A. Krenkel, "Hyperthermia in Ancient Rome," *Arethusa* 8 (1975): 385–86, collected evidence showing that the Romans considered a "broken voice" to be a sign of effeminacy in uncastrated men (e.g., Juv. 2.111, quoted in Chap. 2). It is not possible that, as he proposed, a fashion for high-pitched rhetorical delivery had anything to do with the Romans' notoriously hot baths possibly impairing spermatogenesis: once testosterone has triggered the thickening of the vocal cords in pubescent males, the change is irreversible (cf. Bremer 1958, 110).

42. McCormick 1986, 35–64, 80–130; cf. 11–34; on *Eutr.* 1.252–71 specifically, 48–49.

with its standards, but it consists of eunuchs and the like, "a legion most worthy of Hellespontine emblems" (1.256). As Fargues and Andrews noted, this characterization does not slander Constantinople gratuitously, but refers to a major cult center of Priapus: the traditional association of eunuchs and licentiousness is being played upon.[43] Eutropius is met by a grateful delegation: "dependent" and "defender" indicate their relationship. They embrace. Eutropius delivers a speech in which he "retells the battles." He further declares himself exhausted in public service, and unable to support the weight of domestic ill will (*livori, procellas invidiae*, 1.265–66). Ammianus reports for Constantius's triumphal entry into Rome in 357 the same sequence of progress toward the city, greetings outside the walls by a senatorial delegation, further parade and entrance to the city, and an address to the people; Constantius completed the festivities with games for the populace and a tour of Rome (Amm. 16.10).[44]

The speech Claudian assigns Eutropius could be interpreted positively in context. But Claudian characterizes it as pitiful whining, and concentrates on Eutropius's ignobly quavering voice. Similarly, his description replaces the impressive garments a triumphator would have worn with dust that spatters Eutropius's ravaged scalp and pallid, filthy face.[45] Finally Claudian compares him to a bibulous, exhausted old woman. The glory that a triumph should parade is wholly overshadowed by the demeaning images with which Claudian fills out its basic scheme. Such caricatured pageantry had particular invective

43. Worship of Priapus at Lampsacus on the Hellespont: Pausan. 9.31.2; e.g., *Hellespontiaci . . . Priapi*, Verg. *Georg.* 4.111. Fargues, *Invectives* 61, reported Koenig's suggestion that some of the Eastern units used an image of Priapus on their standards. Andrews 1931, 52–53, declared the collocation "strongly ironical, for of all men eunuchs could least expect some direct benefit from addressing their devotion to a god of fertility and procreation." Compare rather, e.g., Juv. 6.366–78 (women choose to copulate with postpuberal castrates because they are infertile) and references cited by Courtney 1980, 309–11 ad loc.; Guyot 1980, 63–66. Some of the castrates studied by Bremer 1958 retained erectile capacity even without androgen treatment, although "rectal exploration of slightly more than half the cases confirmed that the prostate glands disappear, as stated in other investigations" (110, summarizing case histories taken six to fifteen years after castration). Presumably ejaculate ceases to be produced. Rousselle 1988, 107–28, delineated a positive ideology of castrate sexual activity. It cannot have been actuated by many, but it could reinforce the satirical image. On the other hand, Lucian, *Eun.* 12–13, jokes at castrate sex as an absurdity.

44. Compare too the Eastern army's return to Constantinople, *Ruf.* 2.348–70. On the impact of pageantry within literary descriptions and in real life, see Ramsay MacMullen, "Some Pictures in Ammianus Marcellinus," *Art Bull.* 46 (1964): 435–55 = 1990, 78–106; cf. MacCormack 1981, 17–89; MacCormack 1972.

45. See note 40 on the readings *tineas/tunicas* for *Eutr.* 1.260. Compare the splendor of the triumphator on the column of Arcadius (presumably Fravitta after the defeat of Gaïnas; McCormick 1986, 50, 53, reproduced a sketch and discussed the image).

force in the ceremonious world of late antiquity: Julian rouses fine scorn from the sham imperial proclamation of the usurper Silvanus,[46] for example, and Ammianus of Procopius.[47] Claudian achieves no less with his vivid pictorial commentary.

Manipulation of images is a fundamental artistic technique, which Claudian shares with every literary genre. At a simple but by no means unimportant level, these pictures contribute immensely to the liveliness and general interest of the invective. They indelibly establish Claudian's identification of Eutropius as a limited, alien, repulsive being: he is a eunuch, with all the unattractive qualities that castration entails. This is the central theme of Claudian's attack on him, especially in book 1. The figure of the eunuch makes an irreconcilable antithesis with all the honors Eutropius achieves. Creating a vivid sensory impression that will remain in the audience's mind is the imagery's most important task. An example of its effect, with supporting details further elaborated, is given by the contrast of the slavish, effeminate, shameless, sagging, filthy, whining, bibulous eunuch's impersonation of a triumphator. Other pictures directly illustrate specific claims: for example, the contest of Eutropius's masters to drive him from their homes demonstrates actively how undesirable he was as a slave. Some series of images effect a more general commentary. The omens cataloged in the opening lines, with their reminiscences of Lucan, set a horrific mood for the introduction of Eutropius. The revulsion reflects onto him. Scenes of his slavery demonstrate the debasement of his position, and by their vividness fix it as the norm of his character. When Eutropius is finally "freed by contempt" (1.132), the progression of images from his actual infertility to the death that should have disposed of him permanently both advances and interprets events. He remains a "dead body, so many times up for sale" (*totiens venale cadaver*) as he enters imperial service (1.147).

ii. Feminine Motifs

The final image of Eutropius's triumph in book 1 is of a "parched mother-in-law" (*arida socrus*) who travels a long way to see her daughter-in-law and scarcely gets there when she starts demanding wine. The incongruous and gruesomely ludicrous sensory details of the triumph are summarized in a single petty scene of comic low life that conclusively, derisively erases the military victory that Eutropius was celebrating. In the feminine, domestic context to which Claudian translates his scene, glory has no part.

46. Jul *Or.* 1.48C, 2.98D: "effeminate purple"; cf. Claud. *Ruf.* 2.343–47.

47. Amm. 26.6.15 for the crowning *purpureum pannulum*, but surrounding sections more generally. I discuss the manipulation of imperial imagery in proclamation scenes in my paper "The Emperor's New Beard," *Thirteenth Annual Byzantine Studies Conference: Abstracts of Papers*, 1987 (distributed by Dumbarton Oaks, Washington, D.C.).

Any androcentric culture would find emasculation a natural invective tac-
tic.⁴⁸ It demeans the victim because it denies him any capacity for exercising
the masculine virtues according to which he could be esteemed. The scene of
Eutropius's castration literally emasculates him at the beginning of his invective biography. His castration physically effeminized him in fact. And this
physical feminization afforded Claudian many opportunities for literary attack. Eutropius began his career, Claudian claims, as a catamite (1.61–77).
Pathic homosexuality so obviously puts a man in a feminine position, and so
obviously degrades him, to ancient ways of thinking, and so often was charged
in ancient political invective, that already Aristophanes in *Ecclesiazusae* can
turn the conceit on its head with Praxagora's argument that since the best
speakers are the most pathic, women are naturally equipped to address the
Ecclesia.⁴⁹ Cicero accuses numerous opponents of having had older lovers in
boyhood;⁵⁰ Clodius he even claims continues to perform pathically as an
adult.⁵¹ As I have noted, no holds were barred in the political invective of
democratic Athens and republican Rome, whereas attacks of the late empire
stuck closer to the political issue itself; even the *Panegyrici Latini* do not make
this accusation against the usurpers they revile.⁵² But Libanius's invective

48. On classical Athenian views of feminine characteristics, e.g., Dover 1974, 98–102.
Eva C. Keuls, *The Reign of the Phallus: Sexual Politics in Ancient Athens* (New York:
Harper and Row, 1985), argued that Athenian culture systematically enforced male
sexual dominance both literally and as a metaphor for broader social interaction;
reviewers have found individual claims overstated or sloppily supported, but upheld
the value of Keuls's central thesis (e.g., T. Marsh, *Helios* 12, 2 [1986]: 163–69; H. A.
Shapiro, *AJA* 90 [1986]: 361–63). Richlin proposed a Priapic model for the world view
represented by Roman satire ([1983] 1992, esp. 57–63); for commentary see now the
introduction to her second edition, esp. 1992, xvi–xviii. See too "*Mollitia*: Reading the
Body" in Edwards 1993, 63–97, for discussion and further references.
49. Ar. *Eccl.* 112–14, πλεῖστα σποδοῦνται, "they are banged the most"; cf. 228,
βινούμεναι χαίρουσιν ὥσπερ καὶ πρὸ τοῦ, "they love to be fucked, just like before
now, too" (here the crucial claim is that women will govern well because they are
consistent). Cf. *Nub.* 1089–94; etc.
50. Cic. *Verr.* 2.1.32–33; 2.3.159–62 (Verres' son); *Red. Sen.* 11; *Dom.* 126; *Sest.* 18
(Gabinius), 110 (Gellius); *Har. Resp.* 42, 59 (Clodius); *Phil.* 2.3, 44–46, 86; 3.15; 13.17
(Antony). Ps.-Cic. *Inv. Sal.* 21 uses the same term *paelex*, "mistress," which Claudian
calls Eutropius at *Eutr.* 1.62. Cf. Richlin [1983] 1992, 97–98; Ramsay MacMullen, "Roman Attitudes to Greek Love," *Historia* 31 (1982): 484–502 = MacMullen 1990, 177–89
= Dynes and Donaldson 1992, 340–58.
51. Cic. *Har. Resp.* 42; *Pis.* 65. Cf. Richlin [1983] 1992, 98.
52. Barbara Saylor Rodgers suggests to me that *Pan. Lat.* 12[9].4.3–4 (discussed in
Chap. 3.III) could be read with overtones of the licentiousness and deformity assigned
to eunuchs, if *ille Maximiani suppositus tu Constantii Pii filius* be taken to impute
pathic sexuality to Maxentius; but since Maxentius and Constantine are contrasted
particularly as sons and *supponere* commonly refers to substitution of an alien in the

against Philip confirms the natural expectation that pathic homosexuality lost none of its negative connotations in the later empire (Lib. *Prog.* 9.3.4). The fact that throughout time it was notoriously a service of castrated slaves adds social to sexual degradation.[53]

But Claudian does not allege simply that Eutropius was pathically homosexual as a slave. He makes the whole of Eutropius's slave career into a history of rejections. Thus Eutropius, having been a dubious purchase,[54] first appears in slavery as a discarded catamite. Among the innumerable owners through whose hands Eutropius passed in rapid succession, Claudian declares the *miles stabuli* Ptolemaeus "relatively well known. Fatigued by long use of his mistress [*paelicis*], he passes him on to Arinthaeus" (1.60–63). Despite *longo usu*, Ptolemaeus passes in and out of active participation in the poem only slightly less instantly than the hordes of unnamed masters.

Eutropius laments the callous "divorce" in a hilarious burlesque of the deserted woman of elegy and epyllion.[55] The disparity between the clichés he invokes and his own unloveliness highlight his desperation and erotic unsuitability; the experience of frustration mocks him generally. He is petty and incompetent, even in the already debased role of a homosexual "mistress." "Was this, Ptolemaeus, this your faithfulness?" he begins with melodramatic anguish (*haec erat, haec, Ptolemaee, fides?* 1.66). In its repetition, apostrophe, and accusations of perfidy, the outburst recalls Catullus's Ariadne: "Have you left me thus, faithless man, carried from my father's altars, faithless Theseus, on a deserted shore?" (*sicine me patriis avectam, perfide, ab aris, perfide, deserto liquisti in litore, Theseu?*).[56] Ovid's *Heroides* are a catalog of forsaken women,

---

place of a legitimate baby, not to sexual submission (cf. Lewis and Short, *OLD* s.v., and Pacatus's parallel slur on Maximus, *Pan. Lat.* 2[12].31.1), the suggestion must be remote. Tyrants are reviled for active sexual debauchery, e.g., *Pan. Lat.* 4[10].8.3, Lact. *Mort. Pers.* 8.5, *HA Car.* 16.1; cf. Moreau 1954, 2.253.

53. Guyot 1980, 59–63; cf. Mark Golden, "Slavery and Homosexuality at Athens," *Phoenix* 38 (1984): 308–24 = Dynes and Donaldson 1992, 162–78, on how pederastic relationships among Athenian citizen males evaded servile associations.

54. The scene of Eutropius on display (*Eutr.* 1.35–36) may recall Horace's satirical advice to shop for a sexual partner at brothels rather than among matrons, whose clothes cover their bad points (Hor. *Serm.* 1.2.80–95), although there are no close verbal echoes. Cf. Halperin 1990, 92–93 and n. 44, on the similar theme of Xenarchus fr. 4.

55. Another parodic homosexual "divorce" and overblown reaction, mocking conventions of the novel, is to be found in Petron. 79–81: cf. E. Courtney, "Parody and Literary Allusion in Menippean Satire," *Philologus* 106 (1962): 86–100, esp. 93–94, 97. Opelt 1965, 33–38, discussed words women call their abandoners (she referred also to H. Hross, *Die Klagen der verlassenen Heroiden in der lateinischen Literatur*, diss., Munich, 1958).

56. Cat. 64.132–33. Birt 1892, 76, and Fargues, *Invectives* 44 ad loc., compared Clau-

and like most of them Eutropius calls upon his past bonds with the abandoner. His however are limited to sexual service. And where Ovid's Ariadne, for example, excites pathos from the bed that no longer holds Theseus with her (Ov. *Her.* 10.7–16, 51–58), the bed on which Eutropius calls is so placed as to evoke laughter: "Was this the profit of my youth spent in your bosom, and the conjugal bed [*lectusque iugalis*], and sleep so often spent between the horses' stalls [*inter praesepia*]?"

The real nature of Ptolemaeus's office, "soldier of the stable," is debated. Maurice Platnauer emphasized *stabuli* over *miles* and identified him as "a servant in a public post-house";[57] he used the title *stationarius* for this post, which as Cameron pointed out designates rather a local police official, "in any event a very humble" one.[58] Cameron preferred to identify Ptolemaeus as a *comes stabuli*, on the grounds that Claudian terms him "better known" among Eutropius's owners and discusses him at length. The more pressing reason for Claudian to devote time to Ptolemaeus is that his duties afforded an opportunity for humorous exploitation; Claudian returns to him, as Cameron also noted, in order to pun on his name and compare Eutropius to Pothinus, eunuch slave to the Ptolemies (1.480).[59] Conceivably, "better known" could overstate a low rank either to inflate it and justify the attention devoted to this episode, or ironically to emphasize the lowliness of Eutropius's owners. On the other hand, the jokes read more easily, particularly before Claudian's Western audience, if Ptolemaeus was a prominent figure. He was apparently well enough placed to have connections with the consular Arinthaeus.[60] Cameron's identification is the more likely, *miles* merely avoiding a metrical difficulty. The comic point comes from taking *stabuli* literally and making it concrete.

Beds are one theme of the abandoned heroines; marriage is an even more prominent one, whether it had taken place or merely been promised.[61] Eu-

---

dian's line with Stat. *Theb.* 10.812–13 (not 807), "this was, this, the fearsome hand and sword, which I myself insanely gave" (*haec erat, haec metuenda manus ferrumque, quod amens ipsa dedi*). Though the impassioned repetition is the same, in Statius it belongs to Menoecus's mother lamenting over his suicide; it may add a note of epic burlesque. Possibly Claudian echoes more specifically Propertius's Arethusa (4.3.11), but the reading is corrupt: *haecne marita fides* et pact(a)e iam mihi *noctes* PVo; *et pacat(a)e mihi* FL; *et parce avia* N; *et pactae in savia noctes* Haupt (favored by Fedeli [Stuttgart: Teubner, 1984], though he printed the reading of N and judged the corruption ultimately insoluble); *pactae et mihi gaudia noctis* L. Müller; *et primae praemia noctis* Housmann; *alii alia.*

57. Platnauer 1922, 1.142 n. 1.
58. Alan Cameron 1968a, 401; cf. A. H. M. Jones 1964, 600.
59. For Pothinus, see the prosopography of Guyot 1980, 221–24, no. 83.
60. *PLRE* 1.753, Ptolemaeus 2, concurred; Arinthaeus, *PLRE* 1.102–3.
61. Marriage: Dido (Verg. *Aen.* 4.314–16, 324, 496; Ov. *Her.* 7.31, 69, 167), Penelope

tropius's phrase "the conjugal bed" embraces both ideas (*lectusque iugalis*, 1.67).[62] The promises he charges Ptolemaeus with breaking, however, were to free him. Ovid's Briseis, as a slave mistress closely analogous to Eutropius, begs Achilles to keep her as a slave if not a mistress, if only he will keep her with him (Ov. *Her.* 3.75–82). But Eutropius displays no such devotion.

A more material point in Claudian's indictment is that sex was the only thing Eutropius had to offer. He has no other skill or strength with which he might serve. His many resales constitute the testimony of his masters that they found him worthless. Now Eutropius demonstrates why. He wails (*Eutr.* 1.75–77):

> cum forma dilapsus amor; defloruit oris
> gratia. qua miseri scapulas tutabimur arte?
> qua placeam ratione senex?

> Along with my beauty, love has disintegrated; my features' grace
> has lost its bloom. By what art will my poor self save my shoulders?
> On what account may I please in old age?

He faces the same disaster as the wife loved for her beauty in Juvenal's *Satire* 6: "let three wrinkles come up and her skin grow dry and loose, let her teeth get dark and her eyes less great," and her husband will turn her out of the house (Juv. 6.144–46).

Eutropius lacks the other resources on which such women could rely, as he says (*Eutr.* 1.71–74):

> generis pro sors durissima nostri!
> femina, cum senuit, retinet conubia partu,
> uxorisque decus matris reverentia pensat.
> nos Lucina fugit, nec pignore nitimur ullo.

> The hard lot of our kind!
> A woman, when she ages, retains her marriage by childbirth,
> and reverence for the mother pays out the honor of the wife.
> Lucina flies us, and we are not supported by any pledge.

This complaint follows closely Juvenal's complacent observations about the male brides of *Satire* 2: "they are unable to give birth, and by birth to retain

---

(Ov. *Her.* 1.84), Oenone (Ov. *Her.* 5.9–12, 80–88, 108, 133), Hypsipyle (Ov. *Her.* 6.41–46), Hermione (Ov. *Her.* 8.17–42, 101), Deianira (Ov. *Her.* 9.27–35), Medea (Ov. *Her.* 12.162, 192), Arethusa (Prop. 4.3.11–16, 49–50). Promises: Ariadne (Cat. 64.139–48; Ov. *Her.* 10.116–18), Phyllis (Ov. *Her.* 2.31–44).

62. As Birt noted (1892, 76), Dido includes "the conjugal bed" among the items to be included in the courtyard pyre that will destroy her love for Aeneas, Verg. *Aen.* 4.496.

their husbands" (*nequeant parere et partu retinere maritos*, Juv. 2.138). Claudian's *retinet conubia partu* varies Juvenal's phrase only superficially.[63] Both authors make the same point, that the catamite's biological incapacity makes him inferior to women. But in referring to "our kind" Claudian treats Eutropius's castration as dictating his sexual role and consequent devaluation;[64] moreover, he explicitly ranks Eutropius below women. "And indeed, if a woman assumed the celebrated fasces, it would be less disgraceful" (*esset turpe minus*, 1.320–21). There are queens, goddesses, and priestesses but no corresponding roles for eunuchs (1.321–30).[65] Once more the emphasis falls on the eunuch's lost fertility (1.331–32): "A woman is born for fruitfulness and future offspring; this race was invented that it might serve" (*nascitur ad fructum mulier prolemque futuram: hoc genus inventum est ut serviat*).

Although Claudian uses this comparison and devalues Eutropius against women for sexual unproductiveness, he nevertheless continually identifies Eutropius with female types. After he is discarded as a mistress, he passes on to pandering (1.77–97). Claudian declares him "scarcely otherwise" than the proverbially infamous Lais, who, when she can no longer draw lovers of her own, "stands nonetheless. She plays the bawd and girdles other handmaids, and although long-lived, circles the brothel she has long loved; her habits keep the thing her age has lost."

The identification places Eutropius in a long line of sexually desperate repulsive old women derided by ancient poets. In *Ecclesiazusae* three successively more horrible hags battle over the young man to whom a new political dispensation gives them a right (Ar. *Eccl.* 977–1111).[66] An old woman in *Plutus* complains that her gigolo will no longer serve her (Ar. *Plut.* 959–1096). Various nurses in Greek and Roman New Comedy lament their lost youth, drink, and advise their charges to extract from their lovers as much as they can while the

63. Birt 1888, 53, connected Juv. 2.138 to *Eutr.* 1.224, *numquam mater eris, numquam pater* ("you will never be a mother, never a father"). G. B. A. Fletcher, "Imitationes vel loci similes in poetis Latinis," *Mnemosyne* 3rd ser. 1 (1933–34): 198, linked *Eutr.* 1.72 and Juv. 2.138 as I do.

64. *Generis* refers to eunuchs as a class: cf. *Eutr.* 1.332, 415. At no point does Eutropius regret anything that he has done, so he does not truly resemble "an old woman grieving over her misused past" (Christiansen 1969, 94); if he did, he would be displaying a redeeming touch of decency, however tardy. Claudian does not allow such a thing.

65. Claudian here ignores the Galli of Cybele, to whom he refers at *Eutr.* 1.280. The Galli should have been postpuberal castrates, not eunuchs strictly defined (cf. Rousselle 1988, 121–28), but Claudian does not make the distinction. Barbara Saylor Rodgers kindly calls to my attention two passages of which Claudian betrays no awareness, an ironic protest at eunuch-rule in Persia, Ruf. *Hist. Alex.* 10.1.37, and a serious assertion at Plin. *NH* 13.9.41.

66. Jeffrey Henderson, "Older Women in Attic Old Comedy," *TAPA* 117 (1987): 105–29, surveyed "Satirical Images," 117–20.

getting is good; the model is perpetuated in erotic elegy.[67] Horace in the *Odes* threatens unyielding women by forecasting lonely decrepitude[68] and in the *Epodes* rejects decrepit old women who woo him.[69] His gruesome portraits have counterparts in Petronius, the *Priapea*, and the Vergilian Appendix.[70] These awful women and their eternal frustration perennially fueled scornful laughter. Casting Eutropius as a whore who refuses to retire reinforces the invective implications of his divorcée's lament. If sexual submission is demeaning under any circumstances, Eutropius's desire reveals even greater depravity.[71] The analogy of Lais suggests that he wants it personally, not just as an alternative to being beaten; the fear he shows in his lament admits that he is worthless in other servile capacities. Finally, both roles show Eutropius frustrated. He is not good enough at the thing he wants to do to be able to retain it. Frustration is risible. It also condemns.

In Lais's lingering in the brothel and Eutropius's prolonged involvement with socially disapproved sexuality, Claudian may also have thought of Juvenal's Messalina: she too, in an unforgettably lurid description, haunts a brothel overlong and still cannot satisfy her lust (Juv. 6.114–32).[72] Her extremity of desire and the lengths to which it drives her make her more profoundly horrible than the frantic crones. They can always be rejected, but with what she insatiably takes she contaminates the palace. Eutropius too in his future position of imperial minister will stain the palace, but in this immediate context vicarious immorality achieves a compromise with his postsexual condition. The threatening lusts that old women can represent are neutralized. The comparison merely diminishes him. His proclivities are unchanged, but he can no longer indulge them himself. On the other hand, his talents for pandering continue to reveal his essential depravity. "His mind was not slow to the craft, and was capable of his duty" apes high praise, until it is revealed that the art

---

67. E.g., Plaut. *Most.* 157–292; Ov. *Am.* 1.8; Prop. 4.5.

68. E.g., Hor. *Carm.* 3.10, fulfilled in 4.13. Birt 1892, 77, and Fargues, *Invectives* 47, compared the first lines of Hor. *Carm.* 1.25, *parcius iunctas quatiunt fenestras / iactibus crebris iuvenes protervi* ("more seldom do bold youths shake your closed windows with frequent blows") with *Eutr.* 1.92–93, *iam turba procax noctisque recedit / ambitus et raro pulsatur ianua tactu* ("already does the importunate crowd and night's sollicitation fall away, and the door is beaten with a rare touch"). Erotic elegy uses similar images, e.g., Prop. 3.25.11–18 (= 3.24.31–38, reading 3.25 as continuing 3.24: cf. A. LaPenna, "Marginalia," *Maia* 79 [1955]: 134–35).

69. Hor. *Epod.* 8, 12. See discussion of Richlin [1983] 1992, 109–13 and 284.

70. E.g., Petron. 134–38; *Pr.* 57; *Verg. App.* 83 Bücheler, pp. 151–53 Oxford, lines 26–37; cf. Richlin [1983] 1992, 113–16.

71. Richlin [1983] 1992 discussed the general principle in numerous connections, esp. 57–80. Cicero abuses Antony for desire at *Phil.* 2.45, adding a financial incentive which also demeans, but in a different way.

72. Cf. Richlin [1983] 1992, 106–8.

and duty consist of "plotting against chastity" (*nec segnis ad artem mens erat officiique capax omnesque pudoris hauserat insidias*, 1.78–80).[73] Fargues showed that the specific techniques Eutropius practices against chastity echo commonplaces of erotic elegy.[74]

Claudian contrasts Eutropius's skill with the proper role of eunuchs (1.98–100):

> hinc honor Eutropio; cumque omnibus unica virtus[75]
> esset in eunuchis thalamos servare pudicos,
> solus adulteriis crevit.

> From here Eutropius wins honor. When the single virtue among
> all eunuchs is to keep bedchambers chaste,
> he alone grew on adulteries.

Even as a eunuch, Eutropius is an incongruous prodigy. But Claudian no sooner makes this point than he begins to depict a loss of ability in pandering too. Eutropius's master grows hot with anger when his lust is frustrated, and beats him. Eutropius has indeed fallen to the fate he anticipated when he was cast off as a mistress. Again he fails in degrading duties.

He assumes another female role when his old master fobs him off on a new son-in-law as nurse to the bride. Now, ironically, he fills the position that was just described as typical for a eunuch: he has finally become safe for it. Even though hairdressing was conventionally associated with pandering,[76] Eutropius combs his mistress's hair without incident. His duty of holding a basin of water for her, naked while she is washing, parades the annihilation of his sexuality (1.104–7). Claudian completes the process of decay with a general physical description. His imagery advances to death when Eutropius is set free, as I have discussed.

It is as a female fox that Eutropius goes to ground in the palace (*vetulam vulpem*, 1.145), and when he emerges from civil administration into the full daylight of martial endeavor it is as an "Amazonian crone" (*anus Amazon*, 1.240).[77] The enemy is delighted to see that "men are lacking" (*desse viros*,

---

73. Compare Cicero's censures on Verres' freedman Timarchides, *Verr.* 2.2.134–36.

74. Fargues, *Invectives* 46. Ovid gleefully assembles clichés in *Ars Amatoria* (Fargues cited particularly *AA* 1.605–6); cf. Tib. 1.2.94.

75. Birt 1892, 78, and Fargues, *Invectives* 47, suggested that Claudian took *unica virtus* from Juv. 8.20 on the relative worthlessness of family titles and statues. In Juvenal, however, as Courtney 1980, 388, said, "*virtus* is the subject, *nobilitas sola atque unica* the predicate."

76. See note 30.

77. In Book 2 Aurora says Eutropius at first enjoyed strictly private influence within the palace and gradually consolidated his power before invading civil administration,

1.243); devastation ensues. Here the feminization of Eutropius functions simply. Since he is not a man, he cannot possess masculine military virtue. Therefore he cannot achieve victory, though as a shameless "slave and effeminate" he presumes to claim it (1.252; discussed under "Graphic Images").

When Eutropius does claim victory, Claudian snidely compares him to "a dried-up mother-in-law going to see her distant daughter-in-law: scarcely has she sat down exhausted and already she seeks wines" (*arida socrus, lassa, iam vina petit*, 1.269–71). In the clichéd whininess of old women, Eutropius's exertions are diminished and his victory is obscured. Female bibulousness is a recurrent joke in ancient literature. Depending on context, drinking betokens indulgence or cupidity, but also through Dionysian associations fertility and growth.[78] Thus tippling was sometimes associated particularly with old women, in substitution for their perished sexuality.[79] Claudian evokes this aspect through the adjective "dried-up," which recalls the blighted cornfield of Eutropius's scalp (1.116).[80] The "clear liquid" borne by Eutropius so that his bride-mistress may bathe, as he stands naked and excluded, similarly emblematizes the youthfulness and fertility of her sexuality against the age and aridity of his expired, perverse sexuality. A mother-in-law has resigned her sexual function to the next generation. But this one attends not to the future fertility of her family, only to her own irremediable dryness. Liquid imagery relates the passage, which conspicuously emasculates the victory by substituting a female domestic context, to Eutropius's absolute sexual incapacity. His infertility degrades him even below women.

Eutropius's campaign against the Huns is recalled when in book 2 he summons the Eastern courtiers to discuss another barbarian outbreak, the revolt of the Gruthungian Gothic *laeti* under Tribigild. The courtiers immediately begin to quarrel about the theater. Eutropius insists that more serious business is

---

and she relates his military incompetence to Tribigild's rebellion (*Eutr.* 2.553–83). But in keeping with the topical, timeless emphasis of formal invective, in book 1 Claudian puts Eutropius on the judicial throne at once; he proceeds from there to generalship against the Huns (glanced over in book 2, when Eutropius begs off from serving against Tribigild, 2.367) and then the consulate.

78. E.g., Ar. *Lys.* 195–239, *Thesm.* 628–32, 730–59, *Eccl.* 153–59, 227; Aristophanic men drink too, for the same reasons, e.g., *Ach.* 1190–1233. Compare discussion of Kenneth J. Reckford, *Aristophanes' Old-and-New Comedy*, Vol. 1, *Six Essays in Perspective* (Chapel Hill: University of North Carolina Press, 1987), 109–12.

79. E.g., Ov. *Am.* 1.8; Prop. 4.5.

80. This reminiscence is more straightforward than the obviously fertile *aridis aristis* of Cat. 48.5, which Birt 1892, 78 cited ad loc. (Catullus wants more abundant kisses; he uses the adjective to play on the paradoxical ancient etymology of *arista*: see David O. Ross, Jr., *Virgil's Elements: Physics and Poetry in the Georgics* [Princeton, N.J.: Princeton University Press, 1987], 35–36).

at hand. His words recall the Sibyl's rebuke to Aeneas at the gates of Daedalus: "the time demands not these spectacles."[81] The echo sets the tone for the epic parody of the scene, as *spectacula* is transferred from the poignant mythological autobiography of Daedalus on the epical gates to the implicitly tawdry Tereus and Agave of the contemporary stage. If a more popular image of the Sibyl may also be read into the echo, it again puts Eutropius in the role of an exhausted, postsexual woman. Petronius's Trimalchio, for instance, says that he saw the Sibyl so shriveled with age that she lived in a bottle and wished only to die (Petron. 48).[82]

Eutropius excuses himself because of the fatigues of Armenia. "Let them pardon an old man, let them send young men to battles."[83] The refusal parallels Tacitus's account of Tiberius refusing to take the field himself against the revolt of Florus and Sacrovir, on the grounds that having won significant triumphs "in youth," he did not need to seek a vain one "now as an older man" (Tac. *Ann.* 3.47.4). Now Eutropius takes on the guise of a malignant ruler of literary tradition.[84] It reinforces his Domitianic, antiheroic position in the council, as it is modeled on Juvenal's *Satire* 4.

The conspicuous model of Juvenal gives both setting and emphasis to Claudian's points about the irresponsibility of Eutropius and of his council; I shall discuss the scene in greater detail in the next section. The refusal itself bears the literary overtones I have just mentioned, and their subtle effects, but also directly asserts that Eutropius cannot perform the role he has assumed. Armenia is evoked so vaguely as to seem remote beyond relevance.

Eutropius's past military success recedes even further from awareness when

---

81. *non haec spectacula tempus poscere, Eutr.* 2.365–66; cf. Verg. *Aen.* 6.37, *non hoc ista sibi tempus spectacula poscit.* Noted by Birt 1892, 109; Fargues, *Invectives* 121; Andrews 1931, 116.

82. *Eutr.* 2pr.38 calls Eutropius "blind Sibyl," alluding to Theodosius's having sent him to consult the Egyptian monk John for prophecy about the war against Eugenius (cf. Soz. 7.22.7–8).

83. *Ignoscant senio, iuvenes ad proelia mittant, Eutr.* 2.369. *Senio* and *iuvenes* have meaning in their ordinary senses, but they may also reflect a technical distinction, traditionally made by Servius Tullius, between older citizens who were exempt from military service and younger men who were still eligible: Cic. *Rep.* 2.39; Liv. 1.43.1–2. As Roger Tomlin, "*Seniores - Iuniores* in the Late-Roman Field Army," *AJPh* 93 (1972): 262, remarked, this distinction is not to be confused with that between the "senior" and "junior" units of the late Roman field army.

84. Tac. *Ann.* 3.47.4 runs in full: *igitur secutae Caesaris litterae, quibus se non tam vacuum gloria praedicabat, ut post ferocissimas gentes perdomitas, tot receptos in iuventa aut spretos triumphos iam senior peregrinationis suburbanae inane praemium peteret.* I do not mean to suggest a specific verbal echo, but a parallelism of behavior. On Claudian's knowledge of Roman historiography, see Alan Cameron 1970, 331–43 (334–37, 346–47 on Tacitus specifically); cf. Stoecker 1889 (for the minutest possible echoes; 83–97 on Tacitus).

Claudian compares him and the sorry assembly to "a hated nurse" and "im-
poverished girls," whom "she besets and hoarsely warns to seek their feed in
common from the loom. They beg to relax on festal days, to put aside their
chores and see girls their own age. Angered at the work they mess the yarns
with thumb already tired and wipe off their tender weeping with the thread"
(2.370–75).[85] As before, the simile obscures legitimate martial concerns behind
a petty domestic screen. Rendering the participants as women reduces the
scope of their concerns, trivializing them against the harsh irony that Phrygia
may be lost by their inaction. At the same time, Claudian declares that even
Eutropius's own cronies hate him. The nurse's carping bears out and fixes the
assertion. The frivolousness of the courtiers is established at the beginning of
the passage, as they assemble; the more pitiful image here does not cancel out
the earlier criticism of them, but refocuses it so as to make an extra point
against Eutropius.

Claudian applies feminine motifs to Eutropius for several related effects. At
a basic level, he thus exploits Eutropius's ambiguous sexual condition: he is
degraded directly by his sexual submission, and further by the burlesque of
erotic commonplaces that ensues. Eutropius becomes ridiculous, as well as
contemptible, as he wallows about in a role for which his sexual performance
otherwise qualifies him. He falls far short of female standards. Claudian makes
the same contrast more directly in passages that compare his consulate with
the prospect of a woman's (1.320–45). Just as even a workhouse slave would be
a more fitting consul, if only he were a man or had had just one master (1.26–
31), so even a woman is better equipped than Eutropius. At the same time, the
specific female roles in which Eutropius is cast also denigrate him by their
identification: he is a castoff mistress, an impotent whore, a sexless nurse, a
bibulous mother-in-law, an overaged Amazon, and a hated taskmistress. He is
marginalized, and no longer capable of the one thing for which he was ever
suited. Many other criticisms attach to these unfavorable portraits.

I have already discussed a different kind of emasculating motif used commonly in late antique literature, that of wifely instigation (Chapter 3.III).
Claudian uses it indirectly against Eutropius through the figure of Bellona. *In
Eutropium* 2 dramatically suggests that Eutropius provoked Tribigild's revolt
and now cannot handle the crisis. Therefore Bellona's nagging fits into an
argument ultimately attacking Eutropius's government, even though it reflects
immediately on Tribigild. The base greed with which she inspires him adds
insult to the injury of his attack, deepening the criticism. Some of the encour-

85. Marilyn Skinner has suggested to me that Claudian may draw the image from
Erinna's *Distaff*, since Erinna says that she stood at the loom fearing her mother (cf. *AP*
9.190.5; generally, Averil Cameron and Alan Cameron, "Erinna's Distaff," *CQ* n.s. 19
[1969]: 285–88); Fargues, *Invectives* 121, credited it to Claudian's imagination.

agement she offers reiterates emasculating slanders Claudian uses against Eutropius with reference to his Hunnic campaign in book 1 (2.222–25):

> bella dabunt socios. nec te tam prona monerem,
> si contra paterere viros: nunc alter in armis
> sexus et eunuchis se defensoribus orbis
> credidit; hos aquilae Romanaque signa secuntur.

> Wars will give allies. And I would not be so inclined to advise you,
> if you were exposing yourself against men: now the other sex[86]
> is in arms and the world has entrusted itself to eunuch
> defenders. Them do the eagles and Roman signals follow.

Once more Eutropius's literal sexual emasculation is used to deny him prowess in the masculine field of war.

A variant form of wifely instigation metaphorically emasculates Eutropius when Claudian claims that he depends for his position on women. His fall from power is summarized (*Eutr.* 2pr.21–24):

> mollis feminea detruditur arce tyrannus
>   et thalamo pulsus perdidit imperium.
> sic iuvenis nutante fide veterique reducta
>   paelice defletam linquit amica domum.

> The effeminate tyrant is thrust from his womanly citadel
>   and, driven from the bedchamber, has lost his empire.
> Thus when a youth's faithfulness nods and an old mistress
>   is recalled, his girlfriend weeps and leaves the home.

Just as Eutropius himself was literally cast off as a homosexual "mistress" when he was a private slave (1.62), now as a simile the image describes his rejection from power in the empire. The technique of degradation by identification with female figures has already been discussed. The lofty language of "thrust forth," "citadel," "tyrant," and "empire" is undercut by "effeminate," "womanly," and "bedchamber," so that it appears to exaggerate events that are really petty. Eutropius is also forced to "mollify angered daughters-in-law" (2pr.28). Philostorgius and Sozomen say the empress Eudoxia demanded that Eutropius be dismissed;[87] since it was Eutropius who arranged for Arcadius to marry her (Zos. 5.3) and since Claudian can exploit Eutropius's title of *patricius* to call him Arcadius's father (2pr.49–50), she corresponds to the angry daughters-in-

---

86. "Exposing yourself against men" may have obscene overtones, cf. *Eutr.* 1.363; "the other sex" probably means "women," derisively applied to eunuchs rather than designating them directly, cf. *Eutr.* 1.467.

87. Philost. *HE* 11.6, 136.1–18 Bidez and Winkelmann; Soz. 8.7.3.

law of whom Claudian uses a generalizing plural. If Eutropius could be brought down by a domestic squabble, as the feminine reference implies, then it is implied that equally trivial causes supported him.

In book 1 Eutropius testifies that he has exhausted himself against the Huns "with trembling voice, calling on his sister" (1.263). A eunuch's voice is a conspicuous abnormality.[88] It is hard to tell what significance Eutropius's sister might have had for the audience of his triumph, yet evidently he invoked her in his speech. The fact that Claudian could rely on so glancing an allusion to carry meaning, the only time he mentions this sister in book 1, suggests that she was real and generally known in the West. Unfortunately her true relationship to Eutropius is lost. She may have been literally his sister, though continued contact is difficult to reconcile with the innumerable resales that Claudian claims for Eutropius.

Alternatively, Eutropius's "sister" may have been a *subintroducta,* a woman brought into his household in a chaste union sometimes compared to sisterhood. Such unions could give the appearance of scandal, and were continually attacked by church fathers.[89] Manifestly, the practice was not eradicated. Justin Martyr in the middle of the second century reports that a Christian petitioned the prefect Felix to be castrated, "in the interests of persuading you that unrestrained fornication does not exist in our mysteries" (Just. *Apol.* 29.2); Peter Brown related this petition to the Christian "sisters."[90] This pattern of innuendo against *subintroductae* may help explain Claudian's surprising allegation that the emasculated Eutropius maintains an incestuous relationship with "his sister and, if portents are believed at all, his wife" (*soror et, si quid portentis creditur, uxor,* 2.88). As Birt and Fargues pointed out, Claudian's collocation of "sister" and "wife" suggests Juno's exalted role, *et soror et coniunx* (e.g., Verg. *Aen.* 1.47);[91] yet an ironical literary reminiscence neither strengthens nor weak-

---

88. Cf. *Eutr.* 1.261, 340; 2pr.28; e.g., Lucian, *Eun.* 7, 10.

89. The practice is attested from the second century on: see Edmund Venables, "Subintroductae," *A Dictionary of Christian Antiquities,* ed. William Smith and Samuel Cheetham, 2 vols. (Hartford: J. B. Burr, 1880; rpt. New York: Kraus Reprint Co., 1968), 2.1939–41; H. Achelis, "Subintroductae," *Realencyklopädie für protestantische Theologie und Kirche* (Leipzig: J. C. Hinrichs, 1907), 19.123–27. Hostile testimony around the period of Eutropius includes John Chrysostom's *Contra eos qui subintroductas habent* (which J. Dumortier dated ca. 382: "La date des deux traités de saint Jean Chrysostome aux moines et aux vierges (P.G. 47. 495–514. 513–532)," *Mél. sci. rel.* 6 [1949]: 247–52), and *CTh* 16.2.44 of 420 (issued in the West).

90. Brown 1988, 140; Felix is presumably L. Munatius Felix, prefect of Egypt from 150 to 154: *PIR*[2] 5, 2 no. 723, 315–16.

91. Birt 1892, 99, and Fargues, *Invectives* 99. A. E. Housman observed that in Mart. 12.20, obscene overtones reside in the verb "have," not in "sister" ("Why, you ask, Fabullus, does Themison not have a wife? He has his sister"; "Corrections and Explana-

ens the case for a historical identification. If Eutropius's sister can be identified as a *subintroducta*, it also suggests that Justin's man would have failed to squelch rumor by having himself castrated. In any case, Felix refused the petition (Just. *1Apol.* 29.3).

Claudian claims in book 2 that Eutropius's incestuous sister plays the role of a "chaste wife" by entertaining matrons at banquets and "celebrating the vows of her eunuch husband." He loves her, consults with her about the most important matters of state and entrusts to her his palace duties while he revels drunkenly and buys popular applause with largesse of other people's money (2.84–94). In short, he relies on her both to represent him socially and to do his real work; his dependency is of the same type as Typhos's on his wife in Synesius's *De Providentia.* It diminishes him in the same way.

When Claudian speaks of Eutropius's fall in the preface, he maliciously asks whether his sister will follow him into exile or if she now spurns him (2pr.41–44). Synesius claims that Typhos's allies desert him too (Synes. *Prov.* 122D–123A); he follows the pattern of the myth he is adapting to political purpose (cf. Plut. *DIO* 358D), but he also implies that the erstwhile supporters of his victim had felt no sincere regard for him. Eutropius's sister and daughter-in-law are no less fickle. In turn their disloyalty damns Eutropius.

III. Class, Corruption, and Competence

The relations between a minister and his colleagues and subordinates reflect in certain aspects the honesty and effectiveness with which he governs. The fact that Cleon "stole Pylos" from Demosthenes does not immediately affect the Athenian people's profit from the victory, but it does suggest that Cleon is equally ready to cheat them to his own advantage (Ar. *Eq.* 1191–1225). Cicero says that Verres openly dunned the Sicilian censors he appointed for large contributions toward a statue of himself; if they are supposed to be expressing gratitude in this way, he argues, it confirms that the offices they begged or rather bought were not conferred according to public interest (Cic. *Verr.* 2.2.137). Catullus complains metaphorically that Memmius irrumated him, and that Piso has treated Veranius and Fabullus no better (Cat. 28). Synesius claims that at the desperate last gasp of his tyranny Typhos extorted not only taxes from the people but also "a second round of contributions even from his underlings" (Synes. *Prov.* 121D). Eutropius's underlings, including his sister, figure most extensively in book 2, and Tribigild is driven to revolt in large part because of Eutropius's mismanagement (n.b. 2.177–92); but book 1 also treats administrative failings.

---

tions of Martial," *JPh* 30 [1907]: 260 = *The Classical Papers of A. E. Housman,* ed. J. Diggle and F. R. Goodyear [Cambridge: Cambridge University Press, 1972], 2.734–35).

A considerable section depicts misdeeds in peace (1.151–228). Themes of avarice and cruelty intertwine to unite it. The first victim of the new regime[92] was Abundantius, whom Claudian credits with promoting Eutropius into palace service. As he puts it, Abundantius "produced the bane of Eastern affairs, and first his own" (1.154–55). He likens him to Thrasius, the seer who advised Busiris to sacrifice strangers to Zeus and was the first to be sacrificed, and to Perillus, who built Phalaris's bull and was its first victim;[93] Eutropius is implicitly identified with these archetypal monsters of cruelty. Moreover, Eutropius confiscated Abundantius's property. He rages on against vaguely identified but apparently numerous aristocrats.[94] Claudian declares that the arriviste is always most harsh, because he thinks thereby to assert his power: "he strikes all while he fears all" (1.182).[95] But worst of all is the slave "raging against free backs: he knows the groans and knows not how to spare the punishment that he underwent. Remembering his master, he hates the one he beats. Add that a eunuch is moved by no devotion, nor does he fear for family or children" (1.183–88).[96] Eutropius's debased origins unfit him for power, not merely stain him by association. And for a eunuch, "[gold] alone his cut-off lust enjoys . . . no force castrates bloody avarice" (1.191–93). "Lust" and enjoyment on the one hand and "cut-off," "castrate," and "bloody" on the other fuse Eutropius's sexual identity with his capacity for administrative abuse. The reprehensible sexuality of Eutropius's greed, implied by the associations of *libido* (1.191), makes this transfer of a eunuch's affections even nastier than that alleged by Ammianus, "riches alone they embrace, as their most delightful little daughters" (*divitias solas ut filiolas iucundissimas amplectuntur*, Amm. 18.5.4).

Claudian moves from this drastic excoriation to lighter burlesque. Sale of offices was an extremely trite charge in late antique political invective, as well as

92. The motif of inaugural crime if not the diction accords with Tacitus's dramatic sense: cf. *Ann.* 1.6.1, 13.1.1.

93. Both stories are known from many sources, any of which Claudian may have used; the chosen pair of examples and *imbuit* inclined Birt 1892, 80, and Fargues, *Invectives* 53, to single out Ov. *AA* 1.645–58 (cf. Andrews 1931, 43–44). Pacatus calls Maximus Phalaris, *Pan. Lat.* 2[12].29.4.

94. The charge is conventional: e.g., *Pan. Lat.* 11[3].5.3 of Carinus; 12[9].3.6, 4.4 and 4[10].8.3, 31.1 of Maxentius; 2[12].24–29 of Maximus (discussed in Chap. 3.III). On the reality of "Judicial Savagery in the Roman Empire," see R. MacMullen, *Chiron* 1986 = 1990, 204–17.

95. Dufraigne 1975, 181 n. 6, compared *Eutr.* 1.181 with Victor's pompous assertion that Diocletian adopted the title *dominus* out of a vainglory belonging to very humble men raised high; Victor hastily concedes that Diocletian ruled benevolently in fact (*Caes.* 39.5–8).

96. Hall 1985 found *generi*, "family," better attested in *Eutr.* 1.188, but some manuscripts give or are corrected to *generis*, "sons-in-law" as opposed to *natis*, "children by birth." The contrast is slightly neater.

a common abuse in fact.[97] It engendered other abuses: governorships especially offered purchasers the chance to recoup by exploiting their provinces.
The problem was not new: Cicero connects purchase of office and exploitation
explicitly, as does Mamertinus in his panegyric of Julian (Cic. *Verr.* 2.2.138, *Pan.
Lat.* 3[11].19.4–5, 21.1). Synesius exclaims that men who purchased governorships from Typhos pressed extortion yet further, even the younger ones ex-
pecting to lay up funds for a dissolute old age (Synes. *Prov.* 111D). Claudian
realizes the conceit pictorially: he describes Eutropius's sales office, complete
with a posted price list. Once more Eutropius is represented in a sordid role,
now a "huckster" (*caupo*, *Eutr.* 1.198). His past slavery figures too: "having been
sold himself, he longs to sell all things" (1.206–7). He brings the whole Eastern
empire down to his own low level.

The price list emblematizes blatant venality. Lest its fixed prices imply any
limit to Eutropius's greed, however, Claudian adds that he "often" entertains
competitive bidding too, balancing sums against one another on hanging
scales: "with the weight the judge inclines, and a province sinks onto the twin
pans" (1.208–9). Claudian's term *iudex* in context bears its broadest sense,
someone called upon to make a decision.[98] He repeats it in its more technical
sense, a magistrate with judicial authority, when he characterizes Eutropius's
consulate as culminating his ambition to pollute everything, "as general the
battle lines, as judge the courts, the epoch as the consul!" (*dux acies, iudex
praetoria, tempora consul,* 1.286). Retrospectively this passage applies the designation to all Eutropius's civilian activities in office, including his persecution
of Abundantius and other nobles, as described in the earlier section. Yet properly speaking, Eutropius should not have been a "judge" at all: the *praepositus
sacri cubiculi* did not possess judicial competence.[99] The misapplied term underlines a usurped authority. Zosimus reports that Eutropius prepared to sit as
assessor to Arcadius in judgment over Timasius, against whom Eutropius had
incited his accuser Bargus (Zos. 5.9.2–3). When the proceeding caused general
offense, Arcadius retired as judge in favor of a fellow general of Timasius and a
relation of the emperor Valens;[100] this reaction suggests that it was less Bargus's

97. E.g., *Ruf.* 1.180; Eunap. fr. 87M = 72.1 Blockley; Zos. 4.28.3–4, 5.1.2; Procop.
Anecd. 22.7–9; cf. A. H. M. Jones 1964, 390–96, with T. D. Barnes, "A Law of Julian," *CP*
69 (1970): 288–91 on *CTh* 2.29.1.

98. *OLD* s.v. 4.

99. Guyot 1980, 140; W. Enßlin, "*Praepositus sacri cubiculi*," *RE* Suppl. 8 (1956): 562;
Dunlap 1924, 200. A partial exception may have been authority over appeals from
within the Eastern crown lands, in Cappadocia: this territory was transferred to the
purview of the *praepositus sacri cubiculi* some time between 390 and 414 (A. H. M. Jones
1964, 425–26), and it suits Eutropius's unique power in office that he should have
instituted the change (Dunlap 1924, 188).

100. Respectively, Flavius Saturninus 10, *PLRE* 1.807–8; Procopius 9, *PLRE* 1.744.
Bargus, *PLRE* 2.210–11. Timasius, *PLRE* 1.914–15.

low rank that roused objection, as Zosimus states, than Eutropius's close, extralegal, and notoriously malicious interest in the case. Zosimus observes almost as a matter of course that just as Eutropius "held supremacy over all the royal apartments, he was the master of all [Arcadius's] verdict." Claudian passes over Eutropius's persecution of Timasius, but all the judicial atrocities he ascribes to Eutropius prompt the same kind of resentment.[101]

In many of his poems Claudian makes use of the idea that the brother emperors of East and West ideally ruled in harmony a united empire; conversely, he charges enemies with encouraging disharmony.[102] Concord, virtue, loyalty, piety, and justice are the blessings sown by Theodosius that make Allecto want to overturn the world (*Ruf.* 1.52–53, 57); stirring up Rufinus, who could divide Theseus from Pirithous, Pylades from Orestes, or Pollux from his brother Castor (*Ruf.* 1.107–8), appears a more effective alternative. Perversely swearing to Arcadius "through your brother's royal splendor," Rufinus claims that Stilicho's campaign against Alaric constitutes a conspiracy of Gaul against himself. He threatens civil mayhem if Arcadius does not block it by recalling the Eastern army.[103] Stilicho loyally obeys, though obedience dooms Greece (*Ruf.* 2.197–219). The army, loyally unified under him, recognizes their division as the true "specter of civil war" (*Ruf.* 2.236; cf. *Stil.* 2.95–97, *Get.* 516–17), which Rufinus has roused, and vows revenge.

In Gildonem plays the proper fraternal unity of Honorius and Arcadius against the fratricidal rivalry of Gildo and Mascezel. The noun "brother" is used fourteen times in the single book, more than in any other work of Claudian.[104] The proem proclaims "the concord of the brothers returns in full," now that Gildo is dead (*Gild.* 4–5). Theodosius the Great, appearing in a dream, rebukes Arcadius for allowing Gildo to engender "discord" between himself and Honorius and Stilicho (*Gild.* 236), so that Arcadius treats his brother worse than an enemy; Arcadius immediately protests affection for "my kinsman Stilicho" and wishes "Africa to return now more secure to my brother" (*Gild.* 323–24).

Among the incentives that should urge Theodorus to accept the consulate,

101. Informal influence: Guyot 1980, 145–57; Hopkins 1978, 172–96.

102. Some of the relevant passages were discussed by Alan Cameron 1970, 51–54 (Gnilka 1977, 34–35, however, stressed the vague and conventional nature of Claudian's wishes for "similar marriage-torches" for Stilicho's younger daughter Thermantia), 97, 102–3, 110–12. The ideal of fraternal harmony among emperors is earlier upheld by, e.g., *Pan. Lat.* 10[2].9, 11[3].7 (Maximian and Diocletian); 3[11].27.5 (Julian's bearing toward Constantius, despite civil war; cf. ibid. 3.1, 5.2, where the term "brother" accentuates Constantius's unfraternal jealousy).

103. *Ruf.* 2.144–68; Theodosius had led the army west against Eugenius in 394 (cf. Socr. *HE* 6.1.4, Soz. *HE* 8.1.3).

104. *Frater* seven times, and *fraternus* once, in Theodosius's and Arcadius's scene alone, *Gild.* 235–324: Christiansen 1988 s.vv. Cf. Olechowska 1978, 8–10.

Iustitia alludes to this restoration of concord on Gildo's defeat when she mentions "Pietas embracing the serene brothers," Perfidia grieving over broken arms, and Fides rejoicing with Pax (*M. Theod.* 166–72).[105] Claudian catalogs Stilicho's services to Arcadius as well as to Honorius in his second book of panegyric for his consulate in 400 (*Stil.* 2.50–99). He praises him for "not ascribing to the youth anything that an unmoving and undutiful throng might dare, using the royal name as a screen for its own madness" (*iners atque impia turba . . . furori, Stil.* 2.79–81). "Undutiful" and "madness" allude to disharmony between the brothers and friction between their parts of the empire,[106] as "discord," "illicit war," "civil arms," "loyalty in the midst of quarrels of rash men at court," and "the veneration of brothers" in the next lines bear out. Hostile courtiers of Arcadius are responsible for the ills of the realm, not Stilicho.

The unity of the emperors was affirmed by monuments acclaiming both emperors for victories won by the generals of either one: even after the defeat of Gildo, for example, Roman inscriptions honor Arcadius as well as Honorius.[107] In the letter in which as *princeps senatus* Symmachus reports the Senate's declaration of war against Gildo on receipt of Honorius's letter about the uprising, he tells Stilicho "you will find that I have observed the justice of this fact too and have urged the cause of public harmony before our lord Arcadius" (*Symm. Ep.* 4.5.3). Participants stressed the idea of concord, exactly while events most strained it. Concord was the rule in lesser and more pacific matters as well. For example, the Senate's request to erect a statue of Claudian officially was granted by both Arcadius and Honorius.[108]

Such gestures indicate that the ideal of imperial unity was strongly asserted.

---

105. Simon 1975, 204–8, gave literary references but did not remark on the historical implications of the personifications and their actions. Pietas obviously embodies the family loyalty of Arcadius and Honorius. Serenity, as Simon noted, was claimed as a peculiar imperial title. Fides and Pax are generalized over the empire. Perfidia attaches to Gildo in conformity with *Gild.*

106. *Impius* ("undutiful" or even "sacrilegious") specifically fraternal, *TLL* 7, 1 s.v. 621.29–36; specifically civil, 622.3–17; cf. generally and s.v. *impietas* (esp. civil, 613.9–16; entries for *pietas, pius* not yet available). *Furor* referring specifically to civil war or sedition, *TLL* 6, 1 s.v. 1631.24–31, but also, little less clearly, e.g., Cic. *Cat.* 1.1, 15, 31; 2.25; 4.11.

107. *CIL* 6.1187, 6.31256, 9.4051 = *ILS* 795. For discussion of these and related examples, see Mazzarino 1942, 80–91, or 1990, 60–66; McCormick 1986, 111–19.

108. *CIL* 6.1710. Alan Cameron 1970, 249, doubted whether Arcadius was actually consulted (probably rightly: Honorius obviously was not consulted on the weightier matter of Arcadius's proclaiming his wife Augusta in 404, *Ep. Imp. Pont. Al.* 38): conventionally, consent was assumed. The same rule applied even in the appointment of officials in territory definitely within the control of one or the other: Symmachus wrote letters thanking both Valentinian II and Theodosius for his appointment as urban prefect of Rome in 384, for example (*Symm. Rel.* 1, 2).

It made fomenting discord a useful accusation with which to slander an enemy. A fragment of Eunapius gives an instance: in about 405 Arcadius's general Fravitta answers the accusations of the *comes sacrarum largitionum* John and his tool Hierax with the counteraccusation:[109]

> But it is you who are the cause of all the evils, dividing the emperors by your own conspiracy, undermining and shaking this most heavenly and divine work with your devices, and destroying it. It is an all-blessed marvel, an invincible and adamantine bulwark, when emperors in two separate bodies hold a single empire.

After rapprochement between the Eastern and Western courts from 401 to 403, relations had again deteriorated.[110] The fragment shows that even internal rivalries of a single court might find ammunition in the condition of the empire as a whole.

Claudian however preferred to blame an antagonist in the other court. It is Eutropius who "divides a twin court and tries to commit loyal [*pios*] brothers to hatred." Claudian ironically recalls Eutropius's former pandering, telling him "if you look to your old trade, the decent thing is to bring them together" (1.281–84). At one level he rebukes Eutropius for falling below his own morally dubious standard: even a pander ought to do something better for the empire than Eutropius is doing. But, more important, Claudian thus reactivates his earlier allegations and again implies that so debased and immoral a creature as Eutropius has no business meddling in politics at all.

Book 2 develops the idea of Eutropius's political evildoing yet further. Aurora, entreating Stilicho to redeem her, evokes the sale of offices again with a new twist (2.585–90). Because Tribigild's forces are destroying parts of the empire, Eutropius has divided in two the provinces that remain, "lest the vendor lose anything, when his scope has been trimmed back [*orbe reciso*]." His mercenary concern stands out against the general terrors of war the poem describes. It falls far short of the selfless care for his people that ancient theory expected of a ruler.[111] Lactantius similarly describes Diocletian's division of

109. Eunap. fr. 71.3 Blockley. Fravitta, *PLRE* 1.372–73; John, *PLRE* 2.593 (Ioannes 1); Hierax, *PLRE* 2.556. See further Alan Cameron and Long 1993, 236–52.

110. The consulate is a convenient index of official positions: the West did not recognize Eutropius in 399 or Aurelian in 400, did recognize Fravitta in 401, Arcadius in 402 (joint consulate with Honorius), and Theodosius II in 403, and did not recognize Aristaenetus in 404 or Anthemius in 405 (*CLRE* s.aa.). Another valuable document is Honorius's letter to Arcadius of about June 404, *Ep. Imp. Pont. Al.* 38, at 85–88, protesting three specific grievances: the proclamation of Eudoxia as Augusta, the lack of official notice of Alaric's devastation of Illyricum in 403–4, and the arrest of clergy in the controversy storming about John Chrysostom.

111. E.g., Syn. *Reg.* 30C; compare the synthetic sketches of Lester K. Born, "The Perfect Prince according to the Latin Panegyrists," *AJP* 55 (1934): 20–35, and Seager 1983.

provinces as an act of rapacious brutality (*Mort. Pers.* 7.4).[112] "Lest the vendor lose anything" implies that it is Eutropius's own revenues that concern him. Personal greed joins cynicism and corruption in the accusation.[113] Claudian personalizes his charge still more by describing the reduced sphere Eutropius afflicts as "trimmed-back," a term that recalls his own castration (cf. 1.47–48, *recisos . . . mares*).

Aurora observes that the palace is indifferent so long as its amusements are not curtailed (2.584–85). She refers to events like the vacations in Ancyra that prompt Mars's outrage (2.95–110), but more particularly to the "choruses and banquets" that define the competence of Eutropius's court in the council (2.584, 2.322–401). The scene follows the broad structure of Domitian's Council of the Fish in Juvenal's *Satire* 4. It varies it by the facts that this council is called to address a serious question, not a portentously absurd one, and that the councillors are incapable even of aping dignity. Juvenal enumerates his nobles from the relatively respectable ones to the more pungent criminals (Juv. 4.72–118).[114] Claudian's are a baseborn mass, some plebeian, some former slaves still scarred from fetters and their masters' marks (*Eutr.* 2.342–45). The scars evidence not merely slavery, but criminal punishments they have suffered and presumably deserved; implicitly the marks deny their fitness now to "regulate the laws" as they do.[115] All also are exquisite gourmands. Their tastes in impossibly rare foods and diaphanous garments recall satirical targets of Horace,[116] Petronius,[117] Juvenal,[118] Ammianus,[119] and Pacatus;[120] Eunapius too similarly maligns courtiers of Rufinus as a canaille now reveling in undeserved

112. Charlotte Roueché, "Rome, Asia and Aphrodisias in the Third Century," *JRS* 71 (1981): 103–20, redated some divisions from Diocletian's reign to the middle of the third century, but many remain Diocletian's doing; cf. A. H. M. Jones 1964, 42–43, with her modifications.

113. *Eutr.* 2pr.49–50 similarly contrasts true personal greed and alleged public interest.

114. As Mayor 1901, 1.230, and Courtney 1980, 216, noted, Juvenal calls Pegasus "bailiff [*vilicus*] for the city" rather than "prefect" (4.77–78) with thoughts of the condition of the state under Domitian; it is not a personal slur based on class or occupation.

115. Birt 1892, 109, and Fargues, *Invectives* 119, compared Ov. *Am.* 2.2.47, *conpedibus liventia crura gerentem* ("a man bearing shins livid from their fetters"). Claudian, expanding, juxtaposes "black" to "livid" for greater pictorial vividness: *pars compede suras / cruraque signati nigro liventia ferro* ("part marked on their calves by the fetter, and shins livid from black iron," *Eutr.* 2.342–43).

116. E.g., Hor. *Serm.* 2.4, 2.8.

117. Petron. 33–36, 40, 49, 60, 65, 66, 69–70.

118. Juv. 2.64–78; 4.11–33 (besides the Council itself; for related censures compare especially items cited by Mayor 1901, 220 ad 15 *mullum*; 221 ad 26); 6.259–60. Cf. Alan Cameron 1965b for a similar remark in Jer. *Ep.* 66.13 (not 66.15 as printed).

119. Amm. 14.6.9, 28.4.19.

120. *Pan. Lat.* 2[12].33.4.

luxury.[121] According to Claudian, Eutropius's cronies continually recur to the fantasies of the theater, unable to comprehend the real dangers they face.[122]

Claudian emphasizes food for the immediate purpose of stigmatizing the courtiers' characters with satirical concreteness and detail, but the topic also prefaces the particular skills of Hosius, an estate-born slave and Eutropius's *magister officiorum*. Hosius had been a cook, and Claudian characterizes his administrative qualities with a string of appropriate puns (*Eutr.* 2.347–49):

> dulcior hic sane cunctis prudensque movendi
> iuris et admoto qui temperet omnia fumo,
> fervidus, accensam sed qui bene decoquat iram.

> He is sweeter than all of them, for sure, and expert at stirring up
> law-broth, one to mellow everything by putting it on the smoker,
> a hot one, but good at rendering down wrath flambé.

Dulcior and *accendere* are commonly used of personalities and emotions as well as literally of foods and cooking techniques.[123] *Ius* is a homonym I have already discussed;[124] *movere* can mean either to rouse to action or to upset.[125] Fargues supposed that *fumo* was used by metonymy for *flamma*, but smoking is well attested as an ancient culinary technique, particularly for seasoning certain kinds of wine; "smoke" is also a common ancient metaphor for something worthless.[126] In late antiquity, "to sell smoke" came to designate effective or fraudulent influence-peddling.[127] For the metaphor of "reducing" anger by culinary means Birt and Fargues adduced Homer and Catullus.[128] Not only is

121. Eunap. fr. 63 M = 62.2 Blockley.

122. *Eutr.* 2.338–41, 354–64, 402–5. Compare 2.86–87 of Eutropius: the courtiers' irresponsibility echoes his, even though he takes the role of the harsh taskmistress at the meeting.

123. *OLD* s.vv. (and so for all terms discussed here, with additional references as noted). For puns on the double sense of *dulcis*, cf. Plaut. *As.* 614; Ov. *Met.* 13.795. Such passages confirm for Latin the modern sense of a "sweet" personality, for its obligingness; Alan Cameron 1968a, 409, however, preferred to see the result of Hosius's obliging corruption, his popularity (Cameron discussed the other puns of the passage as well; more limited discussions also by Birt 1888, 45 n. 1; Andrews 1931 ad loc.; Schweckendiek 1992, 144).

124. In connection with the hypothesis of Birt 1888 that Claudian in *Eutr.* imitates Lucilius; see Chap. 2.

125. Specifically of political unrest, *OLD* s.v. 11.

126. Fargues, *Invectives* 119; *TLL* 6, 1 s.v. I.B.4 of domestic use (1543.43–63), B metaphorically (1544.3–28; cf. LSJ s.v. καπνός and Ar. *Vesp.* 143–46).

127. Cf. *HA Ant. Pius* 11.1 (cf. 6.4); *HA Heliog.* 10.3; *HA Alex. Sev.* 23.8, 36.2; and *TLL* s.v. *fumus* as noted previously.

128. Birt 1892, 109; Fargues, *Invectives* 121: *Il.* 1.81 χόλον καταπέπτειν; Cat. 68.139 *concoquit iram* (a generally preferred emendation for *cotidiana / quotidiana iram* of the manuscripts, but many others have been proposed).

this concoction of punning terms skillfully served up, pungent and funny in itself, but it also identifies Hosius irretrievably with his former lowly profession. Applying the skills he learned then to political life produces only corruption.

Claudian's technique is the same as in the obscene puns with which a "racier" wit praises Eutropius's administration in book 1 (1.358–70). Cicero makes similar use of alleged popular opinion, complete with puns, in his second oration against Verres (Cic. *Verr.* 2.1.121, discussed previously).[129] Practically every word in the speech Claudian concocts bears a double meaning:

> miraris? nihil est, quod non in pectore magnum
> concipit Eutropius. semper nova, grandia semper
> diligit et celeri degustat singula sensu.
> nil timet a tergo; vigilantibus undique curis
> nocte dieque patet; lenis facilisque moveri
> supplicibus mediaque tamen mollissimus ira
> nil negat et sese vel non poscentibus offert;
> quidlibet ingenio, subigit traditque fruendum;
> quidquid amas, dabit illa manus; communiter omni
> fungitur officio gaudetque potentia flecti.
> hoc quoque conciliis peperit meritoque laborum,
> accipit et trabeas argutae praemia dextrae.

> Do you marvel? There is nothing big that Eutropius does not take to
>   himself
> in his heart. Always new things, always grand things
> does he love, and taste individually with a swift sense.
> He fears nothing from the rear; to cares standing watch on all sides
> he is open, night and day. He is smooth and easy for suppliants
> to move, and in the middle of a passion he is nonetheless very soft.
> He denies nothing and offers himself even to those who don't ask.
> Whatever the spirit desires he cultivates and hands over to be enjoyed;
> whatever you love, that hand will give. In common to everyone
> he performs his service, and his might delights to be bent.
> This too he has brought to birth by his plans and the desert of his labors,
> He accepts the consular robes too as rewards of his clever right hand.

The remarks begin close to praise; indeed Claudian in an apparently straightforward consular panegyric calls Stilicho "upright and ardent to undertake

---

129. Tacitus is fond of voicing political judgments through anonymous commentators, e.g., *Ann.* 1.4, 9–10. Auson. *Cent. Nupt.* brilliantly demonstrates how fertilely obscene puns can be derived from alien contexts.

nothing small" (*Stil.* 1.41–42). But the train of the speaker's remarks through the rest of this speech suggests that Eutropius's love for new things and grand pertains to male lovers. He is voracious. His "tasting" suggests fellatio. "Fearing nothing from the rear" but rather "being open" implies that he enjoys anal penetration. "Care" (*cura*) often bears erotic connotations in elegy.[130] *Mollis* ("soft") and its cognates provided standard Roman expressions for effeminacy as well as complaisance, which also suits this context. *Ira* is wrath but also any sort of passion, including erotic; Claudian includes "passions easy to bend" among Venus's court in his *Epithalamium* for Honorius and Maria (*Epith.* 79).[131] The concluding lines are still blunter. Eutropius not only grants every solicitation but even offers himself unsolicited. Repeated references to his hand intimate that he masturbates clients. The whole passage recurs to Claudian's earlier picture of Eutropius's sexual career and casts his political administration in the same terms. Finally it confronts Eutropius's consulate with his degraded sexuality as effect and cause. The puns glove with wit a final blow that must shock.

The third victim to be mocked by the terminology of his past career, the general and former weaver Leo, condemns himself out of his own mouth. As mention of the courtiers' gourmandise thematically introduces Hosius, so does the comparison of them and Eutropius to a group of poor girls and the "hated nurse" who bids them "seek their feed in common from the loom" introduce Leo's profession. In the council, he takes the role of Juvenal's Montanus by making a bold proposal to resolve the crisis. Like Montanus's, it is bathetically obvious: make a larger dish; march out on campaign. Like Montanus, he sports an immense paunch, which Claudian says substitutes for the sevenfold oxhide shield which as an Ajax he should bear.[132] The comparison holds up the epic grandeur proper to a literary account of the dire predicament of the East, only to deflate it abruptly, along with any other pretensions to grandeur that Leo might attempt. The images Leo chooses in order to exhort the other councillors inadvertently reveal his equally unheroic training as a

---

130. E.g., Sulpicia, [Tib.] 3.18 = 4.12.1; Ov. *Am.* 1.3.16, *AA* 2.746.

131. See also A. Ernout, "*Ira* = ὀργή," in *Omagiu lui Alexandru Rosetti*, ed. Iorgu Iordan (Bucharest: Academia Republicii Socialiste Románo, 1965), 205–7.

132. "Then he was Eutropius's Ajax and widely he roared, not brandishing seven bullocks with a vast shield-boss but that which he had made heavy by perpetual banquets and a sluggish seat among the old women and among the distaffs: his belly" (*non septem vasto quatiens umbone iuvencos, sed . . . alvum*, *Eutr.* 2.386–89); "and Montanus's stomach is present, slowed down by its paunch" (*Montani quoque venter adest abdomine tardus*, Juv. 4.107). Birt 1892, 110, and Fargues, *Invectives* 122, compared Juv. 7.115 for "Ajax rose up" (*adsurgit*, so also Andrews 1931, 118) and *Il.* 7.219–20 for the association of such a shield with Ajax; compare also Ov. *Met.* 13.2, "Ajax rose to them, master of the sevenfold shield" (*surgit ad hos clypei dominus septemplicis Aiax*, cited by Mayor 1901, 1.297, and Courtney 1980, 364 ad Juv. 7.115).

weaver (2.391–401).[133] He demands how long they will sit "shut in feminine chambers"; when *thalami* are spoken of in connection with Eutropius, they refer to the eunuch's ordinary duties as chamberlain, but here they suggest the place where the women of Homeric epic sit and weave while men fight and adventure.[134] Leo warns the courtiers that "a crowd of graver evils is being woven [*texitur*]" while they waste time. He continues, "This sweat seeks me. Never is my right hand slow to the iron" (*me petit hic sudor. numquam mea dextera segnis ad ferrum*). Sweat can be banausic as well as military, and line 385 shortly above shows that "iron" can refer to woolworking tools as well as to the sword.[135] Calling upon Minerva, Leo boasts that he will make Tribigild and the threat he poses lighter than wool, slaughter the Gruthungi like sheep, and restore the Phrygian women to their spinning.

But Minerva favors Leo only in woolwork, not in war. His army is dissolute, leaderless, and lost. They resemble a horse without its rider, a ship wrecked because it does not have its master, or a whale that having lost its pilot fish strands itself on the reefs (2.423–31); the contrast with their former tautness under Stilicho is absolute.[136] Tribigild leads them on with pretended flight, then attacks when they are all sluggish from banqueting. Leo flies, but his bulk sinks him in a swamp. Claudian compares his panicked squeals to those of a

133. Christiansen 1969, 99–100, noted the preponderance of weaving terms and puns in Leo's martial language. On the late antique cloth industry, A. H. M. Jones, "The Cloth Industry under the Roman Empire," *Econ. Hist. Rev.* 2nd ser. 13 (1960): 183–92. In *HA Tyr. Trig.* 8, the usurper and former ironworker Marius boldly proclaims his "steely" resolve, but is undercut by the chapter's introductory note that he reigned for only three days (numismatic evidence suggests a longer sway; *PLRE* 1.562, M. Aurelius Marius 4). Compare too the puns on Regalianus's name, which are said to have won him his proclamation as emperor, *HA Tyr. Trig.* 10.3–7; *PLRE* 1.762, P. C. Regalianus.

134. *Eutr.* 1.99, 130, 156, 473; 2pr.22; 2.553; *Il.* 3.125–28; 6.490–93; *Od.* 1.356–59; 2.93–110; 19.137–61; 24.129–50; cf. also Claud. *CM* 46.12–15.

135. Noted by Fargues, *Invectives* 123, and Andrews 1931, 118. Also in Lucr. 5.1350–60 (where it is averred that men began to weave before women, being naturally superior, but later agreed to leave weaving to women when they went on to harder labors: thus weaving itself constitutes evidence of slackness; cf. Juv. 2.57 of male spinning and my remarks in Chap. 2; Roma proposes male spinning as one impossible inversion of roles that might as well follow from permitting eunuchs to govern, *Eutr.* 1.496–98); Juv. 7.224 (Mayor 1901, 462 ad loc. adds technical references; Courtney 1980, 378).

136. N.b. *Eutr.* 2.412–14. Christiansen 1969, 100, remarked that "he pictures the Westerners as hunters, sailors, and burden bearers, but the Easterners as blind directionless animals." *Priori* however implies, and "their strength changed along with their leader" confirms, that Claudian is contrasting the condition of the Eastern army while it served under Stilicho before Rufinus forced him to return them; they were unwilling to go then (cf. *Ruf.* 2.237–47, 257–77), but now the influence of their present masters has corrupted them. Fargues, *Invectives* 124, noted that Claudian often describes Stilicho's winter campaigns with similar imagery, citing 3 *Cons.* 150, *Stil.* 1.122–37, *Get.* 348–63.

sow Hosius might contemplate butchering, then dissolves the simile in a puff of fragrant steam (2.445–51).

Lighter yet comes Leo's death (2.452–55): a breeze (*levis aura*) strikes the leaves behind him. Leo assumes it is a javelin, and dies of fright.[137] Fittingly, the words "he breathes out his life" (*vitam . . . efflat*) end the passage. It is all air. The fragility of defense under Eutropius's direction could not be more tellingly imaged.

Claudian devotes a last paragraph to recrimination (2.456–61). Leo should never have traded his comb for swords. A weaver's comb and swords are the two items suggested by "iron" in his bold speech before the council: the pun turns back on him. He takes up the challenge as if his ability in one side of the double world they sketch qualified him equally in the other. The event proves that he is fatally limited. "While you avoid your wools," as Claudian chides him, calling attention to the transition, Leo loses both. A final irony is added by the allusion to the Parcae. They are woolworkers too, in their proper sphere, and they have spun Leo's final threads. Claudian stresses Leo's own fault in addressing him as "degenerate": had he not deserted his "ancestral chair" where he used to praise the weavers' threads, he would not have lost its safety.

The same kind of rebuke appears when Claudian tells Eutropius that he would not break up the emperors if he looked to his "old trade" (1.283), which Hall's text describes as the "ancestral work of a pimp" at 1.77.[138] Their public activities are betraying their own natures. Only disaster can be expected to result.[139] Hosius's butchery in the extended comparison that leads into Leo's death scene similarly reasserts the prevailing force of Eutropius's and his cronies' old professions. All alike, they are bound to their native, lowly trades, even when these affinities set one of them against another. Their class allegiance also degrades their present subjects. Yet more important, the unchangeable facts about their natures that class reveals and reinforces make them incapable and disastrous rulers. At the close of the book Aurora confirms what Cybele foresees when war first breaks in Phrygia, that with these leaders, the East is helpless on its own resources.

---

137. I discuss briefly in Chap. 2 Plutarch's similar scene of ludicrous cowardice on the part of Demosthenes at Chaeronea, *Mor.* 845F.

138. Hall accepted *avitum* of the *Isingriniana* marginalia for *acutum* of the manuscripts at *Eutr.* 1.77. The parallel of *Eutr.* 2.457 supports the reading: the epithet "ancestral" need not be literally true for either Eutropius or Leo, but in context suggests that these professions are intrinsically right for them, as opposed to the public endeavors to which they so badly transfer their inborn talents. Schweckendiek 1992, 71–72, defended *acutum* as unexceptionable, rightly enough, but *avitum* adds a second point of accusation.

139. Therefore I cannot agree with Christiansen 1969, 101, that "the effect here is more sadly ironic than satirical" or that Leo is "a man to be pitied."

CLAUDIAN SLANDERS his eunuch along three closely related lines. The first is simply that he is a eunuch. As an unnatural, ugly perversion of humanity, he instantly repels, and Claudian takes full advantage of physical description to augment the disgust.

Second are the effeminizing consequences of his castration. They encourage Claudian to apply to Eutropius feminine images with greater freedom even than in classical rhetoric: at once Eutropius is trivialized, and then still further damned when Claudian points out that even women surpass him. Childbearing justifies them against all else, but Eutropius has no such capability. Both Eutropius's sexual ambiguity and the physical deformities caused by his castration afford Claudian opportunities for pungently derisive humor; the pleasure of laughter allies the audience to him while the joke asserts that Eutropius is alien to them and their well-ordered world, as to the inappropriate roles that he plays. Finally, Claudian suggests that Eutropius's position as a castrated slave has permanently depraved him. He is inhumanly cruel and greedy, both against individuals and in public administration; slavery alone effects callousness and venality, but eunuchry makes them still worse. And again Claudian emphasizes that Eutropius's greed is fruitless because he has no family to provide for (1.222–28; 2pr.49–50). His infertility functions as a motif in every connection.

Moreover, he takes to his court men of equally low origins and even less ability. The techniques of attack Claudian practices on them derive from his attack on Eutropius, and since they are his creatures attacks on them also attack Eutropius indirectly. Even when he is no longer on the scene, both within the narrative as Leo lives up to his disastrous auspices and in the reality of which Claudian complains in the proem, that Eutropius has been exiled and yet the court is still not cleansed, Eutropius's influence lives on. He, the policies he set in motion, and the subordinates he promoted between them are destroying the state.

Claudian exploits wide-ranging ancient gender and class prejudices to deepen more ordinary complaints about corruption and incompetence that could be directed against any minister. He seasons the whole with graphic imagery and elevated, intense language in an acme of late rhetoricized style. The result is unforgettably vivid. It well deserves Alan Cameron's characterization of it as "the cruellest (and most entertaining) invective that has come down to us from the ancient world."[140]

140. Alan Cameron 1974, 144.

PART TWO

The Historical World
of *In Eutropium*

✦

CHAPTER FIVE

Date and Reference

✦

THE DATE OF *In Eutropium* poses problems because different parts of the invective describe different historical events. *In Eutropium* 1 cites the devastation of the East in 398 to show how the sight of a eunuch defender inspires the barbarian enemy with confidence (1.238–51). Eutropius's triumphal return from Armenia that year exemplifies his shamelessness (1.252–54). Yet more shamelessly, the poem continues, in return for his triumph Eutropius demands the honor of the consulate for 399 (1.284–85). Finally it depicts his inauguration in January 399 (1.300–316). The scene fits to conventions of the ceremony images from Claudian's chosen lines of ridicule. He could have composed it in advance, as early as he heard of Eutropius's nomination; but there was no reason to portray the inauguration as past, if the audience knew it would happen later than the time they heard the poem. Eutropius's inauguration must provide a terminus post quem.

The preface of *In Eutropium* 2 celebrates Eutropius's fall and, with malicious pleasantry, forecasts his exile to Cyprus. Eutropius was deposed and exiled in summer of 399.[1] Since Claudian speculates that Eutropius may die on the way to Cyprus (2pr.67–74), the exile seems to have been been reported in the West only recently. Yet it is not necessary to insist that Claudian wrote before Eutropius was dispatched: news as well as exiles took time to travel (see Chapter 6). On the other hand, Claudian betrays no awareness of Eutropius's subsequent recall and execution in the autumn of 399.[2]

In the proem of book 2 itself, Claudian again refers to the exile: "Do you think the court outstandingly cleansed, if Cyprus holds Eutropius?" (2.20–21). The body of the book describes the pomp Eutropius enjoyed as consul in 399

1. The law of deposition, *CTh* 9.40.17, is transmitted as having been issued on 17 January 399, but since Claudian makes plain that Tribigild did not revolt until later that year, Seeck 1895, 1146–47, emended the date to 17 August. I shall discuss the problem in more detail later in this chapter.

2. Philost. *HE* 11.6, 136.14–25 Bidez and Winkelmann; Zos. 5.18.1–2.

149

(2.58–94), that year's spring departure of the court for Ancyra (2.95–100; cf. 2.120–22), the outbreak of Tribigild's rebellion (2.274–78), and Leo's failed campaign (2.409–55). Rumors of Tribigild's progress terrify the court (2.462–73): no sign hints at the resolution of the revolt in Eutropius's exile. At the end of the book, Aurora laments Eutropius's immediate succession to the tyranny of Rufinus (2.539–52) and the destruction wrought by Tribigild (2.562–83). She begs Stilicho to save her from *servilibus regnis* (2.593). Literally, this phrase means "servile kingships." What exactly Claudian designates by the phrase and what more it implies are a crucial and controversial point in the shifting debate.

In his 1876 edition of Claudian, Ludwig Jeep considered only the dates of *In Eutropium* 2 and its preface relative to one another. He argued that *servilibus regnis* could refer only to Eutropius, specifically to his consulate (xxiv). The fact that Claudian shows the East seeking help from Stilicho also seemed to him to imply that Eutropius was still in power, for it reveals no hint of his exile. Thus the end of the poem appeared earlier than the beginning. Jeep considered and rejected the possibility Koenig had hypothesized, that there is a lacuna after line 489, where Claudian might have described Eutropius's deposition: the end of the poem still appears ignorant of it. The kindred suggestion that the poem might be unfinished fails, in Jeep's view, because a continuation would have made Claudian's book impossibly long.

Jeep preferred to believe that the reference in the proem was an interpolation. What he called the "elegy against Eutropius" he decreed had been prefaced to book 2 of the hexameters erroneously by some copyist. Interpolation then attempted to fit the book better to the elegy's frequent references to the exile. Jeep bolstered this hypothesis with the valid observation that nothing in book 2 suggests the "tiny page" (*exigua charta*), which the elegy says "finished the work of Mars" in felling Eutropius (2pr.19–20); he concluded that the elegy could not be meant to introduce the book.

This conclusion, like the contradiction Jeep saw between *In Eutropium* 2 and the elegiac piece transmitted as its preface, relies on his unstated assumption that a unified work must fulfill all the foreshadowing it entails. Conversely, for him works taking more than one part to fulfill such expectations must have been published all together: accordingly he joined *In Rufinum* 1 and 2 and rejected the preface of the second book.[3] Essentially he seems to have held that authors work only in complete units. The premise appeals to many instincts; but there are different senses in which completeness may be understood. I shall return to this point.

Jeep's other arguments prop his solution weakly if at all. The fact that a Vatican codex inscribes the elegy "the second book against Eutropius" and the

3. Jeep 1876–79, 1.xviii; 1872, 620–24 (not 1873 as printed in the former).

second hexametric piece "the third book" means only that the distinct items were numbered separately in that codex, just as the panegyric for Olybrius and Probinus and the *carmina maiora* are numbered sequentially in modern editions.[4] Meter obviously sets off the preface from the books. The numbering of this one codex does not imply that the elegy was recognized in antiquity as an independent poem. Notably, the usual sequence obtains: the preface is not placed after book 2, as Jeep would order the pieces' composition and delivery.[5] Nevertheless, Jeep asserted that the elegy was a separate poem written after book 2. He justified its being so short on the grounds that Claudian, having already written two very long books about Eutropius, had nothing more to say. This argument willfully ignores Claudian's inventive fertility. He had no trouble writing three books on the unimpressive Honorius's different consulates, for example, and three books on Stilicho's one consulate alone.

Jeep assumed that Claudian would report external fact if he knew it, so that silence about Eutropius's exile implies an earlier date. He also took a strong view of the internal consistency of a work, and felt free to postulate gross textual corruptions to salvage it. His postulate has no more than these considerations to support it.

Theodor Birt had a similar view of what was possible in transmission, but he perceived differently the problems of *In Eutropium*.[6] He also made more effort than Jeep to fix an absolute chronology. The publication of book 1 he dated to the early days of 399, shortly after the inauguration described in lines 300 to 316. Not only does it betray no knowledge of Eutropius's fall, it expects Stilicho or Honorius to influence Arcadius against Eutropius. Even this intervention is only requested for some vague future. Claudian's demand that the eunuch consul be sacrificed to avert the omen he bears (1.21–23) is similarly open-ended. Since Eutropius fell and died through neither Western influence nor archaic ritual necessity but at the behest of Gaïnas and Tribigild, Birt argued that Claudian must have written earlier, when other agencies still could be contemplated.

Birt did not see the problems within book 2 that distressed Jeep. He remarked that events internal to the East had in fact produced Eutropius's exile; they are the subject of the poem. Birt judged that Claudian complains in his proem at the insufficiency of exile because he had wanted Eutropius killed. Crucial to this reading is a different understanding than Jeep's of *servilibus regnis* in Aurora's speech. Birt argued that the falling of the axes and jettison of the fasces by Eutropius's lictors at 2.520–21 could only mean that Eutropius

4. *Eutr.* 1 is 18, *Eutr.* 2pr. is 19, and *Eutr.* 2 is 20; for full list, see Abbreviations.
5. Jeep 1876–79, 1.xxvi, admitted the numeration of the "third book" with a "but," apparently conceding the difficulty.
6. Birt 1888, 50–51; 1892, xl.

had been removed from the consulate. Therefore Aurora can refer not to him, but to the domination of Tribigild: that is why she describes Tribigild's revolt to Stilicho (2.567–83) and why she uses military imagery in summoning him ("defender," "arms," "shield," 2.599–602). The "slaves" (*famulis*) at 2.517 to whom the Easterners regret that they have handed themselves over are then the Gruthungi. Birt did not explain, however, what is intrinsically slavish enough about the Gruthungi for the expression to be so understood in the first instance. Book 2 he judged belongs to summer 399, the date of the last event it mentions, namely Eutropius's exile.[7]

The preface of book 2 Birt agreed with Jeep in seeing as a later and separate poem, wrongly interchanged with book 2 in the transmission of the manuscripts. Books 1 and 2 both bitterly oppose the eunuch and call for his death. But in the supplementary elegy Claudian "has made his compromise with the facts and is content that Eutropius should only be banished."[8] Claudian bids him "live on as a reproach to the fates" (2pr.47). The agreement of the two hexametric pieces in tone to Birt seemed to connect them chronologically too: the elegy comes after. But all must have been composed before Eutropius actually did meet his death, thus by September 399.[9]

Martin Schanz, Carl Hosius, and Gustav Krüger substantially followed Birt as to the dates of book 1, book 2, and the preface, but they did not dissociate the preface from book 2.[10] Alfred Carleton Andrews and Domenico Romano followed in their train.[11] Romano specifically placed the first book "in the first half of 399, the second was written in the second half of the same year."

Pierre Fargues in his studies of 1933 concurred with Birt on the dates for books 1 and 2 of *In Eutropium*, but disagreed over the preface to book 2.[12] His logic depended still more on the assumption that the poems accurately represent the time of composition. Book 1 in his view was published in January or February 399, for Eutropius's inauguration appears recent. Book 2 might have been begun shortly after Leo's disastrous end, and would have come out in September, shortly after Eutropius's exile to Cyprus.[13] The preface however anticipates Eutropius's voyage thither. Therefore it was written somewhat before book 2, which says Eutropius is imprisoned on the island. Fargues believed Claudian did use the piece as a preface to book 2. He added that Claudian had no intention to write a further poem about Eutropius's actual fall, for

7. Birt 1892, xl; cf. xxxv.
8. Birt 1888, 51.
9. Birt 1892, xl.
10. Martin Schanz, Carl Hosius, and Gustav Krüger, *Geschichte der römischen Literatur*, vol. 4, pt. 2 (Munich: C. H. Beck, 1920), 16–18.
11. Andrews 1931, 15–16; Romano 1958, 104–5.
12. Fargues, *Claudien* 23–24; *Invectives* 1–2.
13. Fargues, *Claudien* 24 n. 3.

it would have had to reveal that Stilicho's new rival Gaïnas was the one to bring it about.[14]

Émilienne Demougeot adopted Fargues's conclusions with the unexplained modifications that book 1 was recited at Milan in February or March 399, book 2 was written in the first half of September 399 and recited in the second half, and the preface was written only a few days before book 2.[15]

Alan Cameron accorded with the general consensus on book 1, postulating that Claudian began writing it when Western conservatives greeted Eutropius's nomination with disgust, and read it "a few weeks" after his inaugural panegyric on the Western consul Theodorus.[16] In that poem, as Cameron pointed out, Claudian thanks Stilicho for protecting the West so that "here the curule chair is not raped, base names do not fornicate with the Latin fasti; it was granted to strong men, to be borne by the fathers alone, and will not ever bring shame on Rome" (*violata, incestant, fortibus viris, patribus, pudorem, M. Theod.* 266–69). Sexual connotations possible for most of the key terms punch the allusion to a certain unnamed eunuch consul in the East.[17]

As for book 2 and its preface, however, Cameron renewed the difficulties of Jeep. He pointed out that "throughout the poem Claudian has used *famulus, servus, servilis,* and similar words to designate the ex-slave Eutropius";[18] accordingly he felt that Aurora's plea to be rescued from *servilibus regnis* must refer to Eutropius also. Therefore the end of the poem could not have been written after Eutropius's fall. Cameron also urged the fact that Claudian did not manage to claim credit for Stilicho in bringing Eutropius down. This omission contrasts with his legerdemain about the assassination of Rufinus, for example, where he claims a moral vindication carefully distanced from actual complicity: he makes the soldier striking the first blow cry out "with this right hand Stilicho, whom you boast of routing, smites you" (*Ruf.* 2.402–3). Yet Eutropius did fall; the proem's explicit reference to Cyprus remains. Therefore Aurora's entreaty opens up a possibility for Stilicho to intervene, but Claudian found no way to claim that the possibility was realized.

Cameron applauded Jeep's discomfort, but deplored his solution. He proposed instead one he termed less drastic (136–49). Following their chronological reference, he distinguished as "proem" the first twenty-three lines of book 2, that mention Eutropius's exile;[19] the rest returns to the period before Eu-

---

14. Cf. Fargues, *Claudien* 92.

15. Demougeot 1951, 220–23.

16. Alan Cameron 1970, 125–27. Fargues, *Invectives* 1, also noted the allusion in *M. Theod.* I quote the passage in Chap. 6.

17. Simon 1975, 243, noted "men" and "fathers" but missed the others.

18. In fact not exclusively, but predominantly: Christiansen 1988 s.vv., e.g., *famulus, servilis, servire, servitium, servus.* Alan Cameron 1970, 136.

19. Cameron's usage necessarily differs from my analysis of the published poem as a

tropius was inaugurated and then moves forward evenly. This body, Cameron argued, was Claudian's original draft. He designed it to show that the East had made itself so helpless under Eutropius's leadership that only Stilicho could restore it. But between completion and publication, Claudian received word that Eutropius had been exiled. "For both artistic and political reasons the poem could not simply be brought up to date. Yet at the same time it could hardly just be recited as though nothing had happened. So Claudian dealt with the new development in a separate work, cast into the form of an extended preface" (137). Then Claudian received the further word that Eutropius's successors in influence in the East were no more ready than he had been to compromise with Stilicho. He accordingly vituperated the new development, or lack of it, in twenty-three lines he now prefixed to the body of the poem, and published the lot. Cameron cautioned that only a week or so might have passed between writing the main body and the preface, and only a few days between the preface and the "proem." "But in a rapidly changing political situation, a few days can make all the difference" (138). He presumed throughout that Claudian published as soon as possible after writing. If, as he argued in an earlier article, Jerome echoed a phrase of *In Eutropium* 2 in a letter dating to 399, this terminus ante quem would corroborate.[20]

Cameron like Jeep reacted to the chronological reference of specific passages. His answer, like Jeep's, hypothesizes a chain of events to accommodate the observed phenomena; but where Jeep worked with comparatively arbitrary principles relating to textual transmission, Cameron's explanation grew out of his broader interpretation of Claudian's poetry as pragmatic politics. It was the immediate response to a developing situation that concerned him. He left open, however, the question of how Claudian expected his audience to perceive these revisionary layers in the final laminate.

For this omission Cameron was sharply criticized by Christian Gnilka.[21] Gnilka observed that Cameron's difficulties, like Jeep's, rested on a fundamental problem of interpretation: they perceived the different temporal references of these passages as inconsistencies requiring explanation. In assigning the

---

whole (Chap. 1). I group *Eutr.* 2.1–23 with 2.24–94 for their thematic concentration on the omens and obscenity of Eutropius's consulate and their function preparing for Mars's intervention in the first scene. Fargues, *Invectives* 12, made the same division. *Eutr.* 2.24–94 would have served as "proem" in my sense to the poem Cameron proposed as Claudian's original version.

20. Alan Cameron 1965b. The idea that excessive luxury makes even silk garments seem too heavy is a satirical commonplace (with other commentators on relevant passages, Cameron cited Juv. 6.259–60, Amm. 14.6.9, Pliny *NH* 11.77), but Jer. *Ep.* 66.13 (not 66.15 as printed), "for whom a silk garment constituted a burden," *quibus serica vestis oneri erat*, is more than commonly close to Claudian's "even silks themselves constituted a burden," *onerique vel ipsa serica, Eutr.* 2.337–38.

21. Gnilka 1976, esp. 103–11.

production of these inconsistencies to the poet, however, Gnilka judged that Cameron left him guilty of violating the unity of his own work. Gnilka proposed a different approach: regardless of how Claudian came to present the work in this form, how did he mean the whole to be understood?

Gnilka's question is sound, and need not obscure the temporal reference of individual passages. Yet as Gnilka pursued his question, he did so. Where Cameron distinguished phases of composition and failed to consider how the disparate sections functioned together, Gnilka dismissed in advance any lines of inquiry that might have led him to conclude otherwise than that "a poet thoroughly trained in rhetoric, like Claudian, should have been able to draft 'Praefatio' and Proem at the same time" (111). He avoided determining absolute dates, although his other conceptions imply a terminus post quem after Eutropius's deposition (cf. 122–23 n. 73). He did not pass judgment on whether book 2 with the preface followed book 1 after some interval, but stressed that they were meant to pick up where it left off (109 n. 24).

Gnilka explained away the apparent discrepancies within book 2 by arguing that the fulminations of the proem set an interpretative context for Aurora's plea. Stilicho should be understood to refuse, but Claudian has refrained from saddling him with the need unheroically to explain why (107). Gnilka did not hint what temporal reference he read in the final scene; but whether it is pictured as occurring before Eutropius fell, so that the proem reports its aftermath, or contemporary with the proem's present tense, the proem shows why Aurora's request could not be met.

The hypothesis that Claudian chose to present a situation which then required some face-saving measure to redeem it, ill fits Gnilka's doctrine of artistic consistency. But any objection to argumentative inconsistency on Gnilka's part is overpowered by the strong aggressive role he assigned to the poem overall. In his view, the proem indicts the whole Eastern empire: first, it elevated Eutropius, but also more generally it made reconciliation with the West impossible even once Eutropius was out of the way. Gnilka argued this case at length, and its implications go far beyond the present question of date; I shall return to the political issue in Part III.

As for the formal aspects of his case, Gnilka argued that Claudian regularly breaks off an event just at its climax. He proposed that Claudian so breaks here; the reader is left to infer the negative result.[22] But Claudian's numerous scenes of divine supplication never demand of the reader such labor. Most are answered in the narrative. Roma asks the consulate for the sons of Probus; Theodosius grants it willingly (*Ol. Prob.* 136–73). Jupiter reassures Roma and Africa when they beg for relief from Gildo (*Gild.* 17–213). Then he dispatches

---

22. Gnilka's argument tends to this conclusion, though he does not quite state it; his extremely polemical tone often obscures positive suggestions he might have intended.

the elder and younger Theodosius, who instantly win Honorius's and Arcadius's assent to punishing Gildo and seeing the unity of the empire renewed (*Gild.* 235–351).[23] Iustitia calls Theodorus to the consulate; he expresses modest reluctance, but obeys (*M. Theod.* 135–97). Personified Provinces urge Roma to press the consulate on Stilicho; she does and soon sees "that she has obtained the consul she desired" (*Stil.* 2.218–377). Here she adds an anticipatory request, that Stilicho celebrate his consulate in Rome (*Stil.* 2.386–407). Claudian does not spell out Stilicho's consent, but Fama's message implies it (*Stil.* 2.408–13), and Claudian's third book and preface in honor of this consulate confirm that Stilicho did visit the capital in triumph. Diana bids her nymphs gather wild animals for Stilicho's games, and they do till the book ends (*Stil.* 3.237–369). Roma beseeches Honorius to return to the capital for his sixth consulate; he too complies.[24]

Even the one request that is not explicitly fulfilled within the poem containing it, Roma's request that Stilicho visit Rome, is presented in the understanding that it can be fulfilled. Indeed there is every confidence that each request will be. Gnilka's interpretation would make *In Eutropium* the one place in which a specious request is posed to be frustrated. Gnilka claimed nothing that would make Aurora appear undeserving in any way. She is defeated only by an irony that must be carried over from the opposite end of the book. Even the defeat itself must be inferred. Such reticence would be anomalous in a poet of Claudian's fluency. Characteristically qualified praise is William Barr's, for example: "one of his greatest gifts is the ability to produce the same thoughts again and again, diversified only by elegant variations of language."[25]

23. Notably, Arcadius fully endorses Stilicho and repudiates Gildo, even though the East took no action to quell the revolt (cf. Seeck 1913, 291; Alan Cameron 1970, 110–11): Claudian felt free to represent optimistic wishes rather than strict fact.

24. *6 Cons.* 361–493; Honorius's ceremonial arrival follows. There are also the related cases of Megaera rousing Rufinus (*Ruf.* 1.140–75) and Bellona Tribigild (*Eutr.* 2.174–237). Fargues, *Claudien* 137, detached *6 Cons.* 407–25 from context and viewed it as a more profound request to return the capital to Rome. Taken in isolation, its terms will bear this interpretation, and there is support to be drawn from *6 Cons.* 39–41. But Roma apparently accepts Honorius's reply that he has never denied her, and that he fulfilled her request after victory over Gildo by sending Stilicho as consul in his stead (*6 Cons.* 426–93, dilating in praise of Stilicho). He thus reverts to Roma's complaint in the beginning of her speech, that she had expected to celebrate a triumph for him, as she had requested that he accompany Stilicho to Rome in *Stil.* 2.407. A celebration, not a permanent transfer of the court, is at issue. Where a request made to be granted was not entirely fulfilled, Claudian now goes back and apologizes away the failure.

25. Barr 1981, 21. Cf. Platnauer 1922, 1.xviii, "Claudian's faults are easy to find. He mistook memory for inspiration and so is often wordy and tedious." Glover [1901] 1968, 234, observed, "He can never resist the opportunity to make a list." With more favorable valuation, e.g., Alan Cameron 1970, 269–73, on the lush detail of Claudian's descriptions.

Other than Roma's secondary request to Stilicho in Claudian's second book of panegyric for him, the only parallel scene in which a request is not explicitly addressed within the same poem is in *In Eutropium* 1 when Roma entreats Honorius and Stilicho about Eutropius. Roma's first plea, that the West at least be spared the pollution of the fasces, Claudian's inaugural poem for Theodorus had previously announced as granted (*M. Theod.* 266–69). At no point did the West acknowledge Eutropius as consul.[26] Thus Roma's first request was already known to have succeeded. Her second request is essentially the same as Aurora's: Stilicho should intervene to save the East from crisis set off by Eutropius. Paired with a successful request and in no way introduced by such acrimony as the proem of book 2, Roma's second request appears to have every ground for fair prognostication. Gnilka praises the parallels and complementary details of Roma's and Aurora's requests (106 n. 17); it might be expected that they would bear the same expectation for success, or that an effusive poet like Claudian would mark the irony more directly. Even on its own interpretative ground, Gnilka's argument presents as many difficulties as it solves.

Peter L. Schmidt too in 1976 considered Cameron's proposed scenario for the composition of *In Eutropium* from the literary standpoints of structure, theme, and function.[27] Like Gnilka he underlined the parallelism between Roma's supplication and Aurora's, but he drew the conclusion that Aurora's request like Roma's presupposes that Eutropius is in power; accordingly he concurred with Cameron in judging lines 1 to 23 of book 2 to have been written later. On the other hand, he felt that in abusing the fallen Eutropius the preface duplicates this proem so that "formally they exclude" one another (65). He preferred to judge the preface a separate invective like *Carmina Minora* 23 or 50, mistakenly incorporated into the *Carmina Maiora* by an editor. He cited the incorporation of *Fescenninum* 3 into the *Carmina Minora*,[28] but the case is not really parallel. The Fescennine was interpolated to connect this miscellaneous assortment of pieces to the major body of Claudian's work. It was not interpolated uniformly. The *Carmina Maiora*, on the other hand, had no need to attract additional items. Claudian's other invective epigrams stayed within the *Carmina Minora*, and the preface to *In Eutropium* 2 did not join them. It is firmly established among the major political poems and attached to that book. Furthermore, Claudian was never one to refrain from saying the same thing

---

26. *CLRE* s.a. 399.

27. Schmidt 1976, 59–65.

28. Cf. Alan Cameron 1970, 417–18, and Hall 1986, 68–70; Birt 1892, cxxxv, tabulated the series of *CM* in the manuscripts. Schmidt 1989 did not address this interpolation at any length, but he tended to imply that it could have been made when manuscripts of Claudian began to multiply in the twelfth century, rather than in the initial posthumous publication of Claudian's collected works (411). Unfortunately, the few earlier manuscripts do not contain the *CM* (see Hall 1986, 51–52).

twice in slightly different ways.[29] For example, Cybele's interrupted festival
(2.279–303) transposes to a personalized divine level the preceding pastoral
description of Phrygia being riven by barbarian attack (2.238–78). Common
material between preface and book does not make the preface superfluous
according to Claudian's criteria.

Yet other arguments were made by Siegmar Döpp.[30] He returned to Birt's
inference that the lictor's throwing away the fasces at 2.520–21 means Eutropius's being deprived of his honors. Therefore, when Aurora begs Stilicho
to save her from *servilibus regnis*, she means not Eutropius but "men like
Eutropius." She identifies Rufinus as the first, whose "castrated heir" Eutropius
was (2.550). To such men Stilicho left her, "a joke and a mock for slaves"
(2.535). Thus she reviews her sufferings ever since Stilicho departed for the
West until after Eutropius fell, and calls Stilicho back to save her from any
similar eventualities in the future. Book 2 in its entirety then was written after
Eutropius's fall.

Severin Koster seconded Döpp with the suggestion that Claudian's reference
to Eutropius's statues (2.70–83) alludes to the specific order of the decree
deposing him that they be pulled down.[31] The decree would come to mind
once it was known, ironically since Claudian wishes for the statues to stand
forever as "sure monuments of perpetual shame" (2.78); but since statues were
awarded to public figures very commonly, the wish did not need the decree to
inspire it.[32]

For book 1 Döpp made a more revolutionary argument. He laid weight on
the fact that Roma's request to Honorius not to recognize Eutropius had
already been met by the time Claudian represented her making it. That is, the
scene retrojects the request in poetic justification of an accomplished fact.
Taking this device as a parallel, Döpp argued that when Claudian prays in his
own voice in the proem that the eunuch consul be sacrificed to avert the bad
omen he represents (1.21–23), here too he expresses as a hope an accomplished
reality. Roma's request shows only that Claudian could allude in this fashion to
events outside of his narrative. Döpp completed his argument by finding a
reason why Claudian should have done so: "if Claudian had written and
published the book at the beginning of 399, he would have gotten into trouble

29. Gnilka 1976, 109–11, argued precisely this point to justify dating the preface and
poem together, though many of his examples are of a lesser order.

30. Döpp 1975, 32–34 (briefly in his review of Alan Cameron 1970); 1978 (most fully);
1980, 166–74 (again, summarily).

31. Koster 1980, 331. On the other hand Fargues, *Invectives* 98 n. 77, considered that
Claudian either did not know of the decree or willfully ignored it. Koster followed
Döpp on the dating of both books 1 and 2 (I treat Döpp's arguments on book 1 later),
but returned to the position of Birt about the preface to book 2.

32. Claudian himself received a statue (*Get.* pr.7–14, *CIL* 6.1710); compare the anecdote of Cato the Elder's scorn for statues, reported by Amm. 14.6.8.

with Eutropius, who was at the peak of his career at this time. To demand
Eutropius's head, as Claudian did in 1.23, would have meant declaring war
against the Eastern Empire—that is, beginning a revolution. Therefore, as
Stilicho's advisor Claudian could not have dared making such bold remarks.
Consequently, the first book cannot have been written at the beginning of the
year but only after Eutropius's overthrow."[33]

The objection cannot be allowed. Eutropius already, in far more official
form than court poetry could represent, had enacted precisely the reciprocal
offense against Stilicho: he persuaded Arcadius to call the Senate and have
Stilicho declared *hostis publicus* by official decree (Zos. 5.11.1).[34] Stilicho similarly outlawed Gildo by senatorial vote (*Stil.* 1.325–32), which amounted to a
declaration of war against a minister of the East. This war was actually pros-
ecuted.[35] Nothing barred legally formalized hostilities between the two halves
of the empire. Still less need anything but the policy of his patrons have
hampered the more transitory effusions of a poet. Stilicho was already in as
much trouble with Eutropius as it was possible to be.

Furthermore, Döpp deprived Roma's request to Stilicho of all sense. When
she recommends a whip as the weapon to punish an errant slave, Döpp dismissed it as "a humorous comment after the overthrow."[36] To be sure, Eutropius as a slave faces the whip when his capacities are exhausted: he fears for
his shoulders when as a "mistress" he becomes too old to appeal sexually
(1.76), and he suffers the lash when his pandering fails (1.100–101).[37] But when
Roma tells Stilicho to use the whip, she urges, "Stilicho, why do you put off
winning while competing causes shame? Do you not know that a baser enemy
falls to greater rejoicing?" (1.500–502). "Competing" (*certare*) implies an opponent actively contending against one.[38] If Eutropius has already fallen amid
"greater rejoicing," no reason remains to encourage Stilicho to contend at all.
Helge Schweckendiek observed that the subject of book 1, Eutropius's consulate, concerned Claudian's audience at the Western court only while Eutropius
occupied the honorific post.[39]

33. Döpp 1978, 192.
34. Schweckendiek 1992, 24, pointed out the same problem.
35. Seeck 1913, 285–86, and Paschoud 1971–89, 3¹.113–15, argued persuasively that
Eutropius outlawed Stilicho in response to Stilicho's outlawing Gildo (see discussion in
the Introduction and in Chap. 8.I). With this corrective, on the declaration against
Gildo compare Alan Cameron 1970, 230–34. On the sense of κοινῷ δόγματι in Zosimus, see Alan Cameron and Long 1993, 223 n. 115.
36. Döpp 1978, 192. Curiously, Koster 1980, 315 n. 1143, singled out Döpp's argument
on this passage as decisive.
37. *Eutr.* 1.100–101 includes the same if unsurprising juxtaposition of "beating" and
"back," *verbera tergo*, as *verbere terga* in Roma's speech, 1.507.
38. Cf. *OLD* s.v.
39. Schweckendiek 1992, 25.

Döpp argued that Claudian would not have urged upon Stilicho a course he did not intend to take.[40] Therefore, since Stilicho did not intervene in Eastern affairs in 399, Claudian through Roma's speech can not have been urging this course. Roma's request certainly serves to restate Claudian's constant contention that Roman traditions cannot tolerate the effrontery of a eunuch consul, and it is possible that Claudian did not intend this idea to prompt specific action; I shall treat the questions of his purpose and audience further. But Stilicho's eventual inaction does not prove that he never contemplated intervening. Claudian may, as Cameron argued, provide valid evidence for an intention events suddenly forestalled.[41] Döpp's dating, on the other hand, makes Roma's plea void even before she utters it: she would have to be urging Stilicho to pursue aggression that events had already obviated by removing the proposed object of aggression without any involvement on Stilicho's part. This contorted scenario presents an impossibly unresolved conclusion.

THE PROBLEM OF dating *In Eutropium* has had a long and checkered history. Where does sense survive? Methodological fashion has withdrawn from the nineteenth century's bold hypotheses of textual corruption; indeed, Schmidt considered the mechanics of transmission only superficially. Fargues represented a naive approach to chronological reference, which Cameron demonstrated to break down when it is pressed systematically on individual passages. Cameron analyzed the writing of the poem in terms that suggest no coherent rationale for reading it in its completed form; Gnilka and Döpp argued rationales that fail.

It is time to return to the chronological references themselves, and their function in the parts of the invective. Nothing in book 1 describes as accomplished fact any event beyond early 399. Claudian's call to sacrifice the "prodigy" and Roma's request that Stilicho punish the upstart slave look forward wishfully from the time in which they are represented. Roma's request that Honorius not recognize Eutropius as consul also looks forward as a wish for the future; external evidence confirms that this event, prayed for but not affirmed within the book, took place by the beginning of 399.

It is also known from other sources that in the summer of 399 Eutropius was removed from his unservile offices and later executed. Along with Leo a second general, the Tervingian Goth Gaïnas, had been sent out in the summer against Tribigild. Leo moved directly against Tribigild in Phrygia, while Gaïnas remained behind to protect Thrace and the Hellespont in case Tribigild should

---

40. Döpp 1975, 33; 1978, 192.
41. Cf. Alan Cameron 1970, 138.

elude Leo and circle up in that direction.[42] After Tribigild destroyed Leo and his army, Gaïnas reported to Arcadius that he was too strong to risk engaging. They must come to terms. Tribigild's only recorded demand was for Eutropius to be deposed (Zos. 5.17.5). Other sources report that Eutropius offended Arcadius's wife Eudoxia and she demanded his dismissal.[43] John Chrysostom, in the sermon he delivered literally over Eutropius's cowering form when he fled to the church altar for asylum, refers to enraged soldiers calling for Eutropius's death (*PG* 52.395). The whole set of circumstances suggests wide public outcry, very likely triggered by Gaïnas.[44] Zosimus claims that Gaïnas resented Eutropius's honors (Zos. 5.13.1, 5.17.4–5), Claudian claims that Tribigild resented his own shabby treatment (*Eutr.* 2.174–80, 189–92), and a fragment of Eunapius seems to reflect a belief that they conspired to have Eutropius put to death.[45] First Eutropius fled to John's church and took asylum there.[46] An accommodation was reached, for Zosimus refers to an oath not to put him to death (Zos. 5.18.2); Eutropius left the church for exile in Cyprus, stripped of his honors.[47]

The law that proclaims Eutropius's deposition and exile, 9.40.17 of the Theodosian Code, is transmitted as "issued on 17 January at Constantinople in the consulate of Theodorus," A.D. 399 (*dat. xvi Kal. Feb. Constantinop(oli) Theodoro v.c. cons.*), and addressed "to Aurelian the Praetorian Prefect." But in January of 399 the praetorian prefecture was still held by Eutychian: a steady current of laws addressed to him stretches from 4 September 397 (*CTh* 6.3.4,

42. Zos. 5.14.1–2. Demougeot 1951, 226, suggested that Gaïnas was to guard against similar revolt by Alaric, who virtually could be said to have won his post of *magister militum per Illyricum* by rebelling (so *Eutr.* 2.214–20). Doubtless Alaric was little trusted (Synesius warned against him in 398, for example: see Heather 1988; Alan Cameron and Long 1993, 109–21), but as Paschoud 1971–89, 3¹.128, observed, present suspicion against him is not attested in Zosimus or anywhere else.

43. Philost. *HE* 11.6, 136.1–18 Bidez and Winkelmann; Soz. 8.7.3.

44. So Albert 1984, 43–44. I cite the sermon of John Chrysostom known as *In Eutropium*. *De Capto Eutropio* is so called wrongly: see Alan Cameron 1988.

45. Fr. 75.6 M = 67.10 Blockley reports a message from Gaïnas to Tribigild after they achieved a goal; Zos. 5.13.1–2 reports collusion before the revolt. Since Zosimus based his account on Eunapius, his evidence lacks separate weight but rounds out the interpretation.

46. Ironically, as Socrates and Sozomen emphasize, Eutropius had removed legal authority from asylum; Sozomen ascribes his death to retribution for "this impiety," only incidentally alluding to the historical cause that he had "outraged the Emperor's wife." Socr. *HE* 6.5.2–7; Soz. 8.7.3–5; cf. Joh. Chrys. *PG* 52.392, 395; *CTh* 9.40.16, 9.45.3 (Zosimus 5.18.1 says Eutropius had granted the right of asylum: ἐκκλησίαν, ἔχουσαν ἐξ ἐκείνου τὸ ἄσυλον: error, corruption, or an overcondensed reflection of the right of appeal within the appropriate period, which *CTh* 9.40.16 confirms).

47. Zos. 5.18.1; Philost. *HE* 11.6, 136.14–18 Bidez and Winkelmann; *CTh* 9.40.17.

9.14.3) to 25 July 399 (*CTh* 9.40.18). Aurelian is not otherwise attested in office until 27 August 399.[48] Moreover, Tribigild did not revolt until spring of 399. The transmitted date is impossible. Since John's homily over Eutropius speaks of Easter as some time past (*PG* 52.394), Seeck proposed emending the date of the law to *xvi Kal. Sept.*, that is, 17 August.[49] Assuming the corruption to be restricted to the smallest possible number of elements, that is, the month alone, this correction yields the earliest date that can avoid conflict with Eutychian's well-attested tenure. Eutropius was soon summoned back from exile, however, formally charged with treason, tried by a tribunal presided over by Aurelian, condemned, and executed. Philostorgius says that the offense alleged was of amassing imperial ornaments, which sounds like an easy accusation to trump up against a man who, as *praepositus sacri cubiculi*, would have had charge of such ornaments normally.[50] Zosimus, following Eunapius, ascribes the real motive to Gaïnas.[51]

Stilicho's hand appears nowhere in the machinations that brought Eutropius down. Seeck proposed two different, but not contradictory, hypotheses for inserting him behind the scenes; neither satisfies. One view supposes that Gaïnas was Stilicho's agent.[52] Eunapius alleges, followed by many, that Gaïnas earlier killed Rufinus on Stilicho's instructions;[53] this scenario is extended to Gaïnas's actions against Eutropius and Aurelian, both of whose consulates Stilicho refused to recognize. But Stilicho never realized a tangible benefit in the series of

48. *CTh* 2.8.23; *PLRE* 1.128–29, Aurelianus 3. On the mistaken hypothesis placing more than one person in the prefecture at the same time, which has muddied the understanding of Eutropius's predominance and its aftermath, see now Alan Cameron and Long 1993, 149–61, 175–82, for demonstration that Caesarius not Eutychian succeeded to Aurelian's office in summer 400, against A. H. M. Jones, "Collegiate Prefectures," *JRS* 54 (1964): 78–89 = *The Roman Economy* (Oxford: Clarendon Press, 1974), 375–95; *PLRE* 1.171, Fl. Caesarius 6 and 319–21, Flavius Eutychianus 5; and Liebeschuetz 1990, 253–72 (who cited an earlier, unpublished draft of Alan Cameron and Long 1993).

49. Seeck 1895, 1146–47; cf. Seeck 1919, 103.

50. Philost. *HE* 11.6, 136.19–25 Bidez and Winkelmann.

51. Zos. 5.18.1–3; Eunap. fr. 75.6 M = 67.10 Blockley.

52. Seeck 1894, 456–58. Baynes 1955, 336 (= "A Note on Professor Bury's History of the Later Roman Empire," *JRS* 12 [1922]: 215–16), and Demougeot 1951, 228 (cf. 155–56), took the same position. Birt 1892, xxxv n. 17, suggested that Claudian would need to hide collusion by Gaïnas with Stilicho in silence; yet Claudian was ingenious enough in *Gild.* 380–414 to justify Mascezel's leading an army against his own brother.

53. Eunap. fr. 64.1 Blockley = Joh. Ant. fr. 190 init.; Zos. 5.7.4; cf. Philost. *HE* 11.3, 134.20–21 Bidez and Winkelmann (does not name Gaïnas); Marcellinus, *Chron. Min.* 2.64 (names Gaïnas but does not refer to Stilicho); Jord. *Rom.* 319 (names Gaïnas but does not refer to Stilicho). In Claud. *Ruf.* 2.402–3 an unnamed soldier cries out that retribution should be felt to come from Stilicho, and cuts. Socrates (*HE* 6.1.4–6) and Sozomen (*HE* 8.1.2–3) report merely that the soldiers who had marched west with Theodosius against Eugenius murdered Rufinus on their return because they thought he aspired to the throne and had invited Huns to ravage the East.

downfalls. Eutropius rose when Rufinus fell in 395, and Zosimus asserts that Eutropius worked with Stilicho against Rufinus (5.8.1), but Claudian shows that Eutropius proved to be Stilicho's next enemy (esp. *Eutr.* 2.539–52). When Eutropius fell, Aurelian rose: he received both the prefecture and the consulate for 400. When Gaïnas got rid of Aurelian too, he himself mounted a brief unstable coup.[54] Theodoret shows that Gaïnas was to have taken the consulate for 401 (*HE* 5.32.6). When his coup toppled into open rebellion, the honor passed to Fravitta, the general who defeated him. It is not an unreasonable conjecture that Stilicho might have sought to suborn against Rufinus an officer in the army he was returning to the East; but the conjecture is not supported by any subsequent action. Even if Gaïnas did begin on Stilicho's behalf, he did not continue. Döpp pointed out that "if [Stilicho] really could rely on [Gaïnas] to eliminate the troublesome Eutropius," his help was unnaturally long in coming.[55]

Seeck's second hypothesis identified the "tiny page" that finished Eutropius (*exigua charta,* 2pr.19–20) as a letter from Stilicho.[56] Seeck assumed that Eutropius was forced to request Stilicho's aid against the Persian threat at which Claudian hints (2.474–84).[57] Stilicho would then have written back demanding as a precondition that Eutropius be removed. But as Cameron urged against this scenario, Stilicho never went.[58] Since 396 (*3 Cons.*) Claudian's poetry had been promoting Stilicho's desire to supervise both Honorius and Arcadius. Roma and Aurora in the two books of *In Eutropium* express the same wish. Many scholars have objected that if Stilicho had received any encouragement from the East, it would better suit Claudian's established themes to trumpet vindication, not to hint indirectly.[59] Nor would Stilicho have been wise to waste time on conditions before racing to seize his opportunity; once he gained control, he could impose what he liked. But even supposing he made such a proviso, once it was granted this hypothesis leaves nothing else to keep him back. Suppositions such as Demougeot's "Stilicho thought it politic to neglect the appeal of the endangered East"[60] answer nothing.

54. See Alan Cameron and Long 1993. The praetorian prefecture was given to Aurelian's brother Caesarius, who had earlier succeeded Rufinus as praetorian prefect under Eutropius (*PLRE* 1.171, with the corrections of Cameron and Long).

55. Döpp 1978, 191.

56. Seeck 1913, 311, 565.

57. Seeck also interpreted "the just and the guilty equally pray" (*Eutr.* 2.508) to mean that Eutropius as well as his innocent victims looked to Stilicho; he was followed by Demougeot 1951, 228 n. 570. Alan Cameron 1970, 141, attributed to Birt (without specific citation) the idea that *Eutr.* 2.601–2 could be related to Eutropius's fall as well; Birt 1888, 51 n. 2, interpreted these lines as a plea for help against Tribigild.

58. Alan Cameron 1970, 142.

59. Mazzarino 1942, 213 n. 2 = 1990, 367–68 n. 38; Demougeot 1951, 229 n. 574; Alan Cameron 1970, 142.

60. Demougeot 1951, 229.

Birt identified the *exigua charta* as Arcadius's decree deposing Eutropius (*CTh* 9.40.17).[61] Seeck and Mazzarino rejected this idea on the grounds that "tiny page" is too undignified a thing to call an imperial decree; Demougeot objected that the law merely confirms the deposition after it was effected.[62] But positive formulation belongs to legal language. Moreover, it is to another imperial decree deposing an important minister that Claudian alludes with the phrase. When Tiberius deposes Sejanus, in Juvenal's *Satire* 10, it is with a "wordy and grand letter" (*verbosa et grandis epistula*, Juv. 10.71). Juvenal deals with weighty monsters, Claudian with an overreaching baseborn "half man" (1.171, 2.22). He humorously shrinks the decree to match the moral scale he assigns to its object.[63]

Since Stilicho cannot plausibly be injected into the current of Eastern events, there is no sense in which Roma's and Aurora's requests to him may be said to have been fulfilled. That they had been would have suggested *post eventum* composition. So for example Iustitia prophesies retribution for Rufinus at the end of *In Rufinum* 1 (*Ruf.* 1.368–71), when Claudian in the preface and proem has already referred more plainly to Rufinus's death (*Ruf.* 1pr.15–19, 1.20–23). On the other hand Iustitia's expectation that Honorius will overthrow Persia and India and inaugurate a new Golden Age was never realized. Hermann Funke argued that the vagueness of her second prophecy ought to date the original composition, to which the preface and proem were a later addition: since Claudian does not bring the events of *In Rufinum* 1 up to Rufinus's death, and concludes the proem by requesting the Muses to tell not how Rufinus met his end but how he rose to power, the main body of the book was written before Rufinus died.[64] But Rufinus did die under circumstances that are encompassed by the first part of Iustitia's prediction. The strained arguments and compositional anomalies Funke proposed can all be avoided by

61. Birt 1892, xxxv.

62. Seeck 1913, 565; Mazzarino 1942, 213 n. 2 = 1990, 367 n. 38; Demougeot 1951, 229 n. 574.

63. Alan Cameron 1974, 149, recognized the allusion and noted that Juvenal was popular in Western circles in the fourth century (cf. Amm. 28.4.14; further, Alan Cameron, "Literary Allusions in the *Historia Augusta*," *Hermes* 92 [1964]: 363–77); he deemed *exigua* "an indirect compliment to Arcadius" by virtue of its contrast to Tiberius. I think the joke is primary, but the compliment could be argued if anyone at court took offense at the adjective (it ironically accentuates evil, e.g., at Juv. 1.68 describing the instruments by which a forger of wills makes himself rich). The language of the law codes, to say nothing of panegyric including Claudian's, makes me doubt whether late antique courts considered concision a virtue. Michael Dewar, "The Fall of Eutropius," *Classical Quarterly* n.s. 40 (1990): 582–84, saw contempt in the letter's "tininess."

64. Funke 1984.

admitting that Claudian chose to anticipate an event he knew to have happened, without detailing it.[65]

The fact that Claudian later composed a second book out of details he preferred only to hint at in book 1 is a separate matter. The epic *In Gildonem* ostensibly anticipates a second book describing Gildo's defeat, but Claudian never wrote that book. Even though the one book ends only with the landing of the Roman fleet in Sardinia, its proem like that of *In Rufinum* 1 proclaims the crisis resolved: "Returned to empire is the South, and subject again the vaults of the other sky" (*Gild.* 1–2). Manifestly it was issued as an artistically sufficient entity while still in this state of anticipation. The parallel *In Rufinum* 1 fits the same hypothesis. Foreshadowing completes in the minds of the audience the narrative not actually carried in the poem. By leaving the conclusion of events to the reader's imagination, such anticipation can also lend a sanitizing vagueness to events that might have been too sensitive at the time. The prophesying divinity sanctions the essential fact, and the details are passed by.

Iustitia's more extravagant predictions following from Rufinus's fall (*Ruf.* 1.372–87) push the audience into a farther future, enforcing a more general optimism. The magnificently fabricated paradise Iustitia evokes could never have been expected to be realized literally; it remains conventionally optimistic and inconclusive.[66] With similar effusiveness, when Tiber hears that Olybrius and Probinus have been named consul, he calls for them to supplant Castor and Pollux as a constellation (*Ol. Prob.* 243–53). Even mundane optimism in panegyric often overreaches in its predictions for a future the author did not know when he wrote: for example, Mamertinus claims that the good weather of 288–89 presages that Maximian will defeat Carausius (*Pan. Lat.* 10[2].12).[67] He relied on Maximian's and Diocletian's dutifulness and blessedness as emperors to predict the same success again, equally vainly, when he spoke before Maximian again in 291 (*Pan. Lat.* 11[3].19.4–5).

Synesius's political allegory *De Providentia* provides a further parallel. Synesius explains in his preface to the completed tale that he composed and recited the "first part, as far as the riddle of the wolf" (Synes. *Prov.* 88A), while Aurelian, figured as the good king Osiris in the allegory, was in exile; "the second part was woven on after the return of the best men, who asked that the book not be left incomplete with the story of their misfortunes" (*Prov.* 88B).

65. After I made these arguments in my dissertation of 1989, Nesselrath 1991 argued out a similar position more fully, yielding valuable insights into the dramatic structure of *Ruf.* 1 and 2 (summarized in Chap. 1).

66. Levy 1971, 108–14, collected specific allusions.

67. Claudian with vaguer optimism and the same link between meteorology and empire celebrates sudden good weather at Honorius's sixth consular inauguration, *6 Cons.* 537–42.

That is, Synesius originally designed his first edition to be artistically complete while cutting short the events it narrated before a good resolution was realized, but when it could be anticipated. At the end of this book 1 a god appears and alludes prophetically to two events: a rout of the foreign mercenaries from the city following an attempted heresy and fiery meteorological omens, and the removal of the tyrannous usurper Typhos (*Prov.* 114D–115A).[68] The recipient of this oracle joyfully contemplates "what was to happen about Osiris in the near future, as well as in the years yet to come, when Osiris's son Horus would decide to select the wolf rather than the lion for his ally" (*Prov.* 115B). Synesius thus alludes to the myth beyond the point his narrative reaches. In its traditional form, the dead king Osiris is never restored, but his son Horus overthrows Typhos in turn; Synesius's wolf and lion allude to two variants in the tradition about Horus's preparation for the final battle.[69] Since Synesius alludes so circumstantially to the rout of Gaïnas's Goths from Constantinople as his coup unraveled in July 400, the historical counterpart of the Scythian expulsion in Synesius's tale, it appears that Synesius wrote after the rout. He described the riot that precipitated it and its aftermath in the continuation he wrote later that summer or autumn. But his allusion to Horus and the myth make plain that he expected, if he should ever continue his tale, to write about a successor who would turn Typhos out of office and restore Osiris's policies. The course of historical reality forced him instead to bring Osiris back and try to suggest that he was vindicated against Typhos directly, even though Typhos is never removed from office. At the end of book 2 Synesius still looks to a future when Osiris would be restored fully.[70] This hope was not fulfilled in fact until after Synesius's death.[71] Thus at the close of book 1 he prophesies beyond

68. Liebeschuetz 1990, 269–72, supposed that Synesius wrote book 1 at about the dramatic time its close portrays, before the riot of 12 July 400 (date, *Chron. Marc.* s.a., *Chron. Min.* II.66 = *MGHAA* XI.66), and later revised it incorporating references to the Gothic rout. But the terms in which Synesius describes both his first edition, as a continuous unit within the expanded whole (τό γε πρῶτον μέρος, τὸ μέχρι τοῦ κατὰ τὸν λύκον αἰνίγματος, Synes. *Prov.* 88A), and the second part, as a continuation (προσυφάνθη δὲ τὸ ἑπόμενον [literally, "following"], 88B), resist the imputation of insertions. One would have to unravel and reweave the bolt on the loom to add anything before its end, not simply "weave on."

69. The myth is recounted straight and relatively completely by Plutarch *De Iside et Osiride* 355D–358E and Diodorus 1.14–22, 1.88.6. On Synesius's use of it, see Long 1987 and Alan Cameron and Long 1993, 143–45, 256–60, 311–16.

70. Postponements spread from the middle of the book to its last words: Synes. *Prov.* 125C, 125D, 128A, 128B, 129B; see Alan Cameron and Long 1993, 186–90.

71. That is, Aurelian was named praetorian prefect again in 414 (*PLRE* 2.1250), two years after Synesius must be presumed dead (*PLRE* 2.1048–50; Alan Cameron and Long 1993, 188 and n. 155), *pace* J. H. W. G. Liebeschuetz, "The Date of Synesius' *De Provi-*

the frame of his narrative one event that had happened at the time of writing, and one that had not yet been precluded by other developments, but which never was realized.

The double request of Roma in *In Eutropium* 1 bifurcates similarly. The decision not to recognize Eutropius had already been taken, and indeed Eutropius had entered on his consulate unrecognized by the West when the poem was published. Roma's request symbolically justifies the Western government's action, for it dramatizes the notion that the traditions and ideals of Rome cannot accept a eunuch consul. Her second request similarly authorizes intervention, and opens within the book the possibility that Stilicho should depose Eutropius.[72] But no opportunity ever became available. *In Eutropium* 1 dates itself between the two eventualities: after Stilicho and Honorius repudiated Eutropius's consulate, but before separate Eastern events made it impossible for Stilicho to act against him.

CAMERON URGED essentially the same points against dating the composition of Aurora's speech after Eutropius's fall. She asks Stilicho to protect the East, and he never found an opportunity to do so.[73] But book 2 contains a problem that does not arise in book 1. If, as Cameron believed, it is specifically from Eutropius that Aurora asks to be rescued, the dramatic date at the conclusion of the book falls before the time of Eutropius's exile in August 399, which is described in the preface and proem; the failure of the book's narrated time to catch up to its introduction parallels the structure of *In Rufinum* 1 and *In Gildonem*. But if Aurora asks Stilicho to rescue the East from Eutropius when the audience knows from the same book's preface and proem that Eutropius was already deposed and exiled, without Stilicho's intervention, the book falls either into the futility of Döpp's scenario for book 1 or into Gnilka's strained irony. Claudian successfully exploited foreshadowing in *In Rufinum* 1 and *In Gildonem*, so he should not have expected his audience to forget the preface and proem of *In Eutropium* 1 by its conclusion. There must be some sense in which Eutropius's exile did not prevent the intervention Aurora requests. Her terms need to be examined again.

Her peroration summarizes her plea (*Eutr.* 2.591–602):

in te iam spes una mihi. pro fronde Minervae
has tibi protendo lacrimas: succurre ruenti,

dentia," in *Actes du VIIe Congrès de la Fédération internationale d'études classiques* 2, ed. Janos Harmatta (Budapest: Academiai Kiado, 1983), 39–46, reprised at Liebeschuetz 1990, 269–72. Synesius's own political concerns of course had long lost relevance.
72. These two points are taken up again in Part III.
73. Alan Cameron 1970, 143–44.

eripe me tandem servilibus, eripe, regnis.
neve adeo cunctos paucorum crimine damnes
nec nova tot meritis offensa prioribus obstet.
iamiam flecte animum. suprema pericula semper
dant veniam culpae. quamvis iratus et exul
pro patriae flammis non distulit arma Camillus.
non te subtrahimus Latio; defensor utrique
sufficis. armorum liceat splendore tuorum
in commune frui; clipeus nos protegat idem
unaque pro gemino desudet cardine virtus.

In you now is the one hope for me. In place of Minerva's bough
I stretch forth to you these tears. Aid one who is falling;
rescue, rescue me at last from servile kingships.
Do not condemn all together for the crime of just a few,
nor let a new offense stand in the way of so many earlier merits.
Now bend your spirit. Supreme perils always
grant pardon to a fault. Although enraged and an exile,
in the face of his fatherland's flames, Camillus did not hold off his arms.
We do not take you away from Latium: as defender for both
you suffice. Give us leave to profit from the splendor
of your arms to common advantage; let the same shield protect us
and let a single courage exert itself on behalf of the twinned world.

Aurora's essential theme is a cry for help. She has only one hope. She is collapsing in ruins. She needs to be succored, to be rescued. It is a matter of extreme danger. She seeks a defender. She prays for a shield to protect her and for courage to labor on her behalf.

Aurora echoes Palinurus's cry to Aeneas for burial, "by the sky's pleasant light and breezes, by your begetter I pray you, by the hopes of rising Iulus, rescue me, unconquered one, from these ills [*eripe me his, invicte, malis*]" (Verg. *Aen.* 6.363–65).[74] The associations of this epic scene reinforce Aurora's pathos and nobility. Palinurus loyally and attentively guided Aeneas's ship, but now he suffers because his death has not been resolved by burial. His invocation of Aeneas's father and son call upon Roman traditions back to their Trojan roots and down through history to support his request. Now Aurora suffers not from general ills but specifically insulting "servile kingships." "At last" combines with the echo to extend her sufferings.

Aurora's example of Camillus and the terms "arms," "shield," and "courage"

---

74. *HA Tyr. Trig.* 24 and Eutrop. *Brev.* 9.13.1 assert that Tetricus quoted the same line in surrendering to Aurelian. Barbara Saylor Rodgers (private communication) notes that *eripe* is used similarly also at, e.g., Verg. *Aen.* 2.289, 5.690; Luc. 4.120, but we agree that the echo of Vergil's Palinurus is closest and most compelling.

all suggest a military danger. Indeed, the body of her speech paints the danger posed by the rebellious Gruthungi led by Tribigild. Aurora names them and describes them precisely (2.576–79): they were once a Roman legion, settled after defeat by the Romans on Roman land under Roman law, and now they are ravaging Lydia and Asia. Her present defense is useless, she continues (*Eutr.* 2.580–83):

> nec vi nec numero freti; sed inertia nutrit
> proditioque ducum, quorum per crimina miles
> captivis dat terga suis, quos teste subegit
> Danubio, partemque timet qui reppulit omnes.

They are supported by neither force nor numbers; but the generals'
  inactivity
and betrayal feeds them. And through their crimes the soldier
shows his back to his own captives, whom he subjected, the Danube
witnessing. He fears a part, who has driven back them all.

The Gruthungi are now labeled "captives" and Theodosius's victory over them in 386 is specifically evoked.[75] "Inactivity" aptly characterizes Leo's generalship as Claudian narrates it (2.409–31). "Betrayal" does not otherwise figure in Claudian's version, although other sources writing longer after the outbreak of Tribigild's rebellion unanimously allege that he and Gaïnas had colluded all along.[76] Claudian makes no hint that Gaïnas was involved at the start. His scene of Bellona and Tribigild claims imagistically that Tribigild naturally recovered his barbarian ferocity as soon as Eutropius failed to lull him with sufficient gifts.[77] Yet Claudian too might well see betrayal in Gaïnas's refusal to engage Tribigild; Eunapius reports kindred suspicions against Gaïnas's conqueror Fravitta in 400, for example, because he had not captured him as well.[78] Greater hindsight led the later authors to make stronger claims, so that they infer collusion even before Tribigild's forces began to revolt.

Thus Aurora demonstrates that she can expect no good from the resources she has available. Nor are others likely to become available, for the court is indifferent to the plight of the land so long as its own revenues are unharmed; indeed, a remedy has already been discovered in dividing into two the prov-

---

75. Cf. Seeck 1913, 208, 519; Stein and Palanque 1949–59, 1.194, 521.

76. Synes. *Prov.* 108C (with Alan Cameron and Long 1993, 223–33, 316–23); Eunap. frr. 75.6, 75.7 M = 67.10, 67.11 Blockley (Blockley 1981–83, 2.147 n. 153, suggested that fr. 76 M = 67.7 Blockley too might relate to Gaïnas and this alleged conspiracy); Zos. 5.13–18; Socr. *HE* 6.6.4–6; Soz. *HE* 8.4.1–3; Philost. *HE* 11.8, 138.14–27 Bidez and Winkelmann.

77. Cf. *Eutr.* 2.177–80, 189–93, 194–229 (Bellona's speech), 316–24 (Tribigild's recovery of pride).

78. Eunap. fr. 82 M = 69.4 Blockley.

inces that remain, "lest the vendor lose anything, when his scope has been trimmed back" (2.585–86). "Vendor" epitomizes Claudian's description in book 1 of Eutropius as "infamous huckster of offices" (1.198). His unforgettable sales office even has a posted price list of provinces and amounts (1.201–5). Accordingly, Aurora's complaint here must have been perceived as referring closely to Eutropius, and so to a period when he was still in office.[79] No transition interposes before Aurora begins to beseech Stilicho directly, so that the immediate context places her appeal in the same time frame. But the earlier references to Cyprus make this time retrospective. The narrative does not catch up to the time marked at the book's beginning.

Birt and Döpp precluded this discrepancy when they argued that "the lictor throws the fasces to the ground and shudders, and the infamous axes fall of themselves" (2.520–21) describes Eutropius's expulsion from the consulate. But their interpretation is excessively legalistic. In the previous paragraph Claudian likens the Easterners to children who ignore their father's absence when it frees them from their studies to play, but cry for him when an unjust power takes advantage of their weakness (2.509–15). The thrust of the passage, as of Aurora's plea, is that the Easterners are unable to help themselves. By alluding to Eutropius's deposition in this connection Claudian would wreck his thesis, for then he would show the Easterners taking some action on their own behalf. The most they can do is to recognize how they have let themselves into trouble. The horrified lictor, discarded fasces, and collapsing axes figure in a series of picturesque allegations that fear of Tribigild or worse has finally brought this realization home. It begins, "all confess that they deserve torture or death, because they handed themselves over to slaves and deserted Stilicho" (2.516–17). Whatever the merits of the reason he gives, Claudian must be conceded to exaggerate the confession itself. Next he claims that the Easterners gradually recognize what their former madness has made them do, and avert their eyes; here the emblems of office identify the consul they created. Then he compares them to Maenads spattered with Pentheus's blood, recognizing his head and grieving at the realization. This image too exceeds the present reality. The gestures of the lictor and axes evoke Eutropius's consulate. But although revulsion and spontaneous collapse are less patently overwrought images than torture, death, and the ripping apart of a live body, they too show emotions, not a real deposition. Aurora's "vendor" still occupies his shop.

Aurora's reference to Camillus, if it can be pressed, also suggests that Eutropius still prevailed when Claudian wrote the passage. As she says, Camillus was still "enraged and an exile" when called upon to save Rome from the

---

79. The allusion was recognized by Fargues, *Invectives* 136 n. 586. Andrews 1931, 134 nn. 586–88, identified Eutropius, but mistakenly referred the administrative abuse to taxes.

Gauls.[80] She begs Stilicho "not to damn all by the crimes of a few and not to let a new offense stand in the way of so many earlier merits." May he be swayed, since "supreme perils always grant pardon to a fault" (2.594–98). The fault in question is no vague matter of generalized hostility, but the specific and concrete decree of the Eastern Senate naming Stilicho *hostis publicus*.[81] There is no evidence that this decree was revoked before the general law deposing Eutropius abolished all his *acta* (*CTh* 9.40.17). Stilicho might be expected to resent the former enactment even after it was repealed, so reference to it does not clearly identify the date. But Camillus occupied a position equivalent to Stilicho's while his status as "public enemy" was still in force. Again, this passage tends to refer Aurora's speech to Eutropius's continued predominance.

On the other hand, Cyprus in the preface and proem explicitly evokes Eutropius's downfall and exile (2pr.52, 72, 76; 2.21). It is axiomatic that a poet releases his own work only in a form he feels to function adequately for his present purpose. Thus, for example, Donatus recounts that Vergil gave readings of parts of the *Aeneid* that still possessed half lines, completing some as he performed, but at his death wanted it burned: it sufficed as a work in progress, but he did not wish to be immortalized by flaws he had not had time to correct.[82] "Vendor" best suggests that Claudian wrote Aurora's speech while Eutropius was still in office, but the historical context in which the completed *In Eutropium* 2 was published must abrogate this specificity. Similarly, despite Camillus, Stilicho must be imagined to base any hesitation on bad experience now past.

But substance must remain in Aurora's request. What does she mean by *servilibus regnis?* Unquestionably, as Cameron argued, the primary association in *In Eutropium* of words meaning "slave" is with Eutropius.[83] At the beginning of book 1 Claudian rebukes Fortuna for befouling the consulate "with a servile crime" (*servili crimine*) and, at that, picking a slave worse than the ones on chain gangs (*compede*) or in workhouses (*ergastula*; 1.26–28). Among slaves (*famulis*), he continues, what distinction there is marks out one who has served only one master; but Eutropius's masters are legion (1.30–33). Claudian pictures the scene of Eutropius's frequent sales, using the terms "he changed accounts," "buyer," "price," and "for sale," qualifying it all "while he could be

---

80. On the facts behind this popular tradition (e.g., Amm. 21.16.13), see Friedrich Münzer, "M. Furius Camillus," *RE* 7 (1912): 324–48 (specifically 329–31). The narrative asserts directly that the Easterners fear Stilicho's resentment, but fear the present threats of Tribigild and Persia so much more that they long for him anyway (2.502–8).

81. Zos. 5.11.1. Fargues, *Invectives* 137 n. 594, multiplied the "few" so that "it is a matter of Eutropius, of his partisans, and in a general way of enemies to Stilicho who were located at the Eastern court."

82. Donatus (Suet.) *Vita* 31–34, 39–41 (*Vita Donati* 107–25, 153–65 Hardie).

83. Alan Cameron 1970, 136, quoted previously.

sold" (1.33–38). As their result, Eutropius has bent his repeatedly transferred neck to the yoke, and his ancient servitude (*servitium*) has been constantly renewed, never ceased but frequently begun (1.42–44). This paragraph demonstrates only the beginning of the ways Claudian belabors his point. Abstract generalization, comparison to other slaves, evocation of aspects of slave life, and direct assertion all focus on Eutropius.

Similar instances recur throughout both books;[84] I shall cite only a few more examples. Claudian dwells with epigrammatic relish on the fact that Eutropius became an imperial minister when he had been rejected from private service. The terms "slave" and "attendant" (*servi, ministrum*, 1.142–44) contrast with Eutropius's new role. Eutropius's ferocity as a judge is more savage than any wild beast, as is to be expected of "a slave raging against free backs" (*servi, libera*; 1.183–84). When he returns in triumph from campaign in Armenia, Claudian is outraged at his shamelessness: "indeed, at what will a slave and an effeminate feel shame?" (*servum mollemque*, 1.252). As consul Eutropius joins his former master Arinthaeus in the fasti; Claudian underlines the affront to class with explicit references to masters and slaves (*erile, servus, domino*, 1.478–80). He uses the word *servus* only in *In Eutropium*. In book 2 Mars repeats the charge that Eutropius as consul "spatters the age with servile stains" (*maculis servilibus*, 2.132). Tellingly, Tribigild rejects Eutropius's tardy attempt at conciliation because once he has tasted the sweetness of booty, "he refuses to serve a slave" (*se famulo servire negat*), and rejects the gifts of the fearful (2.318–20).

Servire in this line comes closer than anything else in the poem to associating the Gruthungi with slavery, as would be necessary to underpin Birt's identification of *servilibus regnis* with them.[85] Birt in fact cited not this passage but the remorse of the Easterners "who entrusted themselves to slaves, deserting Stilicho" (*famulis*, 2.517), identifying the *famulis* as the Gruthungi. The second passage gave Birt an easy verbal step from *famulis* to *servilibus regnis*, but the identification itself is not cogent. Although Tribigild occasions the Easterners' fear, the Persians cap him as its object (2.474–84). The "threatening neighbor" who seeks to evict the fatherless and formerly heedless children in Claudian's immediately preceding simile also suggests Persia rather than rebels within the empire (2.509–15). As the context fails to impose a clear suggestion of the Gruthungi, it is more to be expected that the audience would have

84. Without even considering less direct suggestions such as masters or selling, Christiansen 1988 s.vv. *famulus, servilis, servire, servitium, servus* produces the following list of relevant lines: *Eutr.* 1.26, 30, 43, 57, 125, 142, 149, 150, 175, 184, 252, 332, 345, 479, 503, 509; 2pr.61, 62; 2.69, 132, 319 (bis), 352, 517, 535. At 1.250 because of Eutropius the East is enslaved to barbarians (*servire*), and at 2.201 Bellona wishes for captive Greek slaves (*famulas*). 2.593 contains *servilibus regnis*.

85. Birt 1888, 51–52 n. 2.

applied *famulis* to a slavish person in the position Stilicho might have occupied, namely Eutropius. The other passage, however, Tribigild's response,
might be claimed to presuppose that the Gruthungi ordinarily were the Romans' slaves. But as a standard against which to interpret either *famulis* in line
517 or *servilibus regnis* in 593, this norm is weaker than the fact that Tribigild
explicitly repudiates it. As far as the safety of the East is concerned, the problem is precisely that the Gruthungi have ceased to be slaves and become bold
plunderers. Tribigild's *famulo* clearly refers to Eutropius.

But Eutropius is not the only slave in the poem. Claudian presents Hosius
and Eutropius at Eutropius's council meeting (*Eutr.* 2.350–53):

> consident apices gemini dicionis Eoae,
> hic cocus, hic leno, defossi verbere terga,
> servitio, non arte pares, hic saepius emptus,
> alter ad Hispanos nutritus verna penates.

> Twin peaks of Eastern sovereignty they sit,
> this one a cook, this one a pander, their backs furrowed with beating,
> equal in servitude, not in skill; this one more often purchased,
> the other a homeborn slave reared under Spanish household gods.

Slavery equalizes them, so that they can be "twin peaks of Eastern sovereignty."
"Servitude" and the technical term *verna* are explicit. Backs scarred with beat-
ings conventionally emblematized slaves at least as far back as classical comedy.[86]

The whole assembly of Eutropius's courtiers consists of plebeian generals
and others who, "their calves marked by the fetter and livid shins by black iron,
rule the laws, although a printed face resists and betrays itself by its title"
(2.342–45). Again, scars mark the slave.[87]

Slavery and Eutropius's subordinates function, but differently, in Aurora's
history of the East from the time Stilicho marched west against Eugenius. She
opens by charging that he has left her to be "a plaything and laughingstock for
slaves" (2.535); yet since she does not otherwise refer to Eutropius's slave history, the generalizing plural *famulis* joins with *servilibus regnis* in ambiguity.
Rufinus began her troubles. Then when she hoped to have Stilicho back,

---

86. Cf. Peter P. Spranger, *Historische Untersuchungen zu den Sklavenfiguren des Plautus und Terenz*, 2nd ed., Forschungen zur antiken Sklaverei 17 (Wiesbaden: Steiner,
1984), 47–51, 84–87 (although he focused on Plautus and Terence he addressed Greek
traditions as well); Opelt 1965, 159–89.

87. Old convention said that runaway slaves' faces were marked by branding (reflected by Platnauer 1922, 1.211; Andrews 1931, 115; Koster 1980, 338), but C. P. Jones,
"Stigma: Tattooing and Branding in Graeco-Roman Antiquity," *JRS* 77 (1987): 139–55,
argued that tattooing predominated.

Eutropius suddenly leapt into predominance. At this point Aurora applies the language of slavery to herself. Rufinus's death brought a "brief and false liberty" (2.543–44). She hoped again to be governed by the "reins" of Stilicho (*regi, habenis*, 2.544–45). She found she had changed only the sex of her master (*domini*, 2.552).

Eutropius's service as imperial chamberlain at first contained his malice within bounds appropriate to a eunuch, "but afterward, when he had driven out good men and kept the dregs, he chose worse allies: his worthy underling Hosius stood on one side, Leo on the other. His confidence grew and an uncovered lust to command burst into open flame" (2.557–60). Though bearing primarily its general sense, *libido* like "bedchamber" (2.553) potentially echoes the sexual undertones of "castrate" and "the sex of my master" when Eutropius succeeds Rufinus (2.550, 552); at any rate it is the sexual or generally debased character of the eunuch that Aurora emphasizes, rather than slavery specifically. Correspondingly, she does not recapitulate Hosius's and Leo's past careers, but she does name them in synecdoche for all Eutropius's "dregs." She notes briefly how degradation radiates from Eutropius and then at greater length describes the barbarian incursions, before returning to the frivolous unconcern of the court (2.584), the cynical doubling of provinces, and her final plea.

Eutropius's court and he together frame the crucial alarm that motivates Aurora's speech. He remains the salient figure, but in contrast to book 1 Claudian's focus includes smaller satellites as well. This breadth is intrinsic to the whole of book 2. It must have functioned in its interpretation even if the preface and proem did not make clear that Claudian delivered the whole after Eutropius was exiled; but incidentally it allows his reference to be diffused enough to accommodate the fact that he did.

Some degree of retrospective blurring had always been part of Claudian's scheme. Aurora's picture of Leo and Hosius flanking Eutropius is necessarily retrospective, for on any hypothesis Leo was dead by the time Claudian wrote the main body of *In Eutropium* 2. His campaign is capped by his death. It demonstrates the central claim Claudian argues: the East cannot protect itself. His case demands that the image of Leo's incompetence must extend to the East as a whole. While Eutropius remained in power to be a target, the debacle of Leo's campaign would have reflected on him primarily; but with Eutropius gone it casts its damning light on the whole administration.

Admittedly, it is Hosius whom the body of *In Eutropium* 2 specifically identifies as a former slave who rules the empire with Eutropius, and Hosius most likely fell with his superior. Thus history would have excluded the two most outstanding slaves of Claudian's piece from the reference of *servilibus regnis*. Claudian asserts in the preface that "the whole band perishes along with its leader" (2pr.16). Indeed Hosius is not recorded in office after 15 December 398.[88] But not all of the "dregs" can really have been siphoned off at once. Aurelian remained out of office during Eutropius's ministry, but the West no more recognized his consulate than his predecessor's.[89] From Stilicho's point of view he appeared in the same light as Eutropius. Doubtless lesser officials remained too. In the second book of his panegyric in honor of Stilicho's consulate, delivered at the beginning of 400, Claudian describes "an unmoving and undutiful throng that shields its own madness with the royal name," whose effronteries Stilicho does not ascribe to Arcadius (*Stil.* 2.79–81). Once again, a general hostility is evidenced.

Servilibus regnis, and *famulis* at the beginning of Aurora's speech, must be understood to embrace the Eastern administration overall in its continued incapacity to deal with current internal barbarian problems. Only after Aurelian's brother Caesarius succeeded him to the prefecture was the series of crises begun by Tribigild's revolt finally resolved. During the course of 400 Gaïnas revolted. Near the end of 400 Caesarius's general Fravitta routed him beyond the borders. At least until then, Claudian might legitimately claim that Eutropius's successors had not set the security of the East on any more solid ground than he had. The idea that they had failed continued to form a basis for Aurora's appeal to Stilicho for help.

IN THE PROEM Claudian complains in his own voice that Eutropius's exile has not solved all the East's problems (*Eutr.* 2.20–23):

> at vos egregie purgatam creditis aulam,
> Eutropium si Cypros habet? vindictaque mundi
> semivir exul erit? quis vos lustrare valebit
> Oceanus? tantum facinus quae diluet aetas?

> Yet do you yourselves believe the court has been outstandingly cleansed,
> if Cyprus holds Eutropius? Will a half man's exile
> be the rod of manumission for the world? Who will be the Ocean with
>   power to purify
> you? What age will wash away so great a sin?

88. *CTh* 10.22.4. Anthemius (*PLRE* 2.94) is not attested as *magister officiorum* until January 404, but he must have exercised considerable influence before winning the prefecture itself in summer 405: in 405 he was already consul. Such an honor implies several years of prominence. The position of *magister officiorum* is an obvious vacancy, since no other name is attested after Hosius. It is reasonable to suppose that he replaced him at once. (So Alan Cameron and Long 1993, 108–9 and n. 11.)

89. *CLRE* s.a. 400.

The notion of time diluting the transgression embodied by Eutropius reverts to the idea of the pollution his consulate imposes on the time, which was sounded in book 1 (esp. 1.1–23, 284–86). The next part of the proem of book 2 takes it up again specifically. The thematic link justifies the retrospective shift in dramatic date. Although the proem follows the preface in setting *In Eutropium* 2 overall in a later temporal context, it makes plain that the exile, a penalty rather than an adequate remedy, belongs to the same chain of problems begun by Eutropius's inauguration. Similarly, lustration by the ocean is not a gratuitous extravagant image, but picks up the hope of the preface that Eutropius may drown on his way to Cyprus. The ocean, which is regularly associated with purificatory rituals,[90] would then literally wash away the contaminant. This imagistic link too binds the preface and completed book of *In Eutropium* 2.

Fargues argued very literally that since the proem refers to Eutropius on Cyprus and the preface only to his journey there, the proem must date later than the preface; Gnilka answered this argument equally literally.[91] He protested that the proem located Eutropius on Cyprus only in a conditional clause. A simple condition implies nothing as to the fulfillment of its protasis. It cannot be pressed to chronological decisiveness one way or the other.

The crucial function of the conditional sentence is to turn attention away from Eutropius himself, wherever he may be at the moment, to the court he left behind. Claudian blames Tribigild's revolt on him, so that he epitomizes all the incompetence Claudian indicts. As a eunuch in impossibly high honor he naturally emblematizes the corruption and prodigiousness Claudian marshals as emotive weapons. Consular auspices provide a way deeply embedded in the Roman consciousness to associate his miasma with the entire year. Thus even though personally outdated as a target, Eutropius remained a figure through whom to focus a general attack. The preface retains the personal focus, its light tone dismissing the banished eunuch from serious consideration. The proem redirects the focus of the book: first, more harshly, on the real problem that Eutropius represents; second, more broadly, on the whole East. It confirms in advance the potential breadth of Aurora's complaint.

To SUMMARIZE briefly, I am inclined to believe with Cameron that Claudian conceived and composed the larger part of *In Eutropium* 2 while Eutropius was still the evil genius of the East. But form requires that the preface have been presented along with the main book; moreover Claudian incorporated reference to Cyprus into the book as well. These parts cannot be separated from the

90. So Fargues, *Invectives* 94 n. 23 ad loc.
91. Fargues, *Claudien* 24 n. 4; Gnilka 1976, 108–9 n. 22.

completed poem as presented. Nor should they be.[92] They perform the vital function of refocusing the themes elaborated in the main part of the book onto a broader target.[93] Although the terms of Aurora's speech immediately suggest the period of Eutropius's predominance, they can be extended to cover its sequel also. Supplications by personified divinities necessarily step out of strict historical reality into the universalizing world of images; this transposition aids the necessary blurring of Aurora's complaint. Its inherent splendor leaves a suitably grand impression for a conclusion; Claudian would not have wanted to revise very much.

92. Janson 1964, 73, adduced much evidence demonstrating the well-known fact that "an introduction is usually composed after the actual work"; but in all cases presented with it, and closely related to it.

93. Gnilka 1976, 103, made essentially the same point in a negative way: Claudian would not attack the Eastern court in the proem if Eutropius were the only target of the invective.

CHAPTER SIX

Eastern Information
at the Western Court

✦

THE FACT THAT events happened does not alone establish that Claudian referred to them and manipulated them. First he needed access to information.[1] Even more than *In Rufinum*, *In Eutropium* concerns the East. How well Claudian knew the affairs of the Eastern empire, the dealings of Arcadius's court, and Eutropius's personal history limits the degree of detailed accuracy he could attain. In turn, it is within the limits of his knowledge that he selected which items to present and in what light to cast them.

Claudian also must have written with an eye toward the knowledge and interests of his audience, or he would have wasted his efforts. Ammianus obviously exaggerates somewhat when he proclaims disgustedly that the Roman aristocrats of his day "hate learning like poison" and read nothing but Juvenal and Marius Maximus (Amm. 28.4.14); nonetheless, it may well be believed that not every hearer fully appreciated all the richness of Claudian's literary allusions, or even all his citations of Roman history. But they should have been able to grasp the substance of his references to contemporary events.

One extant passage from Eunapius's *History* specifically discusses communications between West and East at precisely this period. Its position among the *Excerpta de Sententiis* indicates that it represents a historiographical digression with which Eunapius introduced the final crisis of Eutropius's administration, Tribigild's revolt.[2] It deserves to be quoted extensively:

1. I gratefully thank Michael McCormick for discussing many of the problems of this chapter with me.

2. Eunap. fr. 74 Müller = 66.2 Blockley. Blockley appended fr. 75 M in smooth succession, as the palimpsest appears to do (noted by Paschoud 1971–89, 3¹.327). I quote up to the last sentence of the fragment as Müller divided it, where Eunapius begins to state how he has handled the evidence. Paschoud 1971–89, 3¹.120–21, questioned but refused to exclude the possibility that it introduced a book of Eunapius; so too Blockley 1981–83, 2.147 n. 149, but without discussion.

In the time of the eunuch Eutropius it was not possible to write accurately into narrative anything to do with the West. For the distance and length of sailing made reports late and dead from time, as if they had been stricken by some chronic, protracted disease. Travelers or officials,[3] if any belonged to the group privileged with knowledge of public affairs, each revealed it with a view to favor or hate or what would give pleasure, according to his own will. And if one brought together as witnesses three or four of them who said contrary things, there was a great struggle and hand-to-hand war of arguments that would take its start from heated and inflammatory words. These were: "from where do you know this?" "where did Stilicho see you?" "would you have seen the eunuch?" so that it was work to unravel the tangle. Nothing to account was to be gotten from merchants, who lied about most things, or as many as they wanted to profit from.

Eunapius canvasses several different possible sources of information, and finds all of them unreliable. Time alone should not create problems for the historian, but while time passed memory and expectations might distort the traveler's report. Meanwhile, events might develop differently from what he had been able to expect when he left. Favorable or hostile prejudice might lead even those who knew more to edit their reports; merchants, of course, were expected to look to their profits. But all of these types of individual traveled from one part of the empire to the other, and could bear some worthwhile information.

The quarreling over news that Eunapius depicts reveals a lively general interest, as well as competition for prestige among the informants. A fragmentary passage of Ammianus shows Roman aristocrats listening avidly to a former official who tells tales of court (Amm. 28.4.20). Eunapius too, though he goes on to profess dispassionate accuracy vindicated by time, plainly reflects in his account the interests and partisanships with which he had watched events unroll.[4] Present concern still more obviously moves Claudian.

3. The manuscripts read πλαττόμενοι καὶ στρατευόμενοι; Boissevain emended πλαττόμενοι to πραττόμενοι, accepted by Blockley 1981–83, 2.102; Niebuhr to πλανώμενοι, accepted by Paschoud 1971–89, 3¹.326. Blockley interpreted πραττόμενοι as "officials" and στρατευόμενοι "soldiers," which is a logical pairing, although clearer indications of a political context would allow greater confidence in the former (see LSJ s.v. πράσσω III.5). But as Paschoud noted, in the later empire formerly military terms designated the civil services as well (3¹.120, 230): στρατευόμενοι may designate military or civil "officials." πλανώμενοι therefore seems preferable, with Eunapius distinguishing travelers on private or on imperial business.

4. On the revolt of Tribigild, which devastated Eunapius's native Lydia, Gibbon 1897–1902, 3.366 (chap. 32 n. 21) memorably characterized Zosimus's condensed adaptation as "a copious and circumstantial narrative (which he might have reserved for more important events)."

Another fact implicit in the counterquestions Eunapius reports is that attention focused on high court circles where political decisions were made. Also manifestly, he is not talking simply about official reports of the actual decisions, or this sort of controversy would not have arisen. He and his informants were looking at the stories behind the decisions and official actions, for the personalities and intrigues that shaped them. Such material apparently received the better part of Eunapius's attention in his *History*;[5] it certainly makes up the balance of Eastern information presented by Claudian's *In Eutropium*.

One class of official communication between parts of the empire, which sent some of these informants on their journeys, concerned occasions for "public rejoicing." Book 8, title 11, of the Theodosian Code groups together five laws on this topic, dating from 364 to 389: they specifically mention consular announcements, reports of victories, and declarations of peace. The information that Eutropius was to be named consul in the East for 399 was obviously crucial for *In Eutropium*. Into the fifth century, both Eastern and Western consular nominations were always communicated to the other court before the day of inauguration on January 1, so that both could be announced together.[6] A consul was first announced unilaterally, by the East, only in 411; the formula "and whoever should have been announced" was used to hold the place for the Western name to be filled in when it was transmitted later in the year.[7] This practice subsequently became standard in both halves of the empire. In 399, the year of Eutropius's and Theodorus's consulate, the Eastern nomination must have been reported to the Western court on schedule during 398, for Claudian's inaugural panegyric for Theodorus alludes pointedly to Stilicho's and Honorius's decision not to recognize the other consul. Claudian congratulates Theodorus that (*M. Theod.* 265–69)

Nothing is permitted to envy, while Stilicho takes care for the world,
he and his celestial son-in-law. Here the curule chair is not raped,

---

5. See Blockley 1981–83, 1.6–16.

6. On the consular practices discussed here, see *CLRE* 13–35.

7. Seeck 1919, 26, postulated that the formula was used as early as 406, in order to explain the misdating of *CTh* 8.4.26 to 415 (*Honorio x et Theodosio vi Augg. conss.*, the transmitted reading): he supposed that it was issued in the form *dat. xiii kal. Mart. ipso Aug. vi et qui fuerit nuntiatus conss.* and falsely supplemented. He proposed emendation to 406, *Arcadio A. vi et Probo conss.* The problem with the transmitted date is that the law is addressed to Anthemius, whom the *Chronicon Paschale* indicates had been replaced by Aurelian before the end of 414 and whom no other law attests in office after 18 April 414 (*CTh* 9.40.22). *PLRE* 2.93–95, Anthemius 1, accepted Seeck's emendation. The authors of *CLRE* did not discuss *CTh* 8.4.26. In default of other evidence for earlier use of the formula, Seeck's proposal seems unnecessarily drastic. The law could as easily belong to another year of Anthemius's long prefecture and have been misdated for another reason: for example, the year could belong to the date of posting, whose formula has dropped out (cf. Seeck 1919, 79–88; *CLRE* 77–84).

base names do not fornicate with the Latin fasti;
these things were granted to strong men, to be borne by the fathers
alone, and will not ever bring shame on Rome.

This glancing allusion challenges the audience to recognize whose "base names" were not "fornicating with the Latin fasti." Claudian's preface names the "eminences and majesty of the Roman Senate" among his audience (*M. Theod.* pr.7). In an extant letter Symmachus excuses himself from going to Milan to attend (Symm. *Ep.* 5.5); although he declined, the letter confirms that Roman senators were invited. Communication between court circles at Milan and senatorial circles at Rome was frequent during Stilicho's primacy, both by travel and by letter.[8] Yet even at Rome, an inscription is preserved that dates itself to 399 by postconsulate from 398; the first dated inscription from Rome to name Theodorus consul was cut on 10 April.[9] Inscriptions monumentalize the usages of the moment, for unlike other media they cannot easily be changed to conform to a later standard. If stonecutters even at Rome had to resort to dating by postconsulate, it demonstrates that no official announcement was conveyed to the ancient capital in advance. The senators may have heard about the nomination through informal means; if they had not, Claudian's panegyric would certainly have prompted them to ask.

In his panegyric for Stilicho's consulate of 400, Claudian has Roma praise Stilicho for keeping the West unpolluted by even the knowledge of how the East shamed the consulate the year before (*Stil.* 2.291–311). In three different ways she states that he did not allow the Senate to debate Eutropius's nomination: "You who consult our Fathers on all matters are silent about monstrosities. In the end no oracles on driving out the shame violate the sacred assembly, nor does my Senate House debate the fatal name." Alan Cameron has drawn attention to how this passage contrasts with others in which Claudian praises Stilicho for submitting matters to the Senate's authority.[10] In each of them, as Cameron showed, Claudian makes a virtue out of the fact that Stilicho exploited constitutional forms so as to co-opt the Senate in potentially unpopular measures. In *De Consulatu Stilichonis* 1.325–32, it was the declaration of war on Gildo; in *De Consulatu Stilichonis* 3.99–119 it was the condemnation of magistrates in Africa who had supported Gildo. When it came to

8. See Matthews 1975, 253–70.

9. Dating by postconsulate in 399, at Rome: *ICUR* n.s. 4.12543 (supplementing the fragmentary month-name so that it dates the inscription in December) = *ILCV* 4539 (supplementing to date in November); the editors of *CLRE* suggested a date in January on the tacit but reasonable assumption that dates would no longer be told by postconsulate once the current year's consuls were known (662). Dating by Theodorus in 399: *ICUR* 1.471; cf. *CLRE* s.a.

10. Alan Cameron 1970, 230–37.

recognizing Eutropius, however, "to have hesitated was equal to crime."[11] That is, Stilicho decided unilaterally not to recognize Eutropius, and Claudian makes a virtue out of his refusing to give the Senate a chance to complicate matters.

There were precedents for repudiating a consulate, but they affected consuls proclaimed by usurpers, or dated back to the rivalries of the decaying Tetrarchy and the sons of Constantine I, when too there were issues of accepting or rejecting emperors.[12] It was a drastic step. Stilicho would have risked his prestige greatly against the chance that the Senate would balk. Indeed Cameron suggested that Claudian would only have brought up the subject of the independent decision and tried to justify it if there had been some protest: no evidence in the other instances when recognition was denied suggests that the Senate was consulted then. Claudian's allusion in the panegyric for Theodorus and all *In Eutropium*, lengthily, publicize the idea that Eutropius's consulate is an impossible affront which can only be repulsed summarily. They provide arguments and a model of opinion that favors rejecting the consulate. Yet even if Claudian's work sought to forestall criticism of Stilicho's policy, his suggestions did not necessarily succeed completely.

In Claudian's second book of consular panegyric for Stilicho, Roma declares that "Any profane page that came from the initial shore of Phoebus was destroyed, for me, before the strait, lest foul examples of the fates injure the chaste ears of Italy" (*Stil.* 2.301–4). She vehemently asserts her ignorance: "that public madness deserved concealment . . . the portents are unknown to the Gabini[13] . . . I never learned or sensed that he had been elected" (*Stil.* 2.305–9). Yet other remarks framing these allow more ambiguity. Roma speaks of the news as "a story not made known to me by any facts; scarcely did Rumor laugh at so great a crime" (*Stil.* 2.293–94). Furthermore, "we did not even believe it" (*Stil.* 2.311). "Story," "rumor," "scarcely laughed," and "we did not believe" all

---

11. *par sceleri dubitasse fuit, Stil.* 2.301, with Heinsius's emendation for *par sceleris, pars celeris, pars sceleris* of the manuscripts. Birt 1892, 213, preferred *pars sceleris*, citing Verg. *Aen.* 7.266, *pars mihi pacis erit . . . tetigisse*. Although the syntax would be similar, the line in Vergil comes from Latinus's reception of the Trojans: Birt omitted *dextram . . . tyranni* (i.e., Aeneas's right hand), and Latinus is about to offer Lavinia to Aeneas. In sense, the echo is alien, and Heinsius's emendation yields clearer grammar.

12. See *CLRE* 24–26 and under the relevant years (307–13, 346; then 399, 400, 404, 405, 424, 451–53, 456, 458–59, 461).

13. Claudian names the Gabini to evoke traditional Roman values generally also at *Stil.* 3.83. They are more particularly associated with a ritual style of girding the toga, the *cinctus Gabinus*: see *OLD* s.v. *cinctus* and references there. Notably, Verg. *Aen.* 7.612 identifies the *cinctus Gabinus* as the proper style for the consul when opening the Gates of War; Claudian uses it of clothing more with generally traditional rather than specifically ritual overtones at *3 Cons.* 3, *4 Cons.* 6, *6 Cons.* 594.

suggest dim or incredulous awareness, contradicting strict claims of ignorance.

"Scarcely laughed" echoes the reaction of the West Claudian portrays in *In
Eutropium*: "a lighter rumor flies through the towns and laughs at the unspeakable" (*Eutr.* 1.347–48); a "more serious" voice and "a racier second" react,
the second mockingly praising Eutropius through a string of obscene puns
(*Eutr.* 1.350–57, 358–70). "The unspeakable" bears the same reference to Eutropius's consulate, here and in Roma's thankful congratulations to Stilicho:
"nor does a letter come to publicize the unspeakable" (*Stil.* 2.295–96). Rome,
in real life, had heard about Eutropius's nomination, at least in part through
Claudian's references to it. But awareness remained strictly unofficial, as was
demanded by the Western government's policy of not recognizing it.

Official communications did not break down during the year. For 400
Stilicho and Aurelian were announced together in the East, while all Western
inscriptions indicate that Stilicho alone was recognized.[14] In panegyric of
Stilicho Claudian mentions "the unmoving and undutiful throng [behind
Arcadius's throne] that holds out the royal name to cover their own madness":
Stilicho sees through their machinations, and remains unshaken in loyalty to
Arcadius himself (*Stil.* 2.79–81). But Claudian does not refer more directly to
Stilicho's refusal to recognize Aurelian along with himself. On the other hand,
the Eastern decree naming Stilicho *hostis publicus*, which would have pre-
cluded recognition of him, must have been revoked along with Eutropius's
other *acta* when he was deposed.

If the communication of consular nominations was not obstructed by the
hostility between Stilicho and Eutropius, other types of information presumably also continued to be transmitted normally. Eutropius's victory over the
Huns in 398 must have been reported, either separately or in conjunction with
the news that he had won the consular nomination as well. Michael McCormick has observed that after the debacle of Adrianople in 378, the dynasties of
Valentinian and Theodosius made the most of all the victories they could.[15]
They announced even minor victories, not only in the territories affected but
also in the other emperors' territories. Credit for a victory was shared among

14. *CLRE* s.a.; add *Ann. Épigr.* 1985 no. 57, *VI X kal(endas) decemb(res) Fl(avio)
Istelicone v(iro) c(larissimo) cons(ule)*, i.e., 18 November 400 or 405 (cf. *CLRE* s.a. 405; I
thank Alan Cameron for this reference). *P.Oxy* 44.3203.1 of June or July 400 still used
the postconsulate of Theodorus, who after Eutropius's *damnatio memoriae* had become the sole consul of the East as well as the West for 399. Unfortunately, the name of
the month is missing from the only other dated papyrus from the year, *SB* VI.9359.1–2
= *P.Lund.* VI.10 (with the corrections of Roger S. Bagnall and K. A. Worp, "Chronological Notes on Byzantine Documents, IV," *BASP* 17 [1980]: 15, it reads ὑπατ[είας Φλ
Στελίχ]ωνος καὶ Αὐρηλιαν(οῦ) τῶν λ[αμπροτάτων . . .] κθ). In the West, Stilicho is
first attested as consul by *ILCV* 3387 of 8 January 400.

15. McCormick 1986, 115–19.

all current emperors. So for example in 398 the Roman Senate honored both Arcadius and Honorius over the defeat of Gildo, even though Gildo nominally transferred his allegiance to Arcadius when he withdrew it from Honorius (*CIL* 6.1187, 31256). No parallel dedication is preserved in Constantinople, but some announcement of victory must have been made and acknowledged by the Eastern court, since Africa returned to the West. The Western government also confiscated and retained control of Gildo's estates.[16] Cameron remarked that Claudian's *In Gildonem* offers a version of events by which Arcadius might accept the defeat and yet save face.[17] Victory announcements are well attested for all periods.[18]

It is likely that Eutropius's Hunnic victory was celebrated in Constantinople by festivities of much the form Claudian pictures, with its parodic coloring adjusted (*Eutr.* 1.252–71). A parallel is provided by Fravitta, who received both a triumph and the next year's consulate after his victory in 400 over the rebelling Gothic general Gaïnas.[19] Since Claudian travesties conventional practices, it cannot be proven that he knew specific records of this very celebration, but neither does his conventionality prove that he did not have such records. They might even have been included in official reports. Similarly, Claudian's parodic images of Eutropius's consular celebrations called for no more than imagination, verbal flair and familiarity with the standard features of such ceremonies, but could reflect reports of actual ceremonial proceedings (1.300–316, 2.62–90).

Other evidence about communication between the Eastern and Western courts in this general period dates to years after 399. In a letter of about 404 Honorius complains to Arcadius about certain Eastern policies.[20] Among them, "we have revealed before you with dutiful affection that it pains us, even above the destruction of Illyricum as it dies [as Alaric and his Goths raided], why you did not want us to be made aware of these injuries to the state on your side, and that they were announced to us by other sources rather than by the letters of Your Piety." Honorius reminds his brother that "rumor," "the nature of men," and "left-handed loquacity" inevitably fasten upon such news. Presumably such unofficial, disparaged, but eloquent sources inform him now. Yet military affairs as well as decisions of policy would normally have been

16. See Demougeot 1951, 185–90. Laws concerning the confiscated property appear as early as summer 399 (*CTh* 7.8.7, 7.8.9, 9.42.16, 9.42.19); cf. Seeck 1919, 76–77, 104.

17. Alan Cameron 1970, 110.

18. References are assembled by McCormick 1986, 41 n. 22, 190–93 esp. nn. 7, 19.

19. On Fravitta's triumph, see Eunap. fr. 78 M = 68 Blockley; McCormick 1986, 50 and 53; Alan Cameron and Long 1993, 199–223.

20. *Ep. Imp. Pont. Al.* 38. I quote and paraphrase from sections 1–2. On Alaric in Illyricum, see Demougeot 1951, 281–83; bibliography on the authenticity and date of the letter, 335 n. 647.

transmitted officially. Honorius's complaint both refers to and exemplifies the usual means of such communication, the imperial letter. The laws of the Theodosian Code occasionally mention these "sacred" or "divine" letters between emperors; the same terms also describe letters to subjects in which the emperors appointed them to office or responded to administrative inquiries and questions of law.[21] The bearers obviously numbered among the official travelers Eunapius mentions, who also transmitted information informally.

Since it was standard practice, it is likely that imperial letters reported the Hunnic raids that Eutropius finally repelled, Tribigild's revolt, and Leo's failure to suppress it. Claudian was in a position to have used such letters as primary sources of information. High-ranking travelers pursuing various purposes would also be likely to pass through Honorius's court and could have supplemented the official reports from their own knowledge. The conformity of Claudian's account with separate, Eastern sources argues for his general accuracy.

In 408 Honorius advised his praetorian prefect Theodorus that[22]

> The public enemy Stilicho had devised a new and unaccustomed thing, to fortify the shores and harbors with numerous guards so that access to this part of the empire should not be open to anyone from the East. Moved by the irregularity of this matter, and so that the passage of various merchandise may not become more infrequent, we direct by this ordinance that the pernicious guarding of shores and harbors cease and that the possibility of going and returning be unencumbered.

This law was issued on 10 December 408, some three and a half months after Stilicho had been executed on suspicion of treason against Honorius and Theodosius II, in the wake of Arcadius's death that May.[23] The next law of the title shows that Theodosius II instituted similar measures in order to impede usurpers and barbarian rebels (CTh 7.16.2).[24] Guards are deployed on land to stop traffic from ships in harbor to further destinations.

Specific evidence is lacking as to when and why Stilicho instituted his blockade, but, although Honorius mentions that trade was blocked, it is easier to imagine that Stilicho was concerned with politics. A likely connection is with

21. Sacri/ae or divini/ae apices or litterae, e.g., CTh 4.4.7, 6.32.2, 7.4.24, 7.16.2. Some similar usages in literary texts are assembled in TLL 2.227.81–228.10 s.v. apex I.10. On imperial correspondence, see generally Millar 1977, 203–72, 313–41.

22. CTh 7.16.1, issued at Ravenna 10 December 408; Theodorus 9, PLRE 2.1086–87 (probably the son of the Western consul of 399).

23. See Zos. 5.31–34 (dating Stilicho's death to 22 September; the Cons. Ital., Chron. Min. 1.300, give 23 September); Soz. HE 9.4; Philost. HE 12.1.

24. Compare too CTh. 7.16.3 of 18 September 420, against the transport of "illicit merchandise," presumably having military uses, "to the barbarian nations."

his attempts after 405 to annex eastern Illyricum to the West.[25] Zosimus reports that Stilicho interrupted this design in spring 407 when he heard simultaneously the false rumor that Alaric, now his *magister militum*, had died and the news that the British usurper Constantine had crossed into Gaul (Zos. 5.27.2).[26] Constantine continued to inspire enough anxiety a year later to keep Honorius in the West after Arcadius's death (Zos. 5.31.4). The interval of time between Stilicho's execution and Honorius's law about his blockade, and Honorius's remark about "irregularity," suggest that merchants were obliged to protest before Honorius abolished the blockade: the tensions that had inspired it were still strained. Regardless of why Stilicho had imposed it, clearly it did hinder ordinary commerce between the two halves of the empire. The very existence of problems implies that some degree of commerce was ordinary. With it of course moved unofficial news, probably not entirely as unreliable as Eunapius complains. As for official news, Theodosius provided for it to be screened by his blockade, not prevented; yet screening would necessarily inhibit official and especially informal communication by official messengers. Stilicho's blockade must have had similar consequences.

It might be expected that when Stilicho was *hostis publicus* in the eyes of the East, a similar blockade would have been instituted against him. But none is evidenced. Indeed, the fact that the East recognized the consulates of Theodorus in 399 and of Stilicho in 400, even when the West did not recognize their counterparts, demonstrates that communication was not blocked.

Laws were routinely communicated across the empire. Imperial letters responded to individual inquiries. Legal initiatives taken from the level of the court were broadcast down the through the ranks of imperial administration. One emperor's laws were not automatically valid in the territory of the other, but the law codes occasionally preserve full evidence of their being received or posted in one half of the empire when they had been issued in the other.[27] Evidently they were circulated, like the imperial letters discussed earlier, at least to inform the other government of current policies and potentially to be adopted as well. Presumably formal posting announced that a law had been accepted into force locally.

This evidence is particularly valuable because it indicates how long informa-

25. See Baynes 1955, 337 = "A Note on Professor Bury's History of the Later Roman Empire," *JRS* 12 (1922): 216–17; Alan Cameron 1970, 59–62.

26. For convenient collections of references and summaries of scholarship on the many controversies about Stilicho's accord with Alaric and his other plans at this period, see Paschoud 1971–89, 3¹.196–200, 205–7, 217–29; on Constantine, see C. E. Stevens, "Marcus, Gratian, and Constantine," *Athenaeum* n.s. 35 (1957): 316–47.

27. On late antique law, see generally A. H. M. Jones 1964, 470–79. Jones assembled evidence for all laws that indicate places of both issuance and reception, 1162–64 nn. 75, 76, with additional discussion 402–3. I rely principally on his account.

tion could take to travel from one place to another, as well as demonstrating the fact that it did. It must be noted however that communication of laws from one court to the other, the route for transmission of information most relevant to Claudian's comments upon Eutropius, is attested extremely rarely. Generalizations can only be tentative.

From the death of Theodosius to the death of Arcadius (395–408), only two laws preserve a full record, neither involving travel from one half of the empire to the other. Section 6.4.32 of the Theodosian Code was issued in Nicomedia on 26 June 397 and was not received at Constantinople until 31 July. The twelfth Sirmondian Constitution took 192 days from 15 November 407 to travel from Rome to Carthage. In this case the lapse of time was caused partly by the fact that the law was issued so late in the year, after the sailing season closed; but the mere 92 days from 18 October 365 that it took another law to travel from Paris to Carthage shows that better could be done even in winter (*CTh* 11.1.13). In fact, as A. H. M. Jones has observed, what sparsely preserved evidence there is shows that laws took greatly varying intervals to travel from one place to another. Incalculable "bureaucratic delays" often consumed as much time as the actual journeys of couriers. Jones contrasted Valentinian III's *Novel* 21.2, issued at Rome 26 December 446, received 27 December, and posted in Trajan's Forum 28 December, with the same emperor's *Novel* 10, issued at Ravenna 20 February 441 and not officially received by the praetorian prefect in the same town until 14 March.[28]

Nevertheless, laws did travel regularly, and the few that record places and dates of reception constitute the best evidence for the many that do not. For travel between East and West, the evidence includes:

> *CTh* 9.1.1 of 316, 4 December at Serdica to 7 March 317 at Corduba, 92 days
> *CTh* 14.24.1 of 328, 1 March at Nicomedia to 6 April at Rome, 36 days
> *CTh* 3.5.6 of 335,[29] 15 July at Constantinople to 19 April 336 at Hispalis, 278 days
> *CTh* 6.4.8 and 6.4.9 of 356, 11 April at Milan to 9 or 10 May[30] at Constantinople, 29 or 30 days

28. A. H. M. Jones 1964, 402.

29. Assuming with Seeck 1919, 183, that as the word order suggests the one consular date given applies to the date "received"; if to the date "issued" then with A. H. M. Jones 1964, 1161 n. 76, the law belongs to 336 and was received in 337.

30. *CTh* 6.4.8 is transmitted as *dat. iii id. April. Med(iolano), lecta ab Araxio proconsule die vi id. Mai.*, 6.4.9 as *dat. iii id. April. Med(iolano), lecta ab Araxio proconsule die vii id. Mai.* Seeck 1919, 202, dated both of them and *CTh* 6.4.10 (which says merely *dat. vii id. Mai.*) as read on *vii id. Mai.*, i.e., 9 May. A. H. M. Jones 1964, 1161 n. 76, dated both *vi id. Mai.* but said 9 May in his text, 403. *PLRE* 1.94 (Araxius) accepted the discrepancy of the transmitted dates.

CTh 14.1.1 of 360,[31] 24 February at Constantinople to 15 May at Rome, 80 days

No evidence suggests that laws were transmitted to the opposite capital faster than to other centers. Laws issued in Illyricum show intervals of 35 to 82 days for travel to Rome.[32] The paucity of evidence forbids inferring from the two items that do appear during the joint reign of Honorius and Arcadius that laws traveled unusually slowly then. They probably followed their normal course. Traveling times appear typically to have ranged from one to three months. Longer intervals suggest that "bureaucratic delays" were encountered, which in turn suggests that communications of laws were not given urgent priority.

The route that official communications took in most instances was the *cursus publicus*. After Julian reformed this imperial post system, only emperors and praetorian prefects had unlimited access to it; but even so, many official purposes kept it busy.[33] Passes brought individuals to court to confer with the emperor or his ministers or other groups gathered there, or to attend court festivities; provincial embassies traveled by the post to present the emperor with their petitions, and bishops used it to attend church councils.[34] Moreover many private citizens managed to use it with or without passes, to travel or transport goods over long distances. As Jones remarked, the title *De Cursu Publico*, whose provisions attempt to control rampant overuse, is "one of the longest in the Theodosian Code" (833).

Official communication was not limited to the imperial courts. Magistrates of every level naturally had to maintain contact with their subordinates, and reciprocally; of course internal communication followed the divisions of the imperial administration, so that they did not normally transmit information between East and West, but circulated it within the administrative territories. For ordinary purposes, emperors used the special corps of *agentes in rebus*, the highest officials used their own corps of couriers, and lower officials used whatever subordinates were handy.[35] In more special circumstances, emperors

---

31. Seeck 1919, 47 (and Gothofredus, as Th. Mommsen noted approvingly, *Theodosiani Libri XVI cum Constitutionibus Sirmondianis* [Berlin: Weidmann, 1905], 1.771), so emended on grounds of the location of the emperor: *Constantio x et Iuliano Caes. iii conss.* rather than *Constantio viiii et Iuliano Caes. ii conss.* (357) as transmitted.

32. *CTh* 2.16.2, 2.17.1, 6.22.1, 8.16.1, 11.30.18, 11.30.28, 16.10.1; cf. 7.22.1 received at Regio.

33. A. H. M. Jones 1964, 830–34 and notes, 1344–49; also 1160–61 n. 74 on Julian's regulations; cf. Edgar Pack, *Städte und Steuern in der Politik Julians*, Coll. Latomus 194 (Brussels: Latomus, 1986). For a fuller account, see Erik J. Holmberg, *Zur Geschichte des Cursus Publicus* (Uppsala: A.-B. Lundequistska, 1933), and, particularly on the speed of the *cursus publicus*, Ramsay 1925.

34. A. H. M. Jones 1964, 1346 n. 15.

35. A. H. M. Jones 1964, 401–2, 1160–61 n. 74.

also used higher officers or members of their domestic staffs. Eutropius served Theodosius I as a special messenger to John, a prophetic monk in the Thebaid, for example, while Theodosius was preparing his campaign against Eugenius. Sozomen records that Theodosius "sent Eutropius, one of the palace eunuchs whom he trusted, into Egypt to bring him back if possible; or if he refused, to learn what must be done." John correctly foretold that Eugenius would be defeated and would die, and that Theodosius would die soon afterward (Soz. *HE* 7.22.7–8).[36]

This campaign transferred large numbers of troops from East to West; other temporary moves took place when Stilicho campaigned in Greece against Alaric, and when the expedition under Mascezel was sent against Gildo in 398. Naturally soldiers and others attached to the troops bore extensive official and unofficial information into new places. And, of course, the army as well as the civilian administration operated with a regular flow of internal communication.

The church like the imperial administration generated its own flow of internal communication, which was transmitted to individual centers through a network of letters, messengers, and more permanently transferred personnel. Private individuals also traveled on their own and sent letters by means of private travelers, merchants, or anyone else they could find.[37]

Claudian composed a dedicatory poem for the gift of a saddle girth woven for Arcadius by Stilicho's wife Serena (*CM* 48).[38] It attests that members of the imperial family exchanged gifts between the courts. Claudian also refers to land and property that Stilicho left behind in the East when he came to the West with Theodosius in 394 (*Stil.* 1.297–98). He doubtless maintained correspondence with agents who managed the property. It is likely that some other members of each court had similar personal ties in the other part of the empire, through which they too could have shared information.

All these activities represent fairly commonplace travel between the regions of the empire. Travel between East and West was not always involved, and long journeys were probably always less frequent than those within a single area.

36. Cf. Ruf. *HE* 11.32, Pallad. *Hist. Laus.* 35.

37. Letter corpora provide abundant evidence, Matthews 1974 a useful discussion focusing on the letters of Symmachus; A. H. M. Jones 1964, 824–72 (chap. 21, "Industry, Trade and Transport") and 894–910 on church finance also surveyed much relevant material.

38. Hall entitled *CM* 48 according to Claverius's suggestion that the poem entitled "On the Girth of a Royal Horse Sent to Honorius Augustus by Serena" in R (which manuscript alone specifies the emperor) was in fact written for a gift to Arcadius; but he noted at *Carm. Spur. Susp.* 4 that R might have been right to group this poem with the other as a pair, one for Honorius and one for Arcadius. Alan Cameron 1970, 407–9, argued to the same conclusion, in favor of deeming both poems authentic.

But enough may be presumed to have provided for a regular flow of information from one place to another. Any traveler for any purpose, whether official or unofficial, civil, military, ecclesiastical, diplomatic, mercantile, or personal, always bore with him at least an awareness of the effects of events or policies on his immediate milieu; if he had contacts with the high circles where events and policies were debated, he often knew much more. His knowledge might well be incomplete or, as Eunapius complains, partial or prejudiced in the telling. But tell he could and did, and was heard eagerly. Eunapius complains in order to excuse omissions in his history, following a commonplace apologetic impulse, but he also boasts of how much he has accomplished. A fragment that seems to belong shortly before the long fragment I quoted at the beginning of this chapter begins, "If some other manages to write up [the same subject], I marvel at him for his valor; may he seem valorous to me, for the sake of his endurance!" It continues in a similar vein.[39]

The regular members of the court and the important visitors who certainly made up Claudian's audience for the consular panegyrics, and probably for his other poems on public themes as well, were bound by their position to be particularly interested in Eastern court news. They were also more than commonly likely to have access to official bulletins. Thus they could be fairly knowledgeable, although a full range of details is never guaranteed. Claudian's testimony in *De Consulatu Stilichonis* 2 indicates that the court could screen official bulletins from wider circulation, and Honorius's letter of 404 indicates that official bulletins may not always have been sent when they might have been appropriate. But it appears that official channels for information between the two courts were not blocked in the period around Eutropius's consulate. An individual in Claudian's privileged position could be very well informed about current events in the other half of the empire; some members of his audience, at least, shared his knowledge.

39. Cf. Eunap. fr. 73 M = 66.1 Blockley. Protestations of inadequacy as a literary *topos*: cf. Janson 1964, 124–49; Curtius 1953, 83, 410–12.

PART THREE

The Literary and Historical Worlds Meet

✦

CHAPTER SEVEN

Claudian's Audiences

✦

PART I OF MY STUDY considers the artistic entity of Claudian's *In Eutropium*, Part II the circumstances with reference to which Claudian wrote and the quality of the information he could exploit. One more element remains to be explored before I can discuss to what effects the literary invective beast, unleashed into the historical arena, savaged its victim Eutropius: the audience before whom this performance was enacted. Claudian not only wrote about public figures and politically important events, he also made his works known to people who had pragmatic interests in these subjects. The nature of their interests must have shaped the reactions they felt. They responded also to the way in which Claudian addressed their interests. Cameron applied the label "propaganda" to this process; Gnilka decried the concept, with particular attention to *In Eutropium*. In order to put the debate on a firmer footing, it will be necessary to outline how propagandistic discourse operates upon its audiences. Finally, because an idealized conception of the Roman state and its traditions supplies Claudian with a gauge against which he continually disparages Eutropius, I shall sketch how sources close to his primary audience reflect this ideal. Cameron criticized earlier scholars for seeing in Claudian's images of Roman culture a romantic espousal of ideals of the late Roman senatorial aristocracy, where he identified a tool by which Claudian sought to manipulate the aristocrats on Stilicho's behalf. Gnilka's reading of *In Eutropium* effectively makes Roman tradition a touchstone Claudian uses to repudiate the East. Rome was a powerful symbol for citizens of the later empire; the identifications they made begin to adumbrate the ends to which Claudian could employ it.

1. Identifying Western and Eastern Audiences

The common political interest of all Claudian's major poems except *De Raptu Proserpinae* encourages the presumption that Claudian in them addressed essentially the same audience. The similar scale of the individual books offers some support for the idea that they were presented in similar circumstances. More conclusively, some of Claudian's prefaces for the panegyrics and the other political poems describe his audience clearly enough to show that it was the same. In the preface to his panegyric for Honorius's third consulate, Claudian mentions "lordly ears," the palace, and, above all, "the Augustus as judge" of what he sings (3 *Cons.* pr.17–18). Within the unprefaced panegyric for Honorius's fourth consulate, Claudian describes a gathering of Italian nobles, famed Spaniards, learned Gauls, and Roman senators; past tenses describe moments in the inaugural ceremony, but present forms suggest that the same audience still attends Honorius to hear Claudian's poem cap the rites (4 *Cons.* 577–83).[1] For Theodorus there are gathered "learned companies"[2] of "so many nobles": "the eminences and majesty of the Roman Senate, and the men in whom Gaul rejoices," and representatives of all the world that is subject to Honorius (*M. Theod.* pr.1–8). When he has to present a panegyric in honor of Honorius's sixth consulate, Claudian says that he has dreamed "of bringing my songs before the feet of highest Jove; and as the dream shows favor, the powers were applauding for my words" (6 *Cons.* pr.14–15). Now he finds that his dream has come true (6 *Cons.* pr.23–24): "There is the prince! there the summit of the world, on a level with Olympus! there, just as I remember them, the awful crowd, the gods!"

In his preface to *In Rufinum* 1, Claudian characterizes similarly the "sacred company" that has gathered to hear his lyre (*Ruf.* 1pr.16); the circumstances of his other invective seem especially likely to extend to *In Eutropium*. Claudian's preface to *Bellum Geticum* mentions his panegyrics and his epic *In Gildonem* in the same breath, now adding this poem to his achievements (*Get.* 1–10). He mentions the bronze statue that the Senate dedicated to him on the emperor's permission. Now "the same eminences renew for me the gatherings I desired." Manifestly he puts the two historical epics on the same footing as the ceremonial poems. "The same" and "renew" indicate that both generically distinct types of performance addressed the same audience. The preface of *In Rufinum*

1. Absence of a preface need not indicate that a poem was not performed publicly. J. B. Hall, reviewing Lehner 1984, connected the fact that 4 *Cons.* and *Gild.* lack prefaces with the fact that Stilicho was *hostis publicus* in the East when they were written, and proposed that in the face of this political ban "it was deemed politic not to flaunt Stilicho's achievements at a gala performance before an invited audience" (*CR* 37 [1987]: 184–86). This argument could extend to *Eutr.* 1, but not to *Ol. Prob.* or to *Stil.* 1 and 2, where every reason for publicity appears, and no impediment.

2. For *M. Theod.* pr.1 *doctae . . . catervae* of the manuscripts, Hall considered most authoritative, also a variant reading in R, Birt 1892, 175, preferred *tantae* of R on the grounds that the prestige rather than the learning of Claudian's audience is at issue. The rest of the preface makes this emphasis abundantly clear, but a compliment to their discernment need not be out of place.

2 specifies only one member of the audience, Stilicho (*Ruf.* 2pr.13–14); the others, including the preface of *In Eutropium* 2, discuss different matters.[3] Without explicit testimony it cannot be absolutely proven that they too addressed a similar group, but the point seems as certain as parallels can make it.

Less certainty can be attained on the question of whether any of Claudian's poems, *In Eutropium* in particular, were also distributed to Eastern audiences after being read before the Western court. Some Westerners who had come east to serve Theodosius remained behind within the Eastern administration when he campaigned against Eugenius in 394. The most prominent of them, however, died or returned to the West within a few years. Theodosius's praetorian prefect of the East, the Gaul Rufinus, whom he assigned to supervise the Eastern government for Arcadius,[4] was assassinated on 27 November 395 (Socr. *HE* 6.1.4). Dexter, *comes rerum privatarum* in the East in 387, returned to the West and appears as praetorian prefect of Italy in 395.[5] John Matthews argued that the Gaul Claudius Lachanius, Rutilius Namatianus's father, is to be identified with the Claudius who was urban prefect of Constantinople in 396, but nothing further is known of him until 417, when Rutilius visited a commemorative statue of him in Pisa.[6] Otto Seeck identified Theodosius's *magister peditum* Timasius as a Spaniard and relation of Theodosius's wife Flacilla.[7] After serving with Theodosius against Eugenius (Zos. 4.57.2), he returned to the East. In 396 Eutropius suborned the criminal Bargus to accuse him of treason and had him exiled to the Oasis, where or on the lam from where he died (Zos. 5.9).[8] Flacilla's nephew Nebridius was identified by Karl Friedrich Strohecker as the proconsul of Asia of that name in 396; he died by 400, when Jerome wrote a letter of consolation to his widow Salvina (Jer. *Ep.* 79).[9] On the

3. Parravicini 1914 categorized the themes of the prefaces to Claudian's public poems. The preface to the epithalamium for Palladius and Celerina says that the bridegroom and the bride's father requested the poem (*CM* 25pr.).

4. Zos. 4.57.4 (quoted in the Introduction); cf. 4.51.1; Claud. *Ruf.*, esp. 1.137, 2.336–453; Eunap. frr. 62, 63 M = 62.1, 62.2 Blockley; Joh. Ant. frr. 188, 190 *init.*; Oros. 7.37.1; *PLRE* 1.778–80, Flavius Rufinus 18.

5. CRP, *CJ* 7.38.2, 3 July 387; PPO Italiae, seven laws from 18 March 395 (*CTh* 8.5.53) to 1 November 395 (*CTh* 6.4.27) and Jer. *Apol. adv. Ruf.* 2.23; Strohecker 1963, 116; Chastagnol 1965, 290; *PLRE* 1.251, Nummius Aelianus Dexter 3.

6. Claudius PVC (*PLRE* 2.300, s.nom. 1) is attested in office by *CTh* 6.26.8 of 15 February 396 and 15.13.1 of 25 December 396; see Matthews 1971, 1082–83, and cf. *PLRE* 1.491, Lachanius.

7. Otto Seeck, ed., *Q. Aurelii Symmachi quae supersunt*, MGHAA 6, 1 (Berlin: Weidmann, 1883, rpt. 1961), cxxxvii–cxxxviii; followed cautiously by Strohecker 1963, 114, and Chastagnol 1965, 289. *PLRE* 1.914–15.

8. Bargus, *PLRE* 2.210–11.

9. *CTh* 11.30.56 (= *CJ* 7.62.28, 22 July 396), *CJ* 11.50.2 (transmitted without date; cf. Seeck 1919, 132); Strohecker 1963, 114–15, was followed by Chastagnol 1965, 289, but the editors of *PLRE* did not identify the imperial nephew (1.620, Nebridius 3) with the

other hand, Claudian attests that Eutropius's *magister officiorum* Hosius came from Spain (*Eutr.* 2.353). His description of him as an estate-born slave of Spanish *penates* suggests that he gained entry to imperial service from Theodosius's household.[10] While so many other Westerners drained away from Eastern service after Theodosius's and Rufinus's deaths, Hosius allied himself closely to Eutropius. He is not likely to have been a profitable addressee for covert distribution of Claudian's invective against his principal.[11] Yet his continued presence at the Eastern court underlines the possibility that Arcadius could also have inherited from his father other, less famous functionaries who originated in the West. They did not make a mark in history by responding to Claudian's call, but the lack of result may not mean that no solicitation was tried.

Even without personal origins in the West, members of the Eastern administration would normally have possessed some fluency in Latin, and a professional interest in current politics. Latin was still the official language of imperial government.[12] Not long since, at least, it had been the primary language of some members of the court. Alan Cameron drew support from Libanius for the idea "that Rufinus's unpopularity owed not a little to his imperfect command of Greek" (Liban. *Epp.* 784, 1025).[13] Ihor Sevcenko has demonstrated

---

proconsul (2.774, Nebridius 1). Salvina, *PLRE* 1.799 (she was Gildo's daughter, Jer. *Ep.* 120.1.15).

10. Strohecker 1963, 116; Chastagnol 1965 limited himself to senatorial Spaniards in well-attested imperial posts outside of Spain between 379 and 395, thus for the East he treated only Timasius, Nebridius, and Dexter, whom I have just mentioned, and Cynegius, who died in 388 (*PLRE* 1.235–36, Maternus Cynegius 3; cf. John Matthews, "A Pious Supporter of Theodosius I: Maternus Cynegius and his Family," *JTS* n.s. 18 [1967]: 438–46).

11. Conceivably, Claudian might deride Hosius in *Eutr.* 2 to avenge a rebuff of *Eutr.* 1 (Hosius did not attract notice by any other preserved literary source, *PLRE* 1.445); but the possibility cannot be demonstrated.

12. *CJ* 7.45.12 of 9 January 397 permits governors to issue judgments in either Latin or Greek. Seeck, arguing that the question of using Greek could arise only in the East, preferred the reading of manuscripts naming the addressee *proconsuli Asiae* (to *proconsuli Africae* accepted by Krueger), and discarded Gothofredus's report from a lost manuscript that the law was issued at Milan (Seeck 1919, 132; cf. *PLRE* 2.637, Iulianus 3). Stein and Palanque 1949–59, 1.295–96 (cf. notes, 569) followed Seeck, deeming the law one of the earliest concessions to Greek-speaking populations; their other evidence dates from the reign of Theodosius II. John the Lydian blames the first great inroads against Latin on Cyrus of Panopolis (PVC 426; PVC II et PPO 439–41; *PLRE* 2.336–39), but reports that Latin remained the predominant official language in Europe until John the Cappadocian did away with it (PPO 531–41; Stein and Palanque 1949–59, 2.433–49, 480–83, 784 and n. 6; *PLRE* 3.627–35, Fl. Ioannes 11): Joh. Lyd. *Mag.* 2.11, 3.42, 3.68. See now Michael Maas, *John Lydus and the Roman Past* (London: Routledge, 1992).

13. Alan Cameron 1970, 242.

that in the late fourth century, on the one hand, it was rare enough to be noteworthy if an official spoke both Greek and Latin, but on the other perhaps less rare than in earlier periods.[14] Native Greek speakers were learning Latin in order to advance themselves.[15] They too would have been able to read Claudian's poems if they were circulated to them. It may not be expected that all these administrators had imbibed the full richness of the Latin literary traditions on which Claudian draws, but neither should it be assumed categorically that none of them could appreciate any of it.[16]

A third class of potential recipients of Claudian's work in the East includes friends and associates with whom Westerners corresponded. Stilicho, for example, left land and property behind him when he came to the West with Theodosius in 394. Claudian affirms that among the threats he weathered in the throes of Gildo's rebellion, "You were unworried, although they held your wealth and lands and your distinguished homes. Light was this forfeit, nor did public interests ever yield to a private cause" (*Stil.* 1.297–99). Evidently Stilicho's Eastern property was confiscated when he was declared a public enemy, just as Rufinus's was after his death, Gildo's after his defeat, and Eutropius's after his deposition.[17] Yet while Stilicho still retained this property, he must have corresponded with agents who managed it.

Orosius mentions meeting "a certain Narbonensian man, of illustrious office under Theodosius," in Bethlehem on a visit to Jerome in 415 (Oros. 7.43.4). Matthews identified him speculatively with the Marcellus Hosius succeeded as *magister officiorum* and located him back in Gaul in the period following Rufinus's death; nonetheless, the visit certainly attests that this official main-

14. Ihor Sevcenko, "A Late Antique Epigram and the So-called Elder Magistrate from Aphrodisias," in *Synthronon*, Bibliothèque des Cahiers Archéologiques 2 (Paris: Librairie C. Klincksieck, 1968), 32–34.

15. The prosopography in Kaster 1988, 233–379, of grammarians known between A.D. 250 and 565 includes several Latin grammarians working in the East. Hemmerdinger 1966 conveniently collected references attesting the use of Latin in Constantinople from 324 to 585. Henrik Zilliacus, *Zum Kampf des Weltsprachen im oströmischen Reich* (Helsingfors, 1935; rpt. Amsterdam: Hakkert, 1965), remains a fundamental study. Cf. Petit 1955, 363–70; Liebeschuetz 1972, 242–55; with caution, Gilbert Dagron, "Aux origines de la civilisation byzantine: Langue de culture et langue d'État," *Revue historique* 489 (1969): 23–56.

16. Kaster 1988, 23, briefly exampled educated perspectives activated in social connections.

17. Confiscation of Rufinus's property, *CTh* 9.42.14, Symm. *Ep.* 6.14, Zos. 5.8.2. Confiscation of Gildo's estates, *CTh* 7.8.7, 7.8.9, 9.42.19 (cf. Seeck 1919, 76–77, 104); presumably they were declared forfeit by the decree that outlawed him, but confiscation could be enforced only after his defeat. Stilicho's Eastern property was vulnerable (Claudian omits observing that Stilicho would have made himself vulnerable had he tried to come East to defend it). *CTh* 9.40.17 directs Eutropius's goods to be confiscated.

tained connections in the East after his term of service.[18] Personal affairs of many kinds helped keep open channels of communication.

It might seem that communications from the Western court would have been too hazardous to receive while its chief minister was considered a public enemy by the East. But consular dates in the papyri show clearly that the Eastern court did receive Western consular nominations for 399 and 400 and did announce them together with the Eastern consuls: there was no break in official communications. Even potentially subversive messages could have been conveyed under cover of the official dispatches. Libanius's letters reveal several instances when he published speeches privately, by reading them to a small group or forwarding written copies to individuals, rather than by public delivery.[19] The transparently autobiographical character in Synesius's *De Providentia* "did not expose his work to the public" but only "entrusted" it to select audiences (Syn. *Prov.* 113B–C). A verbal echo identifies the "manly words" thus discreetly launched as Synesius's *De Regno*.[20] By circulating their more controversial views privately in this way authors avoided the dangers of publicity, while still expressing themselves before the audiences they could best expect to be sympathetic. If these addressees were persuaded, they could then use their influence to seek the desired ends.[21] Similar discreet targeting would have been the best way to present anything like *In Eutropium* to an Eastern audience.

Means existed whereby Claudian's work might have been transmitted to the East: operating channels of official communication opened the route to unofficial communication, and controversial literary documents are known to have been distributed successfully to select audiences in this period. On the other hand, even if it is from *In Eutropium* 2 that Jerome borrowed a phrase characterizing effeteness, which would mean that he saw the book in Bethlehem before the end of 399,[22] he would have received it from his friends in Rome specially; his echo does not reveal a broader effort to publicize Claudian's work in the East.

Claudian does not otherwise surface literarily in the East until the sixth century. The chronicler Marcellinus proves that *In Eutropium* was known in Constantinople. For the year 399 he records, "This Eutropius of all eunuchs was the first and last consul. Concerning him the poet Claudian says: 'All

18. Matthews 1971, 1083–87, 1091–93, 1097–99; *PLRE* 1.551–52, Marcellus 7.

19. The evidence is collected and discussed, together with the problematical speeches of social criticism under Theodosius I, by Petit 1956 and Liebeschuetz 1972, 24–31.

20. λόγων ἀρρένων in Syn. *Prov.* 113B–C recalls *Reg.* 1C, ἀρρενωπούς; see further Alan Cameron and Long 1993, 127–33.

21. Norman 1969–77, 2.94, made these points in connection with Libanius's oration *Pro Templis* (*Or.* 30). The fear of publicity shows well in Liban. *Epp.* 33, 283.

22. See Alan Cameron 1965b and my note, Chap. 5 n. 20.

prodigies have given way, when a eunuch is consul.' "[23] The quotation shows that Claudian chose his theme well: the anomaly he expressed so trenchantly was still perceived.

Latin writers in sixth-century Constantinople borrowed phrases and images from other poems, showing that Claudian's works were known generally.[24] John the Lydian branded him "the Paphlagonian," meaning "windbag."[25] Claudian's panegyrics frequently and not surprisingly influenced Latin panegyrics in the East as they did in the West. On the other hand, although Theodor Birt and Christian Lacombrade have argued a close relationship between Claudian's panegyric for Honorius's fourth consulate and Synesius's *De Regno*, these two works share only commonplace ideals of kingship, which apply similarly to the young emperors they describe.[26] Claudian contributed to later Latin authors felicitous models for expressing these traditional concepts. Marcellinus too borrows a pungent line.

Unfortunately, none of these sources can confirm that Claudian's poems were transmitted to the Eastern capital shortly after each was written, as should be expected of any attempt to influence Eastern politics through them. They could equally well have traveled in collected editions after Claudian's death. Indeed, the latter possibility is supported by the fact that Corippus, for example, echoes passages from unpolitical *Carmina Minora* and *De Raptu Proserpinae* as well as from the panegyrics.[27] Yet neither can the possibility be excluded that single poems reached contemporaries as well. Not every individual leaves literary traces of the works he has read; and the people whose

23. *Chron. Min.* 2.66, quoting here *Eutr.* 1.8. On Marcellinus see references cited in the Introduction, n. 1.

24. Alan Cameron 1970, 244–46, characterized the borrowings briefly. Birt 1892 collected *loci similes* throughout his text. Within *Eutr.*, of Byzantine writers he cited Prisc. *Perieg.* 992 at *Eutr.* 1.354 for the mention of Carmania, but the point is not very distinctive: cf. Dion. *Perieg.* 1083 cited by Fargues, *Invectives* 70 ad loc. At *Eutr.* 2pr.29, *innumeri glomerantur eri*, "his numberless masters mass together," Birt cited Cor. *Iust.* 3.53, *innumerae glomerantur aves*, "numberless birds mass together"; Averil Cameron, ed. and comm., *In laudem Iustini Augusti minoris: Flavius Cresconius Corippus* (London: Athlone, 1976), 62, compared Corippus's line rather with *CM* 27.76, *innumerae comitantur aves*, "numberless birds accompany [the Phoenix]." Claudian's two passages are fused. Birt's other *loci* for *Eutr.* are earlier or Western. Averil Cameron's other *loci similes* for Corippus note Claudian's panegyrics frequently.

25. Joh. Lyd. *Mag.* 1.47; Birt 1892, iii–v, cited parallels for the metaphorical sense of "Paphlagonian" from late authors, Procop. *Anec.* 16.7 and Pallades *Anth. Pal.* 11.340, besides the locus classicus Ar. *Eq.* 2.

26. Birt 1885, xvi–xxii; Lacombrade 1956; cf. Alan Cameron and Long 1993, 137–38.

27. Opening to a page almost at random, I note that Averil Cameron (*Corippus*, 39) cited *Rapt.* 1.75ff. on Cor. *Iust.* 1.89ff., *3 Cons.* 58 and *CM* 30.80 as well as Verg. *Geo.* 262 on *Iust.* 1.108, and *Rapt.* 1.91 on *Iust.* 1.111.

political influence might have been sought by means of Claudian's poems were men of affairs rather than writers.

II. Approaching the Audience: The Problem of Propaganda

The preface of *In Rufinum* 1 and the other available testimony suggest that members of the Western court gathered to hear literary vilification in much the same way as they did to hear literary encomium. It was performed publicly before important people. In the East Claudian's work was transmitted more individually. Jerome read in isolation in Bethlehem; if Western messengers brought the poems to more influential people at court, on the model attested by Libanius and Synesius, they would have read them privately, before small and discreet groups at most.

Both types of audience indubitably knew something in advance of the subject Claudian took for *In Eutropium*. Any Eastern hearers lived under Eutropius's sway. The Western court had heard recently Claudian's panegyric of the year's other consul. At a minimum, they knew from that poem as well as from more prosaic consular announcements that Theodorus's Eastern colleague was not being recognized. Now they were to be given a picture of him. As a formal invective, *In Eutropium* 1 neatly follows the structure of a consular panegyric while making dispraise out of each of its topics. Claudian evokes the format's usual, encomiastic associations so as to affront them by his peculiar subject. The contrast derisively emphasizes how unfitted Eutropius is to his lofty honors and thus, in Claudian's argument, how unfit for them. For instance, when Eutropius is robed as consul Claudian begins conventionally, "How beautiful was the sight"; then he upsets the convention by likening Eutropius to an ape, "imitator of the human face," that a boy has dressed up in silk while leaving his back and buttocks bare (*Eutr.* 1.300–307),

> as a joke for the dinner-tables: with breast upright the wealthy creature steps, and disfigures itself with its brilliant garment.

> ludibrium mensis; erecto pectore dives
> ambulat et claro sese deformat amictu.

The brilliant garment of Claudian's panegyric form and all his resplendent ornament disfigures Eutropius as he portrays him in it. The inverted form serves its occasion perfectly.

The final version of *In Eutropium* 2 responds to fresh news that Eutropius is deposed and exiled. The preface breaks the announcement dramatically, for the benefit of any who had not heard it already and to evoke again the surprise of those who had (2pr.1–4):

Qui modo sublimes rerum flectebat habenas
   patricius, rursum verbera nota timet
et solitos tardae passurus compedis orbes
   in dominos vanas luget abisse minas.

He who just now used to bend the exalted reins of affairs,
   the patrician, fears again the lashings he has known,
and, about to suffer the familiar circlets of a tardy fetter,
   grieves that his threats against his masters have vanished unfulfilled.

The first line evokes a lofty eminence. "Patrician" matches it, but it is plunged
into the second line to confront, starkly, Eutropius's renewed abasement. The
verbs of emotion adopt Eutropius's perspective as he anticipates punishment.
They do not generate sympathy, however, for he grieves only at having his own
malice forestalled. He is still the same monster, the slave raised to "rage against
free backs" that Claudian's first book of invective had portrayed (1.184).

Book 2 itself broaches the consequences of the exile:[28] the character of the
court now that Eutropius is gone and, implicitly, what relations with it the
West might expect to enjoy. Transitions of power naturally engender speculation about how the new regime will deal with old relationships. Claudian has
Aurora describe similar circumstances after Rufinus was assassinated, when
"the world was beginning to be united by fraternal rule" and she entertained
hopes of Stilicho governing, before Eutropius forestalled him (2.543–52). Regardless of whether any citizens in the Eastern empire really did want Stilicho
to take control of its affairs, it is likely that Westerners who blamed Rufinus for
a rift looked to the East in hopes of greater cooperation. Easterners too must
have wondered what changes would ensue. The fragment of Eunapius quoted
in the preceding chapter reveals, while Eutropius was in power, general curiosity about political affairs in both courts. Now in the face of a new change
Claudian addresses similar curiosity. He examines the contemporary political
situation, and he makes specific judgments on it.

The unquestionable, immediate political relevance of Claudian's subject had
the ability to pique his audiences' interest, irrespective of his work's poetic
qualities. Nonetheless, Claudian's artistry is deeply implicated in giving voice
to political positions. Many modern critics deny that any work lacks social
relevance or functions purely at aesthetic levels. To quote but one famous
figure, George Orwell stated his presumptions forcefully: "that propaganda in
some form or other lurks in every book, that every work of art has a meaning

---

28. The original conception of book 2 Cameron postulated, which remains the core
of book 2 (Alan Cameron 1970, 134–49; cf. Chap. 5), anticipated that Tribigild's rebellion might topple Eutropius (see Alan Cameron 1970, 143); ramifications for a
Western audience are similar to those of the book as completed.

and a purpose—a political, social and religious purpose—and that our aesthetic judgments are always coloured by our prejudices and beliefs."[29] Propaganda thus diagnosed extends to virtually any kind of communication that resonates in a recipient's personal or interpersonal life. Orwell asserted that reception does not unravel social and aesthetic considerations; still less need they be entirely separable for the artist, who ultimately makes expression and artistry coincide. Withal, the social component of a work necessarily often consists in implicit values and assumptions. Claudian, by directly promulgating political statements, makes the question of how much his work constitutes propaganda open and specifically political.

Complicating the problem is the fact that the term "propaganda" often bears strong social implications of its own; Orwell's declaration was provocative. Gnilka vehemently rejected Cameron's application of the term to Claudian's work. He interpreted it: "Claudian is a 'Propagandist.' In practical terms, this means that he is scarcely given credit for an independent conviction, much less a greater intellectual conception of his own. He merely reacts, to voices of criticism of Stilicho or . . . to instructions of the administrator, without however at least standing in an inward relationship of commitment to this person." Moreover, Gnilka assumed that calling Claudian a propagandist denies that he shared the values and interests of his contemporaries or used them expressively in his poetry.[30]

Gnilka's drastic view of propaganda excludes, as by definition, any interplay of artistic qualities in a work. It profoundly distorts Cameron's application of the term, for he did not make such exclusions.[31] Meanwhile, several studies of Roman literature in the Augustan period have investigated, under the rubric of propaganda, how literature may communicate and foster attitudes about political relationships; these attitudes in turn can favor political actions. If the term is understood as shorthand for such a problem, more complex than Gnilka allowed it, it frames a productive approach. I. M. LeM. DuQuesnay found "The Propaganda Value" of Horace's conspicuously apolitical or even antipolitical *Sermones* 1, for example, in that their quietism encourages con-

29. George Orwell, "The Frontiers of Art and Propaganda," broadcast talk in BBC Overseas Service, 30 April 1941, published in the *Listener*, 29 May 1941, rpt. in *The Collected Essays, Journalism and Letters*, vol. 2, ed. Sonia Orwell and Ian Angus (New York: Harcourt, Brace and World, 1968), 126. Critics influenced by Marxism especially emphasize that literature is political in that it negotiates ambient relationships of social power: e.g., Terry Eagleton, *Literary Theory* (Minneapolis: University of Minnesota Press, 1983).

30. Gnilka 1976, 100–101; cf. 1977, 27–28.

31. Besides commenting on Claudian's artistry incidentally amid other arguments, Alan Cameron 1970 devoted a chapter to "Techniques of the Poet" complementing another on "Techniques of the Propagandist."

sent to Octavian's government.[32] It would be perversely wrong to suppose that the *Sermones* do not employ the resources of genuine art, or do not reflect meaningfully on friendship and other features of the good life, including the form and nature of well-written satire, just because at a political level their implications bear a coherent message. Conversely, it would be no less wrong to deny that this message is also conveyed. It is in using labels like "propaganda" to curtail texts' complexity of meaning that criticism cripples literature. Andrew Wallace-Hadrill in a brief essay on "Propaganda and Dissent? Augustan Moral Legislation and the Love-Poets" usefully framed the problem in terms of how poets articulate, with whatever intent, acceptance or rejection of Augustus's social policies and therefore also of his role in promoting them.[33] The essays on *Roman Poetry and Propaganda in the Age of Augustus*, edited by Anton Powell, variously explore the ways in which Augustan poets positively and negatively incorporate facets of Augustan ideology in their works.[34]

An important study by Jacques Ellul provides a general taxonomy of operations that propaganda, broadly conceived, can embrace.[35] Ellul studied specifically the "modern propaganda" of twentieth-century technological society. As distinct from "primitive stages of propaganda that existed in the time of Pericles or Augustus," as he put it (4), modern propaganda systematically exploits scientific insights into individual psychology and group sociology, recently developed theoretical principles of propaganda, and the technology of mass transportation and mass media; these last, mechanical resources make it possible to assemble and communicate with large groups simultaneously, and keep the individual continually immersed in a propagandistic environment (89–90). Naturally propaganda has always tried to exploit susceptibilities inherent in the society of its time. Ellul explored techniques used by technological societies for expressly political purposes, but he concerned himself especially with the propaganda of a technological society as such.[36] Nevertheless, he

32. DuQuesnay 1984; cf. Zanker 1988, 265–95, on how imagery concordant with Augustan social objectives penetrated private life.

33. *Klio* 67 (1985): 180–84. On the term "propaganda" cf. Andrew Wallace-Hadrill, "Image and Authority in the Coinage of Augustus," *JRS* 76 (1986): 67; against the distractions of exclusively political readings, G. Karl Galinsky, "Ovid, Vergil, and Augustus," in *Ovid's Metamorphoses: An Introduction to the Basic Aspects* (Berkeley: University of California Press, 1975), 210–65.

34. Powell 1992.

35. Ellul 1965. He drew on numerous more limited studies, a sampling of which is collected in Katz et al. 1954.

36. To take some summary statements from the preface (Ellul 1965, xvii): "Propaganda is called upon to solve problems created by technology, to play on maladjustments, and to integrate the individual into a technological world. Propaganda is a good deal less the political weapon of a regime (it is that also) than the effect of a technologi-

made several distinctions in the realm of propaganda that can be applied usefully to ancient texts and politics.

First, Ellul defined four applications of propaganda, according to context and aim (xiii). "Psychological action . . . seeks to modify opinions by purely psychological means"; it usually addresses the propagandist's own group. "Psychological warfare" uses psychological means to destroy the morale of an enemy group by leading its members to question the validity of their own beliefs and actions. "Re-education and brainwashing [involve] complex methods of transforming an adversary into an ally which can be used only on prisoners." Finally, "public and human relations . . . are propaganda because they seek to adapt the individual to a society, to a living standard, to an activity. They serve to make him conform, which is the aim of all propaganda." All involve manipulating attitudes, but there is great variation in the manner in which the propagandist approaches the propagandee and, implicitly, in his own relationship to the attitudes he is trying to instill.

The range of variation is made more plain by Ellul's definitions of four pairs of modes of propaganda. The distinctions are drawn antithetically, but the modes themselves may complement one another in practice. With "political propaganda" a government, party, administration, or pressure group exerts influence in calculated ways, seeking to change the behavior of the public and achieve a precise, usually limited goal. The themes utilized often are political, the ends always (62). "Sociological propaganda," on the other hand, spreads itself throughout a whole society, perpetually validating its lifestyle. By this means the group integrates individuals into itself and may seek to impose itself on other groups. Members express sociological values spontaneously and comprehensively (62–67). The consistency of their attitudes also serves subgroups using political propaganda for specific ends in action, because the same impetuses will move the entire group in the same way. Ellul even spoke of sociological "pre-propaganda" seeded by specific groups in order to create such a climate.[37]

Ellul also distinguished "agitation propaganda" from "integration propa-

---

cal society that embraces the entire man and tends to be a completely integrated society."

37. Ellul 1965, 15, 30–32, 66; cf. 299–302 on the more specific "pre-action response" also taught by propaganda so that in a later particular instance of political propaganda, an intermediate moment between the immediate stimulus and the ultimate goal may be bridged. In the semiological terms discussed by Foulkes 1983, 22–27 (following Charles Morris, *Writings on the General Theory of Signs* [The Hague: Mouton, 1971]), both the general climate created by sociological propaganda and the pre-action responses correspond to "interpretants," a term defined as "a disposition to respond in certain ways under certain circumstances."

ganda." Intense, relatively brief bursts of agitation incite action. Agitation propaganda always takes an adversarial stance; thus war and rebellion are its natural arenas, but a ruling body may also use it to catalyze radical change by making a scapegoat of an internal enemy (71). Integration propaganda operates over a long term and reproduces itself. It induces the individual to find his own interests fulfilled in the collective interests of the group. In this way it also causes him to behave according to stable patterns (75). This description closely resembles that of sociological propaganda: the categories frequently cover the same phenomena, "integration" considering primarily the socializing effect, and "sociological" the pervasiveness of the material.

"Vertical propaganda" is the most obviously manipulative. It is devised and wielded from above, on an essentially passive group of propagandees from whom the propagandist is always separate (80). "Horizontal propaganda" is generated within an ostensibly egalitarian group. It leads the individual through rational encounters and dialectic so that he consciously brings himself to embrace the propagandized values. Education is co-opted in the service of propaganda (81–84).

"Rational" and "irrational" propaganda can be distinguished by the emphases of their appeal to the individual, but in practice they are almost always fused. "Purely impassioned and emotional propaganda" is used rarely, because propaganda is more effective if it enables the propagandee to justify himself in following it: that is, it must direct the way in which he relates his actions to reality. Even an emotional appeal should ground itself on facts. Conversely, few individuals actually remember large numbers of facts as such. Instead, they retain a general, emotional impression which the facts produce. Therefore even rational propaganda must guide the way the facts that it presents are interpreted (84–87).

Ellul's taxonomy allows a full description of the methods employed by a text, in a way that the label "propaganda" alone does not. Gnilka conceived only of strictly vertical, political propaganda, and of the propagandist as a mechanical functionary of authorities above him. It is only one possible combination within the range of propagandistic activities. Horace's *Sermones*, on DuQuesnay's showing, serve political ends through the modalities of sociological, integrationistic propaganda; thus too the elegists' erotic poetry tends to subvert Augustus's social reforms. Both constitute "psychological action" verging on "public relations." When patrons with ties to governmental authorities support poets whose work favors governmental objectives, as Maecenas connected Vergil and Horace with Augustus, some vertical trickle-down of governmental suggestion may be suspected; indeed, the *recusationes* of Augustan poets call attention to their being urged to write public verse. Yet they represent themselves as rejecting the proposals, and the more subtle messages they do promulgate are spoken with professedly horizontal voice. Their contributions to the political discourse of their day appear differently from the manifestly vertical declarations of imperial coinage, monuments, or ceremony.[38]

Cameron considered the propagandistic function of Claudian's poetry in terms of interest and benefit. He found that Claudian consistently, coherently publicizes Stilicho's acts and aims, and endorses them.[39] Claudian is not a "senatorial spokesman," as earlier studies viewed him, because he does not represent the interests of the Senate consistently. For a significant example, *In Gildonem*, written shortly after victory over Gildo, does not credit the Senate with any initiative for the war, although the later panegyric for Stilicho's consulate praises him precisely for submitting the declaration of war to the Senate's vote (*Stil.* 1.325–32).[40] In *In Gildonem*, on the contrary, Roma and Africa beseech Jupiter, Jupiter dispatches the elder Theodosius to Honorius, Honorius announces his intentions to Stilicho, Stilicho modifies the plan, and the expedition is mounted. All action relies on the gods, Theodosius's family, and Stilicho.

As she supplicates Jupiter, Roma sketches an autobiographical history of the tribute of African grain, which Gildo now denies her (*Gild.* 49–55):

postquam iura ferox in se communia Caesar
transtulit et lapsi mores desuetaque priscis
artibus in gremium pacis servile recessi,
tot mihi pro meritis Libyam Nilumque dedere,
ut dominam plebem bellatoremque senatum
classibus aestivis alerent geminoque vicissim
litore diversi conplerent horrea venti.

After fierce Caesar transferred to himself the common
prerogatives, and morals declined, and I, grown unaccustomed to my
    original
arts, withdrew into the servile lap of peace,
they gave me Libya and the Nile for my many merits,
so that they might feed a sovereign people and a warrior senate
with summer fleets, and, from the twin shore
in turn, different winds might fill my granaries.

38. The distinction is made, for example, by Griffin 1984, esp. 200–206; Maria Wyke, "Augustan Cleopatras: Female Power and Poetic Authority," in Powell 1992, 115, distinguished directly vertical from indirectly, or horizontalized, vertical propaganda, as " 'primary' versus 'secondary' propaganda."

39. I paraphrase a sentence from Alan Cameron 1970, 49.

40. Alan Cameron 1970, 232, 362–63.

Ammianus 14.6.5–6 shows with what different emphasis an otherwise similar picture can be drawn:[41]

> Therefore the venerable city, after having subdued the haughty necks of savage nations and passed laws, the foundations and eternal tethers of liberty, like a frugal parent, both prudent and wealthy, permitted the Caesars, as her own children, to administer the rights of their patrimony. And long since, the electoral tribes have been allowed to be at leisure and the centuries at peace, and there are no conflicts over votes; instead the calm of Numa Pompilius's time has returned. Nonetheless, through all the shores and parts of the earth that there are, she is upheld as mistress and queen, everywhere the Senate Fathers' white hair is revered along with their authority, and the name of the Roman people is respected and honored.

In Ammianus's vision too the Caesars rule, but instead of their seizing authority, Rome grants it by a sort of family succession, "as to her own children." Republican bodies enjoy rest and peace without negative qualifiers like "servile," which Claudian's Roma uses in *In Gildonem*.[42] The old age of the state and the authority of the Senate are universally honored. Claudian's Roma, in contrast, calls her people "sovereign" and the Senate a "warrior," and says that the grain tribute was awarded as her merits deserved, but she makes plain that all real power rests with the emperor. She does not represent the first emperor as her child, receiving an inheritance, but as an aggressor: he transfers the powers of the state to himself absolutely. The emperors give the tribute as largess. This Roma says that she declined morally and militarily from her original strength. Her quiet is not well-earned repose, as in Ammianus's image, but "servile" torpor. She does not even mention the Senate, which otherwise was remembered as the corporate governing authority of republican Rome and which best kept the semblance of its earlier powers under the emperors; implicitly, it is enervated along with the personification of the state.

When Jupiter promises that Honorius will quash Gildo, Roma recovers her youthful vigor (*Gild.* 205, 208–12); still all hopes rest on the imperial family. The Senate plays no role. Similarly, the glorious vision of Rome with which Claudian celebrates Stilicho's consular visit there generally parallels Ammia-

---

41. Demandt 1965, 118–47, discussed Ammianus's full correlation of Rome's development to stages of human life (14.6.4–6), comparing at length Sen. ap. Lact. *Div. Inst.* 7.15.14–16 and Flor. pr.4–8, and other literary antecedents more briefly.

42. Sen. ap. Lact. *Div. Inst.* 7.15.15–16 emphasizes Roma's refusal to bear "servitude" to the kings as she reached maturity and threw off their "yoke of haughty domination," and the loss of that "liberty" in "old age . . . a sort of second infancy" after civil wars destroyed the republic.

nus's image without including the Senate (*Stil.* 3.130–81).[43] The city herself, "parent of arms and laws," won her glory in the republican past. Active verbs throughout the first half of the section chronicle her erstwhile aggression and success. She refused to accept defeat at Cannae and Trebia. "To her rule of peace we owe it that the world is our home."[44] She will escape decadence and eventual defeat, the common lot of Greek, Persian, and Macedonian civilizations. Yet, for the cause why she will escape, Claudian adduces divine protection answering reverence for old prophecies of Roman greatness, not any continued action by the city nor yet the virtues of Senatorial government. Climactically (*Stil.* 3.174–76),

> Her do you guard, glorious Stilicho, together with the gods,
> with your shield you protect her, the native country of both kings and
>   generals,
> and especially your own.

The city of Rome becomes Stilicho's native land by virtue of his son Eucherius's having been born there. Her role is essentially passive. Stilicho ranks with the gods by fairly routine aggrandizement; the glories of the ancient capital enhance the value of what he is said to defend, as well as conciliating a truly native audience to identify him with themselves and concur in his praise. Yet the city remains, though hallowed, no more than a repository of traditions. Claudian does not identify the Senate with those traditions strongly enough even to mention it.

Cameron demonstrated that Claudian treats the Senate as a reverenced fossil even in the three passages of *De Consulatu Stilichonis* that praise Stilicho's relations with it (*Stil.* 1.325–32, 2.291–311, 3.99–119).[45] The three instances cited, Stilicho's resuscitating the Senate's right to declare war, his keeping it unsullied by even momentary contemplation of Eutropius's consulate, and his restoring to it jurisdiction over provincial officials, deserve praise because each act professedly venerates sacred ideals of the Roman state that the Senate represents. Cameron underlined the pragmatic designs and consequences of Stilicho's three acts of reverence. The reverence itself, tellingly, takes radically different

---

43. Fuhrmann 1968, 551–53, found *Stil.* 3.130–81 to express all the crucial features of the un-Christianized late antique conception of Rome; Alan Cameron 1970, 352–61, discussed it as a literary feat. Cf. section III, "The Myth of Rome."

44. *Huius pacificis debemus moribus omnes quod veluti patriis regionibus utitur hospes,* Claud. *Stil.* 3.154–55, as translated by Platnauer 1922, 2.55.

45. Alan Cameron 1970, 230–37; compare discussion of *Stil.* 2.291–311 in Chap. 6. Gnilka 1977, 46, maintained that in *Stil.* 2.291–311, "Claudian portrays a solid fact in such a way that it redounds to the honor of the minister as well as of the Senate," but proposed no argument to refute Cameron's position.

forms. In declaring war and passing judgment on magistrates, the Senate played an active role. When on the other hand the Senate's sanctity must be protected from defilement (*Stil.* 2.298–300, 303–4), it is relegated to utter passivity. It is a touchstone against which the counterfeit, eunuch consul rings false: Roma calls it "my Senate House" (*Stil.* 2.300) to emphasize how monstrously un-Roman Eutropius is and how much Stilicho upholds the traditional Roman values. Claudian deploys it as a symbol, to Stilicho's advantage. In this case the technique is obvious. Yet Claudian used the Senate as a symbol just as much in the other two passages, for he asserts that it acts solely under Stilicho's grant. "The custom ignored through so many ages, Stilicho restored" (*Stil.* 1.328–29). "For the virtues of an era white with age, Stilicho extends the opportunity, and a people forgetful of its ancient height of power, he stirs up into its use again" (*Stil.* 3.106–9). They depend on him even to reawaken the memory of power.

Symbols, as Ellul stressed, are the essential tools of psychological propaganda (23, 163–64). Cultures continually invest certain entities with symbolic power, and imprint these symbols upon individuals (34). The more actively an individual participates in the life of his culture, the more his thought is shaped by its symbols and the more susceptible he is to manipulation of them (111). In the late fourth and early fifth centuries, a quintessentially Roman constellation of symbols shines forth from numerous texts. Rome itself is central, because the city is concrete and discrete, as well as evocative; its lucid simplicity makes it a particularly convenient symbol. Less tangible concepts are summoned up by it, both giving the city its power as a symbol and defining subsidiary symbols. These concepts comprehend the quality of being Roman, and the republican institutions and history that shaped the Roman state and Roman traditions. They correspond to what Ellul termed a myth.

The language in which myths are described tends to be deeply emotional. Ellul called them "all-encompassing, activating images: a sort of vision of desirable objectives that have lost their material, practical character and have become strongly colored, overwhelming, all-encompassing, and which displace from the conscious all that is not related to it. Such an image pushes man to action precisely because it includes all that he feels is good, just, and true" (31). His examples put this effusive description into perspective: "In our society the two great fundamental myths on which all other myths rest are Science and History. And based on them are the collective myths that are man's principal orientations: the myth of Work, the myth of Happiness (which is not the same thing as the presupposition of happiness), the myth of the Nation, the myth of Youth, the myth of the Hero" (40). Usually individuals do not perceive these numinous concepts propelling them through everyday life. Yet much individual and societal behavior can be analyzed in terms that resolve ultimately into similar profound aspirations. Most people would agree that ideals bound up with them can be stirring. Ellul emphasized the power of social myths because that power explains how agitation propaganda can unleash such furious action when it exploits basic societal ideals. He repeated that propaganda must work within the "dominant cultural values" and "structural elements of society" if it is to succeed.[46] The basic forces can be tapped by means of symbols. Normally, however, they remain dormant even while a program of sociological propaganda manages them; in the absence of a comprehensive program such as Ellul contemplated, they would be activated only at random, with limited scope on any particular occasion.

iii. The Myth of Rome

Rome worked strongly on the sensibilities of the later Roman Empire. Roman government and culture had been founded there. They extended their reach across the Mediterranean still tied closely to that one place, and Romans continued to emphasize the connection: so, for example, it is the city Claudian describes in his panegyric for Stilicho as resiliently and tenaciously conquering far-flung peoples, and receiving them into her citizenship (*Stil.* 3.130–59). The city centered all the history, customs, and ideals by which Roman civilization defined itself. By mere mention of it or its personifying goddess could be summoned up a full range of cultural values: in Ellul's terms, it was a symbol invested with the myth of Roman civilization. Romans for the most part doubtless felt more particular, immediate motivations for their actions. But they could also look through them to this transcendent idea and glory. They evoked it continually.

In an important article on the concept of Rome in late antiquity, Manfred Fuhrmann observed that even the most favorable of the assessments of Rome in traditional, pagan terms recognize that it no longer served as the center for imperial government.[47] François Paschoud, in an independent study of how pagan and Christian authors used the "myth of 'eternal Rome' " (10) to define a national consciousness in the face of barbarian encroachments from the later fourth to the mid-fifth century, commented that removal of imperial government seemed to liberate the city for her ideological role: "the Eternal City saw her moral prestige increase when she had lost her practical importance."[48] This

46. Ellul 1965, 39; more generally, 30–43, 62–67, in which it is also observed that propaganda can modify the tenets of a society, but must work indirectly and gradually, through means like sociological propaganda.

47. Fuhrmann 1968, 549–50, on Symm. *Rel.* 3; cf. 550, on Ammianus, and 553, on Claudian.

48. Paschoud 1967, 11.

transcendent image was rooted in republican and earlier imperial writing, of course; but the retrospection of late antiquity gave it distinctive form.[49]

Ammianus Marcellinus conscientiously reports events at Rome in each year covered by his history, even though, he remarks, "I think it possible that foreigners, when perhaps they come to read this, if that should happen, will wonder why, when the discourse turns to showing things going on at Rome, it is a tale of nothing but riots and taverns and other pettinesses like these" (Amm. 14.6.2). Insignificant though he acknowledges activities there to be, for him Rome still defines the center of the empire in a way that no other city can.[50]

Two lengthy digressions on the degeneracy of the city's population show what Ammianus thinks the center should mean (Amm. 14.6, 28.4).[51] For the most part, he inveighs against a commonplace litany of vices. The first passage alleges that the rich seek immortality through statues rather than by establishing a reputation for virtue, flaunt their wealth with extravagant carriages and clothes, and violate hospitality by sequential insincerity, neglect, and parsimony. They parade about Rome with armies of slaves, including eunuchs (Amm. 14.6.16–17, quoted in Chapter 4.I). They prefer entertainment to culture, so much that mime actresses and their hangers-on were allowed to remain in the city when scholarly foreigners were expelled, and women who should be established matrons are still unmarried dancers. Even the rich angle for legacies and violate friendship in hypochondriacal anxiety but do anything for the sake of a handout. The poor loiter in taverns or around theaters, gamble and fight, make disgusting snorting noises,[52] and gape after the races. Claudian claims that Eutropius and his court share most of the same base tastes (cf. *Eutr.* 2.84–87, 341, 356–64). In the second passage Ammianus recapitulates these complaints and adds vainglory of ancestry, cruelty to slaves, pleasure-tripping,[53] adulation of the unworthy and their false pride (cf. *Eutr.* 2.58–94), superstition, malicious litigation, theater claques, and gluttony.

49. Besides Paschoud 1967 and Fuhrmann 1968, on the traditional background of late antique images of Rome see the compilation of Wilhelm Gernentz, *Laudes Romae* (Rostock: Adler, 1918); Dölger 1937; Carl Koch, "Roma Aeterna," in *Religio: Studien zu Kult und Glauben der Römer*, ed. Otto Seel, Erlanger Beiträge zur Sprach- und Kunstwissenschaft 7 (Nürnberg: Hans Carl, 1960), 142–75 (revised from *Paideuma* 3 [1944–49]: 219–40 and *Gymnasium* 59 [1952]: 128–43, 196–209); Ulrich Knoche, "Die augusteische Ausprägung der Dea Roma," *Gymnasium* 59 (1952): 324–49.

50. Cf. Matthews 1986: he suggested that Ammianus chose to live in Rome and to write in Latin essentially because, to apply the terms of my argument, Ammianus himself subscribed to the myth of Rome.

51. On Ammianus's Roman digressions, see Matthews 1989, 414–16 and n. 28; Paschoud 1967, 59–67; Pack 1953; Hartke 1951, 51–74; Thompson 1947, 108–20.

52. Add Amm. 14.6.25 and Synes. *Prov.* 92B to the passages collected by Campbell Bonner, "A Tarsian Peculiarity (Dio Prus. Or. 33)," *Harv. Theol. Rev.* 35 (1942): 1–11.

53. *Eutr.* 2.95–102 too complains at a vacation masquerading as a military campaign.

Some distinctive comments focus Ammianus's diatribes. The first is introduced by a metaphorical biography of Rome (Amm. 14.6.3–6, quoted earlier). In notable contrast to Claudian's biographical metaphor of Rome in *In Gildonem*, Ammianus portrays the city as aged but truly venerable. The state grew by conquest in youth and maturity and now, in old age, retires to enjoy the filial care of the emperors and the reverence of the world. As John Matthews remarked, "This is not an image of decline, far from it; as Rome enters old age, her 'children' in the pugnacious shape of the Roman emperors, carry on the mission."[54] "But," Ammianus continues tartly, "this magnificent splendor of the assemblies is injured by the uncivilized frivolity of a few who do not reflect on the place where they were born but have fallen, as if licence were granted to vices, into misdeeds and abandon" (Amm. 14.6.7). If the fault of the "few" comes from their failure to "reflect on the place where they were born," Ammianus implies that respect for the traditions of Rome ought to inspire them to behave better. Morality and patriotism are united. Both are informed by a sense of history.

Similarly, those who exaggerate the dimensions of their estates "clearly do not know that their ancestors, through whom Roman greatness was so extended, were not conspicuous for their wealth but through the most savage wars, not differing from the common soldiers in their wealth or food or the cheapness of their clothes, overcame all obstacles by their manliness" (Amm. 14.6.10). It is impossible to tell whether Ammianus assigns this ultimate cause of success, *virtute*, its classical meaning, "courage," or the moral sense that was gaining currency in his period, "virtue." Both suit his complaint. As in the previous case, Ammianus assigns the problem to a want of knowledge or consideration. Contemporary Romans behave badly, while they should be inspired by a patriotic sense of history. Moral exempla from Roman republican history make the same points: Cato rebukes the desire for commemorative statues; Valerius Publicola, Regulus, and Scipio illustrate the poverty of Roman heroes (Amm. 14.6.8, 11). The former anecdote conveys a wittily expressed, timeless admonition that gains authority from its ascription. The latter group inspires solely because of the heroes' standing in the Roman past.

In the second diatribe Ammianus complains that the Roman nobles "hate learning like poison" and inexplicably read only Juvenal and Marius Maximus, "when, in view of the breadth of their honors and families they ought to read constantly many different things" (Amm. 28.4.14–15). Once more, study recaptures an illustrious past that sets moral and intellectual standards.

Ammianus periodically reverts to the city of Rome partly in order to evoke its traditions and recall these standards, in moral commentary on the events of his history and on the present day. Devices like the few examples I have selected

---

54. Matthews 1989, 250.

recur throughout the work.[55] It is striking and significant that even though Rome had ceased to be the political capital of the empire, it still remained a symbol by which Ammianus could expressively suggest moral judgments of emperors and citizens. As Paschoud observed, "The fact that the historian follows models for the exterior structure of such passages does not indicate in any way that the subject matter does not correspond to his true opinion."[56]

Symmachus is famous for the conservatism expressed in his *Relatio* 3, written in 384 to request that the Altar of Victory be restored to the Roman Senate House.[57] He argues that the past must not be set aside, because the same forces that brought the Roman state to greatness are still needed to protect it. "We seek again the standing of religions that long profited the republic. . . . Who is so much a friend to the barbarians that he does not feel the need for the altar of Victory!" (Symm. *Rel.* 3.3).

Many more sentences elaborate this fundamental idea, and some conjure more specifically with Rome's power over the sentiments. Constantius's visit to the city in 357 is recalled. Although Constantius was the first to remove the altar, Symmachus insists that he respected the privileges of the Vestal Virgins, replenished the priesthoods with nobles, continued to support "Roman ceremonies," and showed interest and admiration when he visited the ancient shrines (*Rel.* 3.7).[58] Symmachus makes a more direct and passionate appeal

55. See for example the sensitive discussion Matthews 1987 focused on Amm. 15.7.3–5, in answer to Erich Auerbach, "The Arrest of Peter Valvomeres," in *Mimesis* (Berne, 1946; rpt. Princeton: Princeton University Press, 1974), 50–76. Blockley 1975, 157–67, cf. 191–95, gave fundamental discussion to Ammianus's didactic use of exempla. Ammianus cites Greek and even a few external figures as well as Roman ones, so this function is not limited to the evocation of Roman traditions: compare general comments that erudition should accompany rank, e.g., Amm. 14.6.1; 16.7.5, 9.2; 21.16.4; 25.10.15; 31.14.5.

56. See Paschoud 1967, 59–67; on the relevance of rhetorical forms to substance, cf. Alan Cameron 1964, 27. Paschoud supposed Ammianus confronts current Roman mores with the ideal of the city merely from personal frustrations; Blockley 1975 marked out an important new direction for the study of Ammianus by discovering in him a positive, didactic purpose.

57. On Symmachus's petition and the response of Ambrose, see Richard Klein, ed., *Der Streit um den Victoriaaltar. Die dritte Relatio des Symmachus und die Briefe 17, 18 und 57 des Mailänder Bischofs Ambrosius*, Texte zur Forschung 7 (Darmstadt: Wissenschaftliche Buchgesellschaft, 1972); Barrow 1973, 1–23, 34–47; Matthews 1975, 203–11; Vera 1981, 12–53; François Paschoud, "Le rôle du providentialisme dans le conflit de 384 sur l'autel de la Victoire," *Mus. Helv.* 40 (1983): 197–206. Paschoud 1967, 71–109, discussed Symmachus's attitude to Rome as representative of the senatorial aristocracy (Matthews 1975, 203–11, noted correctively that public funding of state cults was integral to their practice and efficacy, and that Ambrose distorts Symmachus's financial arguments polemically). On Symmachus's whole corpus of letters, see Matthews 1974.

58. Amm. 16.10.13–17 also emphasizes Constantius's admiration for the monuments of the city, including the shrines of Tarpeian Jove, the Pantheon, and the Temple of the

through prosopopoeia when personified Roma implores respect for her years and the rites that brought her to them (*Rel.* 3.9).

The emotional force of Symmachus's personification of Roma is demonstrated by the fact that Ambrose, who uses ridicule and insinuation to answer Symmachus's other points, sets this one aside by asserting that Rome in fact pleads differently (Ambros. *Ep.* 18.7).[59] In his version she insists, "I have submitted my sphere to other doctrines." She is happy to convert in her old age, and calls her pagan youth barbarian: "This thing alone I used to have in common with the barbarians, that previously I did not know God." Pride in and identification with Rome are reinforced by her negative reference to the non-Roman.

Symmachus uses the same device when he complains that the ornate carriage assigned to the office of *praefectus urbi* by Gratian is "foreign" as well as overbearing (Symm. *Rel.* 4). "Your Roma does not endure the provocations of pride," he further reminds the emperors. The personification has learned her lesson, naturally, from the exempla of republican history: Tarquin was haughty and even Camillus offended by using a quadriga as dictator, but Publicola won honor by bowing his emblems of office before the popular assembly. These traditions have expressed and shaped a character shared by Symmachus, his Roma, and the Roman people, probably all included in the first-person plural of the final injunction. Symmachus expects it to admonish the emperors. He succeeded, for his *Relatio* 20 concerns the return to the proper stores of silver intended for decorating the ostentatious carriage, when plans to make it were abandoned.

These two authors roughly contemporary with Claudian exemplify attitudes that can be traced much further afield. Somewhat earlier, Aurelius Victor compiled a group of imperial biographies from Augustus to the twenty-third year of Constantius's reign, A.D. 360 (Vict. *Caes.* 42.20).[60] His material is the stuff of which historical exempla are made. With marked nostalgia, he remarks regretfully that the *ludi saeculares* celebrating the centennials of Rome are no longer observed (*Caes.* 28.2).[61] Even more strongly, the Greek historian Zosi-

---

City, but he does not mention the traditional cults or the Altar of Victory. François Paschoud, "L'intolérance chrétienne vue et jugée par les païens," *CrSt* 11 (1990): 561 n. 44, observed that pagan apologists routinely contend that good emperors have tolerated religious plurality.

59. Fuhrmann 1968, 554–58, described the personification's adoption first by Ambrose, then by Prud. *Contr. Symm.* Vera 1981, 38–39, cited examples of Roma personified (Amm. 14.6.5 however, not XVI, 6, 5 as printed).

60. See Bird 1984 on Victor generally, 60–70 on his view of "Rome and the Provinces."

61. See Dufraigne 1975, xix.

mus, possibly following Eunapius, blames neglect of the festival for the decline of the Roman state (Zos. 2.7.1–2).[62]

Somewhat later than Claudian, Macrobius devoted a literary Saturnalia to Roman antiquities and especially to Vergil. His homage to Roman traditions operates on more levels than just the subject matter of the discussion. He set the work as a dialogue among noble Romans of the previous generation, Symmachus, Praetextatus, and their circle; at the beginning of the book he evokes the model of Cicero's *De Republica* (Macrob. *Sat.* 1.1.4). Alan Cameron remarked on this fact, and noted the attendant implication that Macrobius was looking nostalgically back at a generation that lived up to the cultural ideals inherent in the discourse.[63] The virtues of this last generation of great Romans are reinforced by being cast into the literary structure of another exemplary Roman. And just as Cicero's interlocutors discuss the constitution of the Roman state, Macrobius's recall and reaffirm through their conversation a fundamental cultural heritage.

Closer in time to Claudian but far remote from Rome itself, Synesius at Arcadius's court in Constantinople calls on explicitly Roman standards and traditions in his address *De Regno*. He complains that "barbarian" sequestration of the emperor has done "the affairs of the Romans" incomparable harm; he holds up imperial and republican Roman paradigms as well as Greek.[64] Throughout the tirade against barbarian soldiers in Roman service that occupies a key part of the speech, Synesius freely and clearly interchanges "Romans" and the first-person plural.[65] The fact that he used the speech, despite its ostensible form as a discourse on kingship addressing Arcadius, to woo a group of disaffected former high officials rankling under Eutropius's administration shows what power the symbol of Rome held in the East.[66] In his political works Synesius never acknowledges the separate existence of the Western emperor or the Western part of the empire, and yet he identifies with the name of Rome and Roman traditions completely. Furthermore, he expects his hearers to do the same.

62. See Paschoud 1971–89, 1.79, 191–92; cf. Zos. 4.59.3, Paschoud 1971–89, 2².470–73; Paschoud 1975, 139–47.

63. Alan Cameron 1966b, esp. 28, 35.

64. Syn. *Reg.* 14C, 16A (imperial luxury and decay); 17D–19B (recent emperors exemplifying martial virtue); 24A–B (Spartacus and Crixus, exemplifying slave revolt); 19B–D (Roman and Athenian constitutional history); 20B–D (Agesilaus and Epaminondas exemplifying austerity).

65. Individual examples at Syn. *Reg.* 21B, 22D, 22D–23A, 23B, 24B–C, 25C–D; see Alan Cameron and Long 1993, 302–3 and n. 10.

66. This view of the speech is not conventional, but is the only one that explains its many anomalies. See now Alan Cameron and Long 1993, 103–42. Cf. Dölger 1937 on the Byzantine sense of inheritance of Rome.

These few examples could easily be multiplied, extended over time, and explored in greater depth, but they already indicate the power and the prevalence of the symbol of Rome specifically in Claudian's period. These writers worked on the assumption that mention of the city and of incidents in its history would strike a particular note to which their audiences would respond. They expected comprehension or even action. The practical goals urged by means of the symbol are obvious and direct in Symmachus and Ambrose and veiled by a fictional but still hortatory setting in Synesius. These authors in the first instance exemplify the political propaganda of special interest groups. Particular use of the symbol also renews its general existence. Ammianus's and Macrobius's goals are more intellectual and literary, but they too consciously invoke the symbol with specific purpose. It conveyed fundamental elements of a cultural self-definition. It could be readily identified, and at some level it could inspire. In short, it pointed to a social myth in Ellul's sense. In his terms, the literate and politically prominent groups that produced and read such works as I have been discussing were continually reiterating the myth through spontaneous, horizontal sociological propaganda. In turn, this literature integrated the group: that is, it reconfirmed belief in the myth.

Consequently, the mere fact that Claudian too evokes the myth of Rome in his poetry[67] in itself says nothing about his allegiances or purpose. The traditional view, repeated by Gnilka against Cameron, maintained in effect that Claudian joined the senatorial aristocracy of Rome in sociological propaganda and occasional attempts to influence Stilicho and Honorius. The position of *tribunus et notarius* that Claudian attained should rank him in the administrative aristocracy of the Roman imperial service, but it has been maintained that the ideals voiced in his work ally him more profoundly to the Senate; François Paschoud even called Claudian a convert from Hellenism to Roman traditionalism.[68]

But Ellul identified the importance of myth not only in the fact that sociological propaganda reinforces it, but still more in that it represents a reservoir of power on which all propaganda needs to draw. He even suggested that, with enough preparation, propaganda could shape myths for later exploitation.[69] In whichever way the myth is given form, it is useful for the propagandist only if it is subscribed to by the members of the group at which he aims his propaganda, and if they can be made to thrill to it as deeply as Ellul's definition requires. They too will give voice to the myth, often passionately; the propagandist must express no less passion, if he is to stimulate the force he hopes to use. Ellul underlined the fact that the members of a group give their alle-

67. Christiansen 1971 collected passages and references to other discussions.
68. Paschoud 1967, 134.
69. Ellul 1965, 31–43, 86, 117; cf. xviii, 25, 65–67, 247.

giance to a leader because they identify him with themselves (96–97). In particular, they must feel that he shares their aims and beliefs. But while he conveys to them the essential message that he does believe with them, vertical propaganda may also guide their views into the pattern of objectives he has formulated. Propaganda may be detected in a text by its manipulations.

The telltale manipulations appear elusively. If propaganda succeeds, the aims of the leader and the group coincide. As Ellul said (italics his), "Governmental propaganda *suggests* that public opinion *demand* this or that decision; it provokes the will of the people, who spontaneously would say nothing. But, once evoked, formed, and crystallized on a point, that *will* becomes the *people's will*; and whereas the government really acts on its own, it gives the impression of obeying public opinion—after first having built that public opinion" (132). The group adopts as its own the views that are promoted, and the promotion will have had to play upon sentiments already existing within the group, in order to carry its further objective. Therefore gaps between the propagandist and the group will appear as little as possible when propaganda is operating. It is a very delicate task to determine whether a given text expresses the interests of a group simply, or whether it is designed by an agency in some way distinct from the group in such a way as to exploit the group's special interests and steer them in a particular direction. Sociological propaganda, generated spontaneously by the group, also steers, but it steers individuals into the group and validates the interests of those who have joined it.[70] Essentially vertical propaganda that exploits social myth and sociological propaganda that perpetuates the myth are intimately related. A crucial difference exists between them, however: the one urges the mass toward an extrinsic goal, whereas the other exerts purely centripetal force.

The inconsistencies that Cameron detected in Claudian's praise of Stilicho's relations with the Senate in the three books of *De Consulatu Stilichonis* indicate most tellingly Claudian's fundamental allegiance. Assuredly members of the Senate revered their own order and all that it stood for. It is to be expected that they would sympathize with any profession of respect. But when the respect is expressed in contradictory ways, or when it demands silent passivity of the revered body, it seems not to reflect desires originated by the body itself. The activity of originating desires is antithetical to such relinquishing of control.

70. Foulkes 1983 made a fascinating investigation of "Capitalist Integration Myths" in modern literature (chap. 6; other interesting studies are referred to there), notably in the analysis of Beatrix Potter's *Squirrel Nutkin*, 50.

CHAPTER EIGHT

Stance and Purpose

✦

BOOKS 1 AND 2 OF *In Eutropium* are set apart by their different dynamic structures as formal invective and epic. They respond to different circumstances. This chapter explores the apparent aims of the responses. Book 1's systematic stepwise progress through argument, while exploiting various irrational prejudices, pursues the essentially rational end of persuasion. As Ellul noted, rational and irrational elements operate most effectively in concert. Book 2's epic momentum is better suited to agitation.

Both books evoke Roman social myth. A crystallized image of Roman tradition belonged to the cultural self-consciousness of any Roman, but modern scholars have always judged that the senatorial aristocracy of the city of Rome looked to it especially attentively. Their corporate identity was vested in the body that had continuously influenced the conduct of the Roman republican state, during the period of its greatest growth. Identified with Roman achievement, the Senate itself became a symbol. In the late antique empire, its prestige both shaped and was in turn reinforced by the traditionalism of individual senators, as for example the correspondence of Symmachus abundantly illustrates.[1] Claudian's passionate affirmation of Roman values has led scholars to identify him as a spokesman for a defined senatorial cause, but both books of *In Eutropium* bear out the evidence of *De Consulatu Stilichonis* that Claudian uses this language of ideas to present objectives of Stilicho to the senatorial class in the form it might find most palatable.

In Eutropium wrestles with a dilemma over the relations maintained by Honorius's and Arcadius's governments, which had not been resolved by the time either book was published. Claudian maintains that Eutropius made

---

1. In private letters as well as the *Relationes* briefly discussed in Chap. 7.III. See Matthews 1974, and for a broader perspective Matthews 1975, esp. 1–31, Paschoud 1967, 71–109.

cooperation between the two halves of the empire impossible. When book 1 was written, Eutropius's consulate seemed to show that he controlled Eastern affairs absolutely, so that an acceptable concord could not be restored unless by very drastic action. Tribigild's revolt and Eutropius's deposition and exile later in 399 seemed to open possibilities reflected in book 2 for a new accommodation. Neither book, however, participates in exchange: both address the sympathies and capacity for action of a Western, but not an Eastern, audience.

1. *In Eutropium* 1

The Senate's control of events was relinquished, or rather the Senate was not granted the semblance of control, at the decision not to recognize Eutropius's consulate. The formal structure of *In Eutropium* 1 subverts a consular panegyric to climax on just this issue. According to the proem, all monstrous omens are outdone, not so much by a eunuch's having attained power over half the empire, but by his having been named consul (*Eutr.* 1.8). His personal history and malfeasance in office, all consequences of his castration, support the contention that he is not fit for the Romans' supreme honor. It caps his career. A crowning series of comparisons, *teleiotate synkrisis*, holds up the new prodigy of a eunuch consul, with his vile career, against paradigms of mythology, religion, and nature. Roma invokes the Roman past in the book's epilogue, recapitulating its argument against Eutropius's consulate as her central theme. Symbolically in the consciousness of the audience as well as literally in the narrative, Roma reaffirms Eutropius's disqualifications. She declares with the voice of Roman tradition that they must disqualify him, and she authorizes the decision not to recognize him.

Roma's argument against recognizing Eutropius is propagandistic, in the sense that it has potential to influence attitudes toward him, his consulate, and its recognition, rather than the facts themselves. Claudian's own, earlier panegyric for Theodorus shows the request to have been already fulfilled. There too attitudes to the recognition could be swayed by the poem, rather than the policy already determined. When Claudian adduces the fact that Eutropius's consulate is not being recognized to prove that "nothing is permitted to spite [*invidiae*], while Stilicho looks out for the world, he and his starlike son-in-law," he transparently asserts that they decided to repudiate Eutropius's consulate not out of spite or jealousy, but out of thoughtful care for the Roman world (*M. Theod.* 265–69, quoted in Chapter 6). Stilicho and Honorius alone appear as responsible for defending the hallowed office. Even when "the eminences and majesty of the Roman Senate" are gathered to hear, they are not credited with any action (*M. Theod.* pr.7). The preface does not mention Stilicho and Honorius, which may mean, as Fargues suggested, that they did not attend the recital.[2] If not, Iustitia's crediting them for not recognizing Eutropius can only direct the sentiments of the aristocrats present: the primary message, by definition, addresses those who hear it first. Roma's plea in *In Eutropium* 1, published later although set at the moment Eutropius was inaugurated, applauds Stilicho's and Honorius's decision similarly. It justifies a unilateral action before an audience that was not consulted when the decision was made.

Other elements of Roma's speech too manipulate the aristocratic audience as well as or more effectually than they could manipulate Stilicho and Honorius. Roma commends Honorius's victories over barbarian tribes in Britain and the Gauls, enrolling him in the proud traditions of Roman victory. In addressing him as "conqueror of the Germans" she particularly evokes the ancient victory titles that were first applied to generals of the republic (*Germanice, Eutr.* 1.395). Michael McCormick has pointed out that these titles were used only in written contexts, not in ordinary exchanges or even ceremony; thus Roma's vocative is conspicuously literary and archaizing.[3] Such references flatter Honorius, but they also justify his reign and Stilicho's bloodless success with the German tribes in 396 by asserting that they fulfill traditional martial ideals.

Flattery might please a monarch personally, but in this case it introduces a request he has already granted. The conciliation that the narrative frames as hortatory proves superfluous to its ostensible purpose. The secondary audience of this imperial flattery, the assembled nobles before whom Honorius is called "conqueror of the Germans," is more meaningfully targeted.[4] Imperial policy required extensive cooperation of the great landholders, for access to their resources of manpower, produce, and accumulated wealth.[5] They tended conservatively to idealize ancient Roman military principles, as necessary and sufficient to maintain Roman greatness without the need to draw on their reserves.[6] Two of the clearest recitals of these ideals are the advice Claudian

2. Fargues, *Claudien* 15. Yet the argument from silence cannot be conclusive: Claudian does not preface some public poems at all, and not all his prefaces indicate his audience.

3. McCormick 1986, 114–15; cf. 21–22; Them. *Or.* 10.140a–b (1.213.1–8 Schenkl and Downey); Pacat. *Pan. Lat.* 2[12].5.4.

4. Visual representations and ceremony, by articulating the majesty of late antique emperors, substantially reinforced it: MacCormack 1981 is a fundamental study; see too, e.g., McCormick 1986 on the imperial ideology of victory, or Zanker 1988 on the power of images in the age of Augustus.

5. These points are emphasized by, e.g., Matthews 1975, 268–70, 276–78; cf. Mazzarino 1942 = 1990, 165–79.

6. Concessions to barbarians affronted the presumption of Roman superiority, and subsidies required expenditure, so that hostility to barbarians converged with ideology (see, e.g., Bayless 1976; Ruggini 1968; Christiansen 1966). Yet blanket opposition to

depicts Theodosius giving Honorius in the panegyric for his fourth consulate (*4 Cons.* 320–52) and the advice Synesius incorporates in his *De Regno* (*Reg.* 12B–14B).[7] Synesius claims that bad advisers bar Arcadius from even hearing such estimable precepts, but Claudian frames them as a natural heritage; his scene implies that Honorius is bound to embody all Theodosius's prowess and success, as both blood and paternal training enjoin. Reassurance that their rulers fulfilled the ideals the aristocrats embraced would help conciliate them to governmental policies. Claudian relentlessly magnifies Honorius's and Stilicho's successes. About the mission of 396 he marveled to Honorius in 398, "what others were able to earn by long wars, this journey of Stilicho's gives you" (*4 Cons.* 458–59).[8] Roma's address in *In Eutropium* repeated the idea in 399, and Claudian continued to claim it as a spontaneous victory in his panegyrics for Stilicho's consulate in 400 (*Stil.* 1.188–245; cf. 2.243–46, 3.13).

Roma rejoices at Honorius's glory and condemns Eastern "jealousy." She ascribes Gildo's revolt to its inspiration (*Eutr.* 1.396–400):

> But what am I to do? Jarring East envies fortunate
> deeds, and crimes rise up from Phoebus's other
> axis, lest the realm work together with its entire body.
> I do not mention Gildo's perfidy, received with great
> praise, and the Moors propped by Eastern strength.

These fulminations obviously play on fears and resentments roused in the West and particularly at Rome when Gildo transferred Africa's allegiance and grain tribute to the East. It would be easy for popular opinion to infer that the beneficiary instigated the change. Gnilka insisted that Claudian must be expected to have shared common sentiments of his time, from which the label of propagandist would unjustly detach him;[9] yet even sincerely held ideas can yield partisan advantages.

---

barbarians, however active it became as a prejudice, was never a viable policy: see now Alan Cameron and Long 1993, esp. 109–42, 199–252, 301–36.

7. J. R. Asmus, "Synesius und Dio Chrysostomus," *Byzantinische Zeitschrift* 9 (1900): 91–104, traced how Synesius follows Dio in *Reg.* For broader context, cf. Francis Dvornik, *Early Christian and Byzantine Political Philosophy: Origins and Background,* Dumbarton Oaks Studies 9, 2 vols. (Washington, D.C.: Trustees for Harvard University, 1966); Dvornik discussed Synes. *Reg.* specifically at 2.699–705. Alan Cameron 1970, 322, observed against Birt 1885, xvi–xxii, and Lacombrade 1956, that Synesius's and Claudian's parallels stem from a highly traditional literary education, pursued by both in Alexandria at about the same time. Alan Cameron 1970, 431–34, sketched the afterlife of Claudian's version in medieval treatises of Advice to Rulers. On the rhetorical utility of such advice, cf. Alan Cameron and Long 1993, 137–38, 273–74.

8. The campaign and its date were discussed by Alan Cameron 1970, 96–97; Döpp 1980, 102 n. 5; Barr 1981, 85; Lehner 1984, 84–88.

9. Gnilka 1976, 100–101, and 1977, 36, maintained that Claudian could well have

Focusing attention on the idea that the East roused, welcomed, and supported Gildo preempts consideration whether Honorius and Stilicho might have followed a bad policy and provoked Gildo's actions. No such suspicion is positively attested; but parallels imply that high officials could face opprobrium for any sort of interior or exterior disturbance. Synesius's *De Regno* attacks Eutropius both along lines conventionally taken against court eunuchs, that they enervate the emperor with luxury and isolate him from his people, and specifically for his policy toward Alaric.[10] In *In Eutropium* 2 Claudian similarly derives Tribigild's rebellion from Eutropius's mismanagement (2.177–80). His earlier invective against Rufinus alleges that he encouraged barbarians to attack the East (*Ruf.* 1.308–22, 2.22–53).[11] Julian in justification of his revolt publicized the claim that Constantius paid the Alamanni to invade Gaul (Jul. *Ath.* 286A).[12] The usurper Maximus exploited resentment against Gratian for favoring Alans, and against Valentinian II and Theodosius for using barbarians in their armies against him.[13] Damage could always be done by charging that

---

feared that Alaric would try to sack Rome when he invaded Italy in 402, as Claudian claims at *Get.* 530–49 (cf. *6 Cons.* 211–12, 531–36, and on Alaric, Heather 1991, 208–18). Alan Cameron 1970, 183–84, argued that the fear misread Alaric's true intentions, and that Claudian "carefully fosters the myth" because it magnifies gratitude to Stilicho. Claudian need not have had special insight into Alaric's plans for the advantage to operate.

10. Barnes 1986, 107–8, identified the crucial allusion to Eutropius in Syn. *Reg.* 15B: "introducing the senseless element, and stripping in front of them" (πρὸς ἐκείνους ἀπογυμνούμενοι). Eutropius's office of *praepositus sacri cubiculi* traditionally involved valeting the emperor, so that the otherwise bizarre accusation suits him alone. The charge comes in the middle of a long section castigating the "senseless luxury" amid which Arcadius lives; luxurious isolation of an emperor is used as a motif attacking the eunuchs who serve it, e.g., *HA Alex. Sev.* 45.4–5, 66.3; *HA Aurel.* 43.4 (cf. 43.1); Jul. *Ath.* 274A–B; cf. Stroheker 1970; Hopkins 1978, 172–96; Guyot 1980, 160; Albert 1984, 53. Synesius attacks Eutropius's barbarian policy at *Reg.* 22A–26C; Heather 1988 made the important discovery that he describes specifically Alaric's Goths. See now Alan Cameron and Long 1993, 107–42.

11. See Levy 1971, 87–89, 125–26, and the parallel allegations he cited; Alan Cameron 1970, 71–75.

12. Cf. *Pan. Lat.* 3[11].6.1; Liban. *Or.* 12.62, 13.35, 18.107, 113; Amm. 21.3.4–5; Socr. *HE* 3.1.38; Soz. *HE* 5.2.23; Joachim Szidat, *Historischer Kommentar zu Ammianus Marcellinus Buch XX–XXI, Teil II: Die Verhandlungsphase, Historia* Einzelschrift 38 (Wiesbaden: Steiner, 1981), 88–91. Blockley 1972, 441 n. 26, too strictly denied reference to this incident by Socrates, who unclearly collapses it with Julian's battle at Strasbourg, and by Sozomen, who curtails Socrates' version.

13. Gratian: Vict. *Epit.* 47.6–7 (including the allegation that Gratian sometimes dressed in barbarian garments, cf. Claud. *Ruf.* 2.79–85, Synes. *Reg.* 23C), Zos. 4.35.2–4; cf. Matthews 1975, 175. Valentinian: Ambros. *Ep.* 24.4 (Ambrose's countercharge, *Ep.* 24.8, shows that Maximus's was propagandistic rather than principled; cf. Heather 1991, 183–84). Theodosius: Pacat. *Pan. Lat.* 2[12].32.3–5 and Zos. 4.39.5 with Nixon 1987, 92–93 n. 110.

one's political opponent somehow precipitated damaging actions by a group which a Roman audience could identify as alien. Regardless of probability, Gildo's rebellion would have provided an opening to anyone who wished to oppose Stilicho's influence; therefore, whether or not the preventative message faced active opposition, to utter it served Stilicho's interest. The silence of opposing voices may only indicate that Claudian's message succeeded.[14]

Both ancient sources and modern scholars incline to believe that Eutropius did collude with Gildo. Zosimus ascribes the revolt entirely to Eutropius's inspiration (Zos. 5.11.2). Seeck thought that Gildo decided on revolt fearing reprisal for not having helped Theodosius against Eugenius.[15] In essence this interpretation develops assertions made by Claudian in *In Gildonem*. Seeck further supposed that Gildo sought out Eutropius. Orosius asserts that Gildo wanted to form an independent kingdom in Africa (Oros. *Hist.* 7.36.3). Mazzarino developed this assertion into a hypothesis that Gildo allied himself to the East out of nationalism, in order to develop greater autonomy.[16] Demougeot considered that Eutropius capitalized on separatist forces in Africa inherent in the Donatist schism and the circumcellion movement, and merely turned the balance by offering Gildo an alternative alliance.[17] Cameron interpreted Claudian's statement in his first panegyric for Stilicho, "conspiring East was nourishing [Gildo's rebellion] with plots; from there edicts emerged that would corrupt the leaders" (*Stil.* 1.276–78), to mean that Eutropius took the initiative.[18] Paschoud judged that Gildo and Eutropius gradually developed a relationship based on common advantage, and that it is neither possible nor very important to determine responsibility for the first approach.[19] Since Gildo did not rebel absolutely but transferred Africa within the administrative hierarchy of the empire from the West to the East, Eastern collaboration at some stage is assured.

Nevertheless, Claudian did not follow this chain of inference in his epic *In Gildonem* immediately after the event. There Gildo revolts from pure personal malevolence, as Roma, Africa, and Theodosius I aver (*Gild.* 66, 70–76, 139–200, 236–88). Roma alludes plaintively to the fact that Egypt's grain has been

14. Of course, in 408 the suspicion that Stilicho sought "to enrich and stir up all Barbary" (*CTh* 9.42.22) figured in his destruction, as well as charges that he wanted to place his son Eucherius on the Eastern throne after Arcadius's death; see Mazzarino 1942 = 1990, 201–26; Demougeot 1951, 397–439; Ruggini 1968; John Michael O'Flynn, *Generalissimos of the Western Roman Empire* (Alberta: University of Alberta Press, 1983), 14–62, lucidly described Stilicho's career.

15. Seeck 1913, 283–85, 554–55.

16. Mazzarino 1942, 265–66 = 1990, 192–94; so also Olechowska 1978, 3–4 .

17. Demougeot 1951, 173–76.

18. Alan Cameron 1970, 120; cf. 113 and Alan Cameron 1974, 139–46. See further discussion.

19. Paschoud 1971–89, 3¹.116–17.

ceded to Constantinople, because it means that she now has no other resources (*Gild.* 60–65, 113). But she does not say that she has been wronged by Constantinople, only by Gildo.[20] The language Roma applies to Constantinople is neutral or even favorable: "when a Rome peer to me arose, and Aurora split off and assumed equal civic robes, the Egyptian fields passed into the portion of the new [Rome]" (*par Roma mihi . . . aequales togas, Gild.* 60–62).[21] Theodosius rebukes Arcadius for letting Gildo dissever the two courts, so that the East is substantially charged with acquiescing to sedition; but Arcadius immediately repudiates Gildo and wishes Africa to return to Honorius (*Gild.* 320–24). The situation is remedied, if the imputation not absolutely denied.

Honorius assembles his army. His speech to them and their mutual encouragement as they set forth characterize the expedition as opposing solely Gildo and his Moors. Honorius hints only slightly that the East may be concerned (*Gild.* 429–33):

> With a just and great triumph
> destroy the blots of civil war; let the Eastern world know
> and let it be common knowledge, that the Gauls are defeated by their
>   cause, not by strength.
> And though he has collected all of Barbary, let him not terrify
> you.

Singling out the East, however briefly, in this context must rebuke Eastern acceptance of Gildo. But what could have been sounded clamorously as righteous protest, Claudian subordinates to memory of the victory over Eugenius that Theodosius won with the Eastern army. He makes Honorius assert not rivalry with the East, but equal partnership in Theodosius's legacy. Now, as the proem notes (*Gild.* 1–16), by a resoundingly swift victory the West has vindicated itself.

Norman H. Baynes called *In Gildonem* "an eirenicon between East and West."[22] Arcadius need only accede to the repudiation Claudian places in his mouth, of a province that by the time the poem was published he had already lost, and full unity of the brother emperors could be restored. This reading leaps directly to the potential reception of *In Gildonem* in the East. Yet presumably Claudian published it before a Western audience first; his vaunting proem takes an emphatically Western perspective. *In Gildonem*'s political function in

20. *Pace* Gnilka 1976, 113 n. 35.
21. Hall 1985 printed *Aegyptia rura / in partem cessere* novam, following F_2PRW_1 ("... into the new division"), but the stemma of Schmidt 1989, 407, locates Γ and L closer to the archetype along two separate lines of transmission, and they like other manuscripts generally approved by Hall read *novae* (*nothi* n_1).
22. Norman H. Baynes, "Stilicho and the Barbarian Invasions," *JRS* 12 (1922): 207–29; rpt. in Baynes 1955, 326–42, here 335; so too Alan Cameron 1970, 110–11.

the West should be considered too. As in Claudian's panegyric for Honorius's fourth consulate, family heritage and personal enthusiasm claim for Honorius prowess he never put into action: he burns to take up his grandfather Theodosius's mission against rebellious Moors (*Gild.* 324–51). Stilicho argues that Gildo is too base for Honorius to bother to fight in person. He proposes detailing Mascezel instead, but by the time Honorius addresses the troops, Mascezel drops from view. The Western army (*Gild.* 415–23) alone is glorified by the victory. Claudian vehemently congratulates Western military pride and implicates Honorius in it as much as possible. Both gestures consolidate Western confidence. Claudian also places before his Western audience the claims that Arcadius would eagerly disavow Gildo and that Honorius would choose to regard the revolt as a purely Western matter. He insists that on neither side was the harmony of the brother emperors genuinely threatened.

Claudian has shifted from this perspective by the time of his first panegyric for Stilicho's consulate. He distinguishes Gildo and Africa, as "the South," from "Eastern parts" also stirred up by "raging Mars" (*Stil.* 1.269–70). Arcadius's administration based in Constantinople and dominated by Eutropius is specifically implicated in the war. Claudian blames the East for "conspiring" with Gildo, "nourishing" his rebellion "with plots," and being the point of origin for "edicts that would corrupt the leaders" (*coniuratus alebat insidiis Oriens. illinc edicta meabant corruptura duces, Stil.* 1.276–78). The first two charges suit equally instigation of the revolt by Gildo or by Eutropius. Cameron identified the corrupting "edicts" as the Eastern decree outlawing Stilicho, which, following Baynes, he dated to Stilicho's second campaign against Alaric in Greece; this condemnation would have solicited Gildo to transfer his allegiance.[23] Paschoud argued, following Seeck, that the Eastern decree outlawing Stilicho rather answered the Western decree outlawing Gildo for his revolt.[24] However moribund senatorial influence in imperial politics had become (cf. *Stil.* 1.328–29, 3.106–9, quoted in Chapter 7.II), the Western Senate inherited a tradition of authority the Constantinopolitan Senate lacked.[25]

Regardless of the decrees' relative chronology, however, the context of Claudian's reference to "edicts that would corrupt the leaders" better suggests a different set of mandates. The Eastern administration accepted Africa. It must have confirmed Gildo's rank by some official pronouncement. Claudian reviles this specious legality a few lines before he mentions the "edicts" (*Stil.* 1.271–73):

23. Alan Cameron 1970, 113 and 86, 176 on the East's outlawing Stilicho; Baynes 1955, 334–35; Zos. 5.11.1–2.

24. Paschoud 1971–89, 3¹.113–15; Seeck 1913, 285–86; cited in the Introduction.

25. A. H. M. Jones 1964, 329–30 and 1132 n. 18, distinguished specious formal consultation of the Roman and Constantinopolitan Senates from substantive policy-making.

quamvis obstreperet pietas, his ille regendae
transtulerat nomen Libyae scelerique profano
fallax legitimam regni praetenderat umbram.

Although dutifulness cried out against it, Gildo had transferred to the
    Eastern regions the title
of governing Libya, and over his sacrilegious crime
deceitfully extended a cloud of legitimate rule.[26]

Eastern appointments for Gildo and his officers would specifically "corrupt" the loyalty of formerly Western officials. The West's then making war against Gildo as an appointed Eastern minister would have provided an even clearer cause than Stilicho's aborted campaign against Alaric, for the Eastern Senate to declare him an "enemy to the state." On this interpretation of the "edicts," the East is censured for "conspiring" with Gildo and insidiously supporting his rebellion to the extent of legitimizing his acts formally, if not validly to a Western perspective.[27]

So too Claudian's third panegyric for Stilicho's consulate rebukes the East for receiving Gildo (*Stil.* 3.81–86):

Not now does [Rome], suppliant of the puffed-up East, use legates to lay
    claim
to Libya that has been taken away from her, or beg (vile
to say it) her own slaves; but relying on Gabinian strength,
with you as leader, Roman wrath at last avenges itself.
She herself commands the standards, and the toga-clad consul gives
    orders
to one who is going to war; the eagles await the Senate's decrees.

Although in *In Eutropium* terms for "slaves" generally denote Eutropius and his henchmen (see Chapter 5), Roma's commanding the military standards and senatorial decrees' regulating the eagles that decorate the standards describe rather the combat against Gildo. The fact that these slaves are Roma's "own" implies Gildo and Africa, since they through the grain tribute were supposed to serve Rome. Roma never lays claim to Eutropius (cf. *Eutr.* 1.414–65). Accordingly, the "exile of [Roman] dominion in servile fields," which

26. *Pietas* emphasizes the violation of the two courts' fraternal unity, cf. Chap. 4.III. "Gildo" translating *ille* picks up *Austrum* and "the Eastern regions" for *his* picks up *partes . . . Eoas* of *Stil.* 1.270. I transfer "legitimate" from "cloud" to "rule" for the sake of English idiom.

27. "After the battles of Libya, Eastern crime subsides" (*Stil.* 1.7–8), describes Eastern acquiescence in return of Africa to the West more readily than inspiration of the revolt, *pace* Alan Cameron 1970, 120.

Claudian soon proclaims redeemed (*Stil.* 3.126), also refers to rebellious Africa and its grain fields.[28] The East is rebuked for overweening presumption in retaining Africa. If Claudian's audience, rightly or wrongly, blamed Eutropius for setting Gildo on, nothing Claudian says would disturb this idea.[29] But he does not go so far as to make the accusation.

In Eutropium, distinctively, blames Eutropius: not only does he embody baseness, depravity, cruelty, avarice, corruption, incompetence, shamelessness, and all the other qualities that Claudian ascribes to him in the main body of the poem and that Roma recapitulates, above all his monstrous anomalousness which offends the traditions of the Roman state and its highest honor, but also he has initiated hostilities against the West. Claudian's contemptuous picture of how ill Eutropius succeeded against his barbarian invaders (*Eutr.* 1.242–51) ties him specifically with Roma's claim that the East "envies" Honorius's and Stilicho's success against the Western tribes (1.397). Beyond absolving them, the charge that Eutropius incited Gildo mobilizes against Eutropius Western resentment over the revolt.

Now Claudian asserts what he so carefully denied in *In Gildonem*: the revolt did threaten the harmony of the empire. He still detaches guilt from the Western army's war against an Eastern minister by identifying Gildo's transfer of his office as the first aggressive act. Now he adds the claim that Eutropius propelled Gildo. The terrible charge of sowing disunion between the courts attaches to the current invective victim, just as Claudian earlier used it against Rufinus (*Ruf.* 1.107–8, 2.235–39; cf. *Eutr.* 2.539–41). Roma blames Eastern jealousy for preventing "the realm [from] working together with its entire body"; she cites Gildo's revolt as the first instance of this disruption (*Eutr.* 1.396–400).

Roma's other memories of the Gildonic war in this address redound to Honorius's and Stilicho's credit. "Your, or your father-in-law's, never unforeseeing virtue" saw that Rome was provisioned from other sources when Gildo cut off Africa (1.402). Roma enacts the city's gratitude to the rulers: when the personified beneficiary declares them the ones who should be thanked, the scene directs the audience's gratitude on Rome's behalf. The flattery may gratify Honorius and Stilicho and encourage them to preserve Rome in case a similar crisis should arise again, but it more substantively touches the rest of the audience. It confirms them in their support of the regime. Roma closes the *prolalia* of her speech by reaffirming Honorius's victoriousness (1.410–11; cf. 391–95). Typically and significantly, she ignores Mascezel.

28. Platnauer 1922, 2.50 n. 1, tentatively suggested Constantinople.

29. Alan Cameron 1970, 117–23, expounded the hostile aspects of references to the Gildonic war in *Stil.*, based on an insecure identification of the "edicts that would corrupt the leaders" (*Stil.* 1.277–78). The somewhat blunter blame attaching to cooperation rather than instigation functions similarly, but no new evidence here determines whether Gildo or Eutropius moved first.

That Claudian should reinforce Western pleasure in how smoothly the crisis passed need not imply that there was any significant dissent. Gildo seriously undermined the constitution of the partitioned empire. John Matthews argued that Theodosius's having addressed laws to officials in Africa during Eugenius's revolt means that "Gildo was 'constitutionally' quite correct in supporting Arcadius rather than Honorius."[30] But Theodosius's administrative relations during the period of usurpation are not fully parallel with those he instituted by establishing his two sons as resident successor Augusti in the two halves of the empire. Then he sought to reassert his right over the whole. And as Matthews noted, the duty of the African *annona* to Rome was respected even in 393.[31] Contemporaries probably sensed the threat to Rome itself yet more acutely, both because the Roman plebs rioted whenever there were shortages[32] and because of Rome's symbolic value: the grain tribute had long acknowledged the sovereignty of the conquering city, which in turn defined the ideal self-image of the state.[33] Efficient substitution of other sources of grain alleviated the immediate crisis, and victory over Gildo quickly resolved its political cause. All the West must have felt tremendously relieved and proud. But an essential function of propaganda is to capitalize on success, and to steer the resultant positive emotions.

The remainder of Roma's speech concerns Eutropius directly. She turns to her main subject dramatically, focusing at once on the central theme of the whole book (1.412–14):

ecce repens isdem clades a partibus exit
terrorisque minus, sed plus habitura pudoris,
Eutropius consul.

Lo! an unexpected scourge emerges from the same parts:
it will have less terror but more shame,
Eutropius the consul.

"Scourge" reestablishes from the proem of the book the threat of impending disaster posed by the "prodigy" of the eunuch consul. "Shame" and degradation are the most prominent aspects in Claudian's central theme of Eutropius's eunuchry, but some "terror" is also evoked by Eutropius's judicial savagery (1.151–90) and incompetence at defending the East (1.229–51). The generalized

30. Matthews 1975, 272 n. 7; cf. 245 and *CTh* 1.12.4, 9.7.9, 10.19.14 (not 10.19.4), and 12.1.133.
31. See in general A. H. M. Jones 1964, 696–99.
32. See Kohns 1961; Ruggini 1961, 152–76; cf. Matthews 1975, 19–20.
33. As *Gild.* 52–55 indicates ("they gave me Libya and the Nile for my many merits," quoted in Chap. 7.II). *Luc.* 3.65–70, which Olechowska 1978, 146, compared ad loc., emphasizes the dependency of the Roman plebs: Caesar uses the grain tribute to enslave them (cf. *Luc.* 3.54–58).

source of the "scourge" recalls the similarly impersonal geographical statement "from Phoebus's other axis crimes arise" (1.397–98) and its link of Gildo with Eutropius. Though the individuals referred to are not obscured, the generalized phrases do suggest broader recrimination.

Roma hastily clears herself of having ever tolerated eunuchs. They represent "Arsacid arrogance" in the court and "Parthian" corruption of Roman morals (1.415–16), but at least they used to be decently confined to personal service on the emperor. So much they could manage (1.420–24):

> Their life was no guarantee of trustworthiness, but their sluggishness of mind
> was a safe pledge. Let them preserve locked-up jewelry,
> let them take care of Tyrian robes: let them fall back from the face
> of empire. The majesty of the state does not admit of being handled
> by an effeminate heart.

Roma's slur on all eunuchs' integrity, like much of the rest of her speech, repeats ideas that Claudian deploys in the main body of the invective. Thus, for example, does Claudian proclaim Eutropius unfit for eunuchs' typical duties as guardians of the wardrobe while he grows old in servitude: "his faithless mind forbids that he watch over gold, clothing, secrets: for who would want to entrust a bedchamber to a pimp?" (1.128–30). Roma concentrates on how much Eutropius affronts the traditions of Rome when he presumes to step out of seclusion, from the imperial bedchamber into public life. She invokes "war-waging Italy" (1.429–30), "brave Latium" (1.431–32), Honorius, his victories and herself (1.435), Tiber, Dentati, Fabii, the Campus Martius, Aemilii, Camilli, Brutus and the consulate, the war against Lars Porsenna, Horatius and the bridge, Mucius Scaevola and the fire, Lucretia committing suicide, Cloelia swimming the Tiber, the overthrow of the Tarquins, the Decii, the Torquati, the ghost of Fabricius, Regulus Serranus, the Scipios, Caius Lutatius Catulus, Marcellus, the Claudii, the Curii, Cato, companies of Bruti and Corvini, "the togas that Hannibal and Pyrrhus had to tremble at" (1.462–63), the special robes and "Latin axes" of the consulate (1.464–65), the senatorial title "Fathers" which eunuchs would falsify (1.470–72), the curule chairs, countless leaders over the years in preterition, the fasti, the fact that the consulate is the one magistracy the emperor accepts and the fact that he shares it with the Senate, the fasces, records of omens,[34] national dress, Roman conquests, con-

---

34. Hall 1985 printed *Eutr.* 1.490–91 *tradita libris* / nomina ("names handed over to books," i.e., the consular fasti again, cf. 1.478), preferring the reading of J_3 (variant reading) F_{20} (before correction) J_6 (after correction) σ. *Omina* ("omens"), however, is given by Γ and L among Hall's other generally superior manuscripts (also a variant reading in R), which in particular the stemma of Schmidt 1989, 407, has validated. (The

sular auspices, Pompey's defeat of the pirates, Crassus's victory in the Servile War, and, finally, Stilicho's Gothic victories[35] and the destruction of Gildo and his Moors, which she also credits to Stilicho. She includes virtually every conceivable allusion to Roman greatness. She mentions Stilicho's victories by way of personalizing her request that he quash Eutropius, but the context they keep elevates them to the same rank as the other, ancestral victories she cites. Their proud associations are enlisted to Stilicho's advantage. But of course Roma's allusions function chiefly to marshal the Romans' tradition-bound sense of national identity against Eutropius. He is contrasted to every item and disqualified from any meddling with them.

Against the immense weight of Romanness, Roma sets not only Eutropius but also the East. As Claudian does in his own voice when he compares the idea of a eunuch consul with that of a woman consul (1.320–45), she argues that Eutropius is unfit on grounds of other roles that eunuchs do not hold (1.424–29):

> Never even on the sea have we seen
> a ship obey the tiller of a eunuch master.
> Are we so easy to despise, and the world cheaper
> than a keel? Aurora, who delights in bearing
> such things, and cities used to womanish scepters:
> may eunuchs possess them!

Even more forcefully than in the earlier passage, rule by a woman appears as something shameful. Claudian earlier identifies the Medes, the Sabaeans and "a great part of Barbary" as being ruled by women, so that this allusion pushes eunuch leaders outside the Roman Empire; but Aurora is regularly Claudian's

---

vague *omnia*, "all things," is given by R and a few lesser manuscripts.) Alan Cameron 1968a, 403, argued that the idea of omens being polluted is not meaningful, but bad omens are tied up with Eutropius's pollution of the consular auspices (cf. 1.317–19, 2.40–58; in her speech Roma evokes the auspices shortly, 1.494). Schweckendiek 1992, 107, observed that omens could not really face a threat of being buried in dark fog or trampled, from which Roma begs Honorius to protect the items in question; but the books Claudian connects to the omens embody the Roman tradition of respect for omens and the gods' will. The brachylogy is not difficult to understand.

35. The last word of *Eutr.* 1.504 has been contested, but Alan Cameron 1968a, 403–5, demonstrated on historical, literary, and paleographic grounds that *agnosco fremitum, quo palluit Hebrus* must be correct; cf. Schweckendiek 1992, 109–10. *Hebrus* was printed by Hall 1985 and Birt 1892, although Birt changed his mind to *Eurus* in the index verborum he edited later for the same volume. *Eurus* was preferred by Andrews 1931 and Koch 1890, 567–68. Fargues, *Invectives*, preferred *Haemus*. All readings are proffered by manuscripts, *Eurus* by the best of them on stemmatic grounds (cf. Schmidt 1989, 407): an early corruption was emended better by some than by others.

personification of the Eastern part of the empire.[36] Most tellingly, in *In Eutropium* 2 Aurora begs Stilicho to save her from Eutropius and demonstrates that she does not delight in bearing him. But now Roma condemns her.

Lines 427–34 were cited by Gnilka in refutation of Cameron's contention that "Claudian's anti-Eastern comments are confined to *Eutr.* ii and *Stil.* i–iii— that is to say to the last quarter of 399. They are absent even from *Eutr.* i."[37] I quote the remainder of the passage, picking up where my last quotation stops (1.429–34):

> Why do they brand war-waging Italy
> with shared blemishes and contaminate its austere people
> with injurious scandals? Let foreign pollutions be driven
> far from brave Latium, and let the disgrace not cross
> the Alps; in only the fields where it first sprouted let it root fast.
> Let Halys record it, let it be recorded by reputation-scorning Orontes.

The thought begun in line 434 goes on to beg Honorius "by yourself and by your triumphs" to keep the Tiber ignorant of this defilement of the consulate, the honor it used to award to Dentati and Fabii. Thus here too Claudian contrasts the martial West, which respects the Roman traditions and can feel shame, with the complaisant East.

Döpp endorsed Gnilka's interpretation and added lines 396–400, in which Roma accuses Eutropius of fomenting Gildo's revolt (quoted earlier).[38] Döpp also adduced lines 308–16 envisaging Eutropius's inauguration and 471–74, in which Claudian rails at an effeminate senate. In fact the former says nothing about the Eastern empire. The Senate "accompanies polluted fasces," the lictor is "more noble than the consul," and Eutropius boasts about his mission to the hermit John on behalf of Theodosius.[39] Eutropius is the only object of censure. Neither does the latter passage describe the Byzantine Senate, as do somewhat similar images in the second book and its preface (2pr.57, 2.133–39), but a fantasized senate of eunuchs who will follow Eutropius's precedent: he is their "leader." "Frequent the tribunal rather than bedchambers, convert your habit and learn to follow curule chairs, not matrons' chariots," makes the reference plain by alluding to eunuchs' normal duties. Therefore the adjectives in "false Fathers" and "infertile Senate" function literally. Only the connection with Gildo really stirs a general accusation against the East.

"Jarring East,"[40] "crimes rise up from Phoebus's other axis" (1.396–98),

---

36. *Ruf.* 2.100, 3 *Cons.* 69, 4 *Cons.* 130, *Gild.* 61, *Eutr.* 2.527 (she speaks 2.534–602), *Stil.* 1.155, 6 *Cons.* 84, *CM* 30.116; simply the goddess Dawn, *Epith.* 270, 4 *Cons.* 561, *Stil.* 2.473, *CM* 53.34, *Rapt.* 2.46, *Carm. Spur. Susp.* 14.1.

37. Alan Cameron 1970, 367; Gnilka 1977, 39; cf. Gnilka 1976, 114.

38. Döpp 1978, 196 n. 31.

39. Eutropius's mission to John, Soz. *HE* 7.22.7–8, partly quoted in Chap. 6.

40. 4 *Cons.* 484 and *Get.* 565 clearly use *discors* to mean "tending to destroy concord";

"Aurora, who delights in bearing such things," "foreign scapegoats," and "Orontes who disdains reputation" (1.427–28, 431, 434) in these two passages disprove the simple assertion in Cameron's claim that Claudian does not attack the East in *In Eutropium* 1. But a more fundamental point remains, toward which his interpretation tends nonetheless validly. Claudian attacks the East because of Eutropius; therefore his comments are incidentally, rather than fundamentally, "anti-Eastern." Gildo's rebellion roused genuine resentment, which Claudian could use to advantage; since the East had committed itself to naming Eutropius consul, Claudian could not protest the nomination without making some comment on the nominator. Lines 427–34 are the most important part of Roma's speech and indeed of all *In Eutropium* 1 for determining the attitude Claudian takes toward the East in the book. It is apparent that Aurora "delights to bear such things" as governance Roma would not wish on a ship, because she has rewarded Eutropius with the consulate. "In only the fields where it sprouted, let [the scandal] stick." Nor does Claudian note here any sign that the East's endurance of Eutropius is cracking. Continued support of him dooms it, as far as the book is concerned.

But to say that Claudian wished to protest Eutropius's consulate does not really explain the fundamental purpose of *In Eutropium* 1. There must be a reason for the attack. The possibility that Claudian found the idea of a eunuch being consul personally disgusting, offensive to his sense of Roman tradition, and potentially disastrous as an omen can never be excluded, but neither would that explanation exclude more pragmatic concerns. Since so much of the poem and so many related passages in other poems so clearly aim at Stilicho's advantage, his interests claim attention on this point. Eutropius had, as Claudian has Aurora express it in book 2, inherited Rufinus's position as Arcadius's chief minister and Stilicho's chief opponent in the Eastern court (2.550). He obviously did not allow Stilicho to exert control over Eastern affairs. He certainly welcomed and possibly prompted Gildo's change of allegiance, under which "deceitfully extended cloud of legitimate rule" (*Stil.* 1.273, quoted earlier) Gildo's grain embargo profoundly threatened the stability of the city of Rome and of Stilicho's administration. The plebs rioted and burned the house of Symmachus, who had participated in outlawing Gildo;[41] Stilicho's senatorial

---

in *Ruf.* 2.100, however, "by such storms is discordant Aurora pressed" refers to the just-reported complaints of the Eastern populace against Rufinus and wishes for Stilicho. But although *discors Aurora* here and *discors Oriens* in *Eutr.* 1.396 are very close verbally, the coincidence is not strong enough to override context and create an allusion to Eastern popular disapproval of Eutropius. Claudian makes that claim only in book 2. (These four are the only passages where Claudian uses the adjective.)

41. Symm. *Epp.* 6.61, 66; 8.65; 9.81; cf. Otto Seeck, ed., *Q. Aurelii Symmachi quae supersunt*, MGHAA 6, 1 (Berlin: Weidmann, 1883; rpt. 1961), lxx–lxxi; Arnaldo Marcone, ed., *Commento storico al Libro VI dell'epistolario di Q. Aurelio Simmaco*, Biblioteca di Studi Antichi 37 (Pisa: Giardini Editori e Stampatori, 1983), 141–42, 146–48;

support doubtless suffered too. Meanwhile, Eutropius answered the decree by having Stilicho outlawed and, furthermore, confiscating his Eastern estates.[42] Numerous grudges had accumulated over extended time. If the consulate of a eunuch offended the sensibilities of Roman traditionalists, including senators threatened by riots and insecurity, it provided a perfect opportunity to divert their resentment to him and vilify him as the common enemy.[43]

A more particular motivation also appears, as Alan Cameron has outlined.[44] At the point capping Eutropius's *praxeis*, Claudian exclaims (1.284–86):

> In return for achievements such as these, Eutropius
> demands the year, lest all by himself he fail to pollute anything:
> as general the battle lines, as judge the courts, the epoch as the consul!

That is, Eutropius was given the consulate as a reward for the Hunnic campaign that Claudian has just depicted as an absurd debacle.

The campaign against Gildo, whose success Claudian hails ringingly, had also been mounted in 398. For Stilicho's consulate of 400, Claudian's panegyric depicts personified Provinces asking that Roma force him finally to accept the honor (*Stil.* 2.217–68). The first to speak, Hispania, urges his connections with the royal house. Italia speaks last of the group, welcoming the inaugural celebrations. Central are the requests of Gallia, Britannia, and Africa, who praise in turn his victories benefiting them each. They urge the most persuasive, substantive particular occasions for awarding the honor of the consulate; significantly Africa speaks the climax, adducing her rescue from Gildo. When Roma obtains the Provinces' desire, she adds her own request that Stilicho celebrate his consulate in her city. She too gives as reason his care for her during Gildo's revolt. Gildo's revolt had threatened the authority of the Western government. His defeat provided the most impressive victory of Stilicho's administration to date, and what would normally have been the occasion of a consulate. In Claudian's panegyric for Honorius's sixth consulate in 404, Roma says she had expected Honorius to celebrate the victory over Gildo in the city; Honorius replies that he sent Stilicho to fill the curule chair in his stead (6

Matthews 1975, 268–69. Sergio Roda, ed., *Commento storico al Libro IX dell'epistolario di Q. Aurelio Simmaco*, Biblioteca di Studi Antichi 27 (Pisa: Giardini Editori e Stampatori, 1981), 211–12, dated Symm. *Ep.* 9.81 to rioting in 395–96.

42. Unless the East outlawed Stilicho first, for his campaign against Alaric (but cf. discussion in the Introduction and earlier in this chapter); Stilicho would feel the same resentment under either sequence of events. Confiscation of Stilicho's property, *Stil.* 1.297–99, discussed in Chap. 7.I.

43. Freud [1905, rev. 1912] 1960 emphasized the pleasure felt by those to whom a tendentious joke is told; Claudian exploits the power of this feeling, beyond the power of shared hostility alone, to ally his audience with himself as the joker (cf. Richlin [1983] 1992, 59–63).

44. Alan Cameron 1970, 124–25; Albert 1979, 639, concurred strongly.

Cons. 361–83, 431–33). Thus years after the event, Claudian still declared that Stilicho earned his consulate by suppressing Gildo's insurrection.

Yet as Cameron remarked, Stilicho did not take the consulate of the coming year, 399. He apparently remained a "public enemy" in the East until all Eutropius's official actions were revoked when he was deposed in summer 399 (*CTh* 9.40.17). This status doubtless would have invalidated in Eastern eyes any consulate he took. The fact that all previous decisions not to recognize consulates were associated with imperial rivalries and usurpations made nonrecognition potentially even more damaging. Stilicho did not choose to face the risks. He missed an opportunity to enhance his own prestige in the West with a triumphal consulate reaffirming the glory of victory. The jealousy which Claudian avers Eutropius felt for Stilicho's British and Gallic victories, to such an extent that he vengefully stirred up Gildo (*Eutr.* 1.391–95),[45] reverses neatly: Stilicho may well have envied Eutropius's freedom to take the reward of a consulate for his success against the Huns in Armenia. He could strike back only by seeing that Eutropius's celebration was void in Honorius's territory.

At the level of technicality Stilicho could bar recognition of Eutropius more or less arbitrarily, since no more cooperation than Honorius's was required. But since the absence of an Eastern consul would necessarily come to public notice, the refusal to recognize must be justified. Claudian served this end three times within the year. His inaugural panegyric for Theodorus uses personified Iustitia to declare that Stilicho and Honorius had justly preserved the high office from disgrace. *In Eutropium* 1 elaborates. *In Eutropium* 2 points to the disasters that the East suffered for inaugurating a eunuch consul, and credits Stilicho, alone, for preserving Rome's honor from cognizance of the "vile name" (2.126–32).

As Stilicho avoided the ignominy of not being recognized as consul himself and sought to reverse it on Eutropius, he took other risks with the Western public. They upheld the ideal of imperial unity, which demanded that Arcadius's and Honorius's administrations work together as a harmonious partnership. Claudian focused the opprobrium of his epic about the Gildonic war tightly on Gildo in order to identify him as both the originator and limit of all constitutional threat. If the Western army attacked an official of the East, it was because Gildo had perverted the structure of imperial government, and Arcadius himself would repudiate the rearrangement. Once the rebellion was quashed, "We have joined Europe to Libya. The concord of the brothers returns in full" (*Gild.* 4–5). Refusing to recognize the Eastern honor of Arcadius's chief minister could be construed as a diplomatic act of civil war. Honorius's advisers might well have feared damage to his relations with Ar-

45. Brittania's allusions in *Stil.* 2 to Tethys, Picts, and Saxons correspond with Roma's briefer summary in *Eutr.* 1 (Brittania adds Scots), and so do Gallia's references to Franks, Germans (Roma uses the victory title), and the Rhine, *Stil.* 2.240–55.

cadius. Anyone who wished to attack Stilicho was sure to accuse him of causing a rupture. Once more Claudian insists that the danger of disharmony
originated elsewhere. Now he claims that Gildo was spurred to revolt by the
East, specifically by Arcadius's honored minister. Roma identifies the purpose,
"so that the realm not work together with its whole body" (*Eutr.* 1.398). The
balance of Roma's speech and of the entire poem argues that Eutropius's
consulate itself, because of what he is, represents an attack on the traditions
and ideals that define the Roman state. Barring this malignancy from the West
patriotically defends the values of the cultural myth.

Claudian uses these values as a medium of ideological communication with
the Western aristocracy. He renews the tradition as he reuses it, emphasizing
and perpetuating the values of his audience which can best be turned against
Eutropius. Roman public office is affronted by a slave, especially one of the
depraved sexuality attributed to Eutropius as a eunuch. Eutropius's successful
campaign in Armenia is said to have displayed spectacular feebleness, but
Stilicho's peaceful German mission reflects in Honorius true Roman valor and
success. Roma especially evokes the defining figures of Roman cultural identity, whereas she says that Eutropius as a eunuch represents the dissolute
arrogance of Persia (1.415–16).

Fargues claimed that Claudian's injunction in Roma's speech to Honorius
and Stilicho, "Let Halys record [Eutropius's name on Eastern fasti], let Orontes
record it who disdains reputation" (1.434) expresses the resentment of the
Roman senatorial aristocracy toward Constantinople, "for having eclipsed the
ancient capital of the empire."[46] Fargues stepped a great distance from Claudian's text. The Senate is not invoked in this connection, but the Tiber, the
Campus Martius, and "years given" to modest Dentati and Fabii and to Aemilii
and Camilli who have saved the state. Claudian means consular elections. His
Roma exclaims, "Is your power, Brutus, now presented to Chrysogoni and
Narcissi?" (1.440–41). The mention of Brutus alludes to the consulate again.
Chrysogonus and Narcissus were notoriously powerful ex-slaves, freedmen
respectively of Sulla and Claudius.[47] A second point against Fargues's interpretation is that neither the Halys nor the Orontes flows near Constantinople.[48] This line does not target the Eastern capital. Claudian is once again

46. Fargues, *Invectives* 77 n. 434; cf. *Claudien* 136–39 (concerning the basis in *6 Cons.*
on which Fargues claimed that "the senatorial aristocracy keenly wished for the emperors to return to Rome, and envied Constantinople's brilliant fortune," see my
remarks Chap. 5 n. 24).

47. The prospect of the consulate formalizing, even honoring, their irregular political power scandalizes ancestral Roman class prejudice. See Friedrich Münzer, "Cornelius 101: L. Cornelius Chrysogonus," *RE* 4 (1901): 1281–82, and Otto Stein, "Narcissus
1," *RE* 16 (1935): 1701–5.

48. James Zetzel suggests to me that the reference to Orontes alludes to Juv. 3.62, "a
long time ago has Syrian Orontes flowed into the Tiber." Thus Claudian incorporates

contrasting the consulate of a eunuch with the noble Roman past. He rebukes the East at large for its support of Eutropius.

Gnilka emphasized strongly Claudian's disparagement of the East. He refined the traditional view of Claudian's work to assert that *In Eutropium* "raises the traditional criticism of Roman 'Anti-hellenism' to a new political level: to the level of 'Anti-byzantinism.' "[49] Gnilka based his argument primarily on the more extensive vilification of book 2, but he also claimed that Claudian developed this theme in book 1. Roma's dismissal of Aurora and cities ruled by women to pollution from which "war-waging Italy," her "austere peoples," and "brave Latium" must be defended, as I noted previously was his prime example (1.427–33). But he also claimed that "usages such as *Eous rector* (1.105), *dedecus Eoum* (1.239), *facinus Eoum* (1.371) attest to the thoroughgoing effort to let the vileness of the individual rub off on the whole."[50] That is, they make Eutropius symbolize the entire Eastern realm. I have argued conformably with Gnilka that the figure of Eutropius focuses a more comprehensive attack in book 2 (Chapter 5). But the contexts in which these phrases appear in book 1 do not fully support Gnilka's meaning.

In the first passage, the title "ruler of the East" contrasts Eutropius's future power with his present duties as lady's maid. According to the social prejudice that Claudian evokes, the fact that Eutropius has been a hairdresser disqualifies him from governing anything. The adjective "of the East" merely indicates the extent of power which he nevertheless has obtained, outrageously. The East is not blamed.

The second passage may even tend to redeem the East. "The disgrace of the East" is Eutropius acting as an overaged Amazon in its defense. Mars blushes and Enyo averts her eyes. If the East too is shamed, it must still preserve sensibilities decent enough that they may be offended. Roma implies that a capacity to feel shame is a reason to be defended from it (1.429–35, quoted earlier); she says that Aurora is shameless, but as Gnilka noted in a different connection, Claudian does not worry about consistency between different rhetorical effusions.[51] Each separate statement must be analyzed on its own terms. Roma shows the natural revulsion a "disgrace" inspires; nothing in the phrase "disgrace of the East" or in its context suggests that the East would not feel as disgusted as Mars and Enyo, or Roma. Unlike the West and Roma, the

---

from his literary traditions another complaint of Roman cultural traditionalism against foreign contamination.

49. Gnilka 1976, 119.

50. Gnilka 1976, 114; cf. his concept of "collective guilt" (111) discussed subsequently.

51. Gnilka 1976, 108: he compared Claudian's wish that Constantinople be washed away by the sea, with his soon subsequent wish that Eutropius's statues stand in Constantinople forever to commemorate their shamefulness (*Eutr.* 2.37–39, 77–78). On these wishes see further discussion.

East cannot ward off Eutropius because he is already there, which may indeed be all that the adjective conveys.

Gnilka's third passage better identifies Eutropius with the East, but here the "crime of the East" is Eutropius's consulate, the crucial issue of Claudian's whole attack. The East nominated Eutropius: therefore it must be condemned for promoting the obscene, criminal monstrosity of a eunuch consul. But the condemnation is circumscribed by the issue.

Eutropius's *anatrophe* establishes permanently Claudian's moral portrait of him. Transition away from it into his *praxeis* is effected by a subsidiary proem on the theme "there is a point where disdain helps too much" (1.137): Eutropius is able to insinuate himself into the service of the palace, paradoxically, because he is too worthless to be allowed to continue in private service. The first sentence of the *praxeis* proper, introducing the downfall of Abundantius, still looks back to the *anatrophe* and the paradox it has produced: "Perceive whom they beg to connect to the Latin fasti: one of whom even eunuchs feel ashamed!" (*cernite, quem Latiis poscant adnectere fastis: cuius et eunuchos puduit!*, 1.151–52). Gnilka pointed out that the unnamed subject of *poscant* is made responsible for the demand; he identified it as the Easterners.[52] Claudian singles out Abundantius. He "brought forth a bane on Eastern affairs, and first upon himself" by promoting Eutropius, who soon turned on him. The fact that Eutropius's promoters bring doom on themselves speaks worse of him than it does of them. Later Claudian says that "Eutropius demands the year" in reward for his Hunnic campaign (1.184–85): this report does not erase the generalizing plural in line 151, but it weakens its already slight significance. Numinous forces stand behind the undesignated plural too, diluting it yet further. In the proem Eutropius as a eunuch consul is a prodigy, therefore an object embodying some warning of the gods (1.14). In the subsidiary proem to his *anatrophe* he is a cruel joke of Fortune (1.24).

The fact that "the shining white Senate House, perhaps his masters too, accompanies the polluted fasces," which Gnilka cited also (*candida pollutos comitatur curia fasces, forsitan et domini*, 1.308–9),[53] does not really inculpate them; it merely underscores the inappropriateness of Eutropius's position. The juxtaposed adjectives "shining white" and "polluted" clash vividly.[54] Claudian goes on to remark that the lictor, a slave who will be freed in one ceremony of the inauguration, is more noble than the consul (1.309–10). He compares Eutropius in his consular robes before this party, to a monkey that a boy has dressed in silk while leaving his back and buttocks bare in order to amuse dinner guests (1.300–316). The grotesqueness of it is ludicrous, but neither the dinner guests nor even the boy is blamed for behaving badly. Only the monkey

52. Gnilka 1976, 114 n. 39.
53. Gnilka 1976, 114 n. 39.
54. As Fargues, *Invectives* 66 n. 308, remarked.

and Eutropius are mocked, for their true natures are not concealed by their rich garments.[55]

In another ceremonial scene, Eutropius's triumphal army is said to consist of eunuchs and the like, who appropriately carry "Hellespontine emblems" (1.256). Gnilka supposed that this image underlined degeneracy in the Eastern army,[56] but it is more fantastic than representational. The eunuch army merely replicates its general, like the eunuch Senate of lines 471–74 (discussed previously). "Hellespontine" describing the standards links the location of Constantinople with Priapus, who was particularly worshiped at Lampsacus. Linked with eunuchs, the association recalls proverbial castrate licentiousness: the eunuch army performs on the battlefield with verisimilar movement but no real effect, just as a Priapic eunuch would perform in the bedroom.[57] The triumph becomes a complete travesty. The populace who greets Eutropius appears the more abject as his "dependent" (1.257), but it is precisely their dependency on Eutropius that Claudian does censure. Eutropius is the one who inserts himself into the inappropriate field of warfare and corrupts it (1.234–37, 271–72):

> But lest any sector
> be free from infamy, or anything remain undared,
> he even prepares to violate arms, and piles up portents
> with prodigies. Impudent senselessness contends with itself.
>
> . . . Why, most foul female, do you insert yourself
> into wars or make an attempt on Pallas of the savage field?

Similarly, Eutropius alone as leader is blamed for making it seem that the East had no men to summon for defense (1.242–43).

Finally, the morality of Ptolemaeus and Arinthaeus, the two masters who use Eutropius for sexual purposes, contrary to Gnilka's assertion receives no comment at all.[58] Claudian's literary traditions censured lechery of all kinds, but identified the pathic side of homosexual activity as particularly degrad-

55. As noted by Christiansen 1969, 93. Fargues, *Invectives* 66 n. 303, compared Juv. 10.194 (which compares the human face in old age to the wrinkled face of an aged monkey) and applauded Claudian's original elaboration of the image.

56. Gnilka 1976, 114 n. 39.

57. See Fargues, *Invectives* 61, and Andrews 1931, 52–53, with Chap. 4 n. 43.

58. Gnilka 1976, 114 n. 39. No new change of master is indicated between when Ptolemaeus passes his "mistress" along to Arinthaeus and when Eutropius takes up pandering, which seems to identify Arinthaeus as the master whom Eutropius supplied with women and who finally gets rid of him as a lady's maid to his daughter (so, e.g., *PLRE* 1.103). Gnilka however assumed that both Ptolemaeus and Arinthaeus used Eutropius as a catamite: the interpretation is less neat but not impossible, for the narrative consists of a series of more or less discrete pictures, which need not be connected closely by the narrative thread.

ing.[59] Claudian stresses this aspect in his treatment of Eutropius. The only comment Claudian makes about Eutropius's seducer master is that "cheated lust" enrages him when Eutropius fails to obtain his object (1.101). All Claudian's attention is focused on Eutropius. When he echoes the laments of an abandoned heroine or vainly urges his past services against a beating, he alone is mocked. To the humiliating connotations of what he has done are added abjectness and insufficiency. There is not a trace of pity. So too, for example, in Seneca's *Apocolocyntosis*, it is Claudius who is degraded when Gaius proves that Claudius is his slave by witnesses who attest that they have seen him beating him (Sen. *Apocol.* 15).[60]

Claudian does say that Eutropius was made the more cruel and avaricious in administration by having been a eunuch slave (*Eutr.* 1.181–93). But again, Claudian does not mean to arouse pity or call for humane treatment of slaves. Eutropius's debased, dehumanizing past simply disqualifies him from any position where decent sensibilities would be appropriate. Claudian expresses distress over Eutropius's castration only because it made him feeble enough to become worthless as a slave, so that ultimately he was set free (1.54–57). Roma disparages the Persian luxury that eunuchs represent, but even so she consents to tolerate them in private service (1.414–24).

In this book Claudian does not exploit "the concept of 'collective guilt,' " as Gnilka defined it: "that Eutropius is a product of Eastern depravity, the accursed eunuch-rule an expression—of course, an extreme, monstrous one—of the more general degeneration."[61] On the contrary, it is Eutropius who corrupts the East. By following him the army has become a troop of eunuchs (1.255–56). The Senate that parades with him as consul will suffer the same fate (1.471–74). By nominating him to the consulate, the Eastern empire has chosen for itself the disastrous augury from which Roma demands that the West be protected. The idea of "scapegoats" in Roma's speech, reinforced by images of "burning" and "injurious disgraces" (1.431, 429, 430), recalls the way the proem of book 1 delves about into the dangerousness of the eunuch consul "prodigy." The proem's conclusion is especially apposite (1.19–23):

> What victim may expiate
> such great wraths? By what throat shall we placate the dire altars?
> With the consul must the fasces be purified, and with the prodigy itself
> must sacrifice be made: whatever the fates are preparing by this omen,
> may Eutropius expiate it with his neck!

59. I discuss specifics in Chap. 3 and esp. Chap. 4; see also references cited there.
60. E. Courtney, "Parody and Literary Allusion in Menippean Satire," *Philologus* 106 (1962): 96, noted the related perspective by which impotence is viewed as a sin against Priapus, not a punishment by the god: incapability puts its sufferer into the wrong.
61. Gnilka 1976, 111.

To whatever extent Eutropius has not already ruined Eastern affairs by ferocious perversion of justice and corruption, as he ruined Abundantius and as he sells offices, he will finish the job through symbolic portentous degradation. If Aurora delights in putting up with such things, let her have them; she may blame herself for the consequences.

Roma follows her primary request with a second, that Stilicho depose Eutropius. Unlike the first, it was not realized at the time this book of invective was delivered, and indeed was never realized. It does not justify a policy retroactively. Such intellectual persuasion, addressing attitudes about political realities, is well served by the stepwise statement and demonstration of Claudian's rhetorical argument in book 1 overall. Roma reinforces Claudian's points, with particular reference to Roman tradition, in the main body of her speech. But now at the end of Roma's speech and the book, Claudian adds a brief flourish of agitation. The idea of taking positive action naturally yields a more exciting sense of mission than the idea of resistance, however nobly maintained against however calamitous a scandal. Roma's second request rounds off the invective impressively.

Roma caps her exhortation with a pre-Roman historical example. The Scythian army with no more than a show of whips routed the rebel "servile youth" who barred them from returning home from their Asian campaigns (1.508–13).[62] Perfectly harmonizing with Claudian's tone throughout the invective, the image enacts contempt. Once again Eutropius is cast as a craven, slavish usurper of position. Stilicho through the image confronts him in the poem's final moment; the Scythians' prowess reflects luster on him as he takes their role of rightful authority, from which he has been but temporarily displaced. While any traditionally minded Roman may have delighted in Claudian's derision of Eutropius, that Stilicho should appear as the master marks him as the particular beneficiary of Claudian's invective.

"Do you not know that a baser enemy falls to greater rejoicing?" Roma asks (1.501–2).[63] Her stirring suggestion is extremely sketchy. Like Iustitia's second prophecy at the end of *In Rufinum* 1, of a new Golden Age under Honorius, it decorates with symbolic, emotional appropriateness rather than sober pragmatism. Yet unlike that prophecy, the course it suggests could be realized. It opens a suggestion. It reiterates Claudian's recurrent claim that Stilicho ought to control both halves of the empire, and it sets this notion into the context of the present predicament. If the chief theme met with great enthusiasm and Eastern events ever permitted action, it might seed some more concrete plan.

62. Cf. Pacat. *Pan. Lat.* 2[12].30.5; Justin 2.5.1–7; Hdt. 4.1–4; discussed in Chap. 3.III.
63. *Pace* Birt 1888, 50, Claudian's wish in the proem that Eutropius "redeem with his neck" the omen that as consul he represents (1.23) is not confirmed by any call from Roma for Eutropius to be killed.

CLAUDIAN DOES NOT canvass even vague possibilities of action with respect to an Eastern audience. Roma bids the scandal of Eutropius's consulate keep to its own half of the empire. She leaves the Easterners nothing to do. Conceivably, Claudian could have appealed to them to repudiate their consul. Synesius's *De Regno* confirms that they shared the same concepts of the Roman state and the same prejudices against eunuchs as those on which Claudian plays. Official malfeasance was universally reprobated; indeed, since the East suffered directly what Claudian presents as Eutropius's injurious *praxeis*, this section might have stirred Easterners specially. But though the emotional effects obtain, when the epilogue channels them into a bid for action the East is treated as inert. It has already committed itself to the contrary course.

The fact that in *In Eutropium* 1 Claudian does not extend his pragmatic goals to the East is the book's most significant measure of relations between the two parts of the empire. Claudian asserts that Eutropius's predominance has broken relations with the West. He does not call for relations to be broken, as Gnilka claimed, but neither does he find sectors of an Eastern audience who might be amenable to subversion, or seek to conciliate them. He asserts that the Easterners lamented Eutropius's domination,[64] but he does not suggest that they resisted it. On the other hand, he does not indict a general decadence for promoting Eutropius; caprice of fortune and negligent disdain of Eutropius's uselessness as a slave have raised him.[65] To be feared are the results. Claudian deplores effects he claims Eutropius has wrought and forecasts worse. The culminating honor of the consulate manifestly implied that Eutropius's predominance was unshakable in the territories controlled by Arcadius. Claudian dismisses them absolutely and monolithically. When he singles out particular individuals or groups, they illustrate elements in an aggregate rather than distinguishing those who suffer under Eutropius from others who support him. The whole part of the empire is committed to honoring him as consul, and therefore Claudian has nothing further to say to its residents: he does not anticipate that his message could affect them as he does expect it to affect a Western audience.

---

64. E.g., "When first the palace held the little old female fox, who did not groan? Who did not feel pained that a dead body, so many times for sale, crept into the sacred service?" *Eutr.* 1.145–47.

65. In fact, Theodosius's and Arcadius's favor elevated Eutropius within palace service. Sozomen identifies "Eutropius, one of the palace eunuchs whom [Theodosius] trusted" (Soz. *HE* 7.22.7–8, quoted more fully in Chap. 6). Zosimus, presumably following Eunapius, says that Eutropius "dominated Arcadius like a grazing beast," and that Arcadius "gave Eutropius the whole management of his realm" (Zos. 5.12.1, 14.1, with Paschoud 1971–89, 3¹.120, 127). John Chrysostom reports that Arcadius wept when the soldiers called for Eutropius to be put to death (Joh. Chrys. *Hom. Eutr.* 4 = *PG* 52.395).

ii. *In Eutropium* 2

In the second book of *In Eutropium*, Claudian both attacks the East far more broadly than in *In Eutropium* 1, and ultimately expresses greater hopefulness that concord with it can be reestablished. The dynamism of the book makes this paradox possible: after the preface and proem, which delineate approximately the present time in which the poem was first delivered, Claudian looks back to trace a process by which, he claims, a purgatory change of attitude in the East is effected. The proem warns that the change must be carried through fully if the present disasters are to be repaired and further disasters averted, but the conclusion exhorts a resolution that remains possible at the time of delivery, even if circumstances have modified the implication of certain of its terms.

Specifically, when Aurora asks to be saved from "servile kingships," she must be understood to complain not only of Eutropius himself, but of the whole administration on which he has set his stamp (*Eutr.* 2.593; see Chapter 5). The harmful policies that Eutropius initiated continue to engender consequences even after he is exiled; Claudian implies that Tribigild's revolt is still escalating, and further violence is feared throughout the East. "What would the year not dare, that belongs to Eutropius?" (2.480–81; see subsequent discussion). In the emotive moral terms Claudian often uses, the corruption begotten by Eutropius and the metaphorical contagion of effeminacy centered on him have penetrated the Eastern empire and must be thoroughly eradicated. But as Döpp pointed out, the fact that Aurora's appeal ends the book in the way that it does presupposes the possibility that these conditions can be reformed.[66]

It remains to be shown in what ways Claudian appeals to whom with this proposal. The preface to book 2 like the proem of book 1 combines the idea of consular auspices with the broader science of omens. Both sections portray Eutropius in the rank of consul as a monstrous portent that should be averted by being turned against itself. Now the wish has been realized. Unlike book 1, the preface shows the East repudiating Eutropius and identifies particular factions with different fates and interests (2pr.11–18):

> The omen unlucky for populations turns against itself too;
> > prodigious honor rages against its author.
> The fasti breathe deep again with the name washed utterly from them,
> > and a healthier court vomits up the ripened corruption.
> His allies dissemble and his fellow conspirators fall back;
> > the whole troop falls along with its leader,
> not defeated in battle, not subdued by siege,
> > lest they perish in a way in which men have perished.

---

66. Döpp 1978, 196.

Eutropius's offensive elevation to the consulate has now brought him down. He himself originated the honor, which as a prodigy foretells general suffering. Now the court is healthier from having vomited up the contagion. Within one couplet Claudian asserts that Eutropius's former allies desert him and yet that "the whole troop" falls along with him. The assertions are difficult to resolve, unless perhaps the rats desert the sinking ship only to be drowned in the wash. Nevertheless, the idea is plain that the court Eutropius seemed wholly to dominate in book 1 has now fragmented amid recriminations. Some at least have fallen with him, although, Claudian scornfully remarks, "not perished as men have perished." They are joined with Eutropius in ridicule for unmanliness as well as in ruin. The surviving main body is congratulated and conciliated by the contrast. If Eastern audiences read it, they would be encouraged to regard the fallen as scapegoats, and to repudiate their policies. The same message in the West affirms optimistic prospects for the future.

The first part of the proem of book 2, like book 1, reproaches the East as a whole for its choice of consul. Claudian opens grimly: "Mygdonian[67] ashes and remnants of the Eastern realm, if any of what is perishing remains" (2.1–2). Even though they have repudiated Eutropius himself, "the omens of your consul remain; sins to be atoned for have persisted, with the fates unmoved."[68] Eutropius is the source of the pollution, but the adjective "your" assigns guilt to the Easterners at large too. Eutropius's effects perniciously survive him and are visited on them. The court remains contaminated (2.20). Even so, however, it has manifestly separated itself from him. Claudian describes this process with brutal metaphors of cautery and amputation (2.11–19). Significantly, the images involve not only an initial point of injury and an infection spreading from it, but also an imperiled but still essentially sound body, which may by these drastic measures be saved. Claudian's opening is alarmist rather than pessimistic. He underlines the urgent need for reform; he does not declare that reform is impossible.

Claudian does not say what the persistent evils are, merely that they bear out the threats that prodigies had foretokened for the year (2.2–4). He returns to a time before the inauguration to discuss the portents. First he graphically describes the impressive omen of an earthquake (2.24–30): the earth roars, hidden caves shake, roofs fall, Chalcedon is moved, the Bosphorus washes from

67. Mygdon was a mythological king of the Phrygians, *Il.* 3.184–86.
68. *Stant omina vestri consulis; inmotis haesere piacula fatis*, *Eutr.* 2.8–9. *Piaculum* is used in this gerundive sense (*OLD* s.v. 3) also at *Eutr.* 1.431 and *Gild.* 390. Alternatively, Fargues, *Invectives* 92 n. 9, glossed, "it is a matter of disasters which expiate baneful prodigies." Claudian uses *piaculum* in the sense "act of expiation" at *Ruf.* 2.517 and 6 *Cons.* 330. Platnauer 1922, 1.185, translated obscurely, "the atonement due to unmoved fate remains fixed"; Andrews 1931, 85, "since destiny is immutable, atonement is still required."

side to side in the channel, and its mouth opens and closes like new Symplegades. The whole corresponds to ancient seismological theory; specifically, Claudian seems to envisage the variety of earthquake that Ammianus calls *mycematiae* (Amm. 17.7.14).[69] "Obviously the Stygian sisters send these signs in advance, and rejoice that populations are being given to them under this consulate" (2.32). The plural "populations" is not specific to any region; the portents of the year can be realized anywhere. Fires and floods ensue. Claudian prays that the one city be destroyed to avert destruction of the entire world. He continues with more miscellaneous omens, recalling the proem of book 1 and linking the books in the contention that a eunuch consul is both a portent of disaster and a disaster that prompts other dire portents.[70] Again, all these signs should have prevented Eutropius's inauguration. "Is anyone so dull of heart that he doubts the year of a castrated consul would be fatal to those parts?" (2.48–49). "Those parts" is pressed to refer to the East by the fact that it was the East which promoted Eutropius. But the last set of omens is not localized as the earthquake is, and Claudian phrases his remark as a general rule. He proceeds to regret the equally general "blind love that inheres in vices" (2.50) and foolhardy "lust" that installed Eutropius despite all (2.52).

These passages from the proem display another great contrast of book 2 with book 1: Claudian now rebukes widespread human vice and perversity distinct from Eutropius, which are responsible for elevating him to the consulate. In subsequent passages Claudian relates these evils more specifically to the East. Senators, plebeians, "nervous generals," and all officialdom flock to pay homage to Eutropius at his inauguration. Their adulation is marked by words associated with fervid excess and self-seeking: to greet Eutropius is the object of eagerness (*studiis*), to grasp his hand the object of ambition (*ambitus*), and "to fix kisses on his deformed wrinkles" the object of prayer (*votum*; 2.64, 66–68). The city is filled with statues of him, labeled with outrageously flattering inscriptions (2.79).[71] His still-living masters should refute fawning acclaim for

---

69. Earthquakes generally, Amm. 17.7.9–14; cf. Pieter de Jonge, *Philological and Historical Commentary on Ammianus Marcellinus XVII* (Groningen: Bouma's Boekhuis, 1977), 198–211; Fargues, *Invectives* 94 n. 25, recognized the hidden caves. The new Symplegades, which Alan Cameron, "Earthquake 400," *Chiron* 17 (1987): 352, dissociated from the earthquake, in fact correspond to Ammianus's "the elements dash together spontaneously, their frameworks undone." Cameron demonstrated that no other evidence confirms the natural inference from Claudian's text, that this earthquake took place in late 398 (so, e.g., Seeck 1913, 305, 563). If there is any reality behind the dramatic picture, it is an earthquake of 396. On the literary antecedents and overtones of cosmic disaster (relevant here too) in Claudian's earthquake and volcanic eruption in *DRP*, see Fauth 1988.

70. Fargues, *Invectives* 96 n. 41, strangely called the reminiscence "clumsy enough."

71. *CTh* 9.40.17 directs all statues and images of Eutropius to be pulled down,

his alleged noble origins, but apparently they do not. The soldiery stomachs great battles being credited to him alone (2.82). He is called "third founder of the city." Claudian exclaims, "Will Byzas and Constantine see this?" (2.83).

This line refutes one element within the assertion that Fargues made in connection with Roma's relegating Eutropius's consulate to the East.[72] If Claudian meant to express abiding resentment that Constantinople had ever been founded and eclipsed Rome, he could not have protested here that Constantinople's founders are affronted by honor done to Eutropius. Strict logic must find some separate lines of attack inconsistent, but they always retain the same fundamental animosities. Here Claudian simply blames Constantinople's present residents for their adulation of Eutropius.

Significantly, it is in this context that Claudian emasculates Eutropius metaphorically by saying that his sister works to secure his power, while he himself stews in drunken luxury at banquets and the theaters (2.84–94; see Chapter 4.II). The passage concludes, "So, is guarding great realms nothing, and is the world mocked that is patient of its yoke?" Claudian protests Eutropius's irresponsibility, not as in book 1 his shameless initiative and aggression. That Eutropius is not imposing himself on the Easterners violently, in this passage, makes their adulation appear the more depraved and perverse.

Mars tells Bellona to avenge these obscenities, with yet more pointed accusations.[73] He begins, "Can we not yet, my sister, not yet cure Eastern softness? Will the corrupt ages never grow firm?" (2.112–14). In a moment's peace after recent warfare, a year has been given to a eunuch. The explicit rebuke of "Eastern softness" is now reinforced by contrast to "Hesperia" (2.124) and Stilicho, who has defended Tiber and Rome from this abomination, and given a refuge to "the majesty of Latium. He has given fasti to which an age spattered with servile blots may flee, deserting the East" (2.130–32). In the East, however, "this court has men so similar. . . . Don't they at least murmur in silent fear? Don't they condemn in spirit? See the applauding Senate and Byzantine magnates and Greek Roman citizens. Oh people deserving their leaders, oh leaders deserving their consul!" (*plaudentem cerne senatum et Byzantinos proceres Graiosque Quirites. o patribus plebes, o digni consule patres!* 2.135–37). Present corruption is exceedingly general. Gnilka noted the echo of Juvenal 3.60–61, "I cannot bear, Roman citizens, a Greek city" (*non possum ferre, Quirites, Graecam urbem*):[74] where Juvenal's Umbricius speaks of Rome invaded by for-

---

specifying bronze, marble, and painted images in cities, towns, and public or private places. The possible Eunapian fragment 65.7 Blockley complains of gold statues.

72. Fargues, *Invectives* 77 n. 434, discussed earlier. Claudian could change attitudes from poem to poem, of course, but Fargues claimed on the contrary an abiding passion.

73. Gnilka 1976, 112, called attention to this aspect.

74. Gnilka 1976, 116.

eigners, Claudian's paradoxical transfer of the adjective heightens the sense of threat. He appropriates the xenophobia of his original and, more important, Juvenal's authority for it.[75] Mars apologizes to his son Romulus for slowness at avenging the fasces, and gives Bellona specific instructions about the Gruthungi, whom she is to incite to revolt. He concludes, "let barbarian arms come to aid Roman shame" (2.159). The very offense that Claudian most damningly charges against Rufinus,[76] stirring up barbarians against Romans, has become a virtuous crusade of Mars, the paternal god of the Roman state, because it will castigate a people that could honor Eutropius. Again, they are responsible and Eutropius is essentially passive.

In the next scene, however, Claudian shows that he has not ceased to blame Eutropius too; Claudian represents him as passive or ineffectual with respect to other groups not to exculpate him but to criticize a different aspect of his administration or to blame them as well. The criticisms accumulate rather than negating one another. Eutropius is named as Tribigild returns "empty of gifts" from seeing him, so that "poverty, which persuades even delicate natures to crimes, inflames his Scythian breast" (2.179–80). Eutropius is indicted for not handling Tribigild properly and for provoking him to revolt.

Bellona's instigation does not invalidate this human cause. She personifies a horror that infuses the revolt and emphasizes its atrocity (n.b. 2.229–32). She also furthers the contention of the previous scene that the East deserves the carnage Tribigild wreaks: she recalls him to conventional norms of barbarian greed and savagery, underlining retribution's severity. And to the scene's criticism of how ineptly Eutropius has treated Tribigild, she adds a second, related complaint that he has treated Alaric too well (2.211–29).[77] Eutropius's barbarian policy is inconsistent, but wrong whichever course he takes. Finally, Bellona reminds Tribigild that he would not be "exposing yourself against men: now the other sex is in arms and the world has entrusted itself to eunuch defenders" (2.223–25). She adds to the idea that Eutropius contaminates the

75. Questions of ambiguity in Juvenal's satiric stance do not affect Claudian's use of the passage (on the questions see W. S. Anderson, "Anger in Juvenal and Seneca," *Cal. Pub. Class. Philol.* 19 [1964] 127–96 = Anderson 1982, 293–361). See Moroni 1982 on how Claudian uses Roman literary reminiscences as such in order to put himself on the side of traditional Roman views. This device renders less problematical the paradox that Claudian uses such expressions in spite of being an Alexandrian Greek himself (Fargues, *Claudien* 139, asserted that "it is known that the prosperity and high fortune of Constantinople inspired envy in the residents of Alexandria," without indicating any basis for this knowledge; Glover [1901] 1968, 240, took the same position and justified it by referring to Egypt's instant surrender to the Saracens).

76. *Ruf.* 1.319–22; 2.22–85, 268–71 (cf. Levy 1971, 125–26); so too Eunap. fr. 64.1 Blockley; Oros. 7.37.1; Socr. *HE* 6.1.6–7; Soz. *HE* 8.1.2; Zos. 5.5.4; Chron. Marc. s.a. 395 = *Chron. Min.* 2.64; cf. Demougeot 1950; Maenchen-Helfen 1973, 48–51.

77. As Gnilka 1977, 38, observed.

army, expressed in book 1 (1.239–43, 254–56), also blame of the people at large
for trusting Eutropius.

The idyllic picture of Phrygia that Claudian paints in the next scene creates
pathos when the barbarians attack. Claudian steps back from incrimination to
the impersonal grandeur of epic when he concludes it, "such then was Phrygia,
which the gods allowed to be burned by Gothic devastations" (2.274–75). Birt
identified echoes of Silius, Vergil, Statius, and Lucan in the surrounding lines.[78]
The barbarians appear, for the moment, as agents of divine wrath. Cybele
recognizes the omen of devastation, mourns and parts from her beloved land
(2.298–99) without assigning blame for the destruction that will ensue.

Claudian does, however. The first word of the next line is *Eutropius*. He
ignores the crisis, perversely since rumor has already publicized the news, and
pretends that judicial measures will suffice to quell it (2.304–9). It is impossible
to prove whether Claudian invented this information or had word from the
East that Eutropius first took this public position on the revolt. Still less can it
be shown, if Eutropius did minimize the revolt, whether he genuinely under-
estimated the rebels' power or was dissembling; it is interesting that Claudian
claims the latter, for in doing so he demonstrates conscious awareness that
misinformation is a tool of political propaganda.[79] His accusation, of course,
blackens Eutropius for lying.

Claudian also ridicules Eutropius's inaction for ostrichlike absurdity. He
explains that the huge Libyan bird runs from hunters's voices, "but now if
footsteps sound from behind, loud and clear, it forgets its flight and stands,
shutting out the light" (2.313–16). Peder Christiansen interpreted this image to
mean that Eutropius "runs from distant dangers but fails to avoid immediate
disaster."[80] But the adverb "now" marks a sequence of event from the ostrich's
hearing the hunters' distant cries to its hearing the footfalls of pursuit, not two
separate scenarios. The idea that the bird has "forgotten its flight" also implies
a sequence. The ostrich stops running and hides, ineffectually, from the same
hunters. Then they can catch up with it. So too Tribigild's revolt catches up
with Eutropius. At the very moment the crisis is upon him, he tries to deny it
exists, so that he yields all possible advantage.

Claudian next reports that Eutropius tried, secretly (*furtim*), to buy off

---

78. *Eutr.* 2.272–73, *dives equis, felix pecoris pretiosaque picto / marmore purpureis
caedunt quod Synnada venis*: Sil. 1.393, *dives agri, dives pecoris*; Verg. *Aen.* 9.26, *dives
equum, dives pictai vestis*; Stat. *Silv.* 2.2.87–89 (not 2.2.28), *Synnade . . . ubi marmore
picto . . . purpureo distinguitur area gyro. Eutr.* 2.276–77, *spes nulla salutis, / nulla fugae*:
Verg. *Aen.* 9.131, 10.121, *nec spes ulla fugae*; Luc. 10.538–39, *via nulla salutis, / non fuga*
(Birt 1892, 106).

79. Cf. Foulkes 1983, 9 (who drew on Michael Balfour, *Propaganda in War, 1939–1945*
[London: Routledge and Kegan Paul, 1979], 427–32).

80. Christiansen 1969, 99.

Tribigild with gifts. But Tribigild has learned "the sweetness of plunder." He haughtily refuses to serve a slave: "for is any honor not vile, from such a consul?" (2.316–22). If this exchange was not invented solely for the sake of the wordplay, "he denies that he serves a slave" (*se famulo servire negat*), it tends to confirm the outward appearance of Claudian's first report that Eutropius tried to ignore the crisis. Appeasement would have been both a reasonable and an unpopular course. Claudian decries Eutropius's accommodation with Alaric (2.211–29), for example, and Synesius accuses his Typhos of wanting to appease the Scythians in *De Providentia*.[81] "Secretly" is verisimilar as it coincides with the public dissimulation Claudian alleges. It also reiterates Claudian's accusations of deceit. Still more than in Tribigild's scene, criticism focuses on specific acts of Eutropius.

Finally Eutropius calls the council, and the Eastern courtiers file in. I have already discussed their frivolity and base origins, and how as Eutropius's creatures they reflect on him (Chapter 4.III). They also are distinguished from him as being even worse: Eutropius is forced to call them to order. He does not suddenly assume a heroic role, however, for he quickly declares his own inadequacy for confronting Tribigild. Instead the fatuous and incompetent Leo springs up and leads a dissolute army off to utter debacle. The chief minister, his court, their chosen general, and the army all show themselves unable to fulfill the public roles to which they lay claim. Fargues termed Claudian's description of the courtiers' servile and criminal scars (2.342–45) "perhaps the first truly original expression of the defects of byzantinism," even though he conceded that Claudian may not depict the courtiers' tastes accurately and wholly falsifies their social origins.[82] Claudian's contemporaries, like him, lived in familiarity with their society's conventions of political abuse (compare Chapter 3). They would have appreciated the expressiveness of his distortions, without worrying excessively over their accuracy. Yet there is no reason why they should have associated the degeneration Claudian alleges so fabulously with Byzantine government as an institution, rather than with Eastern government under Eutropius particularly: it is his vileness the courtiers replicate. Eutropius and his subordinates display deficiencies of personality and class, not region.

The army, on the other hand, has been enervated by influences said to be Eastern: under Stilicho it could endure winter hardships, but now "Byzantine luxury and Ancyran triumphs have broken their strength" (2.415–16). "Ancyran triumphs" refers to the vast parades of vacationers under Eutropius's leadership which at the beginning of the narrative stirred Mars to declare war

81. Synes. *Prov.* 122A; an embassy led by John Chrysostom was sent to Gaïnas in Thrace, Theod. *HE* 5.33.
82. Fargues, *Claudien* 138–39.

(n.b. 2.101–2). This allusion blames the soldiers' condition on Eutropius, accordingly; but "Byzantine luxury" like the "Eastern softness" that Mars rebukes (2.112–13) accuses a whole population. Tribigild attacks while the troops are languid from overeating and boasting in their cups, and routs or slaughters them easily.

This disaster terrifies the court as rumor of Tribigild's further ravages spreads (2.462). Next the Persians are said to be arming against the Roman Empire under a new king (2.477). Claudian ascribes this new development to the bad auspices of Eutropius's consular year: "what would the year not dare, that belongs to Eutropius?" (*quid non audeat annus Eutropii?*, 2.480–81). Andrews translated *annus* as "administration" and made Eutropius the subject of the next verbs: "He struck down our loyal ally, Sapor, and induced the Persians to assault their king; he flung across the stream of the Tigris the torches of the Eumenides to break the peace, lest any quarter escape destruction."[83] Fargues correctly glossed *annus* as "the consulate."[84] Yet although Andrews was literally mistaken, he assigned culpability correctly after the view Claudian takes. He does not claim that Eutropius himself instigated the Persians, but that in a year polluted by a eunuch consul, any disaster may ensue (cf. 1.14–19, 2.47–58). By the same device, for example, Claudian's panegyric for Honorius's third consulate ascribes to Honorius's auspices Theodosius's victory over Eugenius, and his panegyric for Honorius's fourth consulate gives the same credit for both this victory and Theodosius's victory in 386 over the Gruthungi under Odothaeus (*3 Cons.* 87–101, *4 Cons.* 469–637).

At last popular feeling falters (*Eutr.* 2.486–89):

> Hemmed in on every side by barking wars
> at last they recognized the gods as hostile, and the omen
> of their own consul. Dull-minded, they learned late
> the now irreparable damage: the fact was their teacher.

Again the prodigy formed by Eutropius's consulate mirrors divine hostility and causes affliction. The Easterners also recognize that he is their own consul: they are guilty. By implication, as also in the proem, there was a time when they could have averted disaster by canceling the designation. Instead they proceeded to inaugurate him, and now they suffer as the omens foretold (n.b. 2.50–53). The fate that Roma begged in book 1 be averted from the West (1.493–96) has come home to roost. Roma spoke in vague, conventional terms, stressing the sterility and effeminacy of a eunuch; in the lapse of time between the two books, events gave Claudian more concrete charges.

83. Andrews 1931, 127. Alan Cameron 1968a, 410, suggested that Claudian's "Sapor" for Varanes (Vahram) IV is not so much an error as a generic name for a Persian king, as in later authors.

84. Fargues, *Invectives* 129 n. 480.

The Easterners' recognition of guilt extends into a second but closely related matter when their fear of Persia drives them to yearn for Stilicho as their only salvation. Claudian says that they had long dreaded his return, because they expected him to avenge "things that had been done." "Now they all wish that he had come, and they regret the earlier crimes. They hope for this star in such great waves of wars. For this thing just and guilty pray equally" (2.506–8). "All together" who wish, and "all" who "confess that they deserve torture or death because they handed themselves over to slaves and deserted Stilicho" a few lines below (2.516–17) indicate a broadly popular sentiment.[85] Nothing in Claudian's phrases about "things that had been done" and "earlier crimes" assigns guilt explicitly, but the fact that the Easterners fear for themselves shows that they assume it. Their guilt for entrusting themselves to other leaders is general. On more substantive matters, namely outlawing Stilicho and confiscating his property, "the just and the guilty" (*iusti sontesque*) draws the important distinction. Only certain individual Easterners acted against Stilicho; the others sustain the contamination of their guilt. Similarly Aurora begs Stilicho "do not condemn all together for the crime of a few, nor let a new offense stand in the way of so many earlier merits" (2.594–95).

The narrative of the revolt has witnessed a change in attitudes. Where before the whole populace adored Eutropius slavishly, now they "marvel at the prodigies of their own madness, and avert their eyes." The lictor shudders and throws away the fasces and "the disgraced axes collapse of their own accord" (2.518–21). Horrified at what they are forced to acknowledge that they have done, they do acknowledge it. Now they repudiate Eutropius. The adjective "their own" with "madness," and the analogy of the Maenads over Pentheus, suggest that the Easterners truly share responsibility for the consulate, as they do not in the case of Stilicho. But now they desire to change. Aurora begs for absolution on their behalf, so that Stilicho will come and repair the disaster that Eutropius has created.

She traces the history of Eastern maladministration, coincident with hostility toward him. "Rufinus was the first origin of the evil: disharmony between the twin halves existed with him as author" (2.539–41). Eutropius, Rufinus's "castrate heir" (2.550), renewed the East's affliction. Aurora sketches his rise to power. He alone takes an active role. "As patrician and consul he stains the offices he sells; he stains more the ones he holds himself. Now the emblems and the trumpets grow soft. Faintheartedness has flowed into the very swords" (2.561–63). As in book 1, Eutropius induces degeneration. The barbarians invading Armenia, as in book 1, and now the rebels under Tribigild too, joyfully take advantage of the weakness which spreads from him. "They rely neither on force nor number, but the lassitude and betrayal of the generals sustains them";

85. The passages quoted here are discussed in Chap. 5.

they rout Roman soldiers who previously repulsed even greater numbers of them (2.580–83). "Lassitude" clearly refers to Leo and his undisciplined expedition, whose character exactly matches the court (cf. 2.417–39). "Betrayal" suggests the later action of Gaïnas, whom other sources, all later than Claudian, assume to have colluded with Tribigild from the beginning.[86] Aurora reviles the court for its indifference to her losses (2.584). It occupies itself with "banquets and choruses," just as Claudian portrays the council. "Lest the vendor lose anything when the world is cut back," it has cynically divided the remaining provinces in two. Sale of offices identifies Eutropius specifically, both from Aurora's speech and from book 1 (1.196–209, 2.561). Finally she begs Stilicho to relent, urging that "supreme dangers always grant pardon to a fault" (2.596–97). She promises not to remove him from the West, for he is able to protect both halves of the empire with his shield and laboring *virtus* (2.602).

Virtus is the last word of the poem. It means at once "manliness," "courage," and "virtue." It emblematizes the contrast between the virile, martial, capable Stilicho and the effeminate administration of Eutropius, which the narrative of Tribigild's revolt shows to be most incompetent in war. The first words refer to the devastation Tribigild's Gruthungi have wrought in Phrygia: "Mygdonian ashes and remnants of the Eastern realm, if any of what is perishing remains" (2.1–2). The war with Tribigild centers the epic of *In Eutropium* 2. It is so important not simply because, as Birt supposed, Stilicho is being asked to save the Eastern empire from Tribigild,[87] but because Eutropius's influence on the Eastern empire has enabled Tribigild to ruin so much. Tribigild is merely the present symptom of the fundamental disorder.

The main body of *In Eutropium* 2 spreads blame very broadly about the East. All the people indecently adore the repulsive Eutropius. In emphasizing this charge, Claudian even makes it appear that they initiated the perversity of elevating him to the consulate. Ultimately they acknowledge their culpability. Gnilka's "collective guilt" does operate in this book. Phrases like "Byzantine luxury" (2.415–16) suggest endemic laxity. At the same time, more specific, pointed, and profound incriminations show interaction with Eutropius. He does not simply derive from the group as a symptom of its condition. The court embodies the idiot frivolity of luxurious living; the corrupted army and especially the general Leo exemplify its debilitating effects. Both groups are related closely to Eutropius. Claudian is not alone in making these associations. Zosimus, for example, asserts that Leo's familiarity with Eutropius was

86. Synes. *Prov.* 108C; Eunap. fr. 75.6 M = 67.10 Blockley; Socr. *HE* 6.6.5–6; Soz. *HE* 8.4.2; Zos. 5.13.2 (with details of alleged collusion, 5.14.3–18.9); see now Alan Cameron and Long 1993, 226–32. The fact that Claudian alludes to collusion shows that he is not shielding Gaïnas, and that he does not allege collusion from the beginning suggests that it could only be inferred by hindsight.

87. Birt 1888, 51 n. 2; cf. discussion in Chap. 5.

his one qualification for the command (Zos. 5.14.2).[88] Eutropius himself is blamed particularly for dangerous mismanagement of barbarians, just as Synesius criticized him over Alaric in *De Regno*.[89]

Claudian asserts, moreover, that Tribigild's revolt effects a great change; this idea is fundamental to the stance of *In Eutropium* 2. Pathetic fallacy when Mars's spear strikes Phrygia foreshadows the pastoral interlude in which Phrygia is described and mourned by Cybele. It in turn prepares for Tribigild's attack to rouse pity for the afflicted citizens. They are reformed by the crisis. Both those innocent and those guilty of injuring Stilicho pray that he will come to relieve them. All, allegedly, regret their folly in ever rejecting him. Now they acknowledge in horror their responsibility for Eutropius and repudiate him. Aurora asserts that she always wanted Stilicho to direct her affairs, but was frustrated by Rufinus and then by Eutropius. Although she speaks on behalf of the Easterners, out of their new sentiment, she does not correspond precisely to any group of them described in the book, for they all adored Eutropius (2.58–83) and "all" regret having deserted Stilicho (2.516–17). Aurora rather represents the best will of the East, wanting what the Easterners should have wanted if they had not been swayed by "blind love" (2.50). She begs forgiveness for them. She acknowledges the common guilt but, significantly, she abolishes it. The remainder of her history reverts essentially to the position of book 1 toward the East: all its problems stem from Eutropius, who has imposed himself on a helpless population.

Gnilka did not see such a resolution, since he did not allow that Aurora's appeal could redeem Eastern guilt. I have already argued that his interpretation demands more inference by the reader, contrary to the intrinsic suggestions of the text, than any parallel in Claudian's writing justifies (Chapter 5). Although the proem broadens the scope of the invective, and although other passages express a general hostility to the East, in Claudian's rendering Tribigild's revolt both inspires the Easterners to change their minds and rouses sympathy for them so that the audience is led to accept this change. The reversal is an important part of the epic. By discussing the proem of book 2 before the elegiac preface to the book Gnilka allowed its bitterness to color his reading of the preface, so that it seemed merely sarcastic. But Claudian's audiences would have encountered the preface first, so that they would not have missed its separation of the main body of the court from the malignant party that fell with Eutropius. The proem darkens the tone considerably, so as to argue that purification must go farther, but the preface must color it also.

88. Ridley 1982, 105, secluded the passage without explanation; L. Mendelssohn, *Zosimus. Historia Nova* (Leipzig: Teubner, 1887; rpt. Hildesheim: Georg Olms, 1963), 230–31, and Paschoud 1971–89, 3[1].21, gave no indication that there is any reason to suspect it.

89. Heather 1988; Alan Cameron and Long 1993, 109–26.

It will be best, however, to review Gnilka's arguments in more detail.[90] When Claudian reports the earthquake with which the "Stygian sisters" welcome Eutropius's consulate, he concludes the account (2.35–39),

> What punishment, powers,
> do you preserve for sin, the omen of which was composed of so many
> calamities? Would that you, Neptune, might bend to your trident,
> and sink the polluted ground together with its entire guilt!
> One city we yield to the Furies, in place of the world.

As Gnilka observed, Claudian obviously means Constantinople. Chalcedon, the Bosphorus, and renewed Symplegades in the straits identify Constantinople clearly when Claudian describes the earthquake. Manifestly Neptune, god of earthquakes, is already in the process of destroying it. Sacrifice of one city for the sake of the world repeats the same idea of expiatory sacrifice as in book 1, when Claudian avers that "the fasces must be purified by means of the consul, and the prodigy expiated by means of itself: whatever the fates are preparing by this omen, may Eutropius redeem it with his neck" (1.21–23). "Sin" and "omen" here (2.36) recall both books' proems' identification of Eutropius as a polluting prodigy (cf. 2.8–9, quoted previously). If he is a polluting prodigy, it is only natural that he will pollute any territory where he is recognized; the capital city where he was proclaimed and where he mostly resides is most vulnerable to the association. Only a few lines before the passage under discussion, Claudian asks sarcastically, "Do you think the court outstandingly cleansed, if Cyprus holds Eutropius?" (2.20–21). Accordingly, when Claudian calls Constantinople polluted and wishes that it be destroyed, the most natural reading of these lines in their context still connects his vehemence to Eutropius. Claudian says nothing to dissociate the place from the eunuch consul or to attack anything it represents apart from him. It is thus hard to believe that destruction of Constantinople itself is truly, as Gnilka called it, the "chief aim of his anti-eastern polemic."

Gnilka acknowledged that Claudian soon makes a contradictory wish, that the statues of Eutropius with which the streets of Constantinople are filled stand forever as a perpetual reproach (2.77–78). They could hardly stand forever if the city itself were washed away. But Gnilka deemed it inconceivable that Claudian could have changed his mind on a fundamental point within a few lines:[91] the two passages both express, albeit in different ways, the same fundamental disgust with Constantinople. It should be stressed, however, that this disgust in both instances relates closely to Eutropius. Moreover, surface

90. Gnilka 1976, 111–14.
91. Gnilka 1976, 108. I infer the conclusion, which Gnilka did not formulate precisely in this connection, but compare 111.

contradiction does not legitimate discounting only one of the positions taken, as Gnilka effectively dismissed Claudian's wish about the statues but stressed his wish for the destruction of the city. Both must be considered equally rhetorical and extravagant.

Claudian offers parallel passages which show that his extravagance expresses emotion without being meant literally. When Africa supplicates Jupiter in *In Gildonem*, for example, she begins by demanding why he does not immediately unleash the sea against her peoples, or burn away her fertility (*Gild.* 142–45, 148–50):

> I seek to be sunk first: may the seas come, burst forth
> from Pachynus, may my cities subside in unconstrained Syrtes.
> If the fates cannot lead Gildo away from me,
> carry me away from Gildo! . . .
> May the reddened region grow. May the midmost path of burning
> Olympus act upon me too: I shall lie better as a desert,
> unbearing of the plow.

It would completely defeat all the purposes of the poem if Africa and her grain were really to be destroyed. And indeed by the end of the speech she is complaining that her people are scattered in exile: will they never be returned to her? (*Gild.* 197–200). Africa's suicidal exclamations merely indicate how miserable she is under Gildo's tyranny.

Similarly, after their senses have returned to them, the Easterners of *In Eutropium* 2 "all confess that they deserve torture or death, because they handed themselves over to slaves and deserted Stilicho" (2.516–17). Nevertheless, Aurora begs on their behalf that Stilicho not "condemn all for the crime of a few" and that he allow their "supreme danger" to "pardon their fault"; she holds up to him the example of Camillus (2.594–98). If Claudian meant the Easterners truly to accept punishment for their guilt, they should have sacrificed themselves before Tribigild, whom Mars named the avenger of Roman shame for supporting Eutropius (2.159). If history constrained him, he could nevertheless have stressed satisfaction rather than pathos when he describes the first attack: he is scornful when he describes the fall of Leo, for example. But his scorn, in the wake of the attack, is reserved for Eutropius's general. So too Claudian wishes that Constantinople be washed away, only in order to indicate vehemently how disgraced and polluted the city is under Eutropius.

Gnilka was wrong to assert that Claudian keeps the aim of destroying Constantinople always in view. The one passage that he adduced as recalling the proem's wish that Neptune "sink the polluted ground together with its entire guilt" (2.37–38) does so only through a textual emendation of Birt, which Gnilka did not defend. Birt printed lines 2.339–40, describing the tastes of Eutropius's courtiers, thus:

Romam contemnere sueti
mirarique suas, quas Bosphorus *obruat*, aedes.

accustomed to disdain Rome
and marvel at their own houses, which *may* the Bosphorus *flood.*

Manuscripts offer *alluit* ("washes up against"), *abluit* ("washes away"), *obruit* ("floods"), *obstruit* ("blocks"), and *horruit* ("was appalled at").[92] Jeep preferred the somewhat paradoxical *obstruit* of manuscripts he considered inferior witnesses; Andrews, Fargues, and Hall selected the less colorful *adluit/alluit.* Andrews justified his choice on the grounds that it is "an easier reading than *obruat*";[93] Fargues and Hall did not give arguments. The reading is unobjectionable, if trivial, but it does not give the sense that Gnilka's point would require. Nor really does *abluit,* for the indicative describes the washing away as factual, not as Claudian's wish. Moreover, it would be nonsensical, even for these foolish courtiers, to build houses where the Bosphorus regularly did wash them away; the verb would have to bear its weaker sense "wash clean."[94] The regular floods implied by *obruit* pose the same problem in only slightly weaker form; Schweckendiek embraced the reading as an exaggeration criticizing precisely the courtiers' stupidity.[95] Schmidt's stemmatic research gives *obruit* the best authority.[96] Cameron, however, argued in favor of *horruit,* urging the fact that Claudian often uses stupefied bodies of water to comment on events and persons.[97] It can be added that waterfront building had long represented conspicuous luxury in Claudian's literary traditions, and hence excited the criticism of moralists.[98] The elder Symmachus provoked riots by his infamous remark that he preferred not to sell wine to the urban poor but to use it to slake limekilns: he was referring to a method of making waterproof cement useful for making fishponds and other structures that had to withstand constant pressure of water.[99] Such associations add to the simple wonder that Cameron proposed a note of disapproval apt to Claudian's purpose. All agree

92. The apparatus of Hall 1985 lists: "adluit *Heinsius, Barthius* (F_2, *qui* obruit *legit, notat tamen* .i. tangit vel lavat) : alluit *Livineii Vaticanus* : abluit $LL_{11}P_1$, *Isengriniana mg*, abluat *Camers* : obruit P_2Rpc, *cett. mei* [= $\Gamma gPW_1FJ_3n_1$]: obstruit P_2ulO_2ul : horruit (Ppc)$RacO_2$: obruat *Birt.*"
93. Andrews 1931, 133.
94. *OLD* s.v.
95. Scweckendiek 1992, 143, quoting the note ad loc. of Pieter DeJ. Burman, *Cl. Claudiani quae extant varietate lectionis et pepetua adnotatione illustrata a Io. Matthia Gesnero,* vol. 1 (Leipzig, 1759).
96. Schmidt 1989, 407.
97. Alan Cameron 1968a, 407–8.
98. E.g., Hor. *Carm.* 2.18.19–22, 3.1.33–37.
99. Amm. 27.3.4; cf. Rougé 1961, 63–64 (who related the building to baths); Matthews 1975, 20 n. 2.

that Constantinople was remarkable for its concentration of waterfront palaces. Birt, as he noted, based his emendation precisely on Claudian's wish when he describes the earthquake that the Bosphorus overwhelm Constantinople.[100] On textual grounds *obruit* is a better reading, whereas literary and historical considerations support *horruit*; even if these alternatives were not superior, Birt's basis for emendation renders Gnilka's interpretive argument impossibly circular.

Finally, Gnilka's argument that the epimethean regret of the Easterners comes, by definition, too late to redeem them relies on the proem utterly to undermine Aurora's plea at the end. The Easterners themselves might indeed not be able to claim consideration by any practical means, but the very function of divine supplication in a literary representation is to relay their best interests through a higher authority that cannot be refused. Roma, when she begs for any other destruction than the starvation Gildo is inflicting on her, wrings tears from Venus, Mars, Minerva, Cybele, Juno, and all the other gods worshiped by Romans, "and now the Father began to relax his heart" (*Gild.* 132–33). When Africa adds her pleas, Jupiter cuts her off to promise both personified goddesses that Honorius will restore the proper order of things (*Gild.* 201–7). Mallius Theodorus modestly protests to Iustitia that retirement has rusted his ability to deal with public affairs such as the consulate, but he concedes, "It is unjust that anything should be denied to Justice" (*M. Theod.* 189–90). Realities known when *In Eutropium* 1 was performed indicate that Roma's main request, not to recognize Eutropius's consulate, had already been granted by Honorius and Stilicho. The proem of *In Eutropium* 2 widens the application of Aurora's request to Stilicho to save her from "servile kingships," and indicates in advance that she is still under the "servile sway" of Eutropius's successors; but the end of the book must stand as Claudian's concluding words. More action is still required to secure the cooperation of the East with Stilicho's leadership, but, far from completely rejecting the East and all it stands for, Claudian encourages its return.

This message, before a Western audience, interprets Eastern events and announces a renewed interest in exerting influence over the other half of the empire. Book 1, aimed against Eutropius's consulate, was obliged to dismiss the East as immovable. It was not possible to solicit anything more than Western support for this dismissal. But now Eutropius's stability had been undermined. When Claudian began to write *In Eutropium* 2, he responded to news of Tribigild's revolt and hoped that Eutropius could not withstand the crisis. A chance seemed to open by which Stilicho might reassert his interest in the East. Claudian set out to show that although the Easterners once blindly, damnably, promoted Eutropius, they now have learned from the consequences of their

100. Birt 1892, 108.

perversity and would welcome Stilicho as their savior. He also shows that Eutropius has brought the Eastern court and army to such a state that they are incapable of defending the damaged empire: therefore Western help is required. This interpretation of events presupposes that the survival of both halves of the empire was a goal Western audiences would support. Claudian's implications that intervention was necessary and would be welcomed by the East take away the objection that it would be seen as improper interference. The dynamic form of the epic justifies Stilicho's changed intentions by professing that the East itself has changed. It also suits the character of agitation propaganda for propelling action.

While Claudian worked on the book, Eutropius actually fell in consequence of Tribigild's revolt. The Eastern court changed. But although Claudian applauded this development, he also asserted that the East continued to require Stilicho's help. Residues of Eutropius's administration had not been fully cleansed away: therefore the East risked a catastrophic relapse into its diseased condition if interventive surgery was not undertaken (n.b. 2.11–19). Thus Claudian's preface and the first part of the proem reinterpret his basic message in terms of the changed situation of the East, and reaffirm it. The completed book with its preface, presented as a commentary on current realities, is unified in asserting that Stilicho's "single manliness" still is needed to eradicate completely the corruption that has spread from Eutropius (2.602).

Baynes suggested that "at least . . . the latter part of In Eutropium ii" had the potential to function as propaganda in the East for Stilicho's policy.[101] But it is not to be expected that Claudian designed a complete poem with the aim of cutting off half of it for separate circulation: the whole must function if it is to work at all. The preface opens a route for the East to distance itself from its former abjectness under Eutropius. It has ejected him; it is welcomed back into health and normality as he is cast beyond the boundaries of the real world, to be detained by Tritons or rejected by dolphins (2pr.16, 67, 73). The first part of the proem's metaphorical threats about spreading infections can work to alarm the patient into undergoing drastic remedies. The second and third parts of the proem, which characterize the blind folly that proceeded with Eutropius's inauguration as consul and the more indecent adulation with which it was greeted, remind the sufferer of how dreadful the disease was. Mars too speaks of "healing" Eastern softness (2.112). And yet whereas the metaphor of disease can absolve the sufferer, Claudian underlines Eastern complicity in adulating Eutropius and giving him the year.

The law exiling Eutropius, for a contrasting example, abuses Eutropius as an alien source of pollution (CTh 9.40.17):

101. "A Note on Professor Bury's History of the Later Roman Empire," JRS 12 (1922): 271 n. 1 = Baynes 1955, 338 n. 10.

All the possessions of Eutropius, who once was *praepositus sacri cubiculi*, we have annexed to the accounts of our treasury. His magnificence has been stripped off and the consulate vindicated from the foul muck and from the commemoration of his name and its filthy stains [*consulatu a taetra inluvie et a commemoratione nominis eius et caenosis sordibus vindicato*]. These things have been done so that, once every single one of his acts has been rejected, all times may grow silent and the degradation of our age may not be apparent by his being listed [*nec eius enumeratione saeculi nostri labes appareat*], and neither they who by their manliness and wounds extend Roman borders, nor they who guard those same borders by the justice of preserving what is right may groan at the fact that a miry prodigy has befouled by its contagion the divine reward of the consulate [*divinum praemium consulatus lutulentum prodigium contagione foedavit*]. Let him learn that he has been despoiled of the dignity of the patriciate and all lesser honors, which he has polluted by the perversity of his character [*morum polluit scaevitate*]. We direct that all statues, all images, be they of bronze or marble or pigments or of whatever material images may be made, be obliterated from all cities, towns, and public or private places, so that the blot, so to speak, of our age not pollute the gazes of those who look upon it [*ne tamquam nota nostri saeculi obtutus polluat intuentum*]. Therefore, let him be conducted under the supervision of faithful guardians to the island of Cyprus, in which may Your Sublimity know that he has been relegated, so that in that same place, ringed round with ever vigilant care, he may be unable to confound all things together by the madness of his own devisings [*nequeat suarum cogitationum rabie cuncta miscere*].

Eutropius is repeatedly identified with terms for mud, grime, and foulness. He bears all opprobrium; with him it is being purged away. The language of the law reviles Eutropius and excludes him from the human community of the Roman state just as the law itself decrees his deposition and exile. Claudian in *In Eutropium* 2 dwells on pollution as it subsists in the East that Eutropius has defiled. He pillories Eutropius's own administrative and diplomatic fecklessness, especially in provoking Tribigild's revolt. He identifies Eutropius as the center of debasement, the focus of perverse veneration, and the wellspring of fatuous indifference or sheer ineptitude among his fellow ministers. The effects of their maladministration poison the territory they control. All remain in their afflicted state. Purgation will come only when the East submits its passivity to another agent, Stilicho, as Aurora requests.

The process of change in Eastern attitudes prompting this request within the poem, as Claudian describes it, could not conciliate Eastern feelings. Previously, he asserts, they blindly pursued error; that the original error should have been the product of vice (2.50) makes it a thin excuse. Now they have been terrified into contrition, so that they welcome a savior whom they formerly rejected and abused. Even when they desire correction, the desire comes from epimethean regret for sheeplike obtuseness (2.499), childish folly (2.509–11), or insane delusion like that of the Maenads who killed Pentheus (2.522–26). These are harsh images for Eastern readers to apply to themselves; Claudian supplies no reason for them to do so if they did not already feel the same abject reliance on Stilicho that he figures through Aurora's appeal. He could have shown more indulgence for the error of tolerating Eutropius or more sympathy for wrongs suffered from him, but he merely represents the Easterners altered by circumstances to a condition more amenable to Stilicho's ends. He does not woo them, or seek a reaction from them. As with book 1, the Easterners envisaged by book 2 remain essentially static, while action is requested from the West.

Claudian positions Stilicho as savior by simple, mostly implicit, antithesis to Eutropius. Where Eutropius precipitated Tribigild's revolt and the chain of crises that ensued from the revolt, Stilicho is called upon to resolve them. Where "Eastern softness" (2.113) and Eutropius's effeminacy, with its derogatory connotations, mirror one another, Aurora pictures Stilicho as ready to step into the heroic Roman role of Camillus, champion of the state that had injured him (2.597–98).[102] Ultimately she pleads that he defend both halves of the empire at once (2.599–602). Coupling a call for Stilicho to take charge of Eastern affairs with an assurance that such involvement would not take him away from the West also addresses Western concerns.

The strategies of political suasion in which Claudian was involved did not extend to what Ellul termed "psychological warfare."[103] Means of communication were available, by which Claudian's poems could have been transmitted to the East, at least to private audiences; yet Claudian does not seek to undermine Eutropius through them, nor is there other evidence of such solicitation. The "psychological action" exerted by Claudian's representations was designed to operate only within the West. Aurora's appeal and the dynamic movement of the epic lay groundwork for supporting intervention by Stilicho in Eastern affairs that had apparently unraveled in other hands. In fact, Gaïnas saved the East from Tribigild when Eutropius and Leo failed; his deposition of Eutropius still did not promise complete stability, and Claudian closed *In Eutropium* 2 with Aurora's call to Stilicho as resuming the proem's call for further purgation. Even though opportunity to rescue the East never finally materialized for Stilicho, he remains cast, before Claudian's Western audience, as a bulwark who would "suffice as defender for both" West and East (2.599–600).

102. Roma names "savior Camilli" among figures affronted by Eutropius's consulate, *Eutr.* 1.439; cf. 2.54–58.
103. Ellul 1965, xiii; I survey these terms in Chap. 7.II.

CONCLUSION

In Eutropium and the Empire of Rome

✦

CLAUDIAN'S *In Eutropium* is fascinating, both as a work of literature and as a political document. The two categories are by no means exclusive: Brunella Moroni has argued that Claudian's literary reminiscences themselves work propagandistically. They identify Claudian and his poetry as bearers of Roman traditions, and therefore as appropriate authorities for the positions taken in the poems. Claudian's hero Stilicho too is thereby implied to embody traditional ideals, so that his designs are automatically recommended to conservative Roman patriotism.[1]

One who knew Stilicho's background from Claudian would scarcely be aware that he was, through his father, of Vandal blood; Claudian's panegyric for Stilicho's consulate announces that he will not bother to relate the facts of his father's military service or how "his right hand, loyal to Valens, led squadrons with flashing red-gold hair," since being Stilicho's father conferred distinction enough (*Stil.* 1.35–39).[2] Stilicho himself Claudian continually casts into august, Roman molds. Mars, the father of Romulus who ordains Tribigild's revolt in order to avenge the Roman fasti from pollution by Eutropius (*Eutr.* 2.140–42), fights by Stilicho's side against the mingled barbarian tribes set on by Rufinus (*Ruf.* 1.334–53). Iustitia holds out the opportunity to join in council with Stilicho as one that only a madman would reject, as she urges Mallius Theodorus to undertake the consulate of 399 (*M. Theod.* 161–62). Claudian in his own voice asserts that by refusing to recognize Eutropius as consul Stilicho and Honorius have preserved the curule chairs and "Latin fasti" from violation (*M. Theod.* 265–69). The innumerable Roman exempla

---

1. Brunella Moroni, "Tradizione letteraria e propaganda: Osservazione sulla poesia politica di Claudiano," *Scripta philologa* 3 (1982): 213–39.

2. Orosius identifies Stilicho as "born from the race of the Vandals' unwarlike, avaricious, perfidious and deceitful nation" (7.38.1); Joh. Ant. fr. 187 identifies him as "of the Scythian race"; Jer. *Ep.* 123.16 labels him "half-barbarian," indicating that his mother was Roman.

Roma cites to Honorius and Stilicho against Eutropius's consulate in *In Eu-tropium* 1 erect an insurmountable boundary between them and Eutropius; they are firmly embraced among the heroes who define Roman history, just as Eutropius is firmly excluded. So too when, at the conclusion of her speech in *In Eutropium* 2, Aurora invokes the figure of Camillus as a model for Stilicho, urging him to come to save the East despite the slights he has suffered from it in the past, she revivifies the Roman past in him. In both book 1 and book 2 Stilicho foils Eutropius distantly; the contagion of the eunuch consul is not allowed to contaminate him even by antithetical contact. Claudian thus main-tains a distance between Stilicho and Eutropius in the argumentative structure of each book. It reinforces the impression of the moral gulf that he claims significantly to distinguish them.

Claudian's deployment of Roman literary allusion in *In Eutropium* serves the same purpose in the field of Roman culture, a living tradition of memory and self-definition, as opposed to the more abstract resonances of Roman history as such. Because tradition passed down through education, literature, and art encourages Claudian's contemporary audiences to identify their world with the world defined by Dentati, Fabii, Aemilii, Camilli, Brutus, and all the rest, against the Greek-named freedmen Chrysogonus, Narcissus, and Eu-tropius, Roma's historical exempla have persuasive force (1.436–41). Ethnicity, class, and especially the role these figures played in the Roman story all con-tribute meaning to the comparison Roma makes. So too, for example, when Eutropius appears in the ill-fitting guise of a deserted erotic heroine (1.64–77), the role itself marginalizes him even while his inadequacies for it make him the more ridiculous. Vergil's Dido in this position wrung tears from Augustine as a schoolboy in the 360s (Aug. *Conf.* 1.13); but Aeneas had to leave her in order to discharge his duty to the Roman future (Verg. *Aen.* 4.265–76). Eutropius more congruently fulfills the literary roles of impotent whore, bibulous mother-in-law, and hated taskmistress (*Eutr.* 1.90–97, 269–71; 2.370–75).

The council at which Eutropius plays this last part derives its general struc-ture and several specific characterizations from Domitian's council in Juvenal's *Satire* 4. The courtiers assemble as for a council of war, but they are incapable of discussing serious matters. The boldest of them is a corpulent buffoon. The echoes cast Eutropius into the same despotic mold that Juvenal cast Domitian; this translation of role helps gloss over the total absence of Arcadius from the poem. He is entirely removed from the sphere of blame for Eutropius's mis-deeds, so that Claudian says nothing disloyal in criticizing them. In keeping with the epic travesty of Claudian's scene and its Juvenalian model, Leo's stomach appears in the role of the sevenfold oxhide shield proper to an Ajax (*Eutr.* 2.386–89; Ov. *Met.* 13.2). It helps sustain the travesty's intrinsic ridicule of the base characters who people it. As a vivid, sensory image it emblematizes Leo's gluttony, just as the archaic shield emblematizes Ajax's old-fashioned courage and strength. Leo's belly like the shield is immense and heavy; it fends off any noble or even practical consideration of the problem that he undertakes. He dies like a fat pig butchered by a cook, in fear of a light noise from behind him. Hosius is recalled from the council, and the courage Leo thoughtlessly vaunted there is given the final lie. Claudian weaves allusions together into a rich texture, which conveys its own pleasure in Roman literature while serving his particular representations.

Graphic particularity, as of Leo's belly, makes unforgettable the impressions that Claudian gives. Gnilka disparaged the possibility that the clever, learned, and artistic expressions of a poet could ever have had pragmatic effect.[3] It is not unlikely that some of Claudian's erudite play was lost on some of his audience, although some highly educated individuals also occupied positions of power. But Claudian's pictorial and emotive abundance could be appreciated by anyone. Ellul noted that it is precisely the emotional impression created by an interpretation of facts that a person ordinarily retains, not the mass of individual facts themselves.[4] Experiments have demonstrated that, beyond a short term, people retain and are influenced by information to which they have been exposed without remembering that they had initially distrusted its source; Roman historiography witnesses the same process.[5] The artistic vividness Claudian sought for his representations both makes the overall impression more forceful initially and makes particular details more memorable. Not every one can be believed literally, but they would not need to be: cumulatively they express a moral judgment that transcends facts. An audience whose consciousness had been shaped by pervasive rhetorical culture, as was the case among the educated classes of late antiquity, would expect no less. The modern theory of propaganda bears out the tendencies well developed in the practice of ancient political invective.

The generic models Claudian adapts for the two books of *In Eutropium* also serve his political purposes. Book 1 is constructed on a rhetorical pattern that precisely corresponds to the inverted occasion of the poem. Claudian argues against recognizing a consul in the same rhetorical form as that in which a consul normally was acclaimed. He substitutes disparagement for praise in every topic of the rhetorical scheme of encomium to produce a full formal *psogos*. This model is known otherwise in a relatively pure form only from school exercises: practical affairs ordinarily called for invective to focus on

3. Gnilka 1976, 123 n. 74.
4. Ellul 1965, 44.
5. Carl I. Hovland and Walter Weiss, "Influence of Source Credibility on Communication Effectiveness," *Public Opinion Quarterly* 15 (1952): 635–50 = Katz et al. 1954, 337–47. Charlesworth 1933, for example, illustrated how Antony's slanders of Octavian percolated through rumor, lampoon, and graffiti into history and other serious assessments of Octavian's character.

some particular issue, rather than to analyze and abominate an entire character systematically. Claudian's issue, however, the consulate, was a largely symbolic honor that favorable panegyrics typically claimed to seal an entire life. Claudian in his early panegyric for the young Olybrius and Probinus exclaims to them, "You have begun at what used to be the end" (*Ol. Prob.* 67). The situation that called forth *In Eutropium* 1 made inversion of this genre literarily and rhetorically appropriate.

The dynamics of *In Eutropium* 1 and 2 also served Claudian's rhetorical purposes. While he justified Honorius's and Stilicho's decision not to recognize Eutropius, a course already taken, Claudian utilized the relatively static, intellectual persuasiveness inherent to epideixis; he married form to purpose with a sophisticated understanding of the needs and capacities of both. The different form of book 2 is also sensitively suited to its practical purpose. Dynamic epic represents a change that justifies a call to action, and its own motion reinforces the call.

The opportunities of intellectual persuasion and political action to which Claudian responds can only be understood in terms of the circumstances in which he wrote, which are most conveniently delineated by dates of composition. External evidence identifies certain fixed points, more indeed than are available for many ancient works. Eutropius campaigned in Armenia in 398. He was named consul for 399 and inaugurated in Constantinople on the first of that year. He was deposed and exiled by a law of 17 August 399.[6] Finally he was recalled from exile and executed at Chalcedon a few months later. But for precision between these points research still must rely on internal details of Claudian's poems. In consequence, assumptions must be made about how an author could respond to real circumstances. These assumptions can be tested against no more secure basis than analogous literary practice, which has often been understood according to similar assumptions. There is always a risk of circularity; but there are no alternative methods by which to escape the risk. The weight of parallels and probabilities ought not to be dismissed. It is reasonable to assume that Claudian would not have foretokened events in ways that were falsified by events he and his audience knew to have occurred. It is reasonable to assume that he would not waste creative energy on wholly vacuous details. John the Lydian's criticism of Claudian as a blusterer has been echoed by many modern scholars,[7] but the fault they perceive is that of saying the same thing too excessively, not of saying nothing at all.

Claudian has to have composed *In Eutropium* 1 some time after news of Eutropius's nomination reached the Western court in 398; he had it ready to deliver in the early part of 399. Eutropius was still in power. Claudian foretells

6. Date emended by Seeck 1894, 1146–47; I discuss the issue in Chap. 5.
7. Joh. Lyd. *Mag.* 1.47; e.g., Platnauer 1922, 1.xviii, quoted in Chap. 5, n. 25.

disasters for the year contaminated by its consul in vague language referring to Eutropius's slavery and eunuchry. By contrast, in *In Rufinum* 1, Iustitia's more specific threats of retribution for Rufinus correspond with the circumstances of his death (*Ruf.* 369–71): as the book's proem indicates, it was composed after Rufinus was lynched. *In Eutropium* 2 and its preface reflect the progress of events. They explicitly refer to Eutropius's exile. Since they give no hint of the death he actually met, the book and preface seem to have been finished and delivered in late summer or early autumn of 399.

Nevertheless, Aurora's plea to be freed from "servile kingdoms" at the end of book 2 on its own terms best suggests that Eutropius still held power when Claudian wrote it, and that his predominance had as yet only been threatened by Tribigild's revolt. This discrepancy illuminates the process of composition of the book. Claudian left the main body developing to a conclusion that seems most naturally to imply that Eutropius still reigned supreme; if he modified details, he managed it seamlessly. The preface and proem of the book more patently redirect Claudian's complaints from Eutropius individually onto the broader target of the administration that survived him. Since the epic must in any case have focused on Tribigild's revolt as demonstrating how much Eutropius injured the state, and since Eutropius himself did not lead the campaign against Tribigild but entrusted it to Leo, it seems that even the earlier version must have derided Eutropius's subordinates as well as abusing him directly. Gaïnas exploited Tribigild's revolt to have Eutropius deposed, but he and his accessories failed either to stabilize Eastern affairs decisively, or to accommodate Stilicho's interest in them; Claudian, asserting that Stilicho's intervention was still needed in the East, makes Eutropius a symbol for all the incapacities of those who served the Eastern government at about the same time. This dilation of focus of the epic embraced the more complex problems that intervention now faced. After Gaïnas had Eutropius recalled from exile and executed, his own attempt to consolidate power spun out of control into armed revolt; only Fravitta's victory over him ended the possibility for Stilicho to restore the East.

Communications between Eastern and Western parts of the empire were generally good at the end of the fourth century. It appears both that Claudian could have been fairly precisely informed about contemporary events in the East and that his poems had some chance of circulating to Eastern readers. Nevertheless, it does not follow that he chose to represent Eastern policy precisely. It is likely enough, for example, that Eutropius initially treated Tribigild's revolt as a minor disturbance, at least in official announcements.[8] That he minimized the revolt for the purpose of ignoring it, ostrichlike, as Claudian

---

8. Such as imperial letters to the West: cf. Honorius, *Ep. Imp. Pont. Al.* 38.1–2 (discussed in Chap. 6; the present reference is *Eutr.* 2.306–7).

also asserts, is a less fair inference. Similarly, Aurora should refer to some real act when she says that Eutropius has divided provinces in two (*Eutr.* 2.585–88), but it is hard to believe that he truly acted only to preserve his revenues from selling offices, sales having been threatened because territory was lost to Trib-igild's ravages. This alleged motive is no more than a cynical squib: the insult stands in for the serious explanation that report of the fact alone would call for.

In the other direction of communications, although it would have been possible for Claudian's poems to be transmitted to the East, *In Eutropium* 1 and 2 do not reveal any systematic effort to solicit Eastern enthusiasm for their positions. Certain points about Eutropius's oppressions might have appealed to Easterners, and they would not have been less sensitive than Westerners to Claudian's regular appeals to Roman traditions. But in both books the East appears in fixed positions when the West is asked to move: it is irrevocably committed to Eutropius's consulate in the first, and helpless in the second. If the text treats a group as incapable of action, it denies itself a basis on which to appeal to them to take a particular course.

Peder Christiansen has argued that *In Eutropium* marks the point at which Claudian recognized that division between the Western and Eastern parts of the empire was irrevocable, because there at last he speaks of the division as a fact and merely hopes that it can be repaired.[9] Christiansen's argument forced him to regard all the references in *De Consulatu Stilichonis* to Stilicho's protec-tion of both Arcadius and Honorius as purely nostalgic, which weakens it: Claudian is, as Christiansen acknowledged, recounting Stilicho's biography, and he relates Theodosius's charge to look after both sons in the past tense because the event took place in the past. Moreover, Claudian does not limit himself to the past tense in describing Stilicho's care for them. The very passage that Christiansen cited reads (*Stil.* 2.50–55):

> And love bound to the living does not cease to remember
> the dead; the goodwill of the fathers is transmitted to the offspring.
> By it you used to cherish Theodosius, while he held the scepters,
> by it even after his fated end you still cherish him. Nor do you care more
> for your own children than for those he had given to you
> to be admonished and watched over.

Alan Cameron better identified the passage as revealing that "in 400, with Honorius now 16 and Arcadius 23, Stilico [*sic*] had still not retreated a jot from his claim to the regency of both."[10] Closely intertwined with the regency, of course, was the idea of the unity of the empire.

This unity is no less a goal of *In Eutropium*, a fact Christiansen did not deny.

9. I.e., in Aurora's request; Christiansen 1970, esp. 118.
10. Alan Cameron 1970, 152.

But whether or not unity was realized, or to what extent it was realized, the fact that the ideal was upheld indicates that the parts of the empire were not yet ready to see themselves as disunited. If Eutropius's consulate degraded only the East, Roma would not have to argue against it. If the Eastern capital did not in some way represent Rome, Romulus would not need avenging (2.141–43). Mars's use of the old-fashioned term *Quirites* for "Roman citizens," even joined to the adjective "Greek," and his final injunction "let barbarian arms run to aid Roman shame" (2.136, 159) both presuppose the fundamental oneness of the Roman Empire. And if Claudian uses these concepts to appeal to a Western audience, it must mean that he did not believe they were willing to give up on the East entirely. It had demonstrated a need for correction. Intrigues with Gildo had posed a serious problem. Stilicho also perceived a problem of prestige, if Eutropius could enjoy a consulate which he himself was denied by status as a public enemy. His very competitiveness reflects a sense of community between the two halves of the empire.[11] It was important to be honored by both. Of course his reaction, causing the West to reject the designated consul of the East, necessarily strained unity considerably. But strain was felt because unity was still perceived as the norm. Claudian in *In Eutropium* tied the responsibility to forces centering on Eutropius. In the first book his consulate alone was the issue; in the second the general population's adulation of him existed, for dramatic purposes, only to be reformed away and turned into a penitent call for Stilicho at the climax of the epic. All that remained was to correct the rest of the court. Claudian may have recognized that difficulties to unity were increasing. But officially at least he remained optimistic. All the glories of Rome's past might be reconfirmed under the protection of Stilicho; all the glories of both Greek and Roman literary traditions of the unified empire Claudian put into the service of this ideal.

11. The fact that Claudian represents Eutropius rather than Stilicho as the one who "madly divides the twin court" (*Eutr.* 1.281) is typical of propaganda: as Ellul 1965, 58, observed, "[The propagandist] will accuse [the enemy] of the very intention that he himself has and of trying to commit the very crime that he himself is about to commit [for example, of provoking war]. . . . The accusation aimed at the other's intention clearly reveals the intention of the accuser."

SELECT BIBLIOGRAPHY

EDITIONS OF AND COMMENTARIES ON CLAUDIAN

Opera Omnia

Jeep, Ludwig, ed. 1876–79. *Claudii Claudiani Carmina*. 2 vols. Leipzig: Teubner.
Birt, Theodor, ed. 1892. *Claudii Claudiani Carmina*. Monumenta Germaniae Historica Auctorum Antiquissimorum 10. Berlin: Weidmann. Reprint, Munich: Monumenta Germaniae Historica, 1981.
Koch, Julius, ed. 1893. *Claudii Claudiani Carmina*. Leipzig: B. G. Teubner.
Platnauer, Maurice, ed. 1922. *Claudian*. 2 vols. Cambridge, Mass.: Harvard University Press.
Hall, J. B., ed. 1985. *Claudianus. Carmina*. Leipzig: B. G. Teubner.

In Eutropium

Andrews, Alfred Carleton, ed. 1931. *The In Eutropium of Claudius Claudianus*. Dissertation, University of Pennsylvania.
Fargues, Pierre, ed. 1933. *Claudien, Invectives contre Eutrope*. Paris: Librairie Hachette.
Schweckendiek, Helge, trans. and comm. 1992. *Claudians Invektive gegen Eutrop (In Eutropium)*. Beiträge zur Altertumswissenschaft 10. Hildesheim: Olms–Weidmann.

Other Poems

Barr, William, ed. 1981. *Claudian's Panegyric on the Fourth Consulate of Honorius*. Liverpool Latin Texts (Classical and Medieval) 2. Liverpool: Francis Cairns.
Charlet, Jean-Louis, ed. 1991. *Claudien: Oeuvres*. Vol. 1, *Le Rapt de Proserpin*. Paris: Les Belles Lettres.
Consolino, Franca Ela, ed. 1986. *Claudiano, Elogio di Serena*. Venice: Marsilio Editori.
Garuti, Ioannes, ed. 1991. *Cl. Claudiani De Bello Gothico*. L'Aquila: Japadre Editore.
Gruzelier, Claire, ed. 1993. *Claudian. De Raptu Proserpinae*. Oxford: Clarendon Press.
Hall, J. B., ed. 1969. *Claudian, de Raptu Proserpinae*. Cambridge Classical Texts and Commentaries 11. Cambridge: Cambridge University Press.
Lehner, Jakob, comm. 1984. *Poesie und Politik in Claudians Panegyrikus auf das vierte Konsulat des Kaisers Honorius*. Beiträge zur klassischen Philologie 163. Meisenheim: Hain.
Levy, Harry L., ed. 1971. *Claudian's In Rufinum*. Philological Monographs of the American Philological Association 30. Cleveland: Case Western University Press.
Olechowska, Elzbieta M., ed. 1978. *Claudii Claudiani de Bello Gildonico*. Roma Aeterna 10. Leiden: E. J. Brill.
Simon, Werner, ed. 1975. *Claudiani panegyricus de consulatu Manlii Theodori*. Dissertation, Berlin, 1974.

OTHER WORKS

Ahl, Frederick. 1984. "The Art of Safe Criticism in Greece and Rome." *American Journal of Philology* 105: 174–208.

Albert, Gerhard. 1979. "Stilicho und der Hunnenfeldzug des Eutropius." *Chiron* 9: 621–45.

———. 1984. *Goten in Konstantinopel.* Studien zur Geschichte und Kultur des Altertums, n.F., 1. Reihe 2. Paderborn: Ferdinand Schöningh.

Alfonsi, Luigi. 1960. "Nota claudianea." *Latomus* 19: 131–32.

Anderson, Graham. 1993. *The Second Sophistic: A Cultural Phenomenon in the Roman Empire.* London: Routledge.

Anderson, William S. 1982. *Essays on Roman Satire.* Princeton, N.J.: Princeton University Press.

Babcock, Robert G. 1986. "A Revival of Claudian in the Tenth Century." *Classica et Mediaevalia* 37: 203–21.

Bagnall, Roger S., Alan Cameron, Seth R. Schwartz, and Klaas A. Worp. 1987. *Consuls of the Later Roman Empire.* Atlanta, Ga.: Scholars Press.

Banchich, Thomas M. 1993. "Julian's School Laws: *Cod. Theod.* 13.5.5 and *Ep.* 42." *Ancient World* 24: 5–14.

Barbieri, Guido. 1954. "Mario Massimo." *Rivista di filologia* n.s. 32: 36–66 and 262–75.

Barnes, T. D. 1978. "Claudian and the Notitia Dignitatum." *Phoenix* 32: 81–82.

———. 1986. "Synesius in Constantinople." *Greek, Roman, and Byzantine Studies* 27: 93–112.

———. 1990. "Literary Convention, Nostalgia and Reality in Ammianus Marcellinus." In *Reading the Past in Late Antiquity,* edited by Graeme Clarke with Brian Croke, Raoul Mortley, and Alanna Emmett Nobbs, 59–92. Rushcutters Bay: Australian National University Press.

Barr, William. 1979. "Claudian's *In Rufinum:* An Invective?" *Papers of the Liverpool Latin Seminar* 2: 179–90.

———. 1981. *See* Editions and Commentaries, Other Poems.

Barrow, R. H., trans. and comm. 1973. *Prefect and Emperor: The Relationes of Symmachus, A.D. 384.* Oxford: Clarendon Press.

Bayless, William N. 1976. "Anti-Germanism in the Age of Stilicho." *Byzantine Studies / Études Byzantines* 3: 70–76.

Baynes, Norman H. 1955. *Byzantine Studies and Other Essays.* London: Athlone Press. Reprint, 1960.

Bernardi, Jean, ed. 1983. *Grégoire de Nazianze. Discours 4–5 contre Julien.* Sources chrétiennes 309. Paris: Éditions du Cerf.

Bird, H. W. 1984. *Sextus Aurelius Victor: A Historiographical Study.* ARCA Classical and Medieval Texts, Papers and Monographs 14. Liverpool: Francis Cairns.

Birt, Theodor. 1885. *De moribus Christianis quantum Stilichonis aetate in aula imperatoria occidentali valuerint disputatio.* Marburg: Friedrich.

———. 1888. *Zwei politische Satiren des alten Rom.* Marburg: N. G. Elwert.

———. 1890. "De velis Iudaeis (Claud. Eutrop. I 357)." *Rheinisches Museum* 45: 491–93.

———. 1892. *See* Editions and Commentaries, Opera Omnia.

Blockley, R. C. 1972. "The Panegyric of Claudius Mamertinus on the Emperor Julian." *American Journal of Philology* 93: 437–50.

———. 1975. *Ammianus Marcellinus: A Study of His Historiography and Political Thought.* Collection Latomus 141. Brussels: Latomus revue d'études latines.

———, ed. 1981–83. *The Fragments of the Classicising Historians of the Later Roman Empire: Eunapius, Olympiodorus, Priscus and Malchus.* 2 vols. ARCA Classical and Medieval Texts, Papers and Monographs 6, 10. Liverpool: Francis Cairns.

Bollinger, Traugott. 1969. *Theatralis Licentia: Die Publikumsdemonstrationen an den öffentlichen Spielen im Rom der früheren Kaiserzeit und ihre Bedeutung im politischen Leben.* Winterthur: Schellenberg.

Bowersock, G. W. 1969. *Greek Sophists in the Roman Empire.* Oxford: Clarendon Press.

Boyle, A. J., ed. 1990. *The Imperial Muse: Ramus Essays on Roman Literature of the Empire, Flavian Epicist to Claudian.* Bendigo, Australia: Aureal Publications.

Bramble, J. C. 1974. *Persius and the Programmatic Satire: A Study in Form and Imagery.* Cambridge: Cambridge University Press.

Braund, Susan H. 1988. *Beyond Anger: A Study in Juvenal's Third Book of Satires.* Cambridge: Cambridge University Press.

Bremer, Johan. 1958. *Asexualization.* Oslo. Reprint, New York: Macmillan, 1959.

Brown, Peter. 1988. *The Body and Society: Men, Women and Sexual Renunciation in Early Christianity.* American Council of Learned Societies Lectures on the History of Religions n.s. 13. New York: Columbia University Press.

Browning, Robert. 1952. "The Riot of A.D. 387 in Antioch: The Role of the Theatrical Claques in the Later Empire." *Journal of Roman Studies* 42: 13–20.

Bruère, R. T. 1964. "Lucan and Claudian: The Invectives." *Classical Philology* 59: 223–56.

Burgess, Theodore C. 1902. "Epideictic Literature." *University of Chicago Studies in Classical Philology* 3: 89–261.

Bury, J. B. 1923. *History of the Later Roman Empire from the Death of Theodosius I to the Death of Justinian.* 2nd ed. 2 vols. London: Macmillan. Reprint, New York: Dover, 1958.

Cairns, Francis. 1972. *Generic Composition in Greek and Roman Poetry.* Edinburgh: Edinburgh University Press.

Cameron, Alan. 1964. "The Roman Friends of Ammianus." *Journal of Roman Studies* 54: 15–28.

——. 1965a. "Wandering Poets: A Literary Movement in Byzantine Egypt." *Historia* 14: 470–509. Reprinted in Cameron 1985, chap. 1.

——. 1965b. "St. Jerome and Claudian." *Vigiliae Christianae* 19: 111–13.

——. 1965c. "Eunuchs in the *Historia Augusta.*" *Latomus* 24: 155–58.

——. 1966a. "A Biographical Note on Claudian." *Athenaeum* n.s. 44: 32–40.

——. 1966b. "The Date and Identity of Macrobius." *Journal of Roman Studies* 56: 25–38.

——. 1968a. "Notes on Claudian's Invectives." *Classical Quarterly* 62 n.s. 18: 387–411.

——. 1968b. "Theodosius the Great and the Regency of Stilicho." *Harvard Studies in Classical Philology* 73: 247–80.

——. 1970. *Claudian: Poetry and Propaganda at the Court of Honorius.* Oxford: Clarendon Press.

——. 1974. "Claudian." In *Latin Literature of the Fourth Century,* edited by J. W. Binns, 134–59. Greek and Latin Studies: Classical Literature and Its Influence. London: Routledge and Kegan Paul.

——. 1977. "Paganism and Literature in Late Fourth-Century Rome." In *Christianisme et formes littéraires de l'antiquité tardive en occident,* edited by Manfred Fuhrmann, 1–40. Fondation Hardt, Entretiens 23.

——. 1985. *Literature and Society in the Early Byzantine World.* London: Variorum Reprints.

——. 1988. "A Misidentified Homily of Chrysostom." *Nottingham Medieval Studies* 32: 34–48.

Cameron, Alan, and Jacqueline Long, with a contribution by Lee Sherry. 1993. *Barbar-*

ians and Politics at the Court of Arcadius. Transformation of the Classical Heritage 19. Berkeley: University of California Press.

Cameron, Averil. 1985. *Procopius and the Sixth Century.* Transformation of the Classical Heritage 10. Berkeley: University of California Press.

Cameron, Averil, and Amélie Kuhrt, eds. 1983. *Images of Women in Antiquity.* Detroit: Wayne State University Press.

Charlesworth, M. P. 1933. "Some Fragments of the Propaganda of Mark Antony." *Classical Quarterly* 27: 172–77.

Charpin, François, ed. 1978–91. *Lucilius. Satires.* 3 vols. Paris: Les Belles Lettres.

Chastagnol, André. 1965. "Les espagnols dans l'aristocratie gouvernementale à l'époque de Théodose." In *Les empereurs romains d'Espagne,* Colloques Internationales du CNRS 1964, edited by A. Piganiol and H. Terrasse, 269–92. Paris: Éditions du CNRS.

Christes, Johannes, ed. and comm. 1971. *Der frühe Lucilius: Rekonstruktion und Interpretation des XXVI. Buches sowie von Teilen des XXX. Buches.* Bibliothek der klassischen Altertumswissenschaften, n.F., 2. Reihe, 39. Heidelberg: Carl Winter.

Christiansen, Peder G. 1966. "Claudian versus the Opposition." *Transactions of the American Philological Association* 97: 45–54.

———. 1969. *The Use of Images by Claudius Claudianus.* The Hague: Mouton.

———. 1970. "Claudian and the East." *Historia* 19: 113–20.

———. 1971. "Claudian and Eternal Rome." *Antiquité classique* 40: 670–74.

———. 1988. *Concordantia in Claudianum: A Concordance to Claudianus.* Alpha-Omega Reihe A 47. Hildesheim: Olms–Weidmann.

Cichorius, Conrad. 1908. *Untersuchungen zu Lucilius.* Berlin: Weidmann. Reprint, Zurich: Weidmann and Niehans, 1964.

Clarke, Amy, and Harry L. Levy. 1976. "Claudius Claudianus." In *Catalogus Translationum et Commentariorum,* edited by F. Edward Cranz and Paul Oskar Kristeller, 3.141–71. Washington, D.C.: Catholic University Press.

Classen, C. Joachim. 1974. Review of Levy 1971. *Gnomon* 46: 175–82.

Conti Bizzarro, Ferruccio, and Roberto Romano, trans. 1987. *Omelie per Eutropio. Giovanni Crisostomo.* Quaderni di *Koinonia* dell'Associazione di Studi Tardoantichi 9. Naples: M. D'Auria.

Courcelle, Pierre. 1948. *Histoire littéraire des grandes invasions germaniques.* Paris: Hachette.

Courtney, E. 1980. *A Commentary on the Satires of Juvenal.* London: Athlone Press.

Creed, J. L., ed. 1984. *Lactantius. De Mortibus Persecutorum.* Oxford Early Christian Texts. Oxford: Clarendon Press.

Crees, J. H. E. 1908. *Claudian As an Historical Authority.* Cambridge Historical Essays 17. Cambridge: Cambridge University Press.

Cremona, V. 1948. "Originalità e sentimento letterario nella poesia di Claudiano." *Studi pubblicati dall'Istituto di Filologia Classica di Bologna* 1: 37–70.

Curtius, E. R. 1953. *European Literature and the Latin Middle Ages.* Translated by William Trask. Bollingen Series 36. New York: Pantheon Books.

DeGaiffier, B. 1957. "Palatins et eunuques dans quelques documents hagiographiques." *Analecta Bollandiana* 75: 17–46.

Delmaire, Roland. 1989. *Largesses sacrées et Res Privata: L'Aerarium imperiale et son administration du IVᵉ au IVᵉ siècle.* Collection de l'École française de Rome 121. Rome.

Demandt, A. 1965. *Zeitkritik und Geschichtsbild im Werk Ammians.* Dissertation, Marburg. Bonn: Habelt.

———. 1970. "Magister militum." *Real-Encyclopädie der classischen Altertumswissenschaft* Supplementband 12: 553–790.

Demougeot, Émilienne. 1950. "Le préfet Rufin et les barbares." *Annuaire de l'Institut de Philologie et d'Histoire Orientales* 10: 185–91.

———. 1951. *De l'unité à la division de l'empire romain 395–410.* Paris: Librairie d'Amérique et d'Orient.

Dessen, Cynthia. 1968. *Iunctura Callidus Acri: A Study of Persius' Satires.* Illinois Studies in Language and Literature 59. Urbana: University of Illinois Press.

Dilke, O. A. W. 1970. *Claudian, Poet of Declining Empire and Morals: An Inaugural Lecture.* Leeds: Leeds University Press.

Dölger, Franz. 1937. "Rom in der Gedankenwelt der Byzantiner." *Zeitschrift für Kirchengeschichte* 56: 1–42. Reprinted in *Byzanz und die europäische Staatenwelt,* 70–115. Ettal, 1953. Reprint, Darmstadt: Wissenschaftliche Buchgesellschaft, 1976.

Döpp, Siegmar. 1975. Review of Cameron 1970. *Anzeiger für die Altertumswissenschaft* 28: 28–34.

———. 1978. "Claudian's Invective against Eutropius as a Contemporary Historical Document." *Würzburger Jahrbücher für die Altertumswissenschaft* n.F. 4: 187–96.

———. 1980. *Zeitgeschichte in Dichtungen Claudians.* Hermes Einzelschriften 43. Wiesbaden: Steiner.

Dorfman, Ralph I., and Reginald A. Shipley. 1956. *Androgens: Biochemistry, Physiology and Clinical Significance.* New York: Wiley.

Dover, K. J. 1974. *Greek Popular Morality in the Time of Plato and Aristotle.* Oxford: Blackwell.

Duckworth, George E. 1967. "Five Centuries of Latin Hexameter Poetry: Silver Age and Late Empire." *Transactions of the American Philological Association* 98: 77–150.

Dufraigne, Pierre, ed. 1975. *Aurelius Victor. Livre des Césars.* Paris: Les Belles Lettres.

Dunlap, J. E. 1924. "The Office of the Chamberlain in the Later Roman and Byzantine Empires." In *Two Studies in Later Roman and Byzantine Administration,* by A. E. R. Boak and J. E. Dunlap, 161–324. New York: Macmillan.

DuQuesnay, I. M. LeM. 1984. "Horace and Maecenas: The Propaganda Value of *Sermones* I." In *Poetry and Politics in the Age of Augustus,* edited by Tony Woodman and David West, 19–58. Cambridge: Cambridge University Press.

Dynes, Wayne R., and Stephen Donaldson, eds. 1992. *Homosexuality in the Ancient World.* Studies in Homosexuality 1. New York: Garland.

Edwards, Catharine. 1993. *The Politics of Immorality in Ancient Rome.* Cambridge: Cambridge University Press.

Ellul, Jacques. 1965. *Propaganda: The Formation of Men's Attitudes.* Translated by Konrad Kellen and Jean Lerner. New York: Alfred A. Knopf.

Fabbri, P. 1938. "L'oriente nella poesia di Claudiano." In *Atti del IV congresso nazionale di studi romani 1935,* 1.545–52. Rome: Istituto di Studi Romani.

Fargues, Pierre. 1933. *Claudien: Études sur sa poésie et son temps.* Paris: Librairie Hachette.

———. *Invectives. See* Editions and Commentaries, *In Eutropium.*

Fatouros, Georgios, and Tilman Krischer, eds. 1983. *Libanios.* Wege der Forschung 621. Darmstadt: Wissenschaftliche Buchgesellschaft.

Fauth, Wolfgang. 1988. "Concussio Terrae: Das Thema der seismischen Erschütterung und der vulkanischen Eruption in Claudians 'De Raptu Proserpinae.'" *Antike und Abendland* 39: 63–78.

Foulkes, A. P. 1983. *Literature and Propaganda*. London: Methuen.

Fowler, Alastair. 1982. *Kinds of Literature: An Introduction to the Theory of Genres and Models*. Cambridge, Mass.: Harvard University Press.

Freud, Sigmund. 1960. *Jokes and Their Relation to the Unconscious*. Translated by James Strachey from the German edition of 1905, revised 1912. New York: Norton.

Fuhrmann, Manfred. 1968. "Die Romidee der Spätantike." *Historische Zeitschrift* 207: 529–61. Reprinted in *Rom als Idee*, edited by Bernhard Kytzler, 86–123. Wege der Forschung 656. Darmstadt: Wissenschaftliche Buchgesellschaft, 1993.

Funke, Hermann. 1984. "Zu Claudians Invektive gegen Rufin." *Illinois Classical Studies* 9: 91–109.

Galletier, Édouard, ed. 1949–55. *Les Panégyriques latins*. 3 vols. Paris: Les Belles Lettres.

Garbugino, Giovanni, ed. and comm. 1990. "Il XXVI libro di Luciliano." *Studi noniani* 13: 129–236.

Garuti, Giovanni. 1979. *Claudiani de Bello Gothico: Introduzione al "De Bello Gothico."* Edizioni e saggi universitari di filologia classica 23. Bologna: Pàtron.

Gibbon, Edward. 1897–1902. *The History of the Decline and Fall of the Roman Empire*. 7 vols. Edited by J. B. Bury. London: Methuen and New York: Macmillan.

Gleason, Maud. 1986. "Festive Satire: Julian's *Misopogon* and the New Year at Antioch." *Journal of Roman Studies* 76: 106–19.

Glover, Terrot Reaveley. 1901. "Claudian." In *Life and Letters in the Fourth Century*, 216–48. Reprint, New York: Russell and Russell, 1968.

Gnilka, Christian. 1973. "Götter und Dämonen in den Gedichten Claudians." *Antike und Abendland* 18: 144–60.

———. 1975. "Beobachtungen zum Claudiantext." In *Studien zur Literatur der Spätantike*, edited by Christian Gnilka and Willy Schetter, 45–90. Antiquitas Reihe 1, 23. Bonn: Habelt.

———. 1976. "Dichtung und Geschichte im Werk Claudians." *Frühmittelaltlerichen Studien* 10: 96–124.

———. 1977. Review of Cameron 1970. *Gnomon* 49: 26–51.

———. 1982. "Mixta duplex aetas. Zu Claudian *In Eutr.* 1,469–70." *Rivista di filologia e d'istruzione classica* 110: 435–41.

Griffin, Jasper. 1981. "Genre and Real Life in Latin Poetry." *Journal of Roman Studies* 71: 39–49.

———. 1984. "Augustus and the Poets: 'Caesar qui cogere posset.'" In *Caesar Augustus: Seven Aspects*, edited by Fergus Millar and Erich Segal, 189–218. Oxford: Clarendon Press.

Griffith, John G. 1969. "Juvenal, Statius, and the Flavian Establishment." *Greece and Rome* 2nd ser. 16: 134–50.

Gruzelier, C. E. 1990. "Claudian: Court Poet As Artist." In Boyle 1990, 299–318.

Gualandri, Isabella. 1969. *Aspetti della tecnica compositiva in Claudiano*. Milan, Varese: Istituto editoriale cisalpino.

———. 1973. Review of Hall 1969. *Rivista di filologia e d'istruzione classica* 101: 235–43.

Guilhamet, Leon. 1987. *Satire and the Transformation of Genre*. Philadelphia: University of Pennsylvania Press.

Guyot, Peter. 1980. *Eunuchen als Sklaven und Freigelassene in der griechisch-römischen Antike*. Stuttgarter Beiträge zur Geschichte und Politik 14. Stuttgart: Klett-Cotta.

Hall, J. B. 1969. *See* Editions and Commentaries, Other Poems.

———. 1983. "Claudian." In *Texts and Transmission*, edited by L. D. Reynolds, 143–45. Oxford: Clarendon Press.

———. 1985. *See* Editions and Commentaries, *Opera Omnia*.

———. 1986. *Prolegomena to Claudian*. Bulletin Supplement 45. London: Institute of Classical Studies.

Halperin, David M. 1990. *One Hundred Years of Homosexuality and Other Essays on Greek Love*. New York: Routledge.

Hardie, Alex. 1983. *Statius and the Silvae: Poets, Patrons and Epideixis in the Graeco-Roman World*. Liverpool: Francis Cairns.

Hartke, Werner. 1951. *Römische Kinderkaiser; eine Strukturanalyse römischen Denkens und Daseins*. Berlin: Akademie-Verlag.

Heather, Peter J. 1988. "The Anti-Scythian Tirade of Synesius' *De Regno*." *Phoenix* 42: 152–72.

———. 1991. *Goths and Romans, 332–489*. Oxford: Clarendon Press.

Hemmerdinger, B. 1966. "Les lettres latines à Constantinople jusqu'à Justinien." In *Polychordia. Festschrift Franz Dölger*, edited by Peter Wirth, 174–78. Byzantinische Forschung 1. Amsterdam: Hakkert.

Hofmann, Heinz. 1988. "Überlegungen zu einer Theorie der nichtchristlichen Epik der lateinischen Spätantike." *Philologus* 132: 101–59.

Holum, Kenneth G. 1982. *Theodosian Empresses: Women and Imperial Dominion in Late Antiquity*. Transformation of the Classical Heritage 3. Berkeley: University of California Press.

Hopkins, Keith. 1978. *Sociological Studies in Roman History*. Vol. 1, *Conquerors and Slaves*. Cambridge: Cambridge University Press. Reprint, 1980.

Hunger, Herbert. 1978. *Die hochsprachliche profane Literatur der Byzantiner*. 2 vols. Handbuch der Altertumswissenschaft 12, Byzantinisches Handbuch 5. Munich: Beck.

Huxley, H. H. 1954. "Claudian, In Eutropium 2.336–8." *Mnemosyne* 4th ser. 7: 339.

Janson, Tore. 1964. *Latin Prose Prefaces: Studies in Literary Conventions*. Studia Latina Stockholmiensia 13. Stockholm: Almqvist and Wiskell.

———. 1979. *A Concordance to the Latin Panegyrics*. Hildesheim: Georg Olms.

Jeep, Ludwig. 1872. "Nachträgliches über die Handschriften von Claudian's Raptus Proserpinae." *Rheinisches Museum* n.F. 27: 618–24.

———. 1873. "Die älteste Textesrecension des Claudian." *Rheinisches Museum* n.F. 28: 291–304.

———. 1876–79. *See* Editions and Commentaries, *Opera Omnia*.

Jones, A. H. M. 1964. *The Later Roman Empire*. 2 vols. Reprint, Baltimore: Johns Hopkins University Press, 1986.

Jones, A. H. M., J. R. Martindale, and J. Morris, eds. 1971–92. *Prosopography of the Later Roman Empire*. 3 vols. in 4 pts. Cambridge: Cambridge University Press.

Jones, C. P. 1978. *The Roman World of Dio Chrysostom*. Cambridge, Mass.: Harvard University Press.

Jones, F. M. A. 1990. "The Persona and the Dramatis Personae in Juvenal Satire Four." *Eranos* 88: 47–59.

Kaster, Robert A. 1988. *Guardians of Language: The Grammarian and Society in Late Antiquity*. Transformation of the Classical Heritage 11. Berkeley: University of California Press.

Katz, Daniel, Dorwin Cartwright, Samuel Eldersveld, and Alfred McClung Lee, eds. 1954. *Public Opinion and Propaganda: A Book of Readings.* Society for the Psychological Study of Social Issues. New York: Dryden Press.

Kennedy, George A. 1983. *Greek Rhetoric under Christian Emperors.* Princeton, N.J.: Princeton University Press.

Kenney, E. J. 1962. "The First Satire of Juvenal." *Proceedings of the Cambridge Philological Society* 188 n.s. 8: 29–40.

Kernan, Alvin P. 1959. "A Theory of Satire." In *The Cankered Muse: Satire of the English Renaissance,* 1–36. New Haven, Conn.: Yale University Press. Reprinted in *Satire: Modern Essays in Criticism,* edited by Ronald Paulson, 249–77. Englewood Cliffs, N.J.: Prentice-Hall, 1971.

Knoche, Ulrich. 1949. "Ein Sinnbild römischer Selbstauffassung." In *Symbola Coloniensia Josepho Kroll sexagenario A.D. VI Id. Nov. A. MCMIL oblata,* 143–62. Cologne: B. Pick. Reprinted in *Vom Selbstverständnis der Römer: gesammelte Aufsätze,* edited by Franz Bömer and Hans Joachim Mette, 125–43. Heidelberg: Carl Winter, 1962.

———. 1975. *Roman Satire.* Translated from the 3rd German edition (1971) by Edwin S. Ramage, bibliographical supplement by Wolfgang Ehlers. Bloomington: Indiana University Press.

Koch, Julius. 1889. "Claudian und die Ereignisse der Jahre 395 bis 398." *Rheinisches Museum* n.F. 44: 575–612.

———. 1890. "Claudianea." *Philologus* 49: 567–70.

Kohns, Hans Peter. 1961. *Versorgungskrisen und Hungerrevolten im spätantiken Rom.* Antiquitas Reihe 1, 6. Bonn: Habelt.

Koster, Severin. 1980. *Die Invektive in der griechischen und römischen Literatur.* Beiträge zur klassichen Philologie 99. Meisenheim am Glan: Hain.

Krenkel, Werner, ed. 1970. *Lucilius. Satiren.* 2 vols. Leiden: E. J. Brill.

Kroll, W. 1940. "Rhetorik." In *Real-Encyclopädie der classischen Altertumswissenschaft* Supplementband 7: 1039–1138.

Kurfeß, A. 1941. "Zu Claudius Claudianus' Invektiven." *Hermes* 76: 93–95.

Lacombrade, Christian. 1956. "Notes sur deux panégyriques." *Pallas* 4: 15–26.

Lassandro, Domenico. 1981. "La demonizzazione del nemico politico nei Panegyrici Latini." In *Religione e politica nel mondo antico,* edited by Marta Sordi, 237–49. Contributi dell' Istituto di storia antica 7. Milan: Università Cattolica del Sacro Cuore.

Lehner 1984. *See* Editions and Commentaries, Other Poems.

Levy, Harry L. 1946. "Claudian's *In Rufinum* and the Rhetorical Ψόγος." *Transactions of the American Philological Association* 77: 57–65.

———. 1948a. "Claudian's *In Rufinum* and an Epistle of St. Jerome." *American Journal of Philology* 69: 62–68.

———. 1948b. "Claudian's Neglect of Magic as a Motif." *Transactions of the American Philological Association* 79: 87–91.

———. 1958. "Themes of Encomium and Invective in Claudian." *Transactions of the American Philological Association* 89: 336–47.

———. 1971. *See* Editions and Commentaries, Other Poems.

Liebeschuetz, J. H. W. G. 1972. *Antioch: City and Imperial Administration in the Later Roman Empire.* Oxford: Clarendon Press.

———. 1990. *Barbarians and Bishops: Army, Church, and State in the Age of Arcadius and John Chrysostom.* Oxford: Clarendon Press.

Lieu, Samuel N. C., ed. 1989. *The Emperor Julian: Panegyric and Polemic.* 2nd ed. Translated Texts for Historians 2. Liverpool: Liverpool University Press.

Long, Jacqueline. 1987. "The Wolf and the Lion: Synesius' Egyptian Sources." *Greek, Roman, and Byzantine Studies* 28: 103–15.

———. 1993. "Structures of Irony in Julian's *Misopogon*." *Ancient World* 24: 15–23.

MacCormack, Sabine. 1972. "Change and Continuity in Late Antiquity, the Ceremony of *Adventus*." *Historia* 21: 721–52.

———. 1975. "Latin Prose Panegyrics." In *Empire and Aftermath: Silver Latin II*, edited by T. A. Dorey, 143–205. Greek and Latin Studies: Classical Literature and Its Influence. London: Routledge and Kegan Paul.

———. 1976. "Latin Prose Panegyrics: Tradition and Discontinuity in the Later Roman Empire." *Revue des études augustiniennes* 22: 29–77.

———. 1981. *Art and Ceremony in Late Antiquity.* Transformation of the Classical Heritage 1. Berkeley: University of California Press.

MacDowell, Douglas M. 1978. *The Law in Classical Athens.* London: Thames and Hudson.

MacMullen, Ramsay. 1990. *Changes in the Roman Empire: Essays in the Ordinary.* Princeton, N.J.: Princeton University Press.

Maenchen-Helfen, Otto J. 1973. *The World of the Huns: Studies in Their History and Culture.* Edited by Max Knight. Berkeley: University of California Press.

Maguiness, W. S. 1932. "Some Methods of the Latin Panegyrists." *Hermathena* 47: 42–61.

Manitius, Max. 1890. "Beiträge zur Geschichte römischer Dichter im Mittelalter: Claudianus." *Philologus* 49: 554–60.

Marcone, Arnaldo. 1984. "Un panegirico rovesciato: Pluralità di modelli e contaminazione letteraria nel 'Misopogon' giulianeo." *Revue des études augustiniennes* 30: 226–39.

Marsili, Aldo. 1946a. "Roma nella poesia di Claudiano. Romanità occidentale contraposta a quella orientale." *Antiquitas* 1, 2: 3–24.

———. 1946b. "Personificazioni e quadri allegorici in Claudiano." *Antiquitas* 1, 3–4: 49–55.

Martin, Jean, ed. 1988. *Libanios. Discours II–X.* Paris: Les Belles Lettres.

Marx, Friedrich, ed. 1904–5. *C. Lucilii Carminum reliquiae.* 2 vols. Leipzig: B. G. Teubner.

Matthews, John. 1971. "Gallic Supporters of Theodosius." *Latomus* 30: 1073–99.

———. 1974. "The Letters of Symmachus." In *Latin Literature of the Fourth Century*, edited by J. W. Binns, 58–99. Greek and Latin Studies: Classical Literature and Its Influence. London: Routledge and Kegan Paul.

———. 1975. *Western Aristocracies and Imperial Court, A.D. 364–425.* Oxford: Clarendon Press. Reprint, 1990.

———. 1986. "Ammianus and the Eternity of Rome." In *The Inheritance of Historiography, 350–900*, edited by Christopher Holdsworth and T. P. Wiseman, 17–29. Exeter Studies in History 12. Exeter: Exeter University Press.

———. 1987. "Peter Valvomeres, Re-arrested." In *Homo Viator: Classical Essays for John Bramble*, edited by Michael Whitby, Philip Hardie, and Mary Whitby, 277–84. Bristol: Bristol Classical Press and Oak Park, Ill.: Bolchazy-Carducci.

———. 1989. *The Roman Empire of Ammianus.* Baltimore: Johns Hopkins University Press.

Mayor, John E. B., ed. 1901. *Thirteen Satires of Juvenal.* 2 vols. London. Reprint, Hildesheim: Olms, 1966.

Mazzarino, Santo. 1942. *Stilicone: La crisi imperiale dopo Teodosio.* Studi pubblicati dal R. istituto italiano per la storia antica 3. Rome: Angelo Signorelli. 2nd ed., Milan: Rizzoli, 1990.

McCormick, Michael. 1986. *Eternal Victory: Triumphal Rulership in Late Antiquity, Byzantium, and the Early Medieval West.* Cambridge: Cambridge University Press and Paris: Éditions de la Maison des Sciences de l'Homme.

McGeachy, John Alexander. 1942. *Quintus Aurelius Symmachus and the Senatorial Aristocracy of the West.* Dissertation, University of Chicago.

Merone, Emilio. 1954. "La morte di Claudiano." *Giornale italiano di filologia* 7: 309–20.

Merten, Elke W., ed. 1985–87. *Stellenbibliographie zur Historia Augusta.* 4 vols. Antiquitas, Reihe 4, Beiträge zur Historia-Augusta-Forschung ser. 2, vols. 1–4. Bonn: Habelt.

Meulder, Marcel. 1989. "Timarque, un être tyrannique dépeint par Eschine." *Études Classiques* 57: 317–22.

Millar, Fergus. 1977. *The Emperor in the Roman World (32 B.C.–A.D. 337).* Ithaca, N.Y.: Cornell University Press.

Moore, C. H. 1910–11. "Rome's Heroic Past in the Poems of Claudian." *Classical Journal* 6: 108–15.

Moreau, J., ed. 1954. *Lactance. De la mort des persécuteurs.* Sources chrétiennes 39. 2 vols. Paris: Éditions du Cerf.

Moroni, Brunella. 1982. "Tradizione letteraria e propaganda: Osservazione sulla poesia politica di Claudiano." *Scripta philologa* 3: 213–39.

Nesselrath, Heinz-Günther. 1991. "Zu Datierung und Aufbau des 1. Buches von Claudians Invektive 'In Rufinum.'" *Hermes* 119: 217–31.

Nisbet, R. G. M., ed. 1961. *In L. Calpurnium Pisonem Oratio.* Oxford: Clarendon Press.

Nixon, C. E. V. 1983. "Latin Panegyric in the Tetrarchic and Constantinian Period." In *History and Historians in Late Antiquity*, edited by Brian Croke and Alanna M. Emmett, 88–99. Sydney: Pergamon Press.

———, trans. and comm. 1987. *Pacatus: Panegyric to the Emperor Theodosius.* Translated Texts for Historians 3. Liverpool: Liverpool University Press.

———. 1990. "The Use of the Past by the Gallic Panegyrists." In *Reading the Past in Late Antiquity*, edited by Graeme Clarke with Brian Croke, Raoul Mortley, and Alanna Emmett Nobbs, 1–36. Rushcutters Bay: Australian National University Press.

Nixon, C. E. V., and Barbara Saylor Rodgers. 1994. *In Praise of Later Roman Emperors: The Panegyrici Latini.* Transformation of the Classical Heritage 21. Berkeley: University of California Press.

Norman, A. F., ed. 1965. *Libanius' Autobiography (Oration I).* London: Oxford University Press for the University of Hull.

———, ed. 1969–77. *Libanius: Selected Works.* 2 vols. Cambridge, Mass.: Harvard University Press and London: William Heinemann.

Nugent, S. Georgia. "Ausonius' 'Late-Antique' Poetics and 'Post-Modern' Literary Theory." In Boyle 1990, 236–60.

Olechowska 1978. *See* Editions and Commentaries, Other Poems.

Opelt, Ilona. 1965. *Die lateinischen Schimpfwörter und verwandte sprachliche Erscheinungen. Eine Typologie.* Heidelberg: Carl Winter Universitätsverlag.

———. 1982. "Schimpfwörter bei Claudian." *Glotta* 60: 130–35.

Pack, Roger. 1935. *Studies in Libanius and Antiochene Society under Theodosius.* Dissertation, University of Michigan.

———. 1953. "The Roman Digressions of Ammianus Marcellinus." *Transactions of the American Philological Association* 84: 181–89.

Parravicini, Achille. 1905. *Studio di retorica sulle opere di Claudio Claudiano.* Milan: Scuola tipografica salesiana.

———. 1909. *I panegirici di Claudiano e i panegirici latini.* Rome.

———. 1914. "Le prefazione di Claudio Claudiano." *Athenaeum* 2: 183–94.

Paschoud, François. 1967. *Roma aeterna. Études sur le patriotisme romain dans l'Occident latin à l'époque des grandes invasions.* Bibliotheca Helvetica Romana 7. Institut Suisse de Rome.

———, ed. 1971–89. *Zosime. Histoire Nouvelle.* 3 parts in 5 vols. Paris: Les Belles Lettres.

———. 1975. *Cinq études sur Zosime.* Paris: Les Belles Lettres.

Paucker, C. 1880. "De latinitate Claudiani poetae observationes." *Rheinisches Museum* 35: 586–606.

Penella, Robert J. 1990. *Greek Philosophers and Sophists in the Fourth Century A.D.: Studies in Eunapius of Sardis.* Leeds: Francis Cairns.

Penndorf, Julius. 1911. *Progymnasmata: Rhetorische Anfangsübungen der alten Griechen und Römer.* Plauen: Neupert.

Perrelli, Raffaele. 1992. *I proemi claudianei. Tra epica ed epidittica.* Saggi e testi classici, cristiani e medievali 5. Università di Catania: Centro di studi sull'antico cristianesimo.

Petit, Paul. 1951. "Sur la date du 'Pro Templis' de Libanius." *Byzantion* 21: 295–310.

———. 1955. *Libanius et la vie municipale à Antioche au IVe siècle après J.-C.* Paris: Librairie Orientaliste Paul Geuthner.

———. 1956. "Recherches sur la publication et la diffusion des discours de Libanius." *Historia* 5: 479–509. Translated as "Untersuchungen über die Veröffentlichung und Verbreitung der Reden des Libanios." In Fatouros and Krischer 1983, 84–128.

———. 1957. "Les sénateurs de Constantinople dans l'oeuvre de Libanius." *Antiquité classique* 26: 347–82. Translated as "Die Senatoren von Konstantinopel im Werk des Libanios." In Fatouros and Krischer 1983, 206–47.

Pichon, René. 1906. *Les derniers écrivains profanes. Les panégyristes—Ausone—Le Querolus—Rutilius Namatianus.* Paris: Leroux.

Platnauer 1922. *See* Editions and Commentaries, *Opera Omnia.*

Potz, Erich. 1990. "Claudians *In Rufinum*: Invektive und Laudatio." *Philologus* 134: 66–81.

Powell, Anton, ed. 1992. *Roman Poetry and Propaganda in the Age of Augustus.* London: Bristol Classical Press for the London Classical Society.

Ramsay, A. M. 1925. "The Speed of the Roman Imperial Post." *Journal of Roman Studies* 15: 60–74.

Richlin, Amy. 1983. *The Garden of Priapus: Sexuality and Aggression in Roman Humor.* New Haven, Conn.: Yale University Press. 2nd ed., Oxford: Oxford University Press, 1992.

Ridley, Ronald T., trans. and comm. 1982. *Zosimus: New History.* Byzantina Australiensia 2. Canberra: Australian Association for Byzantine Studies.

Rike, R. L. 1987. *Apex Omnium: Religion in the Res Gestae of Ammianus.* Transformation of the Classical Heritage 15. Berkeley: University of California Press.

Roberts, Michael. 1989. *The Jeweled Style: Poetry and Poetics in Late Antiquity.* Ithaca, N.Y.: Cornell University Press.

Romano, D. 1958. *Claudiano*. Biblioteca di cultura moderna 49. Palermo: Palumbo.

Rougé, Jean. 1961. "Une émeute à Rome au IVe siècle. Ammien Marcellin, xxvii, 3, 3–4: Essai d'interprétation." *Revue des études anciennes* 63: 59–77.

Rousselle, Aline. 1988. *Porneia: On Desire and the Body in Antiquity*. Translated by Felicia Pheasant from the original French publication, Paris: Presses Universitaire de France, 1983. Oxford: Basil Blackwell.

Ruggini, Lellia. 1961. *Economia e società nell' Italia annonaria: Rapporti fra agricoltura e commercio dal IV al VI secolo d.C.* Fondazione Guglielmo Castelli 30. Milan: Giuffrè.

———. 1968. " 'De Morte Persecutorum' e polemica antibarbarica nella storiografia pagana e cristiana." *Rivista di storia e letteratura religiosa* 4: 433–47.

Russell, D. A., and N. G. Wilson, eds. 1981. *Menander Rhetor*. Oxford: Clarendon Press.

Sabbah, Guy. 1978. *La Méthode d'Ammien Marcellin*. Paris: Les Belles Lettres.

Sallmann, Klaus. 1970. "Satirische Technik in Horaz' Erbscheichersatire (S. 2,5)." *Hermes* 98: 178–203.

———. 1974. "Die seltsame Reise nach Brundisium. Aufbau und Deutung der Horazsatire 1,5." In *Musa Iocosa. Arbeiten über Humor und Witz komik und Komödie der Antike. Festschrift Andreas Thierfelder*, edited by Udo Reinhardt and Klaus Sallmann, 179–206. Hildesheim: Olms.

Schmidt, Peter L. 1976. *Politik und Dichtung in der Panegyrik Claudians*. Konstanz: Universitätsverlag.

———. 1989. "Die Überlieferungsgeschichte von Claudians Carmina maiora." *Illinois Classical Studies* 14: 391–415.

Schröter, R. 1967. "Horazens Satire I,7 und die antike Eposparodie." *Poetica* 1: 8–23.

Schweckendiek 1992. *See* Editions and Commentaries, *In Eutropium*.

Seager, Robin. 1983. "Some Imperial Virtues in the Latin Prose Panegyrics: The Demands of Propaganda and the Dynamics of Literary Composition." *Papers of the Liverpool Latin Seminar* 4: 129–65.

Seeck, Otto. 1894. "Studien zu Synesios." *Philologus* 52: 442–83.

———. 1895. "Arkadios." In *Real-Encyclopädie der classischen Altertumswissenschaft* 2: 1137–53.

———. 1913. *Geschichte des Untergangs der Antiken Welt*. Vol. 5. Stuttgart: J. B. Metzler and Berlin: Franz Siemenroth.

———. 1919. *Regesten der Kaiser und Päpste für die Jahre 311 bis 476 n. Chr.* Stuttgart: J. B. Metzler.

———. 1920–24. "Libanius gegen Lucianus." *Rheinisches Museum* 73: 84–101. Reprinted in Fatouros and Krischer 1983, 26–42.

Simon 1975. *See* Editions and Commentaries, Other Poems.

Stein, Ernest. 1949–59. *Histoire du Bas-Empire*. 2 vols. Edited and translated by Jean-Remy Palanque. Paris. Reprint, Amsterdam: Hakkert, 1968.

Stoecker, Ernst. 1889. *De Claudiani poetae veterum rerum Romanarum scientia quae sit et unde fluxerit*. Marpurgi Cattorum: F. Soemmerling.

Stroheker, Karl Friedrich. 1963. "Spanische Senatoren der spätrömischen und westgotischen Zeit." *Madrider Mitteilungen* 4: 107–32.

———. 1970. "Princeps clausus." In *Bonner Historia-Augusta-Colloquium 1968/9*, edited by Johannes Straub, 273–83. Bonn: Habelt.

Struthers, Lester B. 1919. "The Rhetorical Structure of the Encomia of Claudius Claudian." *Harvard Studies in Classical Philology* 30: 49–87.

Sullivan, J. P. 1985. *Literature and Politics in the Age of Nero.* Ithaca, N.Y.: Cornell University Press.

Süß, Wilhelm. 1910. *Ethos. Studien zur älteren griechischen Rhetorik.* Leipzig: B. G. Teubner.

Thompson, E. A. 1947. *The Historical Work of Ammianus Marcellinus.* Cambridge: Cambridge University Press.

Townend, G. B. 1973. "The Literary Substrata to Juvenal's Satires." *Journal of Roman Studies* 63: 148–60.

Van Rooy, C. A. 1965. *Studies in Classical Satire and Related Literary Theory.* Leiden: E. J. Brill.

Vera, Domenico, ed. 1981. *Commento storico alle Relationes de Quinto Aurelio Simmaco.* Biblioteca di Studi Antichi 29. Pisa: Giardini Editori e Stampatori.

Viljamaa, Toivo. 1968. *Studies in Greek Encomiastic Poetry of the Early Byzantine Period.* Commentationes Humanarum Litterarum, Societas Scientiarum Fennica 42. Helsinki: Helsingfors.

Warmington, E. H., ed. 1938. *Remains of Old Latin III: Lucilius; The Twelve Tables.* Cambridge, Mass.: Harvard University Press.

Waszink, J. H. 1972. "Problems Concerning the *Satura* of Ennius." In *Ennius,* edited by Otto Skutsch, 99–147. Fondation Hardt, Entretiens 17. Geneva: Fondation Hardt.

Weston, Arthur H. 1915. *Latin Satirical Writing Subsequent to Juvenal.* Dissertation, Yale University, 1911. Lancaster, Pa.: New Era Printing.

Wiesen, David S. 1964. *St. Jerome as a Satirist: A Study in Christian Latin Thought and Letters.* Cornell Studies in Classical Philology 34. Ithaca, N.Y.: Cornell University Press.

Wilken, Robert. 1983. *John Chrysostom and the Jews: Rhetoric and Reality in the Late Fourth Century.* Transformation of the Classical Heritage 4. Berkeley: University of California Press.

Winkler, Martin M. 1989. "The Function of Epic in Juvenal's *Satires.*" In *Studies in Latin Literature and Roman History,* edited by C. Deroux, 5.414–43. Collection Latomus 206. Brussels: Latomus revue d'études latines.

Zakrzewski, Kazimierz. 1931. *Le parti théodosien et son antithèse. Eos* Suppl. 18. Lublin.

Zanker, Paul. 1988. *The Power of Images in the Age of Augustus.* Translated by Alan Shapiro. Ann Arbor: University of Michigan Press. Reprint, 1990.

21–24. *Stil.*, 182–84, 208, 209–11, 219,
    228–30, 236
consulate
    failures to recognize, 2, 11, 13, 29–30,
        139n, 162, 167, 181–84, 187, 237
    standard procedures, 2, 181

deformity: Greco-Roman attitudes
    toward, 27, 79, 92, 108–9,
    114–16
demons, 102–4
Demosthenes, 68, 70, 71, 72–73
Döpp, Siegmar, 13, 158–60, 163, 170, 234,
    245
DuQuesnay, I. M. LeM., 21, 204, 207

Eastern attitudes: alleged by Claudian,
    40, 41–42, 46, 50, 119–20, 170,
    172, 233–34, 241, 244, 245–46,
    247–48, 250, 252–55, 259–60,
    261–62, 268, 269. *See also*
    Aurora
Eastern court: as portrayed by Claudian,
    13, 41, 50, 56–57, 129–31,
    140–42, 146, 173, 174–75, 213,
    234, 242, 246, 248, 251, 254, 255,
    258–59, 264–65, 267
effeminacy and homosexuality: Greco-
    Roman attitudes toward,
    59–62, 66, 70–71, 74, 75, 76,
    79–80, 81, 88, 93–94, 122–23,
    125–26
Ellul, Jacques, 205–8, 211–12, 218–19, 262,
    265
Ennius, 20
Eudoxia, 10, 62, 132–33, 161
Eunapius, 98, 140–41, 161, 162, 169,
    179–81, 191, 203, 217
eunuchs
    appearance of, 108–9
    employment of, 2, 107–8
    Roman attitudes toward, 29, 35–37, 82,
        93–94, 104–5, 107–9, 115–16, 121
Eutropius
    and Alaric, 10, 249, 251, 255
    and Arcadius, 1–2, 10, 12, 19, 28–29, 62,
        136–37, 235, 244
    career, 1–2, 10–12, 19, 121, 180, 184, 186,
        266

as treated by Claudian, 19, 26, 34,
    38–40, 42, 48–49, 62, 146,
    149–50, 174, 213, 225, 231–35,
    236, 240, 244, 253, 259–60,
    261–62
    civilian official, 27–28, 35–36, 41,
        50, 56–57, 119, 128, 129–31,
        132–33, 134–41, 142–43, 145,
        169–70, 172, 243, 250, 251,
        267–68
    military and triumphal, 28,
        119–21, 128–30, 132, 133, 149,
        230, 237, 238, 241, 251–52
    sexual, 123–28, 131, 139, 241–42,
        264
    slave, 27, 34–35, 112–19, 123–28,
        159, 171–72
consulate, 1–3, 30, 167, 181–84
    as treated by Claudian, 27, 29–30,
        36–37, 40, 49, 62–63, 109–12,
        131, 149, 160, 176, 182–84, 202,
        222, 235, 236, 238, 240, 243, 245,
        246–47, 252, 254, 263, 269
deposition and exile, 2, 12, 149, 151,
    152, 155, 161–64, 199, 203,
    260–61, 266
    as treated by Claudian, 38–39, 40,
        42, 149–50, 153, 171, 175–76,
        202–3, 222, 245–46, 260
and Eudoxia, 10, 62, 132–33, 161
and Gildo, 11, 226–31, 232, 235, 237–38
and Rufinus, 10, 162–63
and Stilicho, 62–63, 90, 162–64,
    235–36
and Theodosius, 2, 190
and Tribigild, 40, 41, 50, 56, 129–30,
    134, 139–40, 169–70, 172, 249,
    250–51, 254, 262, 267
Eutropius's sister, 39, 40, 133–34, 248

Fargues, Pierre, 32, 120, 141, 152–53, 160,
    176, 238, 248, 251
Fravitta, 12, 139, 163, 169, 175, 185, 267

Gaïnas, 12, 151, 160–61, 162–63, 166, 169,
    175, 185, 254, 262, 267
genre: general considerations, 17, 48–49.
    See also rhetorical forms
Gildo, 11, 137, 156, 159, 182, 185, 190, 199,